Nietzsche's Task

LAURENCE LAMPERT

Nietzsche's Task

AN INTERPRETATION OF
BEYOND GOOD AND EVIL

2001

Yale University Press

New Haven/London

Set in Sabon type by Keystone Typesetting, Inc.
Printed in the United States of America.

The Library of Congress has cataloged the hardcover edition as follows:
Lampert, Laurence, 1941–
Nietzsche's task : an interpretation of Beyond good and evil / Laurence Lampert.
p. cm.
Includes bibliographical references and index.
ISBN 0-300-08873-6 (cloth : alk. paper)
1. Nietzsche, Friedrich Wilhelm, 1844–1900. Jenseits von Gut und Böse.
2. Philosophy. I. Title.
B3313.J43 J465 2001
193 — dc21
2001001528

A catalogue record for this book is available from the British Library.

The paper in this book meets the guidelines for permanence and durability of the Committee on Production Guidelines for Book Longevity of the Council on Library Resources.

ISBN 0-300-10301-8 (pbk. : alk. paper)

10 9 8 7 6 5 4 3

Contents

Acknowledgments

I am grateful to Robert Looker and the Looker Foundation for two major grants that enabled me first to begin and then to complete my work on this book.

David Frisby and George Dunn read and commented on my manuscript as it was being written; their contributions have improved my book immensely and I am grateful.

Abbreviations of Nietzsche's Works

A	*The Antichrist*
AOM	*Assorted Opinions and Maxims*
BGE	*Beyond Good and Evil*
BT	*Birth of Tragedy*
CW	*The Case of Wagner*
D	*Dawn of Day*
EH	*Ecce Homo*
GM	*On the Genealogy of Morality*
GS	*Gay Science*
HH	*Human, All Too Human*
KGB	*Kritische Studienausgabe Briefe*
KSA	*Kritische Studienausgabe*
NCW	*Nietzsche Contra Wagner*

PTA   *Philosophy in the Tragic Age of the Greeks*

RWB   *Richard Wagner in Bayreuth*

SE   *Schopenhauer as Educator*

TI   *Twilight of the Idols*

UD   *On the Use and Disadvantages of History for Life*

WP   *The Will to Power*

WS   *The Wanderer and His Shadow*

Z   *Thus Spoke Zarathustra*

Nietzsche's Task

Introduction: Nietzsche's Task

What *was* Nietzsche's task? It was the task of *philosophy:* gaining a comprehensive perspective on the world and on the human disposition toward the world, a perspective that could claim to be true. The older language can still be used if it is rebaptized with Nietzschean meanings: philosophy as the love of wisdom aims to overcome irrational interpretations with rational ones, interpretations guided by the mind, by spirited intellect Nietzscheanly conceived. As a direct consequence of achieving that comprehensive perspective — for his two chief books, *Thus Spoke Zarathustra* and *Beyond Good and Evil,* show that he achieved it — an additional task fell to Nietzsche, the task of *political philosophy:* making a place for that perspective in the lived world of human culture or doing justice to all things in the human disposition toward them. But given the sway of the irrational, making a place for the more rational in the midst of the irrational requires strategic finesse; it is a task for an artful writer who knows his audience and knows how to appeal to them.

Philosophy

In a letter to Georg Brandes explaining the core of his work to one of the first readers to pay it close attention, Nietzsche said, "That they're dealing here with the long logic of a completely determinate philosophical sensibility and *not* with some mishmash of a hundred varied paradoxes and heterodoxes — of that, I believe, nothing has dawned on even my most favorable readers" (8 January 1888). The long logic of that determinate philosophical sensibility can dawn on favorable readers through the study of *Zarathustra*, Nietzsche's most important book, a book he wrote in order to show Zarathustra gaining that perspective, a new teaching on the fundamental fact and a new teaching on the highest value. For Nietzsche's view is both ontological and axiological; comprehending fact and value, it includes a perspective on the way of all beings — to be is to be will to power — and a disposition toward that way — an unbounded Yes and Amen to everything that was and is. *Beyond Good and Evil*, Nietzsche's second most important book, is his second book to be grounded in the long logic of his determinate philosophical sensibility — a book that "says the same things as *Thus Spoke Zarathustra* but differently, very differently" (letter to Burckhardt, 22 September 1886). Both books aim to show that philosophy is possible and desirable, that there are plausible grounds for the mind's assent to a particular interpretation of the whole of things and plausible grounds for the heart's embrace of that interpretation as a teaching to live by.

Political Philosophy

Reviewing the whole course of his authorship in *Ecce Homo*, Nietzsche said of *Zarathustra*, simply and unequivocally, "The Yes-saying part of my task had been solved" (*EH Books BGE*). When *Beyond Good and Evil* says the same things differently, it says them in a book whose explicit purpose is the opposite of Yes-saying: "Next came the No-saying, *No-doing* part of my task." *Beyond Good and Evil* is the first installment in Nietzsche's "great war" of the transvaluation of values, spiritual warfare made necessary against the authoritative opinions of modern times by the newly won affirmative view. Woven into this No-saying book, grounding its No-doing, giving No its rationale and purpose are glimpses of Zarathustra's Yes, and those glimpses are, it seems to me, the most important events in the book. For if the book is an act of war, it is a strategic act, the calculated means to win a war that Nietzsche might seem to have no chance whatever of winning, a war on behalf of a new teaching against the prevailing doctrines of his whole age. How could a solitary thinker win such a war? How could one man change the general taste (*GS* 39) and forge a new conscience (*BGE* 203)? *How?* After announcing *Beyond Good and Evil* as an act of war, *Ecce Homo* did not describe the war but indicated instead the book's strategy for winning it: *Beyond Good and Evil* begins "the slow search for those related to me." It is a search for allies, more exactly, an effort to create allies, for there are none to begin with. Nietzsche's true allies will be won to his affirmative teaching by the artfulness of the No-saying book, by its power to draw its favorable readers into the determinate philosophical sensibility beautifully if enigmatically presented in the book. For what might look at first like a scattering of 296 sections loosely gathered into nine disparate assemblages is in fact a carefully composed and ultimately stirring drama of philosophy's responsibility for the future of the human species. "You must take part and fight," the book implicitly says to the allies it seeks to create (see *BT* sec. 15 final sentences). It commits the crime political philosophy has been guilty of since its origins, it corrupts the young.

Ecce Homo describes the precise task of *Beyond Good and Evil* as "a critique of modernity." In Nietzsche's view, modernity is a complex but understandable process that threatens to culminate in the universal sway of "the autonomous herd" (*BGE* 202), the "final humans" of Zarathustra's speech in the marketplace (*Z* Preface 5), global humanity surviving the death of God within an ideology proclaiming humanity's freedom, equality, and wisdom. According to its preface, *Beyond Good and Evil* is primarily a critique of the penultimate stage of late modernity, a stage it calls "the democratic Enlightenment." But the preface also indicates what the book argues in greater detail: the democratic Enlightenment is a cultural event within a much larger cultural process originally set in motion by Plato. The critique of modernity unfurls into a more comprehensive critique of the whole Western or Platonic tradition, with special focus on its origin and its possible end in a fully successful democratic Enlightenment, Hegel's end of history.

But *Ecce Homo* also states that *Beyond Good and Evil* is more than a critique, for it includes "pointers to a contrary type that is as little modern as possible, a noble, Yes-saying type." The presence of these pointers permits Nietzsche to describe his book in a most illuminating way: it is "a school for the *gentilhomme,* taking this concept in a more spiritual and radical sense than has ever been done." Philosophers once commonly regarded their writings as a school for gentlemen—Nietzsche claims membership in a great tradition whose exemplary members include Plato and Xenophon, Machiavelli and Montaigne, Bacon and Descartes. Plato, one of the founders of this tradition, wrote in part to create a new nobility through a new teaching on virtue, a nobility that would found a regime friendly to philosophy without itself being primarily philosophical. Anti-Platonic in its philosophy, *Beyond Good and Evil* as a school for the gentleman is Platonic in the scope and aim of its philosophical politics. The gentlemen in question, odd as it may seem at first, include scientists and scholars, modern free minds whom the book aims to make allies, for the philosophic leadership of science is perhaps the core element in Nietzsche's philosophical politics. The final chapter, "What Is Noble?" gathers the book's pointers to a nonmodern ideal and shows that the new nobility, a nobility of knowledge seekers, is crowned by the *most* spiritual and *most* radical, the very few philosophers. The political task of *Beyond Good and Evil* is therefore twofold: thwarting the goal of the democratic Enlightenment, the end of history that would be "the end of philosophy on earth."[1] And establishing the interests of philosophy where those interests are reasonably seen as "the highest interests of mankind."[2]

Esotericism

How will the new nobility be schooled? Through a book in which "the refinement in form, in intention, in the art of *silence* is in the foreground" (*EH Books BGE*). The three foreground refinements seem to me to be three aspects of one refinement, the art of esoteric writing deeply rooted in the tradition of political philosophy, particularly in Plato, but enhanced and deployed in a new way by Nietzsche. Nietzsche is an esoteric writer who helps his reader understand the old art of esotericism in a new way (*BGE* 30) and to understand why a new esotericism befits the present age, which is potentially a postmoral age following the ten-thousand-year moral period (32). Philosophy's traditional esotericism, clearly stated by Plato, believed in the indispensability of the noble lie, moral fictions that directed the fears and hopes of citizens into decent, public-spirited practices by appealing to a moral order and calling in moral gods as the punishing and rewarding guarantors of the moral. "That's all over now," Nietzsche says simply (*GS* 357) — now that God is dead, now that modern science has robbed Platonism of any intellectual respectability and made it clearer to everyone that humanity lives out its fears and hopes in a silent, unresponsive universe.

But if it's all over with noble lying, it's not all over with esotericism, as *Beyond Good and Evil* makes evident. Its art of writing trains by temptation, allowing the essential matters to be almost overheard in what is actually said. Almost overhearing induces the reader to strain to actually hear, to recompose the thoughts composed in Nietzsche's mind and made available in the only way likely to persuade, an enchanting way that draws the enchanted reader into assembling the thoughts on his own, making them his own, owning them as they own him in a mutual act of owning. The new esotericism schools a new spiritual and radical nobility in what looks — as every great innovation must —

---

1. Leo Strauss, *On Tyranny* 211; see *BGE* 204 (end).
2. Leo Strauss, *Persecution and the Art of Writing* 18; see *BGE* 211–13.

immoral. But the mask of the immoralist, that exoteric demon, shelters a new teaching on virtue and a new teaching on the good.

And what about that other esotericism in Nietzsche, his much-neglected speech about the gods? Nietzsche ends *Ecce Homo*'s description of *Beyond Good and Evil* by speaking theologically. "I rarely speak as a theologian," he says, a falsehood that alerts the reader to the many speeches on gods and devils in *Beyond Good and Evil:*[3]

> It was God himself who lay down as a serpent at the end of his days' work under the tree of knowledge: he recuperated in this way from being God. . . . He had made everything too beautiful. . . . The devil is only the leisure of God on that seventh day.

Recuperating from the creation of the world in *Thus Spoke Zarathustra*, God becomes the Tempter offering in *Beyond Good and Evil* the forbidden fruit of the tree of knowledge, knowledge of good and evil. As a theologian Nietzsche is a gnostic who knows how to almost quote the Bible, a gnostic who offers a saving knowledge of the world knowing that the gods who now rule require him to appear as the devil. Part of the esoteric task of *Beyond Good and Evil* is to make a new teaching on the divine capable of being heard or taken to heart as one's own. But by whom?

The Free Mind

After completing *Zarathustra* Nietzsche had a clear grasp of his next task, though not of his next title: he had to write a new book for free minds, and he thought it would be a second edition of *Human, All Too Human: A Book for Free Minds* after he destroyed all the copies that remained of the first edition. When it proved impossible for him to recover the unsold copies, he projected the new book as a second volume of *Dawn of Day*. Finally though, after most of it had been composed, Nietzsche decided that the new book in fact had to have "a title of its own (just as it has a color and a sense of its own)." *Beyond Good and Evil* thus received a "dangerous slogan" as its title (*GM* 1.17).[4] The history of Nietzsche's intentions for his new book helps

---

3. A selection: 37, 56, 62, 150, 227, 294, 295.

4. Nietzsche's changing intentions for his new book can be followed in his letters. On a new edition of *HH*, see especially, 15 August 1885 (to Elisabeth); 22 September 1885; 6 December 1885, 24 January 1886 (all to Köselitz). On a second volume of *D*, see January 1886 (to Credner); 30 January 1886 (to his mother); 25 March 1886 (to Overbeck). Two letters on 27 March 1886 declare that the new book will have a title of its own (to Credner and Köselitz).

clarify a key point about it: *Beyond Good and Evil* belongs, anachronistically, to the series of books written for the free mind before *Thus Spoke Zarathustra,* the series that came to an end with *The Gay Science,* Nietzsche's last book before *Zarathustra.*[5] *Zarathustra* is the essential book chronicling the essential gains of the free-minded Nietzsche, his becoming a philosopher with a new teaching on the way of all beings and on an unbounded affirmation of all beings. After completing *Zarathustra,* Nietzsche had to *re*address the free minds; after making his essential gains and communicating them in an impossible book for free minds, he had to write an introduction to it that would force them to consider it and help them to enter it. *Beyond Good and Evil* addresses the free minds in their objective, skeptical, critical temper; its most important chapter, entitled "The Free Mind," contains Nietzsche's basic argument to his indispensable audience: free minds must learn that it is reasonable to bind their minds to a new teaching and that new responsibilities fall to the freely bound minds.[6]

When Nietzsche's task is seen in its full magnitude, it is evident that *task* is too thin a word to encompass it. But *task* inadequately translates the word Nietzsche actually used, *Aufgabe,* whose root is *geben,* or give. Heard literally, Nietzsche's *Aufgabe* is what is given him to do, almost his mission or, in religious settings, his calling.

The Architecture of Beyond Good and Evil

Beyond Good and Evil is a book in nine parts,[7] but, as Leo Strauss observed, it has two main divisions separated by an interlude of "Epigrams

---

5. On the back cover of the first edition of *GS* (1882) Nietzsche had stated that it was the finale of a series of writings whose common goal was to erect a new image and ideal of the free mind.

6. While composing *BGE* Nietzsche had an additional project in mind: the back cover of the first edition announces a book "In Preparation, *The Will to Power. An Experiment in a Transvaluation of All Values. In Four Books.*" As attested by many notes from the time of *BGE,* this book was to be Nietzsche's second *Hauptwerk,* a book that dealt directly with the two teachings Zarathustra was shown discovering, will to power and eternal return, as well as with the implications of those two teachings for the transvaluation of all past values. The complete trajectory of Nietzsche's authorship with its two main *Hauptwerke* must be kept in mind when considering the particular task of *BGE.* Had the second *Hauptwerk* been completed, *BGE* would not be what it now is, Nietzsche's second most important book.

7. Nietzsche called the parts *Hauptstücke,* "chief parts," a designation that distinguishes them from the other *Stücke,* the 296 sections. For convenience I will call the 9 parts chapters and the 296 *Stücke* sections.

and Interludes" and framed by a "Preface" and an "Aftersong." The first division, chapters 1–3, deals with philosophy and religion; the second division, chapters 5–9, deals with morals and politics.[8] Each of the nine chapters (with the possible exception of chapter 4) is composed as a coherent whole, offering an argument more latent than manifest but an argument that must be appreciated if Nietzsche's deepest aim is to be appreciated. Nietzsche said that his teacher, "Ritschl, actually claimed that I planned even my philological essays like a Parisian *romancier*—absurdly exciting" (*EH* Books 2). With study, each of the chapters of *Beyond Good and Evil* comes to seem in its own movement and trajectory—absurdly exciting. The individual sections within the chapters receive their specific gravity from their location in the unfolding argument and from their contribution to it. But not only the chapters unfold as coherent arguments; so too do the two divisions: chapters 1–3 offer a coherent argument about philosophy and religion and the profound relation between them; chapters 5–9 offer a coherent argument about morality and politics culminating in the new nobility. And finally, the whole book is a coherent argument that never lets up: what is discovered about philosophy and religion, about what can be known and what might be believed, necessarily assigns the philosopher a monumental task or responsibility with respect to morals and politics.

The architecture of the book is reflected by its frame, its preface and aftersong—a *Vorrede* and a *Nachgesang:* the nine chapters are introduced by a "preparatory *speech*" and followed by no mere *Nachrede,* or concluding speech, but by a "concluding *song,*" celebratory, edifying singing that anticipates the arrival of Zarathustra.[9] The speech at the opening invites its reader to enter the great adventure awaiting the lovers of truth. The song at the end invites the schooled reader to enter *Zarathustra,* invites newfound friends to friendship with Zarathustra.

8. "Note on the Plan of Nietzsche's *Beyond Good and Evil,*" *Studies in Platonic Political Philosophy* 176.

9. See the end of *Zarathustra:* "Sing! Speak no more!" (the end as Nietzsche thought while writing it), *Z* 3 "The Seven Seals, 7."

Preface: A Task for a Good European

Nietzsche's great preface to *Beyond Good and Evil* was written in June 1885, *before* the book it introduces. Nevertheless, it prepares the chief themes of the book with remarkable precision, beginning with a characterization of philosophy itself and setting out its Western past, present, and future with dramatic conciseness. For Nietzsche, philosophy is what matters most in human civilization, and the history of Western civilization has two outstanding features, each philosophical: millennia of Platonic dogmatism and centuries of modern spiritual warfare against it that have left it in ruins. The present, amid the ruins, is marked by an unprecedented tension of mind and spirit that could yet dissolve into mere contentment and ease. The future, however, if it drew on that great tension, could be transformed if philosophy took up its present task.

"Assuming truth is a woman —, what then?"

What then? Why then there are good grounds for the suspicion that philosophers, truth's vaunted suitors, have been insensitive lovers, dogmatists inattentive to the subtleties of their beloved. Ignorant of erotics, of the logic of seduction, they were lovers so adolescent and crass that it offends good taste to suppose that so refined a beloved as Truth ever yielded herself to them.

Nietzsche opens the preface in a sporting mood, a manly mood challenging previous philosophers as a rival for their beloved. Socrates was the philosopher who claimed the erotic as his one expertise,[1] but the preface and the book that follows challenge both Socrates and his greatest erotic success, Plato, whose seduction by Socrates Nietzsche treats as a corruption. *Beyond Good and Evil* is a book for lovers that opens by proclaiming a contest of suitors for the highest beloved. As a contest of manly lovers, it is a book for warriors who want to be "what wisdom wants us: unconcerned, mocking, violent — she is a woman and always loves only a warrior."[2] Has there finally emerged from the long history of philosophy, the history of the lovers of wisdom, a lover and warrior subtle and dashing enough to succeed in the highest erotic pursuit? If truth is a woman who yields to her fitting lover, there are grounds for the suspicion that the tale of her yielding will be tastefully told, that her lover will not betray her in a way that would bring her shame. There are grounds too for the suspicion that the rivalry among lovers may have made the warrior's dismissal of all challengers less nuanced, less fair than it might have been.

Nietzsche later simply states that truth is a woman and concludes, "One should not do her violence" (220). Violence done to truth is, in that section, the violence of disinterest, investigation of naked truth by inquirers stripped of ego and personality, modern inquirers moved by the ideal of objective science to count philosophy among the disinterested sciences. But Nietzsche had just spoken of philosophy as the highest spiritualization of justice (219), and to do truth justice one must approach her with "love and sacrifice" (220). The chapter in which these things are said is titled "Our Virtues," and at its center it isolates honesty or probity as the one virtue left to us while emphasizing that we should not let our virtue become our stupidity: honest truth telling about passionately pursued truth will itself be a game of seduction.

If truth is a woman, what is her lover's goal? Possession. *Thus Spoke Zarathustra* pictures possession as a marriage, a consummated courtship between Zarathustra and Life, between the inquiring mind and the beloved object of inquiry, a marriage of truth seeker and truth that will generate offspring for centuries. As an introduction to *Zarathustra* for free minds, *Beyond Good and Evil* is a *Vorspiel,* foreplay perhaps, that presents the same goal more soberly; at its deepest point it argues that the truth seeker can successfully draw a reasonable inference about the way of all beings (36). This ontological conclusion has implications for all aspects of human thinking and acting, and the lover who draws it finds himself drawn on to pursue those implications. The new philosophy thus claims a right to stand to our future as dogmatic

---

1. Plato, *Symposium,* 177d; *Theages* 182b; *Lysis* 204c.
2. Z 1 "On Reading and Writing," *GM* 3 motto.

Platonism stood to our past, as a philosophy of the future fit to rule a new age by virtue of the truth gained through its lover's charm, its warrior panache and swish.

The opening play of manliness and womanliness is prelude to the primary theme of the book, the thinker's investigation of nature, but it is prelude as well to an intimately related theme, the celebration of nature, even its divinization. For Nietzsche chooses to end his book in a way that echoes its opening. In the penultimate section (295), he elevates manliness and womanliness in the return of Dionysos and Ariadne, a philosopher god and the beloved whom his love raises to divinity. From beginning to end and in its deepest moments of philosophy and religion, *Beyond Good and Evil* is playful and daring, festive and gallant, the work of a lover and warrior.

"Let us hope"

If the "awful earnestness" of dogmatic philosophers was a poor means for winning truth's heart, earnestness is not discredited, for Nietzsche expresses the chief thought of the preface "earnestly." The demise of philosophical dogmatism leaves "good reasons for the hope" that its millennia-long rule will prove to be a noble childishness, mere apprenticeship. Perhaps dogmatic philosophy will be like astrology, "a promise across millennia," intrinsically worthless but producing a discipline that directs whole peoples and results in something great.[3] For Nietzsche draws a generalization about great things: "It seems" that in order to "inscribe eternal demands in the hearts of humanity," everything great first has to bestride the earth as a monstrous and fear-inducing grotesque. If the noble childishness of dogmatic philosophy was such a grotesque, "let us hope" that it prepared the hearts of humanity for the mature achievement of the most spirited philosophy, let us hope that out of the ruins of Platonism will rise a philosophical edifice worthy of that millennia-long discipline.[4]

The task of philosophy is not to repudiate its childish past but to mature

3. On dogmatism, see *A* 54; *GM* 3.12 ends on the fitting indictment of dogmatism: it "castrates the intellect."

4. Dogmatic philosophy as a fear-inducing grotesque is both Asian and European, Vedanta doctrine and Platonism, but Nietzsche's concentration in *BGE* will be entirely on European dogmatism. Elsewhere he suggests that the trajectory of European spiritual history obeys an internal logic already worked through in Asia. *GM* (3.27) mentions parenthetically that the study of the evolutionary course of the European spirit would gain from the study of India, where "the decisive point" was reached by the Sankhya philosophy that was later popularized by Buddha and transformed into a religion.

gratefully out of it, weighing its ancestry, its genealogy, like a grateful heir thankful for an inheritance richer and finer than any other. But the grateful heir knows that his inheritance includes something singularly dangerous: Plato's dogmatism is "the worst, most durable, most dangerous" of all errors so far. This judgment against Platonism, so full of superlatives, focuses on two of Plato's "inventions," "the pure mind and the good in itself."[5] What is dangerous about Platonism is its epistemology and metaphysics, its view of knowing and being; it imagines that the human mind can be so purified of its prejudices and limitations that a permanent unitary ground of everything could become discernable by it. The book as a whole will argue that the great danger of this epistemology and metaphysics was cultural and political: a philosophy that dreamed this dream proved vulnerable to capture by religion. Platonism paved the way for the rule of religion over philosophy. Platonism is, so far, the decisive event in Western history because its dangerous dream eventually cost the West its greatest achievement: the pre-Platonic Greek enlightenment.

Where do we stand now with respect to the most dangerous error? Seemingly delivered from the nightmare of Platonism, European civilization experiences relief and enjoys a more healthy — *sleep.* Like every civilization, ours sleeps through its defining events, it lives right past them (285). But while our civilization slumbers more comfortably on, a task is granted to a very few: wakefulness to the defining events. Standing in the aftermath of a great war, looking backward, forward, and around, the wakeful do not fight old battles against a Platonism that lies on the ground. "God is dead" — that phase of the war has been won. Focusing on the near, *Beyond Good and Evil* shows how the war must go on in a subtler but more comprehensive way. Now the war is for wakefulness itself, for the very possibility of philosophy amid the temptations of sleep, the pervasive rule of comforting opinion at the end of Platonism that looks like the end of history.

Dogmatic Platonism was antitruth, being so ungracious as to stand truth on her head. But Platonism was also antilife: to speak of a pure mind and the good in itself the way Plato did denies "the *perspectival,* the fundamental condition

---

5. *Geist,* translated *mind* in "the pure mind," is a crucial word that the book helps define in a new way; it comprehends what English separates into *mind* and *spirit.* I will translate it most frequently as *mind,* as in "the free mind." Mind and spirit are not two separate things but aspects of the human soul and body investigated by a "proper physiopsychology" (23). As important as spirit and spiritedness are for Nietzsche, *mind* seems to me what must be thought first by English-speakers in Nietzsche's use of *Geist.* On just how broad and fruitful a notion *Geist* is in Nietzsche, see Roberts, *Contesting Spirit,* 69, 70–74, 90–93.

of all life." Does perspectivity condemn the perspectival knower to insurmountable skepticism about the truth of any perspective? This question dominates Nietzsche's presentation of the new philosophy in the first two chapters. Addressing modern skeptics, free minds, *Beyond Good and Evil* argues for a perspectivity that recognizes a hierarchy of complementary perspectives and ultimately allows, even demands, plausible inferences to testable conclusions. Nietzsche's perspective on the perspectival endorses the perspective from above, from the widest outlook, from the cruelest will to knowledge, from the desire for the enhancement of the human species. Without descending into the fictions of the pure mind and the good in itself, the affirmation of the perspectival finds a way to reasonably affirm perspectives that can claim to be true — including even a perspective on the way of all beings.[6]

While condemning Platonism as a crime against truth and life, Nietzsche elevates Plato himself to the highest possible rank. The author of the worst of all errors is "the most beautiful growth of antiquity," and Greek antiquity is the most beautiful growth of all humanity for Nietzsche. The greatest growth of the greatest age authored the most dangerous of all errors. How did Plato contract the sickness of Platonism? Nietzsche puts his diagnosis in a series of questions arising from a problem that occupied him from the beginning of his career, the problem of Socrates. The tenor and tempo of the preface dictate that the physician's diagnosis be stated as a hypothesis still to be tested, but *The Birth of Tragedy* had already reached the conclusion: the divine Plato was corrupted by Socrates (*BT* 12–15). The book to come separates Plato from Platonism, suggesting that Plato's corruption into dogmatic Platonism was corruption into a politic philosophy, a supposedly salutary public face for philosophy. Nietzsche's Plato is reminiscent of the Plato of another of his underworld heroes, Montaigne, a Plato who, while rightly called a dogmatist, could not possibly have held for true the dogmatisms he thought it salutary that others believe.[7] In a note from the time of *Beyond Good and Evil* Nietz-

---

6. Among the different perspectives are those from below and above (30, see 205: "the view from the top down"), from inside and outside (36), from a narrow base and the broadest base (207); the perspective of "the basic will of the mind" and of the cruel will to knowledge (230); the perspective of the autonomous herd and of the complementary man (207); the perspective of science and the perspective of philosophy (chapter 6); and the perspective Nietzsche chooses to make most definitive, that of sickness or of health, of decadence or enhancement. Important reflections are found in *GS* 374 and especially *GM* 3.12, where objectivity is defined as "the capacity to have one's For and Against *under one's control.*" For a valuable account of Nietzsche's perspectivism, see Cox, *Nietzsche* 109–68.

7. See *HH* II (*AOM*) 408; Montaigne, *Essays,* "Apology," 70–80; "Of Glory," 477.

sche said, "Plato is a man with many caves out back and many facades out front" (*KSA* 11.34 [66]), and in *Beyond Good and Evil* a hermit reports that the philosopher keeps his caves hidden (289). The charges against Plato in the preface prepare the book's subtle reflections on the "philosopher with the greatest strength till now" (191), a philosopher who was a successful actor (7), a philosopher Nietzsche takes as his ultimate model and rival.[8]

"A magnificent tension of the mind and spirit"

The wakeful who stand in the aftermath of a great event in our defining war must learn what that war is and why it must still be fought. A millennial war against Platonism, it took its most recent shape as the centuries-long fight of modern science against the most successful Platonism for the people, Christianity. This modern campaign was only the latest outbreak in the basic spiritual warfare of Western history between Athens and Jerusalem, philosophy and revealed religion, episodes of which are traceable in Nietzsche's historical sketches of Greece and Rome, of Provençal troubadours, of the Renaissance, and of modern science and modern philosophy. With its rapid interpretations of vast historical movements, the preface previews a key element of the book: the spiritual warfare of this *Prelude to a Philosophy of the Future* includes a fight for our past. Written by a philosopher with the "historical sense," it is not a history book with the details filled in. Instead, its history is presented with the brevity and *presto* with which every theme is treated. Gradually, however, the historical claims take shape as a comprehensive reinterpretation of the whole human past dramatically at odds with the progressive modern view. Is it a true interpretation? By causing this question to arise, philosophy challenges science in the way suggested in chapter 6, "We Scholars": to become a philosopher means to achieve the most comprehensive perspective out of which new values are created. Could it be true, as the philosopher Nietzsche claims, that our past is marked by combat between parties so different that they cannot be dissolved in some *Aufhebung* that preserves what is valuable in each? And does this perspective, once gained, transform observers into combatants whose new values make them philosophy's allies in a fight for the European future?

As Europe sleeps on, thinking the crucial fight to be over, Nietzsche thinks the war is entering its most critical phase. It enters that phase coiled into a magnificent tension of mind and spirit "the like of which has never yet existed

---

8. Nietzsche's reflections on Platonism and Plato form one of the running themes of his book; see especially 7, 14, 28, 30, 40, 49, 56, 61, 62, 190, 191, 204, 295.

on earth." The tension is experienced as need and distress, and Nietzsche is grateful, wanting to heighten and direct them. He pictures the tension in a metaphor that governs the rest of the preface: the fight in our past makes the present like a bow drawn taut that can launch an arrow into the most distant future. The taut bow is a frequent image in the surviving fragments of Heraclitus[9] and an important image in *Zarathustra:* "To speak the truth and to shoot well with arrows" defines Persian virtue, Zarathustra's virtue (*Z* 1, "On the Thousand Goals and One"; *EH* Destiny 2). In his speech describing the great danger represented by the present age, by "the final humans," Zarathustra says, "Alas, the time is coming when man will no longer shoot the arrow of his longing beyond man, and the string of his bow will have forgotten how to twang!" The preface of *Beyond Good and Evil* gives Zarathustra's lament a more precise historical focus by stating that two attempts have already been made "in the grand style" to unstring the tense bow and rob the present of its promise: Jesuitism and the democratic Enlightenment.

Two "attempts in the grand style to unbend the bow"

If Jesuitism was the first attempt to unbend the bow of modern tension, our tense present has endured for a long time, extending back to the Reformation and Counter-Reformation. How did Nietzsche understand Jesuitism? An unpublished notebook entry from the fall of 1883 (*KSA* 10.16 [23]) gives a clue, for Nietzsche defined Jesuitism as "the conscious holding on to illusion and forcibly incorporating that illusion as the basis of culture." As a religious order carrying out ruthless warfare against heretics on behalf of a liberal, permissive, ruling Catholicism, Jesuitism was a self-conscious Platonism for the people, a Christian exercise in Platonic noble lying, an attempt to relax the taut bow of the modern European spirit by forcibly incorporating Christian principles it knew to be illusory.

A second important aspect of Jesuitism appears in the one substantial reference to it in *Beyond Good and Evil*, a reference that invokes the preface (206). In a chapter dedicated to defining the philosopher in contrast to the scientist or scholar, Jesuitism is presented as the worst and most dangerous form that can be taken by the scientific or scholarly temper, a poisoned, envious form that "works instinctively for the annihilation of the uncommon human being and tries to break every tense bow or—much rather!—to relax it. Relax, namely, with considerateness, with solicitous hand, of course—, *relax* with

---

9. See Heraclitus, Diels fragments 8, 48, 51, 53, 80. Heraclitus was the philosopher Nietzsche esteemed above all others; see *PTG* 5–8; *TI* Reason 2; *EH* Books *BT* 3; *BGE* 204 is the only mention of Heraclitus in *BGE*.

trustworthy compassion: that's the true art of Jesuitism, which has always well understood how to insinuate itself as a religion of compassion." The uncommon human being Nietzsche contrasts with Jesuitism is its great enemy, Pascal, who was on Nietzsche's mind when he mentioned Jesuitism in the preface: in one of the notes from which he drew material for the preface, Nietzsche named Pascal a "brilliant sign of the terrible tension [of the bow]" and gave his judgment on the outcome of the clash between Pascal and the Jesuits: Pascal "laughed the Jesuits *dead*" (*KSA* 11.34 [163] April-June 1885).[10] Pascal's *Provincial Letters*, Nietzsche suggests, the writings of a solitary genius, helped decide the fate of modern Europe. As Europe was becoming increasingly secular and libertine and politics increasingly dominated by expanding empires ruled by absolutist monarchs and their courts of administrators, Jesuitism had become a powerful movement to align these modern forces with the Catholic Church and bring them and the ruling and educated classes generally under Christian control. Such an alignment required latitude in easing the traditional Christian condemnation of worldly practices and relieving the strict Christian conscience of its sense of the sinful.[11] By bringing Jesuit latitude or laxity into the open, by publicizing the pious fraud of such Jesuit devices as mental reservation and probable opinion, Pascal discredited the whole Jesuit effort to relax the tension between Christianity and modern movements in politics and society. Nietzsche's unpublished comment on Jesuitism and Pascal illuminates the warning of the preface against easing our civilizational tension: the fight against Jesuitism is over, the fight against the democratic Enlightenment is not.

Nietzsche's decision not to publish his comment linking Pascal and Jesuitism illuminates the style of *Beyond Good and Evil*: its art of silence requires readers to draw inferences on the basis of fragmentarily expressed thoughts. On the basis of the references in *Beyond Good and Evil*, Leo Strauss called Pascal Nietzsche's "precursor par excellence."[12] How did Nietzsche stand to his precursor with respect to the uses of tension? The chapter on religion in *Beyond Good and Evil* opens and closes with reflections on Pascal. Its opening

---

10. A few entries earlier in the same notebook Nietzsche lamented that Pascal died thirty years too soon to laugh himself out of Christianity as he had laughed himself and others out of Jesuitism (34 [148]). This comment shows the singularity of Nietzsche's admiration for Pascal: not many readers have supposed that Pascal *laughed* himself out of Jesuitism, however successful the *Provincial Letters* may have been in leading others to laugh themselves out of Jesuitism; neither have many readers supposed that thirty more such years would have afforded Pascal the possibility of a more comprehensive laugh. On Nietzsche and Pascal, see Brendan Donnellan, *Nietzsche and the French Moralists*.

11. On Jesuitism as a modernist movement aimed at holding sway over the ruling educated classes, see Leszek Kolakowski, *God Owes Us Nothing* 44–61.

12. *Studies in Platonic Political Philosophy* 176.

reflection requires the thinker to look down on the highest religious experience from above in order to measure it in thought. The closing reflection requires that history-making actions on behalf of the European spirit be undertaken by a philosopher who stands above any Christian or providential view of human destiny. Pascal is Nietzsche's precursor as a solitary writer of genius opposing a powerful tendency to pacify the European mind, but Nietzsche stands above Pascal, wholly outside Platonism, writing against a more comprehensive enemy.

If Nietzsche stands to the democratic Enlightenment as Pascal stood to Jesuitism, then his ambitions for his book are monumental and precise: he aims to defeat the powerful Platonism for the people that now holds sway by defeating Platonism as such. The central chapter of the book, "On the Natural History of Morality," argues that the democratic Enlightenment is a Platonism for the people that may yet succeed in its effort to relax the tensed bow of the modern spirit. The preface suggests that the democratic Enlightenment finds its chief weapon in a German invention: the printing press or modern media, which, while amusing and diverting the population, create in it the belief that it is the first free and informed population in history. The opponent of the democratic Enlightenment also finds his chief weapon in a German invention: gunpowder, figurative gunpowder, for this is a "war without powder and smoke" (*EH* Books *HH*). The central chapter argues that victory in the war against the democratic Enlightenment can be achieved only by "a new type of philosopher" who effects a "transvaluation of values" (203). His war is a war in which the explosives are words like the word *enlightenment* itself: *The New Enlightenment* is a prospective title often used in the notebooks containing materials that eventually appeared under the title *Beyond Good and Evil* (for example, *KSA* 11.26 [293, 298]; 27 [79]; 29 [40]). Nietzsche's task is itself an enlightenment that carries forward the Greek enlightenment prior to the Platonic strategy that reconciled that enlightenment with popular prejudice. Nietzsche's enlightenment is anti-Platonic; it brings the effects of enlightenment into the open by refusing to hide "deadly" truths behind "noble" lies.[13]

"We good Europeans and free, very free minds"

"I say 'we' out of courtesy," Nietzsche remarked in *Twilight of the Idols* (Reason 5), and it is evident that here too "we" is a singular. But if the *very* free

---

13. See Picht, *Nietzsche* 51: Nietzsche "carries out an enlightenment of the Enlightenment and shows that the completed enlightenment is possible only as the enlightenment of humanity respecting its own history."

mind is singular, "free minds" is plural, and it is clear from chapter 2 that free minds are the audience for whom the book is written, scholars and scientists addressed directly in "We Scholars" and "Our Virtues." Free minds will want to be freer, to be very free, and the book aims at freeing the free mind from prejudices that still bind it to fashionable skepticisms about the possibility of true judgments. But the book has an aim subsequent to mere freeing: it aims to bind the very free minds it creates, bind them to true judgments about the world and true judgments about history, bind them via their science that certifies those judgments. Furthermore, it binds the very free minds to the task those judgments imply: enlisting in the war for human enhancement.

"And perhaps also the arrow, the task and who knows? the goal. . . . ."

Did Nietzsche know the goal when he placed these phrases at the end of the preface? "On the Thousand Goals and One" is the title of the chapter of *Zarathustra* that claimed to understand the thousand goals of the thousand peoples, and that set forth, on the basis of that understanding, a thousand and first goal for a new people, global humanity. It is the goal that falls to a comprehensive philosophy, one that gains an interpretation of the way of all beings and transfigures that interpretation into shared image and festival. *Beyond Good and Evil* is a fishhook baited to attract others to that goal by helping them glimpse its possibility and desirability and inducing them to study *Zarathustra* to understand its character and range.

If bow, arrow, and target[14] evoke Heraclitus and Zarathustra, perhaps they evoke as well the beginning of the preface and frame it in a unifying image: bow and arrow are the weapons of Eros, and to know the target is to know how to use them. The erotic passion that always fired philosophy now steps into the open, opposing the Platonism that acknowledged its erotic source but veiled it in dogmatic moralism. The imagery of eros framing the preface suggests that Platonism's foe is Plato's kin, and the book that follows confirms it. The good European has a lover's mission, restoration of the highest beloved. *Beyond Good and Evil* shows how philosophy is possible again in a postmodern, post-Christian, post-Platonic, world. The end of Platonism is not the end of philosophy.

14. *Ziel,* translated *goal* above, is also the word for target.

On the Prejudices of Philosophers

Nietzsche's *Prelude to a Philosophy of the Future* opens with an assault on philosophy. So prominent as a first impression and so effective in the suspicions it arouses or confirms about philosophy, this first chapter of Nietzsche's book may seem to destroy permanently the possibility of philosophy as a way to truth. But even though philosophy is always prejudiced for Nietzsche — always situated or from a perspective, always interested or driven by passion — that condition need not be fatal to philosophy's task of winning the truth. Subsequent chapters, as well as quieter suggestions within the assault itself, gradually recover philosophy's original greatness and stake a renewed claim to its capacity to win the truth and even, on that basis, to be the legitimate creator of values and the lawgiver to the sciences. If the opening questions question the value of the will to truth and pose the problem of the value of truth itself, the supreme value of that subjective passion and its elusive object are eventually confirmed by such questioning: Nietzsche's book does not end where it begins; it is structured; it opens, advances, and closes — and not just once, though its first opening and its final closing clearly have a priority that befit their prominence. The opening questions about truth point the way into a profound and liberating skepticism about philosophy — the way to "the free mind" — and then to a way out of that skepticism that does not surrender the intellectual conscience. Chapter 1 justifies the assertion of the preface that traditional philosophy now lies in ruins while raising new suspicions against it. Chapter 2, as its title indicates, is a second chapter on philosophy or philosophy's second chapter; it demonstrates how a new philosophy, while sustaining the suspicions of the first chapter, can move beyond mere skepticism or free-mindedness and attain reasonable and comprehensive conclusions about the world. If philosophy is possible again, as chapter 2 argues, the rest of the book follows: religion must be reconstituted on the basis of the new philosophy (chapter 3), and a morals and politics grounded in history and crowned with nobility must be generated to serve and dignify it (chapters 5–9).

The first and best-known chapter of *Beyond Good and Evil* is deconstructive, as its title announces, but peering through the destruction is a calculated argument for a new, constructive view. The lyrical opening section, invoking the tale of the heroic knower Oedipus, announces a turn to a new kind of question for philosophy and sets a mood of heroic risk over the whole enterprise—a warning, yes, but a lure as well to the right kind of reader. Warning and lure are sounded again in the closing section, which invokes the myth of another heroic Greek knower, Odysseus, to herald the great adventure that lies ahead in subsequent chapters (23). Framed within this setting of heroic risk, chapter 1 follows a reasoned trajectory that can be readily mapped. Treating first some general characteristics of philosophy as it has presented itself till now (2–6), Nietzsche sketches a history of philosophy that treats ancient philosophy very briefly (7–9) and modern philosophy somewhat more extensively and with constant reference to philosophy's relation to science (10–14), in particular, the deficient philosophical interpretations of modern science that impede the advancement of science—an indispensable part of Nietzsche's project (15–17). Section 18 poses a challenge met in the remaining sections (19–23), chapter 1 thus closing with a display of strength on the issue of human will: are free minds free?

Four times in chapter 1 the fundamental teaching of will to power is named, first with respect to philosophy itself, then with respect to biology, physics, and psychology: first the comprehensive science and then the sciences of life, nature, and the human soul.[1] And it is the investigation of the final item, the human soul, that promises, in the final section of this chapter, to give privileged access to the reality shared by all beings; in this respect the Nietzschean

---

1. These allusions to a new constructive view are what most distinguish this opening chapter from its counterpart in Nietzsche's earlier book in nine chapters addressed to free minds, *Human, All Too Human,* a book Nietzsche could regard as supplanted because of what these allusions claim.

turn resembles the Socratic turn described in the *Phaedo* and the *Symposium*. And with Nietzsche too it is not simply the human soul that the philosopher investigates but the different character of the soul he finds within himself, the soul of the driven knower. Consequently, chapter 2 begins with considerations of the philosopher's difference and advances to the philosopher's reasoning with respect to the soul, leading ultimately to a conclusion about the way of all beings, the world defined according to its "intelligible character." The new view is presented through an experiment in reasoning whose conclusion is a comprehensive ontology or account of the way of all beings. Once drawn, that conclusion leads inexorably to an experiment in how human life might best be lived. The assault on philosophy thus prepares philosophy's reestablishment, its instauration, as an ontology of will to power and a consequent transvaluation of all values.

Daring to Question the Value of Truth
SECTION 1

"The will to truth": Nietzsche opens his opening section with words philosophy has long employed to name its fundamental drive, a variant on the opening of the preface. But the will to truth provokes in Nietzsche new questions as dangerous as the question of the Sphinx who killed those who dared to answer but answered wrongly. Oedipus solved the Sphinx's riddle because he knew the truth about humanity and, after killing the Sphinx, ascended to rule in Thebes.[2] Both Sphinx and Oedipus, questioner and answerer, the new heroic knower now poses two questions about the will to truth. What are its origins? What is its value? These questions about the origin and value of the will to truth lead to what seems to be the basic and most important issue, "the problem of the value of truth," the now-fundamental problem for philosophy according to this first section. This seemingly new problem draws a superlative from Nietzsche: perhaps there is no greater risk than raising the problem of the value of truth. Like Plato in his allegory of the cave, Nietzsche pictures the risk-taking questioner as "turning around." With Nietzsche the turn is inward, toward the intrepid investigator himself: What causes this drive in himself and why does he value it above all other drives? And why value it even though it puts everything at risk?

Following this opening, chapter 1 is primarily a critique of the old philosophy, and in the next section Nietzsche argues that the old philosophy, instead of raising the question of the value of truth, assumed its supreme value and

2. See Nietzsche's reflections on Oedipus in *BT* 9.

asked only about the origin of this valuable thing. But to assume the value of truth for human beings is to assume that there is consonance or harmony between truth and our natures, that truth is what we are naturally fitted for. By opening mythically on the heroic danger of pursuing the question of the value of truth, Nietzsche intimates that, on the contrary, truth is deadly. And if it is deadly, if truth puts everything at risk, then the old belief of Platonism that truth is what we are naturally fitted for required that the real truth be falsified, lied about. The "truths" of the old philosophy were edifying myths, beginning with the myth that truth is edifying. Our most indispensable lie is our belief in the goodness of truth. The risk in questioning the value of truth lies in the likelihood that it will destroy the falsifications that have sustained human life and force humanity to face truth's deadliness. That truth is deadly is the deadliest truth.

Is Nietzsche, as it "almost seems" to him in his reflection on Oedipus, the first to view truth as deadly? The mythic-heroic tone of the opening perhaps exaggerates the pioneering quality of the investigator, for *Beyond Good and Evil* itself suggests that Plato faced the question of the value of truth. But Plato concluded that truth was too dangerous to be openly proclaimed; the well-being of humanity required that the truth seeker "lie knowingly and willingly," as Nietzsche said in a notebook entry on Plato.[3] Socrates stated at the opening of Plato's *Republic* that it is just to lie to the mad,[4] and the rest of the dialogue intimates that this is the justice of the few sane, the philosopher who recognizes the necessity of the noble lie.[5] *Beyond Good and Evil* opposes Platonism while acknowledging the great difference between Plato and Platonism, between what Plato thought and what he found it desirable for others to believe.

Has it now become desirable to believe the deadly truth? Nietzsche had posed this question often but never more powerfully than five years earlier in *Dawn of Day* (429), where the questions that open *Beyond Good and Evil* are already given an answer, one that ties the risk to historic necessity. In a section entitled "*The new passion*," Nietzsche asks why we fear and hate a possible return to barbarism: not because such a return would make human beings unhappier but because it would make us more ignorant. "Our *drive to knowl-edge* has become too strong for us to be capable of valuing happiness without

3. *KSA* 11.26 [152]; see also 34 [179, 195]; *KSA* 13.14 [116].
4. *Republic* 1.331c.
5. *Republic* 3.414b-c; see also the "willing lie" *Republic* 7.535d-e (cf. 2.382a-b). Nietzsche reflected on the necessary lie very early, in *UD* 10; he raised that issue after presenting the three teachings he regarded as "true but deadly," "the teachings of sovereign becoming, of the fluidity of all concepts, types, and kinds, of the lack of any cardinal difference between man and animal" (*UD* 9).

knowledge or valuing the happiness of a strong well-founded delusion. . . . Knowledge has transformed itself into a passion in us which shrinks at no sacrifice and at bottom fears nothing but its own extinction." The risk faced at the opening of *Beyond Good and Evil* is put in the most extreme form and fully embraced: "Perhaps humanity will even perish of this passion for knowledge! — even this thought has no power over us!" And Nietzsche concludes, "We all want the destruction of humanity rather than the regression of knowledge! And if humanity does not have a *passion*, it will perish of a *weakness*: what would one rather have? That's the chief question. Do we want humanity to end in fire and light or in the sand?" A note prepared for Zarathustra but never published puts the same risk graphically: "*We are making an experiment with the truth!* Perhaps humanity will perish because of it! On with it!" (*KSA* 11.25 [305]). "On with it!" is neither a shrug nor a wish to perish; it's Nietzsche's recognition that there is no choice. Like *Dawn of Day, Beyond Good and Evil* ties the necessity to the times, but it will go further and locate that necessity in nature, in a certain kind of human being. But in risking truth, in attempting to bring opinion into accord with the philosopher's knowledge, *Beyond Good and Evil* displays in its own quiet way the greatest gain of *Thus Spoke Zarathustra:* truth is deadly only to a certain kind of human being while to another kind, *the* other kind, truth is not only enticing but ultimately lovable, the reason for gaiety and festival that could ultimately house the global human community.

Heroic risk and the threat of ruin set the mood of the opening section, but what follows does not succumb to the somber; instead, it exhibits an irrepressible cheerfulness or gaiety, a spirit of comedy that is as much a part of philosophy, Nietzsche intimates, as the spirit of tragedy. Risk appears again in the closing section of the first chapter, in which Odysseus is the model, the great voyager in search of the truth; the threat of ruin is vanquished by exhilaration and good cheer, which buoy the born adventurer setting out on a great undertaking — the adventure of the subsequent chapters, which pursue the questions of the origin and value of truth. *Beyond Good and Evil* began by identifying Plato as the source of our dying dogmatism; chapter 1 opens and closes with allusions to pre-Platonic Greek heroes of wisdom. *Beyond Good and Evil* aims in part to recover a Greek wisdom prior to Socrates and Plato, Homeric wisdom celebrated in tragedy, reformed and restored in Aristophanic comedy, and pursued philosophically by the philosophers of the tragic age of the Greeks. Platonic dogmatism, Nietzsche will indicate, supplanted Homeric or tragic wisdom out of convictions not about its superior truthfulness but about its superior safety. The heroic still risks the Homeric but finds it necessary to go beyond even Oedipus and Odysseus, as Nietzsche states later in a section of "Our Virtues" that defines the heroic virtue of the seeker after knowledge (230).

The dangerous new question that opens *Beyond Good and Evil*—What is the value of truth?—rises again at the end of the final essay of *On the Genealogy of Morality*, the essay on the ascetic ideal. Nietzsche has just quoted at length from yet another formulation of that question, *The Gay Science* 344, and he stops to say, "—— At this point it is necessary to pause and to reflect for a long time." The problem to reflect on is "that of the *value* of truth. —The will to truth is in need of a critique—let us thus define our own task—the value of truth is for once to be experimentally *called into question* (3.24)." Nietzsche then adds a reading assignment for reflection on this new problem: the whole of *Gay Science* 344, "or best of all, the entire fifth book of that work, likewise the preface of *Dawn of Day*." In the *Genealogy* itself, Nietzsche continues to elaborate this problem: in our time the question of the value of truth focuses on science. As an expression of the ascetic ideal, science since Copernicus has contributed to the self-belittlement, even self-contempt, of humanity; it talks humanity out of its previous respect for itself (*GM* 3.25). While science is not able to posit a new value-ideal (3.25), as the heir to Christianity, inheriting its will to truth, science is able to destroy both its progenitor and something broader and deeper as well, morality itself (3.27). It does so by raising the question, "*What does all will to truth mean?*" And Nietzsche adds after this question, "Here again I touch on my problem, on our problem, my *unknown* friends (for as yet I *know* of no friends): what meaning would *our* entire being have if not this, that in us this will to truth has come to a consciousness of itself as a *problem?*" There is one more section to go in *On the Genealogy of Morality*, the final section on the possibility of new meaning imputed to human suffering now that the ascetic ideal has drawn its last consequence, a possibility left open as the book ends.

On the Genealogy of Morality announced on the back of its title page, "Appended to the recently published *Beyond Good and Evil* as a supplement and clarification." The end of the whole work, supplements and all, brings it around again to its beginning, the question of the value of truth. Has no progress been made on the dangerous new question? In continuing to raise repeatedly the question of the value of truth, Nietzsche is not pointing to a question he himself had yet to solve; he is a "hyperborean," he "knows the road," he "has found the exit out of millennia of labyrinth" (*A* 1). He poses the question of the value of truth again and again in order to set the friends he still lacks on a road he has traversed to its end. As *Beyond Good and Evil* will show, raising the question of the value of truth leads not only to the possession of truth but to its affirmation and celebration, no matter how deadly, how demonic, it looks at first. Science, which has served the ascetic ideal, does not in principle have asceticism or denial as its ideal: the denials necessary for a life of knowing can well serve a disposition higher than denial; science, as *Beyond Good and Evil* will show, can be grounded in an affirmative philosophy. And as for the place of humanity in the newly discovered truth, *Beyond Good and Evil* ends by raising the question, "What is noble?" and showing a way to affirm the nobility of the human in the face of a whole tradition of self-belittlement and self-contempt.

The opening question does not remain an open question. Facing up to the deadly question of the value of truth leads ultimately to the affirmation of truth as wholly compatible with the affirmation of life and humanity. The book is a drama that dares to open on what threatens to be the ultimate tragedy but becomes instead, not simply comedy, but a spectacle fit for gods.

Dangerous Maybes
SECTIONS 2–6

The questions of the origin of the will to truth and of the value of truth dominate the opening sections of the first chapter. Clear indictments can be brought against the old philosophy for the prejudiced way it answered these questions, but at this early point only dangerous maybes can be suggested about how the philosophy of the future might answer them. But the dangerous maybes of these opening sections are, later sections make clear, no longer mere maybes for Nietzsche but reasonable conclusions arrived at through responsible experimental method and sufficient evidence — conclusions that can be shared by those willing to risk pursuing the questions that lead to them.

Section 2   The second section erupts out of the first, the old dogmatism rising up to condemn the questioner of the first section and proclaim its own firm faith in truth and the will to truth. The quoted speech of the old dogmatism answers the question of the origin of truth, but its answer is possible only because it refuses to question the value of truth. The speech pronounces the fundamental prejudice of Platonism: truth cannot arise out of error, the high cannot originate in the low, perfection must stand at the origin of all good things like truth. Nietzsche's response offers a brief characterization of Platonism: *"faith in the oppositeness of values."* That dogmatic faith dictated that there be two worlds, a true world of being accessible to the purified mind and an untrue world of becoming. Philosophy invented its own version of a true world but its invention embraced the common or popular view that already divided the world into high and low, sacred and profane. The chief prejudice of philosophers was already the prejudice of the people.

Dualistic dogmatism condemns its opponents: whoever dreams that the true originated in its opposite is "a fool, yes, worse." Worse than fools are criminals (cf. 30) guilty of breaking the law of moral origins promulgated by dualism. Nietzsche accepts the judgment that he's a criminal, a teacher of evil, a tempter offering the forbidden fruit of knowledge of good and evil, the most potent opposites. The temptation is offered temptingly as a dangerous maybe, the possibility that there are no such opposites, that the perspective claiming opposites is a prejudice squinting up from below, that the good may be related to the evil, even essentially the same. Definitive only in its indictment of the dogmatic conviction of traditional philosophy and in its recommendation of radical doubt, this very early section is provisional and programmatic about where that doubt may lead. Only gradually does Nietzsche assemble the reasoned perspectives that point to a defensible philosophical monism able to account for the full range of phenomena, able as well to account for the faith of dualism: dogmatic dualism will come to light as a fully understandable response to a conflict within human beings between heart and mind, between what we wish for and what can reasonably be thought.

What is not doubtful about the evaluations of traditional metaphysics is that they preexist philosophy as the evaluations of the populace to which philosophy merely sets its seal.[6] Metaphysics thus originates with the philosophers' alignment with the populace—it originates with the philosophers' failure to demarcate and make prominent the difference of the philosopher's soul. The study of the soul of the philosopher in its difference opens the path to the fundamental problems in chapter 2. Chapter 1 begins with the philosophers' assimilation to the common run of humanity and the dualism that resulted; chapter 2 begins with the philosopher as an exception, even the exception among exceptions, and leads to the monism that is the reasonable culmination of the study of the philosopher's soul.

Doubt about origins is Nietzsche's first means for undermining the faith in opposite values. Doubt about the value of this faith leads Nietzsche to propose an alternative standard, life itself: "For all the value one might have to attribute to the true, the truthful, and the selfless, it's still possible that the apparent, the will to deception, self-interest and desire will have to be assigned a higher and more fundamental value for all life." But life as a standard hides an ambiguity that Nietzsche will soon articulate: is the standard the preser-

---

6. See the distinction between "the famous wise" and "you who are wisest" in Z 2 "On the Famous Wise," "On Self-Overcoming."

vation of life or the enhancement of life? To argue for the enhancement of life, as Nietzsche will, implies that there is something of more worth than mere preservation, something to which life might properly be sacrificed. While content at this point to submerge the ambiguity, Nietzsche's willingness to run heroic risk already suggests that he is moved by something more primordial than the mere will to live. Gradually Nietzsche will show himself to be an evolutionary thinker who looks back on human history and understands its contours on the basis of survival through natural selection. But the present point in the natural history of humanity is unique, Nietzsche will argue, for as the whole evolutionary process now becomes transparent to the wakeful, the power of mere preservation, its threat to life's enhancement, also becomes visible and makes it necessary to choose enhancement even if it puts preservation at risk. Nietzsche's central chapter, "On the Natural History of Morality," argues that this is the ultimate reason for breaking with Platonism's endorsement of popular prejudice.

Nietzsche's dangerous maybe suggests that "the apparent" or "the illusory" (*der Schein*) may have more value for life than the true. But Nietzsche's understanding of *Schein* rescues it from Platonism's depreciation as mere transitory appearance masking a valuable and permanent reality. Schein names most concretely what shines, shimmers, gleams and, more abstractly, what shows forth, what appears. Given our dogmatic Platonism, Schein is bound to be heard first as the opposite to the true, mere appearance, the illusory. *Beyond Good and Evil* is structured to advance gradually to the conclusion that "the world seen from the inside . . . would be will to power and nothing besides" (36). How is Schein understood in a world of will to power and nothing besides? As Nietzsche says in a note from the time of *Beyond Good and Evil*, "NB. *Schein* as I understand it is the actual and sole reality of things."[7] It is reality from the perspective of ordering subjects like ourselves, who array and construe it in accord with patterns we cannot throw off. *Schein* is the shown-forth reality whose "intelligible character" can be inferred to be will to power; it is not illusory, it is not *mere* anything. "I therefore do not set 'Schein' in opposition to 'reality' but on the contrary take Schein as the reality that resists transformation into an imaginary 'truth-world.' A determinative name for this reality would be 'will to power,' namely, characterized from inside and not from its ungraspable, flowing Proteus-nature."[8] Two perspectives, exterior and interior, two names, Schein and will to power, the same sole reality.[9]

7. *KSA* 11.40 [53] (Aug.-Sept. 1885). This entry, entitled "against the word '*Erscheinung*,'" follows an entry that singles out *Erscheinungen,* or appearance, as a fateful word that hinders knowledge.

8. Ibid. The whole entry runs, "NB. *Schein* as I understand it is the actual and sole

Pursuit of such dangerous maybes, Nietzsche says at the end of section 2, awaits a new genus of philosophers, a non-Platonic genus given that Plato set "all theologians and philosophers on the same track" (191). The new genus "will have some other, turned-around taste and inclination." Are there such philosophers? "Spoken in all earnestness: I see such new philosophers rising up." *Beyond Good and Evil* states this hope at its beginning but gives no evidence that Nietzsche had actually seen a single such philosopher—besides himself. Nietzsche's earnest hope seems to lie in what he can imagine: such philosophers rising up through the books he writes to create them.[10] The philosophers of the dangerous maybes are a Nietzschean genus set on the same track by a turned-around taste and inclination and "baptized" with the anti-Platonic name Nietzsche waits to bestow on them until his two chapters on philosophy are nearly over. They are *Versucher*, tempters and experimenters (42), who pursue the dangerous maybes in the way Nietzsche does; fearless reasoning about dangerous maybes gradually turns them into dangerous probabilities that force one to act.

Section 3   Turning from the true to the truth seeker, from the object to the subject, Nietzsche raises a dangerous maybe about philosophical thinking itself or about the possibility of "pure mind." His manner of studying the philosophers is peculiar: he looks "between the lines and at the fingers"—both forms of looking will be connected with Nietzsche's understanding of philosophic esotericism. Study of this unusual sort led him to conclude that so far from being the opposite of the instincts, "the conscious thinking of a philosopher is secretly guided and forced into determinate tracks by his instincts." Section 3 thus carries forward the chief thought of section 2; radical doubt about the dualism of mind and body initiates the project of understanding just how philosophical thinking might be determined by "valuations or, spoken more clearly, physiological demands for the preservation of a certain

---

reality of things,—that which all available predicates first befit and what relatively would be best characterized with all [predicates], therefore also with the counter predicates. But with words nothing is further expressed than its *inaccessibility* for the logical processes and distinctions: therefore, 'Schein' in relation to 'logical truth'—which is itself however only possible of an imaginary world. I therefore do not set 'Schein' in opposition to 'reality' but on the contrary take *Schein* as the reality that resists transformation into an imaginary 'truth-world.' A determinative name for this world would be 'will to power,' namely, characterized from inside and not from its ungraspable, flowing Proteus-nature."

9. See *TI* " 'Reason' in Philosophy"; Nietzsche ends this important reflection by distilling his view of the distinction between "true world" and apparent world into four theses "which I dare you to contradict."

10. Georg Picht, *Nietzsche* 61–88.

kind of life." Again, life is determinative; again, the survival of the species may dictate that "appearance be worth less than 'truth.'" But again, the dangerousness of such a maybe is clear: it seems to be antilife because it jeopardizes self-preservation.

Sections 2 and 3 of *Beyond Good and Evil* expand and deepen the main thought of the opening section of *Human, All Too Human,* "The Chemistry of Concepts and Sensations." That earlier reflection emphasized the continuity of thought and physiology, stating that the new "historical" philosophy "must no longer be thought separate from natural science, the youngest of all philosophical methods." *Beyond Good and Evil,* too, simply assumes that philosophy will employ the gains of science, here the gains of evolutionary biology: all life processes, including thinking itself, originate in the basic instincts and are directed by them; everything characteristically human, including thinking, evolved as part of the survival struggle of our species. For Nietzsche the gains of modern biology are in part a recovery of an earlier, pre-Platonic biology preserved in Lucretius. Emphasizing "retraining" or learning differently (*umlernen*), these sections unlearn Platonism by adopting the basic reductionism of the pre-Platonic science of the Greek enlightenment: everything is part of the cosmic process, and whatever flourishes is selected by the process itself.

While sharing this general view with *Human, All Too Human, Beyond Good and Evil* announces an essential advance: just as the foundations of modern science were laid by philosophy, so must it continue to be led by philosophy, now by a philosophy that has achieved a reasoned account of the comprehensive way of all beings and of the values affirmative of the way of all beings. Nietzsche's presentation of philosophy's claim to the leadership of science comes gradually, strategically. Perhaps this is indicated by a small change he made in correcting the final draft of section 3 for publication: he chose to replace an ending that contained the words *will to power.*[11] By eliminating that phrase from the final version of this section, Nietzsche may have indicated his sense of the architecture of his book: the first use of *will to power* is reserved for its highest, most spiritual form (9).

Section 4   The dangerous maybe of the brief section 4 concerns what "may sound strangest" in the new philosophy. Once again the issue is the value of truth, expressed here as the view that the falseness of a judgment is not neces-

---

11. *KSA* 14, *Kommentar,* 348. The deleted clauses begin after "nevertheless mere foreground valuations" and run: "thanks to which the will to power carries through [*durchsetzt,* in this context, "allows to survive"] a certain kind of being (this being must look over everything easily, closely, precisely, calculably, therefore fundamentally in the logical perspectives —)"

sarily an objection to it. Instead of taking truth or falsity as the ultimate criterion, Nietzsche locates the value of a judgment in "how far it is life-promoting, life-preserving, species-preserving, perhaps even species-cultivating." Having already traced "the greater part" of philosophers' judgments to instinct and instinct to preservation (3), Nietzsche here adds, with a "perhaps," what will become the decisive standard of measure for him, what cultivates or enhances the species.[12]

Nietzsche's new language sounds strangest on the issue of the true and the good. Platonism assumed that the true was coterminous with the good; Nietzsche's strange language recognizes that the good, construed as the species' advantage, often requires that the false be taken as true. Does the good of the species as Nietzsche construes it, its enhancement, require that the value of the will to truth be limited? Here is the most important issue of the book, the relationship of the true and the good, or the question of the value of truth in light of the enhancement of the species. The complexity of the issue is merely suggested here, where Nietzsche restricts falsification to the insurmountable falsifications of thinking itself: synthetic a priori judgments, logic, mathematics. This aspect of falsification — its epistemic unavoidability — is central to modern philosophy, and Nietzsche will consider it after the proper preparation at the center of chapter 2: given such falsification, given "the erroneousness of the world in which we think we live," can the truth of the world be glimpsed at all (34–35)? Nietzsche answers, Yes, but the truth he infers draws the reaction that *that* truth is anything but species-enhancing (36–37). Such a reaction shows that falsification is more endemic than the necessary falsifications of perception and conception; it extends to the whole realm of values, to the "simplification and falsification" within which human beings choose to live (24). How does the will to truth of the new philosophy stand toward the falsifications of value? The core issue of the book, the relation of the true and the good or of fact and value, is, in the most general sense of the terms, the relation of philosophy and religion. Nietzsche structures the first three chapters to show how intimately the two are related.

Section 5 The recognition of necessary or epistemic falsification in section 4 seems to supply a silent background to what is denounced in section 5: unnecessary or dishonest falsification by moral philosophers advocating their

---

12. The dramatic but as yet unexplained title of Nietzsche's book receives its first explicit clarification at the end of this section: *Beyond Good and Evil* moves beyond the good as customarily construed by refusing to suppose that the true has its origins in the good and is in some way identical with it. The title of the book is also used in 44, 56, 153, 212, 260.

prejudices. Nietzsche claims that philosophers provoke mistrust and ridicule not simply because they're innocent or childish, as the preface claimed, but rather because they're not honest enough. Honesty mistrusts and ridicules philosophers as "advocates who resent that name," lawyers arguing a case in accord with their heart's desire while posing as coldly rational—the desires of the heart seem to take their place alongside the instincts as the hidden masters of thought. The chapter will end on this conflict between heart and mind (23). But if the value of the will to truth is in question, if falsification is unavoidable, if life itself is preserved by falsification, if falsification serves the heart's desires, what status can mere honesty claim? Providing a defense of philosophy's new honesty or candor is a major task of the book; that defense can be laid out only gradually, for it must be comprehensive; it must be tied to virtue (227) but, more than that, it must be tied to the good, to species enhancement.

Section 5 claims that philosophers are "*very* far from having a conscience brave enough to own up to" being dishonest advocates of their moral preferences. A brave conscience will be part of what Nietzsche aims to forge in *Beyond Good and Evil*. At the beginning of *The Gay Science* (2) Nietzsche gave the name "intellectual conscience" to his virtue, treating intellectual conscience as his form of *in*justice: because he acts as if everyone has one, he's unjust to almost everyone, not giving them their due. Here Nietzsche links the bravery of conscience to an additional quality, good taste. The good taste of philosophical bravery admits the truth about itself "in order to warn an enemy or friend"—the good taste of philosophical truth telling lacks lawyerly stealth out of pride, rejecting both of the old grounds for a lack of candor about philosophy: the harm its enemies could inflict on it or the harm the truth could inflict on philosophy's friends. Philosophy's brave good taste admits the truth about itself for another reason: "out of high-spiritedness and in order to make sport of itself." The section began by looking at all philosophers "sportingly" (*spöttisch*, mockingly); good taste requires that it do the same with itself. Out of high-spiritedness the new philosophy risks showing itself to be high-spiritedness; refusing to fake a solemn knowledge of truth, it risks showing itself to be a sport, a hunt, a love affair with the most elusive of beloveds.

Section 6 Nietzsche brings his opening reflections on philosophy to a close not on a dangerous maybe but on a settled conclusion he learned "gradually" about "what every great philosophy so far has been: namely, the personal confession of its originator and a kind of involuntary and unconscious memoir." Great philosophy is profoundly autobiographical; it cannot avoid betraying its grounds in the drives and the wishes of the heart: "the moral (or immoral) intentions in every philosophy constituted the genuine germ of life out of which the whole plant grew every time." This generalization produces a rule of method recommended to his reader: in reading a philosopher one must ask, "To what morality does all this (does *he* —) aspire?" To what morality does *Nietzsche* aspire? *Beyond Good and Evil* has the same reflexive quality exhibited by Zarathustra, who invited judgment by the standards he used to judge others.[13] Later chapters set out the history of morality, the basic moral types, and the drives on which they are grounded, making clear just what the contest of moralities is. In keeping with the implicit invitation of this section, they include many little dialogues that formulate objections and accusations against the morality to which Nietzsche aspires. They provide guidance for determining what is involuntary in the new philosophy, the drives *it* serves, and for judging the degree to which it became conscious of its rule over the wishes of the heart.

Nietzsche claims that "the drive to knowledge" (a variant of "the will to truth") is not "the father of philosophy" but that other more basic drives employ this claim as an instrument. There is, however, one feature common to all the drives: "Every single one of them would like only too well to represent precisely *itself* as the ultimate purpose of existence and as rightful *master* of all the remaining drives. For every drive is *herrschsüchtig:* and *as such* it attempts to philosophize." Every drive is addicted to mastery, it lusts to rule, striving to impose its perspective on all the other drives.[14] *Zarathustra* had made clear that this is no critique; *Herrschsucht,* the lust to rule, is one of the "three evils" Zarathustra reweighs and finds good (Z 3 "On the Three Evils"), the central "evil" basic to the most fundamental human undertakings and to Zarathustra's own undertaking as a thinker and teacher: he confesses that he had earlier called *Herrschsucht* "the gift-giving virtue." In solitude and abstaining from virtuous labels, Zarathustra comes close to giving *Herrschsucht* its true name: the will to power. He withholds that name for reasons intrinsic to the book, husbanding his fundamental words for maximum effect, just as Nietzsche does in *Beyond Good and Evil.*

Having stated that the philosopher is defined by *Herrschsucht,* Nietzsche adds an essential proviso before moving to the history of philosophy: he is speaking only of the very rare great philosophers: "With scholars, with truly scientific human beings, it may well be otherwise — 'better' one may want to

13. See especially the chapters on justice, Z 1 "On the Adder's Bite," Z 2 "On the Tarantulas," "On Redemption."

14. See Z 1 "On Enjoying and Suffering the Passions," and *KSA* 12.7 [60]. Nietzsche's "major point of historical method" in *GM* 2.12 generalizes this claim about drives: "All events in the organic world are an *overpowering,* a *becoming master,* and all overpowering and becoming master is a fresh interpretation."

say." *Better* is not what Nietzsche says: the whole of "We Scholars" is devoted to the difference between philosophers and scholars, arguing that philosophy's right to rule is well grounded. In the present section *Beyond Good and Evil* affirms the possibility and desirability of scientific objectivity. The prophetic excesses of *Zarathustra* do not, as many have argued, signal the abandonment of Nietzsche's esteem for science so apparent in the books of his "scientific period."[15] Instead, beginning with *Zarathustra*, Nietzsche's work exhibits a new claim for philosophy as a spiritual/intellectual achievement more comprehensive than science and fit to lead science. *Zarathustra* chronicles that gain while emphasizing in part 4 what will be argued in "We Scholars": science is an indispensable instrument of philosophy.

By what right can philosophy rule science? By natural right, Nietzsche eventually answers, a right granted by nature construed as an order of rank. Such an answer requires preparation before it can sound plausible, and *Beyond Good and Evil* has just begun: philosophy differs from science, and the difference seems to make science "better" because philosophy is *herrschsüchtig* whereas science can be an objective pursuit of knowledge. If it is better with scholars and scientists, if a drive to knowledge detached from the will to rule really is at work there, then Nietzsche's book, addressed to them, must still meet their standard. Nietzsche is a philosopher writing a book that will be assessed by scholars with respect to its truthfulness. It could have no hope of success if the intellectual conscience could be raised against it.

Philosophy is driven by the lust to rule — this culminating thought of Nietzsche's presentation of the general prejudices of philosophy governs the next sections, for in turning to the history of philosophy, Nietzsche turns to the great philosophies that ruled antiquity: Platonism, Epicureanism, and Stoicism. He treats them with great brevity, focusing on their lust to rule.

Ancient Philosophy: Comedies of the Lust to Rule
SECTIONS 7–9

Nietzsche deals with ancient philosophy in three sections that seem to be reducible to two jokes and a generalization. If this seems a trivializing dismissal, lingering over them provides a corrective: a little comedy penetrates to the heart of the matter.

Section 7   "How malicious philosophers can be!" If philosophers are driven

15. See for example *GS* 46: just after praising Epicurus for something he alone has seen in Epicurus, Nietzsche expresses his wonder at the possibility of science: "There lies a deep and fundamental happiness in the fact that science ascertains things that *stand fast* and that repeatedly hand over the ground for new ascertainings." Nietzsche never abandoned this praise of science; see *A* 47–48, 59.

by a lust to rule, the defeat of their mastering drive can poison them into malice. As an example Nietzsche cites a remark that opens a window on the greatest contest in ancient philosophy, perhaps in philosophy as such, the conflict between Platonism, heir of Socratic moralism, and Epicureanism, heir of Democritus and the Greek scientific tradition.[16] Epicurus's defeat in this fateful philosophical contest doomed Europe to the dogmatic Platonism from which it is only now awakening.

Nietzsche is categorical: "I know nothing more poisonous than the joke Epicurus permitted himself against Plato and the Platonists: he named them *Dionysiokolakes*."[17] Even Nietzsche finds it desirable to partially explain this arcane joke. Literally and stage front, he says, Epicurus's joke calls Plato and the Platonists " 'flatterers of Dionysius,' that is, tyrants' accessories and ass kissers." But behind the curtain it intimates, "They're all *actors,* there's nothing 'genuine' about them (for *Dionysokolax* was a popular label for actors)." Epicurus's poison joke makes its point by adding one iota to the popular name for an actor: Epicurus was moved to malice against Plato and the Platonists because their acting talents successfully won over the tyrant—not Dionysius of Syracuse but the public, the greatest tyrant.[18] If every great philosophy is a passion to rule, it's clear why a discrepancy in acting talent so ate at Epicurus: Plato came to rule through the stage, through great acts of pious fraud that persuaded the majority of the audience that Plato's was the divine philosophy and Epicurus's only a demonic atheism. Later philosophers appreciated Plato's acting talent without poisoned envy: Plato acted as if he believed in immortal souls and moral gods who rewarded and punished them, but philosophers like Montaigne knew Plato could not possibly have held such beliefs, beliefs, Montaigne said, "as useful for persuading the common herd as they are ridiculous for persuading Plato himself."[19] Plato's acting ability gave his philosophy a right to rule that the teacher of *ataraxia* could not help but envy.

16. Kant refers to this conflict between Epicurus and Plato as basic, adding, "Each of the two types of philosophy says more than it knows" (*Critique of Pure Reason* A 472/B500; see also A 853/B881). Nietzsche, who is not an epistemological skeptic, suggests that each knows more than it says.

17. Epicurus, ed. Arrighetti, fr. 93, 18–19.

18. Leo Strauss used Epicurus's joke in a characteristic way. Student of Epicureanism and Platonism, commentator on Aristophanes and Machiavelli, Strauss speaks as an unpoisoned Platonist to make a little joke of his own: altering Epicurus's joke by its added iota, he suggests that today's triumphant postatheism is an impolitic worship of Dionysos. See Strauss, *Studies in Platonic Political Philosophy* 179 and Lampert, *Leo Strauss and Nietzsche* 50–51.

19. *Essays* ii.12, "Apology for Raymond Sebond" 379.

Ruling Platonism saw to it that Epicurus's three hundred books would not continue to damage its stage plays, for it systematically sought them out and destroyed them. The malice of later Platonists makes it impossible to know the extent of *Epicurus's* theatrics—to what degree, for instance, the laughable swerve he introduced into the rain of atoms was mere *Schauspielerei*, assuring worried spectators that because atoms swerved they themselves enjoyed free will. The surviving fragments at least enable us to see the fun Epicurus too had with the gods: he made them look a lot like himself, proving himself a fit philosophical heir to Xenophanes' horses and lions.

Nietzsche's explanation of the motive for Epicurus's joke keeps playfully to the stage. Epicurus's books were written "who knows? perhaps out of rage and ambition against Plato?" It took a hundred years, Nietzsche says, for Greece to go behind the scenes and discover who this garden god Epicurus really was—the poisoned rival of Plato. But he adds, "—Did it actually get behind the scenes?—" The question prepares the next section—the next scene, which also takes place on the comic stage, not behind the scenes but stage front.

Section 8   What mounts the stage in section 8 is what no philosophical actor could ever want, but what no philosophical actor can avoid:

> In every philosophy there comes a point at which the "conviction" of the philosopher mounts the stage: or, to say it in the language of an ancient mystery:
>
> > The ass arrived
> > beautiful and most brave.

Nietzsche's joke, borrowed from Lichtenberg, invokes the origins of Western theater in the mystery festivals dedicated to Dionysos.[20] Did the ass of Epicurus's philosophy ever mount the stage for the Greek world? Nietzsche's joke suggests it did: every philosophy is prey to such disclosure. But the universality of Nietzsche's claim suggests that even actors as gifted as Plato cannot avoid this embarrassment. Because a genuine philosopher is not an actor through and through but harbors some irreducible core of perspectives and purposes, some moral purpose (6), he must eventually share the stage with his fundamental stupidity, as Nietzsche calls it when directing the ass of his own philosophy to mount the stage (230–31).

Beyond Good and Evil does not give a complete account of Nietzsche's appreciation of Epicurus. Instead, it claims that the retiring—and perhaps poisoned—way of the garden god is not a viable option for anti-Platonic

20. *KSA* 14 *Kommentar* 349, on *BGE* 8.

philosophy amid the ruins of dogmatic Platonism (61, 62; see 200, 270). But if Nietzsche's task required that he adopt the engaged theatricality of Plato, he does so as heir to Epicurus and the Greek scientific tradition; elsewhere Nietzsche indicates that "we look Epicurean" because we carry forward the views of Epicurus just as philosophy did in pre-Christian Rome, where "every respectable mind was an Epicurean" (GS 375, A 58). As modern science prevails against Platonism, "Epicurus triumphs anew" (D 72).

Because the next section turns to Stoicism, the chapter devoted to the prejudices of the philosophers seems content to treat Platonism, the worst, most durable, and most dangerous of all prejudices, with nothing more than two jokes. But as Nietzsche brings modern ideas onto the stage, Plato's teaching is reassessed and proves to be greater than the malice of Epicurus could grant and more refined than the wars of modern philosophy made it seem.

Section 9 Section 9 addresses the third major school of ancient philosophers, "you noble Stoics," moral philosophers concerned with the best human life. But their moral teaching presupposed a view of nature, and Nietzsche's account ultimately concerns the relation between nature and human life, the key issue of the whole book. Nietzsche continues to treat ancient philosophy in the language of the theater — the Stoics too are actors — and when he ends this section he seems to engage in some theatrics of his own.

"Live in accord with nature" is the fundamental Stoic commandment. But Nietzsche describes nature as "wasteful without measure, indifferent without measure, without purposes and consideration, without mercy and justice, fertile and desolate and uncertain at the same time, imagine indifference itself as a power — how could you live according to this indifference?" The conflict between human life and nature is made to seem complete: "Life — is it not precisely a wanting-to-be-other than this nature?" Nietzsche calls the Stoics "odd actors" — they rank below Plato and Epicurus because they don't know they're acting. His criticism of them employs the tools of philology: acting as if they read out of nature the canon of their law, they write into nature (vorschreiben, prescribe, dictate) their own morality. Claiming a "love of truth," they falsify nature through a trick of logic: because they know how to tyrannize themselves, they conclude that nature too lets itself be tyrannized — for is the Stoic not a piece of nature?

The criticism of Stoicism ends before the section ends, for Nietzsche turns from the Stoics to draw a generalization about all philosophy. What happened with the Stoics "happens still today as soon as a philosophy begins to believe in itself. It always creates the world in its own image, it can do no other." With these famous phrases from the creation story in the Bible (Gen. 1:27) and from Luther's defiant stand at Worms, Nietzsche prepares his concluding words:

philosophy is the drive to "the 'creation of the world,' to the *causa prima*." Philosophy assigns itself the role our religion assigns to God. But after borrowing memorable phrases from religion, Nietzsche employs one of his own most memorable phrases, the phrase he was planning to make still more memorable as the title for the *Hauptwerk* he was preparing. For the first time in the book, Nietzsche uses the phrase *will to power:* "Philosophy is this tyrannical drive itself, the most spiritual will to power." The first appearance of the phrase *will to power* in Nietzsche's writings after its dramatic presentation in *Zarathustra* is an appearance in its highest possible form, its *geistigste* form, where the context dictates that *geistig* be understood in part at least as godlike or world creating (see 150). Nietzsche had found in philosophy the lust to rule (6), and at the end of his summary treatment of ancient philosophy he links philosophy with the ultimate form of rule, the creation of the world.

In the wording of this section, philosophy is the drive to tyrannize the world, to rule the world through an interpretation of the world. But Nietzsche had just challenged the Stoic view of nature by stating what nature is. What status can his own statement possibly have if philosophy is the tyrannical drive to create the world? Nietzsche's emphatic conclusion about all philosophy goads his audience to ask how the generalization he applies to others applies to him. If philosophy is the most spiritual will to power, isn't his purported description of a nature just another falsifying tyranny? Unless we suppose that by the end of his paragraph Nietzsche had forgotten what he said at its beginning, we must conclude that Nietzsche's first mention of the will to power is itself theatrical and self-reflexive. The calculated tension of this section draws its reader up into the fundamental problem of philosophy, a problem with two dimensions both made visible in this section. Given its understanding of philosophy as tyranny, how can the new philosophy ever arrive at and warrant a true understanding of nature? And even if it could give warrant to its understanding of nature, how could it ever found a teaching for human life on that understanding? — how could you live in accord with nature's fecund indifference?

Beginning here, *Beyond Good and Evil* presents what appears to be a calculated series of declarations about will to power that assert the new view of nature: all the phenomena of nature are ultimately understandable as will to power whether it be the most spiritual phenomenon (9) or living things generally (13) or all so-called material things (22) or the human soul itself (23). Just how will to power is to be interpreted will be indicated gradually as the declarations accrue. Only later — and to the audience selected out by the rhetoric of the first chapter — does *Beyond Good and Evil* present an argument that it has a right to that view of nature and can even claim it as the true view (36). Does Nietzsche's philosophy "believe in itself"? It can do no other. Persuaded by the reasoning on its behalf yet keeping its conclusion "under the police supervision of mistrust" (*GS* 344), the philosophy of will to power is a reductionism that probes and tests all aspects of its implications, especially its implication for human values.

Will to power is mentioned first in *Beyond Good and Evil* with respect to its *geistigste*, its most spiritual / intellectual form. By introducing will to power as a critique of Stoicism, Nietzsche invites its misconstrual as a critique of philosophy generally. But when all the discussions of will to power are considered, it is evident that Nietzsche's opening statement is as far as possible from critique. On the contrary, it is an elevation of philosophy to the highest possible rank: philosophy, spirited and reasoned inquiry into nature and human life, rooted in passion and supervised by a self-legislated intellectual conscience, is the highest form achieved by nature; it is the natural apex of nature, and insight into its character must be recovered if philosophy is to flourish again as it flourished among the Greeks and Romans. Just how philosophy is possible — just how an ontology or an account of the way of all beings is possible given an epistemology that recognizes the falsifying activity of human categorizing — will be approached glancingly as the book proceeds.

"Live in accord with nature!" Stoicism was noble but deceived itself about nature. Can one live in accord with nature viewed as will to power? A naturalized philosophy, the book will argue, aims to naturalize human values, recognizing the cruelty of nature's indifference while striving for a new nobility that cultivates and celebrates nature. What looks like a wholly unpromising view of nature will be displayed as the reasonable grounds for the affirmation of nature and humanity.

Nietzsche's treatment of ancient philosophy suggests that the practical or moral problem of human life in a wholly indifferent universe was faced by ancient philosophy in all three of its ruling forms. Platonism and Epicureanism were schools of acting that taught the few who could bear it one thing and the many who couldn't quite another. Platonism owed its victory to the very outrageousness of its acting, its daredevil promise offered to the many that they could live forever if they behaved for now, the all-too-rash promise that prepared the way for Christianity. Stoicism, on the other hand, was noble but more innocent, an acting school whose leading players did not realize they were living a fiction they themselves had invented.

Modern Philosophy's Platonism: True and Apparent Worlds
SECTIONS 10–15

Section 10   As Nietzsche jumps from ancient philosophy to "today" the will to truth is still the basic issue, but the foreground is occupied by the most prominent problem of modern philosophy: "the real and the apparent world." Nietzsche pictures himself as a listener straining to hear what lies behind the "eagerness and subtlety" with which this problem is pressed upon everyone today and judges that those who hear only a will to truth behind it are not blessed with the best of ears. *Beyond Good and Evil* thus opens one of its main themes: the prejudices of philosophy make it almost impossible to hear competing perspectives. The prejudice that distinguishes between the real and apparent worlds occupies the most important sections of the next two chapters, leading up to sections 34–37; there Nietzsche attempts to make audible to skeptical free minds what is present in that distinction and to demonstrate how one can move beyond it to a plausible claim about the "intelligible character" of the world. Beginning with the present section, Nietzsche argues that behind the enthusiasm for the distinction between the real and the apparent world one can hear a desire for ignorance of the real world. Such ignorance is desirable because it can be remedied with intimations of reality that comfort but do not claim to be knowledge and are therefore invincible to knowledge. Kant is the symptomatic modern philosopher, and Nietzsche takes him at his word: he really did deny knowledge in order to make room for faith.

In isolated, rare instances a genuine will to truth can be at work behind the distinction between real and apparent worlds, but Nietzsche dismisses these instances by saying, "But this is nihilism." This first use of *nihilism* in Nietzsche's published writings employs it as sufficient grounds for refuting a view. Nietzsche's concentration is on other cases, thinkers whose enthusiasm for the distinction between real and apparent worlds is not founded on the will to truth but on mistrust of modern ideas. He expresses agreement with their "instinct" to get away while disagreeing with the direction it takes, its longing for the past: "What do we care about these backward-looking little shortcuts?" With a little more strength such distrust of modern ideas could point in the proper direction: "*Up and out* — and not back! — " At the beginning of his consideration of modern ideas Nietzsche reinforces the trajectory signaled at the end of the preface: the tension caused by the fight against modern ideas enables us to aim forward to the most distant goals. The transition section between ancient and modern thus exhibits respect for a conservatism desiring the return to some former order. But "no one is free to be a crab," Nietzsche "whispered to conservatives" in *Twilight of the Idols* (Skirmishes 43); the instincts of repugnance at the modern are correct but must be turned toward the future.[21]

21. Alisdair MacIntyre is a conservative who takes Nietzsche to be the most repellant modern with views that make a turn backward obvious and imperative. But MacIntyre

Section 11   Perhaps more than any other section in chapter 1, section 11 is the distilled product of continuous work recorded and refined in numerous notebook entries extending over a period of two years, right up to the final version of March 1886.[22] Its lightness of touch, its acuity and depth on matters of extreme gravity and complexity, make it one of the high points of this chapter. For Nietzsche now turns to the most prominent modern form of the distinction between real and apparent worlds, Kant's, and treats this great event in the history of modern philosophy in a decidedly whimsical manner. According to Nietzsche, Kant, "the great delayer" (*EH* Books CW 2), did his sober best to return Europe to the dogmatic slumber almost ruined by modern materialist thought.[23] Wakeful Europeans, understanding Kant's invitation to sleep on, will treat it as a diverting comedy and devote their energy to understanding what Kant wanted to cover up, modern materialism. Nietzsche remedies the active effort to deflect attention away from what Kant himself guilelessly pointed to as the heart of his project: the discovery of new faculties. Sober old Kant corrupted fervent German youth and gave birth to the intoxicating zeal of German romanticism that captured all of Europe as "German philosophy." Nietzsche treats the whole episode with something less than Kantian solemnity: "One grew older, — the dream melted away."[24] Now that it's gone Nietzsche accounts for it in two stages. First, "Why is the belief in synthetic a priori judgments *necessary?*" His answer again utilizes the basic explanatory tool of evolutionary biology: the conviction that supposedly universal and necessary judgments about the world are true was an indispensable survival mechanism for our species. But now, being bound by the will to truth and seeing the provenance and function of such judgments, we immediately conclude that we have no right to them. Second, why was Kant's invention of epistemological and moral faculties so welcomed in modern Europe? As a

---

misinterpreted Nietzsche's antimodernism and the grounds for his move forward, taking them to be merely willful, merely a lust to rule. See MacIntyre, *After Virtue* ch. 9, "Nietzsche or Aristotle." A far more interesting and complex case is presented by Leo Strauss's return to Plato and to Platonic political philosophy; see Lampert, *Leo Strauss and Nietzsche*.

22. Important examples are found in *KSA* 11.30 [10], 34 [62, 79, 82, 185], 38 [7].

23. See *GM* 3.25: "What is certain is that since Kant all kinds of transcendentalists are again playing a winning game. . . . There is no knowing: *consequently* there is a God."

24. Georg Picht demonstrated the inappropriateness of counting Nietzsche among the Romantics: "No one has analyzed the decadent character of romanticism with as much acuteness, subtlety, and severity as Nietzsche. It belongs among the tragic absurdities of intellectual history that his own philosophy has been interpreted by the majority of his followers as if it arose from a position within romanticism." Picht, *Nietzsche* 181.

Gegengift, a poison antidote to poison. The original poison was the materialism that roused Europe into a troubled wakefulness, and Kant's inventions were welcomed because they put the newly aroused senses back to sleep. Having drawn this conclusion with the help of a line from Moliere, Nietzsche closes with an ellipse: awakening from the Kantian dream, we now face the materialism from which it sheltered us. And this is the theme of the next sections, the materialism of modern science in all its unsettling consequences.[25]

With this section, Nietzsche's program for European thought begins to come into clearer focus. In its enthusiasm for distinguishing between real and apparent worlds, modern philosophy betrays its uneasy conscience as a bulwark against modern science. The sensualism Kant opposed stands for the whole of modern science in its self-understanding, a relatively inarticulate and unsophisticated materialism that threatens the whole web of Platonic concepts which still undergird European civilization. Kant belongs to the history of the Platonic fable as a late, pale exemplar, sheltering it in the mists of skepticism (*TI* "How the True World Finally Became a Fable"). The next sections draw the reader further into this history.

Section 12   The central section of chapter 1, section 12 is central in more than number. Its theme is physics and the soul. While its treatment of each is preliminary, it discloses a core aspiration of Nietzsche's thought: to counter the basic prejudice of both Platonic and modern philosophy, faith in opposite values or the distinction between real and apparent worlds, in the only effective way: through knowledge of the world. The views of "the metaphysicians of all ages" (2) can be attacked and corrected by a science of nature that includes human nature. Nietzsche views physics as pre-Platonic Greeks did; it is the science of *physis,* rational inquiry into the way of all beings. But he is critical of modern physics for its materialism and will suggest to physicists a different way of construing nature (22). Physis encompasses psyche, nature encompasses human nature, but the study of the human opens the path to what is true of all beings—Nietzsche will end chapter 1 on a claim that arises out of this center: the study of the soul is once again the path to the fundamental problems (23).

Without changing his theme of true and apparent worlds, Nietzsche turns to

25. On Nietzsche's critique of Kant, see ibid. 69–73, 122–31; Krell, *Infectious Nietzsche* 5–7, 11–18; Ridley, *Nietzsche's Conscience* 1–11, 68–72. Christoph Cox argues persuasively that Nietzsche should not be considered a Kantian by showing how Nietzsche's epistemological formulations can be read as a consistent expression of his naturalism. Nietzsche is not an ontological skeptic, and the refusal to count him a Kantian spares him the elementary contradiction of making knowledge claims about an ostensibly unknowable thing in itself. See Cox, *Nietzsche* 118–20, 140–47, 170–84.

"materialistic atomism," "one of the best refuted things there are." It is refuted not by the antinomies of Kantian skepticism, but by a more adequate conception of the intelligible character of the world. Nietzsche attributes a revolution in physics to Roger Joseph Boscovich (1711–87), an older contemporary of Kant whose main work was published in 1759 while Kant himself was occupied partly by the problems of physics. Instead of positing supposedly ultimate particles of matter as classical Greek atomism did, Boscovich posited the ultimacy of packets or quanta of energy.[26] By reading an eighteenth-century Jesuit physicist a nineteenth-century philologist came to anticipate the revolution of late-nineteenth- and twentieth-century physics from a matter-based model to an energy-based model.[27] Boscovich's revolution still lay in the future, and in a later section Nietzsche lectures modern physicists on this coming revolution in their science (22).

Nietzsche pairs Boscovich with Copernicus as revolutionary modern thinkers and not because of any "Copernican revolution" in the Kantian sense. On the contrary, each is credited with advancing our actual knowledge of the world by overcoming in a reasoned way the overwhelming evidence of *Augenschein*—how things shine forth to the eye. Each refused the evidence of the senses, and neither used that refusal to invent a "real" world. With cosmology and physics, as with biology, Nietzsche situates himself within the gains of

26. The view is already present in Francis Bacon, according to Robert Ellis, one of Bacon's nineteenth-century editors, who mentions Boscovich as a thinker whose theory of force accords with Bacon's. See Ellis's preface to *De Principiis atque Originibus*, Bacon, *Works* 3.70–71.

27. Nietzsche was guided to Boscovich by Friedrich Albert Lange's *Geschichte des Materialismus*, which he first read in 1866 and which deals very briefly with Boscovich (see letter to Gersdorff, end of August 1866). During 1873 and 1874 he checked out of the University of Basel library Boscovich's two-volume work *Philosophiae naturalis theoria redacta ad unicam legem virium in natura existentium* (Vienna, 1759) (see Luca Crescenzi, "Verzeichnis der von Nietzsche aus der Universitätsbibliothek in Basel entliehenen Bücher [1869–1879]"). (See Roger Joseph Boscovich, *A Theory of Natural Philosophy*.) There are only four mentions of Boscovich in the selection of notebook entries in Colli-Montinari; see *KSA* 9.15 [21] (1881); *KSA* 11.26 [302, 410, 432] (1884). Some of the wording in *BGE* 12 goes back to a letter written to Köselitz three years earlier that discusses Boscovich (20.3.82). The decisive importance of Boscovich for Nietzsche is demonstrated by Greg Whitlock in "Roger Boscovich, Benedict de Spinoza and Friedrich Nietzsche: The Untold Story." Whitlock demonstrates that Boscovich's ideas are actively present in numerous notebook entries of 1881–85 in which Nietzsche works toward the comprehensive view of will to power put forward in *Beyond Good and Evil*. Whitlock shows how Nietzsche's dynamic worldview arises out of the mechanistic view as its refinement, and how that dynamic view has ramifications for all aspects of Nietzsche's thought, most particularly his understanding of the human.

modern science. For a philosophical philologist, the current situation has a great historic precedent: the conflict that arose when natural science itself arose, the conflict between the Socratics led by Plato on the one hand and the philosophers of the tragic age of the Greeks on the other hand, philosophers of physis whose reflections on nature culminated in the atomism carried forward by Epicurus. That battle was won by Platonism, but now, with the death of Platonism, the battle is rekindled, and the heirs of Epicurus have at hand the weapons forged by modern cosmology, physics, and biology.

Like his pre-Platonic predecessors and against Plato and Kant, Nietzsche extends science's claims about nature to human nature: Boscovich's energy physics enables the philosopher to "go still further" and "declare war, a relentless war to the death" against all relics of materialistic atomism, especially Christian "soul atomism." Soul atomism was once given heart by arguments for the soul's immortality invented by Plato, who did not himself believe them; now it shelters itself within the ignorance granted by Kantian skepticism. But that view of the soul is annihilated if it can be shown with some probability that to be is to be energy in an always shifting energy field.

Nietzsche stands in the long line of assassins of "the old soul concept," which he traces back to Descartes (54). He mentions a final feature of this assassination "among ourselves," as if he wished to speak privately to a select audience about a secret among assassins: while making war on the disastrous concept of individual eternal souls, it is not necessary to throw away the soul itself and deprive ourselves of one of the oldest and most venerable of hypotheses. Nietzsche names new versions and refinements of the soul hypothesis such as "mortal soul," "soul as subject-multiplicity," and "soul as social structure of the drives and affects," naturalistic versions of the soul that merit "citizens' rights in science."[28]

But the new psychologist is bound to have a less pleasant time of it than psychologists who took Platonism's way of appeasing a folk superstition: he banishes himself into a desert of mistrust. But there will be compensation for "he knows that he will be condemned to *invention* [*Erfinden*]" by this banishment — "and who knows? perhaps to *discovery* [*Finden*]." The new psychology may thus overcome both Plato's *Erfindung* (preface) and the post-Kantian inability to distinguish *finden* and *erfinden* (11). The science of psyche, like the sciences of cosmos, physis, and bios, can make actual discoveries that change

28. See *KSA* 11.40 [21] = *WP* 492 for an extended reflection on beginning with "the body and physiology" in order "to gain the correct idea of the character of our subject-unity, namely as regents at the peak of a communality." For a rich examination of the soul hypotheses of section 12, see Graham Parkes, *Composing the Soul* esp. 346–62.

the way we interpret ourselves and the world. The new study of the natural soul is both dangerous and promising, and Nietzsche brings chapter 1 to its culmination on that vertiginous mix (23): the voyage of some new Odysseus risks the danger of shipwreck for the promise of a whole new continent of discoveries. A proper science of the soul promises a way out of the problem of real and apparent worlds.

The centrality of section 12 illuminates the chapter it centers by casting light backward and forward. It illuminates the previous sections as preparations for the basic problem of knowledge: can the intelligible character of the world be ascertained? And it anticipates answers to this problem through new investigations of physis and psyche.

Section 13   Section 13, the first section after the basic claim about the science of physis and the science of soul, deals with the science of life, biology — "physiology" in the nineteenth-century German usage Nietzsche employs.[29] The section contains Nietzsche's second mention of will to power. Will to power first appeared in its most spiritual/intellectual form, philosophy itself (9); now it appears as the fundamental feature of all living things. The highest human activity is thus one expression of what is basic to all life; as will to power, philosophy is wholly natural, an activity of the human organism continuous with the way of all organisms.

If "life itself is will to power," modern biology must be wrong in making the instinct to self-preservation the cardinal instinct. Nietzsche has already made use of the gains of evolutionary biology and its explanatory principle of natural selection: supposedly permanent features of human consciousness and sensibility are better explained as naturally selected survival strategies of a threatened species (4, 11). But in the science of biology no Copernicus or Boscovich has yet explained the *Augenschein* in a more fundamental way, so Nietzsche makes the announcement himself: self-preservation, a form of standing fast, is observable everywhere but is "only one of the indirect and most frequent *results*" of what is fundamental to life. Rather than preserve or husband itself, "something living wants above all to *discharge* its strength," to let it out (*auslassen*), to express it or expand it.[30]

29. Nietzsche uses *Physiologen* and *Physiologie* in reference to the science of living organisms, or the physical-chemical explanation of the conditions of life and in contrast to *Physiker* and *Physik*. Such terms are required to mark out distinct fields of investigation, even though Nietzsche regards any firm distinction between the organic and the inorganic as a superficiality contributing to or dictated by the faith in opposite values.

30. See *GS* 349: "In nature it is not conditions of distress that are *dominant* but overflow and squandering, even to the point of absurdity. The struggle for existence is

When Zarathustra made a similar announcement he chose a narrow audience: only "you who are wisest" were required to hear it (Z 2 "On Self-Overcoming"). And Zarathustra did not leave it as a bare announcement to them but made preliminary arguments on its behalf that claimed privileged observer's status for himself, and he quoted the essential argument from life itself — or *herself,* given the personifications of "The Dance Song" (Z 2), in which Life intimates to Zarathustra the essential point that she can be fathomed. Only after that encounter and for the only time in the book does Zarathustra invite the wisest to reason with him, thus elevating to supreme importance among the wise this novel claim about "the way of all beings." *Beyond Good and Evil,* with its different rhetorical imperatives, stretches out these items of presentation through the first two chapters, but the goal is the same, to persuade a small audience of especially engaged inquirers to consider a new fundamental hypothesis.

Nietzsche's announcement about life and will to power entails a major point of method in the philosophy of science: method demands parsimony of principles. Nietzsche's application of Ockham's razor makes self-preservation a "*superfluous* teleological principle" because the evident phenomena of self-preservation can be explained as a function of a more fundamental non-teleological force. Teleological interpretation is not arbitrary but serves the same instinctual wishes that posit faith in opposite values and that keep investigations of the human soul at the surface (23).[31] If life itself is will to power, every organism is a dynamic organization of will to power that seeks to discharge its force with no goal or purpose beyond the expression of its force

---

only an *exception,* a temporary restriction of the will to life. The great and small struggle always revolves around superiority, around growth and expansion, around power — in accordance with the will to power which is the will of life." See *TI* Skirmishes 14: "The overall aspect of life is *not* a state of need and hunger, but instead, wealth, bounty, even absurd squandering — where there is struggle, it is a struggle for *power*." See also *KSA* 12.7 [44] = *WP* 649. While praising Nietzsche for getting so much right in understanding human history on the basis of evolutionary theory, Daniel Dennett expresses impatience with him on the chief point. Will to power seems to Dennett to be just another of those "sky hooks" introduced to deliver us from the dangerous truth of evolutionary naturalism. But it is no such thing; instead, it is a way of understanding living things as continuous with all things. See Dennett, *Darwin's Dangerous Idea* 461–67. On Nietzsche's relationship to Darwin, see Cox, *Nietzsche* 223–29.

31. On teleology in Aristotle, see David Bolotin, *An Approach to Aristotle's Physics: With Particular Attention to the Role of his Manner of Writing,* an argument that Aristotle used teleological explanation as a rhetorical device to make science publicly defensible though Aristotle himself held it to be scientifically indefensible.

against other forces.[32] Parsimonious of principles, Nietzsche is a reductionist who posits a single principle as the ultimate explanatory foundation of the observable phenomena of life, while allowing for emergent properties that are unpredictable results of increased complexity and that give life its nuance and mystery.

Section 14   Nietzsche opens section 14 by looking forward to a more subtle physics that will be aware of its status as an interpretation, not an explanation, of the world. Primarily, however, the section looks backward, contrasting modern physics and Plato to Plato's advantage. The issue is: What counts as an explanation? What role do the senses play in explaining the world? Except for the five or six heads in which it is dawning that physics too is only an interpretation of the world, physics failed to learn the lesson of its revolutionaries, Copernicus and Boscovich; it still trusts in *Augenschein* (12), instinctively following the truth canon of popular sensualism. Nietzsche employs the language of the gigantomachia in Plato's *Sophist* (246a-b) to describe that sensualism: it believes that that alone is real which it can see and touch and that every problem should be pursued only that far. The Stranger from Elea attributed this view to the "giants" of philosophy, coarse materialists against whom the "gods" of philosophy must make war. Nietzsche sides with the gods, while holding a view of nature closer to that of the giants. "Precisely in its resistance *against* the adequacy of the senses stands the charm of the Platonic way of thinking, which was a *noble* way of thinking" — no small praise in a book that ends by asking, "What is noble?" and answering that ultimately it is philosophy. The charm of Platonism lay in its pleasure-giving mastery or *Welt-Überwältigung* (overpowering the world), achieved by casting a net of concepts over "the mob of the senses" (*Laws* 689a-b); Platonism too was a spiritual will to power tyrannizing the world in its own image.

Not only physicists follow the popular belief in the senses: so do "the Darwinists and antiteleologists among the physiological laborers" — physics and biology both obey the imperative obeyed by the giants of the *Sophist*: "Where humanity has nothing more to see or grasp, it has nothing more to seek." This may be "the right imperative for a tough, industrious race of machinists and bridge-builders of the future, who have only *coarse* work to do." But the

---

32. See *GM* 2.12: "All events in the organic world are an *overpowering,* a *becoming master,* and all overpowering and becoming master involves a fresh interpretation, an adaptation through which any previous 'meaning' and 'purpose' are necessarily obscured or even obliterated." Nietzsche calls the lengthy explanation of will to power in this passage a "major point of historical method"; it is perhaps the most important single statement on will to power in Nietzsche's published works and provides a detailed critique of teleology.

subtle work of a philosopher, the work of explaining the world, must, Nietzsche implies, respect the noble way of Plato, at least in its subtlety with regard to the popular belief in the senses. Nevertheless, sensualism as a working hypothesis is preferable to any idealism, and the next section offers a refutation of idealism; it does so in order to give physiology a good conscience: it is important for scientific work that folk beliefs be replaced by more refined concepts.

Section 15   In order to proceed with a clear conscience the science of biology needs a philosophical legitimation of its instruments, the senses. Put negatively, it must be liberated from idealist philosophy, which distinguishes real and apparent worlds and depreciates the sense organs as mere appearance. Sensualism, as the previous section argued, cannot serve as a philosophical foundation for physics and biology, but it must nevertheless be maintained in a limited way.[33] Therefore, Nietzsche says (using the language of Kant's idealism), "sensualism at least as a regulative hypothesis, though not as a heuristic principle." The senses interpret the world, but they do not explain it. Any attempt to explain the world — for example, that the world is will to power and nothing besides — must provide the sciences with a good conscience by giving the senses their due. In the meantime, biology can be freed from the bad conscience to which idealism's explanation of the world condemns it by the brief but knockdown reductio ad absurdum argument Nietzsche offers.

In recommending sensualism as a regulative hypothesis, Nietzsche cannot have forgotten what he said about Copernicus and Boscovich and their victories over *Augenschein* (12) or about Plato and his noble stand against the "mob of the senses" (14). In a note relating to this issue Nietzsche said:, "When I think about my philosophical genealogy . . . I recognize a family connection . . . with the mechanistic movement (tracing all moral and aesthetic questions back to physiological ones, all the physiological to the chemical, all the chemical to the mechanical) though still with the difference that I do not believe in 'material' and hold Boscovich to be the great turning point" (*KSA* 11.26 [432] Summer-Fall 1884). Nietzsche is neither an idealist nor a materialist, though he too is a philosopher who aims to furnish a reasonable explanation of the world, one that grounds the interpretations of physics and biology.

Nietzsche's perspective on modern science and its philosophical foundations is beginning to become apparent from his critiques of the prejudices of

33. "And what fine tools of observation we have in our senses! . . . The extent to which we possess science today is precisely the extent to which we have decided to *accept* the testimony of the senses — and learned to sharpen them, arm them, and think them through to their end" (*TI* Reason 3).

modern philosophers. He lauds the antiteleological character of modern science while aiming to be more rigorous and consistent in applying it to the phenomena of life (13). He lauds the attack on fixed essences but judges that it has not been consistently applied either to atoms or the atom's remnants (12). While viewing materialistic monism as in some respects an advance over idealist dualism, he judges it to be too crass or blunt to serve as a world explanation (14). Moreover, modern physics and modern sciences generally are mistaken in thinking that "law-abidingness" constitutes a genuine explanation of nature, though a genuine explanation is nevertheless possible (22). Finally, modern science inconsistently exempts human beings from its nonteleological, materialist account of nature, an exemption Nietzsche will explicitly refuse when he turns to the science of the human soul (23, see also 230). The philosophical foundations of science must therefore be purified or made more rigorous with a unified, nonteleological, explanatory account of the whole of nature: will to power is the animating impulse of all beings.

Popular Prejudice and Philosophy
SECTIONS 16–17

Section 16 Nietzsche turns from the apparent world to the "real" world, the inner world of "immediate certainty" about the "I think" or "I will," dealing with the "I think" in sections 16 and 17 and with the "I will" in section 19.[34] Philosophers who affirm such certainties are "harmless observers" because they assert philosophically what the people already believe they know anyway; the self-observer who questions the certainty of "I think" seems less harmless. In a note that questions the *contradictio in adjectivo* questioned in this section, Nietzsche said, "The first need is for absolute skepticism against all traditional concepts (as *perhaps* one philosopher already possessed it—Plato: naturally he *taught the opposite*" (*KSA* 11.34 [195] April-June 1885). Contrary to what Plato taught, Nietzsche maintains that whenever the people suppose they know, the philosopher has a responsibility to question, every immediate certainty becoming for him a whole series of "truly genuine conscience-questions for the intellect." The questions about the self that lie behind the popular certainties are "metaphysical" in character, but they can be pursued only with a "proper physio-psychology" (23). It seems implicit in the questions Nietzsche poses here that he himself pursued the questions into tentative answers that do not support popular prejudice, an-

---

34. Notes that are precursors of sections 16 and 17 identify them as a critique of Descartes (*KSA* 11.40 [20–25]).

swers based on a comprehensive explanation of things. The questioning of philosophy's prejudices in chapter 1 prepares for the dangerous answers of chapter 2.

Nietzsche ends section 16 with a little dialogue. To someone maintaining the immediate certainty of "I think," a philosopher today could reply, "with a smile and two question marks, 'Sir, it's improbable that you're not in error, but then why truth at all?'" The first section had asked, "*What* in us really wants 'truth'?" Today's philosopher's smiling reply indicates that what is popularly wanted is not truth but certainty, and that yesterday's philosophy has been too ready to oblige.

Section 17   Nietzsche's critique of the certainty of "I think" continues: to say "*I* think" falsifies the facts, as does "*it* thinks," inasmuch as an entity is posited as an interpretation of an activity, a mere grammatical habit leading one to posit a subject for an activity. Logic must make the advance made by physics, or at least by Boscovich, of not positing an entity or "earth-residuum" in addition to the activity. By questioning the popular fictions, logic could, like the physics of Boscovich, contribute to a new understanding of the human self, replacing the soul atomism of Christianity. By exploding philosophy's fundamental prejudice, its perpetuation of the popular faith in opposite values, philosophy could align itself with the primary intellectual gains of modern times and ground those gains in comprehensive principles. Is philosophy capable of this? Is Nietzsche? The next sections address another popular prejudice, free will, and do so as an exhibition of what Nietzsche can do as a questioner.

A Display of Strength
SECTIONS 18–21

Section 18   The short section 18 makes use of a sentence Nietzsche had been copying out in his notebooks since 1882: "About a theory it is truly not the least of its charms that it is refutable — precisely thereby does it attract subtler minds" (*KSA* 10.4 [72], 5 [1, §24], 12 [1, §156]). In publishing it, Nietzsche applies it to a single theory, "the hundred-times refuted theory of the 'free will,'" stating that "again and again someone comes along and feels strong enough to refute it." Someone in fact comes along in the next sections offering a refutation based on the phenomenology of the "I will" anticipated in section 16. As a pause in his questioning of the unity of "I think" and "I will," this little section supplies a perspective on his questioning: in part it is a display of strength. Is Nietzsche worthy of his problems, strong enough for them?

The display of strength is an essay in the Nietzschean manner, a *Versuch* that probes and tempts and puts the experimenter to the test before a critical audience of free minds. The display begins with a tightly reasoned, closely interlocked set of reflections on the old problem of free will (19–21), reflections that carry the reasoner into the most comprehensive possibility, a new account of nature (22), and then into the most dangerous possibility, a new account of human nature (23). The reflections end with a return to the display of strength, for Nietzsche ends section 23 — and the whole first chapter — on a taunt: "There are a hundred good reasons for everyone to keep away from it who — *can!*" The display of strength by the author turns into a test of strength for the reader. Those who have followed Nietzsche through his essay in five sections will not be inclined to accept his invitation to close the book at that point.

Section 19   The crucial section 19 refutes the theory of free will by dismantling the very notion of will as a unitary phenomenon. What philosophers have said about the will is a typical prejudice of Platonic philosophy and of the most recent philosopher, Schopenhauer: they take over a popular prejudice and exaggerate it. Those most moved by *Herrschsucht* (6) permit a word to be *Herr* over them.

Nietzsche's analysis finds three major phenomena dissolved into the false unity of the word *will*. The first is itself a plurality, a series of four distinguishable "feelings" (*Gefühle*) identifiable in an act of will. Second, willing is a thought — a thought that commands and is inseparable from willing. Third and "above all," willing is an "affect" (*Affekt*), an impression to which one is subject, here, the affect of commanding experienced as the sense of superiority resident in commanding. And precisely in this affect, Nietzsche says, lies the truth about what is called "freedom of the will" — the privileging of this one affect among the whole mix of feelings, thoughts, and affects.

The thing "most worthy of wonder" in the complex event of willing is the fact that it includes commanding and obeying.[35] As the obeyer in this duality, one knows the feelings of constraint, impulsion, pressure, resistance, motion — yet this aspect is suppressed, and the habit of enclosing a complexity within the false unity of a single word seduces us into supposing that willing is exclusively commanding. Obliteration of obedience in this complex mix of events has led to a whole chain of erroneous conclusions, Nietzsche maintains, but the one he emphasizes is freedom of the will. "Free will" is a habit of self-congratulation based on inattention, the refusal to notice that the apparent unity of willing consists of a complex of commanding and obeying.

Exclusive focus on the commanding aspect of willing derives from a kind of

35. Nietzsche's first elaboration of will to power emphasized commanding and obeying (Z 2 "On Self-Overcoming").

pleasure, "a growth of the feeling of power," a complex condition of pleasure experienced by the person who commands and identifies himself as the executor of commands enjoying triumph over resistances. These feelings of pleasure are supplemented by additional feelings of pleasure that derive from the whole chain of bodily events by which the command is successfully executed. This complex plurality — "for our body after all is only a social structure of many souls" — is one way in which the soul hypothesis can survive the death of Christian soul atomism (12).³⁶ As in every well-built, happy commonwealth, in the commonwealth of the body and its souls the ruling class identifies itself with the success of the commonwealth: free will is the ruling ideology of the body's politics.

Nietzsche's refutation of the hundred-times-refuted theory of free will leads him to an uncharacteristically categorical conclusion — "In all willing it is absolutely a matter of commanding and obeying" — a conclusion Nietzsche takes as granting a right: "Hence a philosopher should have the right to enclose willing as such within the horizon of morality." But *morality* then means something new: "morality understood namely as the doctrine of the mastery-relationships under which the phenomenon 'life' arose. — " This understanding of morality changes the horizon; morality becomes coterminous with life itself.³⁷ Morality — mastery relations of commanding and obeying — is not a uniquely human phenomenon; humanity is continuous with the rest of life in the fundamental respect. The philosopher thus opens the way to a new science of morality: study of the phenomenon in humans can illuminate the rest of life, and study of the rest of life can illuminate the phenomenon in humans. The conclusion of this section thus makes the cardinal point: what is true of humans in our acts of willing provides access to the whole phenomenon of life. But not even this broadened horizon is encompassing enough; three sections after this one Nietzsche extends the horizon in the most comprehensive way possible to indicate that the analysis of the human will permits conclusions to be drawn about all phenomena. What is on display in Nietzsche's display of strength is the core claim of the new philosophy: a plausible hypothesis about the whole of nature can be drawn from an analysis of the thing we are, a willing thing, a commanding and obeying complexity whose mastery relations begin to give us an inkling of the whole of which we are conscious fragments.

Section 20   Why does Nietzsche interrupt two sections wholly devoted to

---

36. On this social structure, see Parkes *Composing the Soul* 355–59.

37. In later discussions applying the term *morality* to human history, Nietzsche continued to use it in a narrower sense, e.g., the "moral period" of human history (32), or "On the Natural History of Morality" (chapter 5).

the refutation of free will (19 and 21) with a section on philosophical concepts and their rootedness in human experience? The answer seems to be that the question of the free will entails the question of the free mind. Philosophy is the highest aspiration to freedom, but how free can it ever be, given the bondage described in this section?

Quite apart from the passion for system exhibited by some philosophers and scorned by Nietzsche as dishonest (*TI* 1.26), genuine philosophical thinking just is systematic. Individual philosophical concepts do not evolve autonomously but as fragments within broader perspectives that lend their individual components coherence; they are like the fauna of continents in which each species evolves in ways dictated by local conditions. This naturalistic image of philosophy's unfreedom is supplemented by another: planets bound to their orbits. The two images point to a single bondage: the great families of languages are as formative for philosophy as continents are for the evolution of animals or suns for orbiting planets. Can philosophy ever escape its natural bondage and achieve a comprehensive, independent perspective? Nietzsche seems to suggest the means to such liberation when he describes the bondage, and his suggestion links him to Plato. The thinking of philosophers "is less a discovery than a re-recognizing, a re-remembering, a return and homecoming to a distant, age-old collective household of the soul." Philosophical thinking is recollection, but recollection with a natural basis; it is genealogy, a recovery in consciousness of what is written unawares into the human soul by the collective, formative experience of our species. Till now, philosophy has been the unconscious setting forth of the lineaments of that experience; the new philosophy attempts to make that unconscious part of philosophy conscious: "Philosophizing is a kind of atavism of the highest rank." Unconscious atavism becomes conscious atavism, the grateful recovery for consciousness of the formative history of our species by its late offspring.[38]

Does philosophy then become free? Or is the recollection itself continent-bound, orbit-bound? Nietzsche does not answer the reflexive question dictated by his images, but it is evident that insight into what bound philosophy is insight from a perspective. And it is a perspective won, a freedom gained, by a compulsion: the drive for freedom of thought is a passion to which philosophy is subject (230–31); liberation from that subjection would be the death of philosophy and the achievement of wisdom but, in Nietzsche's view, even the gods philosophize (294–95).

The family resemblances of all Indian, Greek, and German philosophy are due to the unconscious lordship and leadership exercised by grammar. This

---

38. This process is further described in *GS* 354.

is the bondage from which the surrounding sections attempt a liberation, bondage to the grammar of "I think" and "I will." But if language is the spell that has kept philosophy within certain orbits, there are more fundamental spells: "the spell of *physiological* value judgments and race-conditioning." If the surrounding sections seek liberation from the lordship of grammar, there seems to be no liberation from the more fundamental spells. Nietzsche's final comment on Locke's superficiality indicates that the refutation of Locke's view of the empty mind is a new defense of innateness, the linguistic and physiological predispositions of our species that the new philosophy brings to conscious awareness.[39] This intervening section thus helps define the basic compulsion of the new philosophy, its passion to understand how thought is subject to physiology; its primary task is therefore a proper physio-psychology (23).

Section 21   Section 21 completes Nietzsche's refutation of free will by invoking a claim about the *An-sich,* the in-itself, the display of strength thus turning out to be a fragment of a much larger set of claims. The new refutation of free will is made possible by a new understanding of knowing and being that refutes the explanatory powers of the old categories and claims fundamental explanatory power for itself. Because of its explanatory power, the new refutation of free will can end with an explanation of why free will seemed persuasive in the first place.

Free will is one aspect of "the best self-contradiction that has been thought up so far," the *causa sui.* Human pride so tied itself to this contradiction that "enlightenment" about free will seems a denial of human dignity. Nietzsche's refutation insults the way humans have prided themselves, but the section ends by suggesting a new basis of pride, not a free will but a strong will. Free will is a fiction of pride; unfree will is a fiction of shame. Belief in free will is the self-contradictory positing of a causa sui; belief in unfree will is "a misuse of cause and effect," part of the human tendency to assign to the world the merely conceptual. Cause and effect are to be employed only as "pure *concepts*" or "conventional fictions" that serve the purposes of "designation and communication, *not* explanation." Such concepts cannot explain because they do not obtain in the *An-sich.* Nietzsche thus claims access to the *An-sich* at the very moment he emphasizes the human propensity to read our own concepts into reality: he repeats the procedure of section 9, forcing the same question of warrant for his claims. Instead of providing that warrant, Nietzsche elaborates the mechanism whereby we attribute to the in-itself "causes, sequence, community, relativity, force, number, law, freedom, ground, purpose": such attribution is an *erdichten,* a fabricating or poetizing. When we poetize this sign-world of ours onto the in-itself, "we're behaving again as we've always be-

39. See *GS* 57 *"To the realists."*

haved, namely, *mythologically*." Our poetizing is a mythologizing, creating powers and entities out of pure concepts by the force of imagination. But "behaving" is *treiben*: to drive, propel, push — poetizing is the forceful imposition onto the in-itself of conceptual tools of designation and communication.

At the end of this account of the mechanism of mythologizing stands a nonmythological knowledge claim: "The 'unfree will' is mythology; in real life it is a matter only of *strong* and *weak* wills. — " The dash separates this assertion from a reading of symptoms that employs the knowledge asserted. Strong and weak wills are explanations, not just conceptual designations; they claim the status denied to cause and effect, law, number. Given this capacity to explain, Nietzsche does what the mythologists could not: he explains the mythology of free and unfree wills in terms of strong and weak wills. This final aspect of Nietzsche's display of strength is more than a refutation, it is an exhibition of a capacity to explain. The emphasis is on himself— "if I have observed rightly here" — and the claims are less than categorical— "almost always." The basic claim is that what a thinker holds "betrays" him, what he says points to what he is. *Who* took the issue of free will to be a problem? Nietzsche has observed two opposed grounds for taking "unfreedom of the will" as a problem, each stemming from an irreducible disposition to take oneself and the world this way rather than that. One way refuses to give up "responsibility" for itself and its merits — not even logical rape and unnaturalness is too high a price to pay for belief in free will. The other way pays a high price for the opposite: unwillingness to take the blame for anything about itself dictates a belief in unfree will.

This is the first glimpse of the fundamental human duality elaborated in the book as the two basic moral types. Each type took the hundred-times-refuted doctrine of free will to be foundational; it lies at the core of our morality because both basic types had a stake in it. But the problem of free will can be explained as the poetry produced by the two kinds of will, strong will affirming: "I am responsible," weak will denying: "I can't be blamed." Chapter 1 thus raises the expectation that a new understanding of the *An-sich* will explain our morality in later chapters.[40]

Nietzsche's symptomatology of will takes a position on freedom and un-

---

40. John Richardson shows how Nietzsche's "power ontology" underlies a new perspective on morality: "When we see that the world's real 'parts' are willful processes defined by their power relations to one another, we see that there are no self-sufficient parts and that things 'condition' one another in an even more penetrating way than determinism had supposed; we learn a new form of that thought, a new fatalism. Yet we also see how these power relations of command and obedience give the basis for a new kind of freedom and responsibility, now not as the equal inheritance of all subjects but as an ideal form of command that some wills may achieve." *Nietzsche's System* 211–12.

freedom; the very exercise of reading symptoms points to a basic unfreedom: views are dictated by dispositions that are simply given. Where humanity is disposed to pride in itself, it has willed the belief that it is responsible for itself; but free will is a self-contradiction. Where humanity has been ashamed of itself it has willed the belief in an unfree will; but unfree will is a misuse of cause and effect. Nietzsche has defined philosophy itself in terms of freedom and unfreedom: as the lust to rule, it is ruled by a passion not to *be* ruled. It is not free not to seek its freedom. In real life, where it is an issue of strong and weak wills, philosophy is the strongest will as well as the most spiritual. The new philosophy, able to refute free will and unfree will on the basis of a new understanding of the *An-sich,* aims at a new pride that will realistically understand how far it can extend its responsibility. As *amor fati* it is free of the need to believe in any self-contradictory *causa sui* and strong enough not to blame any mechanical cause and effect for what it is. It loves its fatedness while striving for the greatest possible freedom.

What is man? — the riddle of the Sphinx returns at the end of the chapter. If not a being with free will that chooses the course for which it is responsible or a being with unfree will that is not responsible, what *is* man? The question implies a broader question, What is nature, the whole of which man is a part? The refutation of free will and unfree will is appropriately followed by section 22, which raises the question of a new view of nature as a whole. That section is followed by the final section, which suggests that the problem of nature itself can best be approached through a proper understanding of the natural being with consciousness, man.[41]

The Popular Prejudices of Physics and Psychology
SECTIONS 22–23

The new philosophy, capable of refuting the prejudice of free will on the basis of a new understanding of nature, is also able to refute the prejudice about nature held by modern physics, the paradigm modern science. And it is able to recognize the moral prejudices and fears of psychology, the science of the human soul that has not dared to descend to its depths. Our sciences of nature and human nature have allied themselves with a disposition that my-

41. The human place in nature is given succinct expression at the end of Nietzsche's account of "The Four Great Errors" in *TI* (the fourth of which is "the error of free will"). Under the title, "What alone can *our* teaching be?" Nietzsche describes the "*great liberation*" implied in the view that "the fatality of our essence cannot be separated from the fatality of all that was and will be. . . . One is necessary, one is a piece of destiny, one belongs to the whole, one *is* in the whole . . . [T]he *innocence* of becoming is restored."

thologizes nature from the standpoint of weak will. The final sections of chapter 1 continue the display of strength begun in section 18 and prepare for the argument of chapter 2 on behalf of a true and comprehensive perspective on nature.

Section 22   Nietzsche asks forgiveness in opening section 22, as he, a philologist, presumes to tell physicists how to think about nature. But the advantage turns out to be all his, for physics too interprets a text and is therefore a branch of philology, the art of interpretation. Trained in exegesis and eisegesis, the philologist can see that modern physics poetized "law" onto the in-itself. But this philologist also takes history as a text and discerns behind modern physics the revolutionary democratic politics of modern times. In the end, however, the philologist assures the physicists that he "asserts the same about this world as you do"—a crucial assurance that a science of nature is possible on philological grounds.

Physicists speak with pride of "the law-abidingness of nature [*Gesetzmässigkeit der Natur*] as if— —"—as if they had discovered that the *An-sich* was obedient to law.[42] The philologist counters with what looks like a philologist's pride: that's only your construal (*Ausdeutung*), and it's bad philology; nature's law-abidingness is not "text" but a prejudiced misreading of the text: "a naive-humanitarian costuming and twisting of meaning." These accusations from a philologist's arsenal are part of the political charge that misreading nature as law-abiding goes "more than halfway to meet the democratic instincts of the modern soul."

The philologist reads the physicists' interpretation as itself a text, one that betrays the motives lying behind it: "Everywhere equality before the law— nature is no different in that respect, no better off than we are." Their desire to read the doctrine of equality into nature is called a *Hintergedanke*, but thoughts lie behind this thought too: enmity or rancor at a recognized inequality plus "a second and more refined atheism." Zarathustra had taken special care to persuade his followers that the teaching of equality is a reaction to intolerable inequality, a forceful preaching intended to right a natural wrong through revenge (Z 2 "On the Tarantulas"). "Hooray for the law of nature!" is a cry of good cheer masking a hatred of nature for generating superior and inferior. The political alliance of modern physics with the democratic instincts of the modern soul is based on a shared opposition to nature; in its doctrine of

---

42. On the dangers of attributing law-abidingness to nature, see the very important reflection on the dangers of mythology—shadows of God (*GS* 108)—that threaten science, *GS* 109: "Let us beware of saying that there are laws in nature. There are only necessities: there is nobody who commands, nobody who obeys, nobody who trespasses."

law-abidingness modern physics opposes *physis*. For all its successful fight against popular Platonism in its religious form, modern natural science in its motives aligns itself with an antinatural prejudice.[43] Nietzsche hints even that the defense of nature against atheistic modern physics could prove to be a vindication of God or gods, and the story he will tell, a physiodicy, turns out to be a theodicy too.

The old philologist has more than accusations to offer the physicists; "someone" might come along with a different interpretation of nature, and what that someone says suggests a competing political alliance. That nameless someone would have the "opposite intention"—he would not be moved by enmity to bring down the naturally advantaged. And he would possess the "opposite art of interpretation" to the art that reads a law-abiding equality into nature. A condensed version of the new reading is offered in words whose inadequacy calls for an apology. That reading too interprets nature in political terms but as a lawless tyranny, "the tyrannically inconsiderate and relentless carrying through of claims of power." Nature is not subject to laws somehow transcendent to it and which it obeys; nature takes its own course in the relentless carrying through of what is intrinsic to every aspect and component of it, claims of power.

The sentence describing the new view breaks suddenly at this point, gathering for a new onslaught from the someone who might come along: "An interpreter who would so set before your eyes the exceptionlessness and unconditionedness in all 'will to power' that almost every word including the word *tyranny* itself would appear finally unusable or even as weakening and softening metaphors—as too human." No interpreter can avoid the all-too-human in describing nature; all must employ language, an instrument generated for survival success by a species lacking other survival advantages, a blunt instrument lacking words for this very different endeavor, this luxury of attempting to describe the fundamental processes of nature (see 268, *GS* 354). The new terms borrowed from the political sphere unsettle those who politicized nature as a law-abiding democracy, but even the new terms are mere metaphors that soften nature's way.

The new interpreter applies to the whole of nature his own term for the fundamental process of nature: the will to power. This is the third time Nietz-

43. Nietzsche here touches a theme present in his notebooks from early to late and expressed in a typical form in Summer-Fall 1884: "'Science' (as it is practiced today) is the attempt to create a common language of signs for all appearances with the purpose of the easier *calculability* and resultant masterability of nature" (*KSA* 11.26 [227] see also [170]).

sche has used *will to power* in chapter 1, and there seems to be an order to the sequence: will to power first appears in its most spiritual form, philosophy; then as the cardinal drive of all organisms; and third as the fundamental feature of all nature—*will to power* serves as the descriptive, if inadequate, name for the highest, the living, and the whole. Reality is of one kind, according to the view being introduced, and the philosophy that gains insight into that is in a position to ground the fundamental sciences of life and of *physis* in the most comprehensive way. *Will to power* appears once more in this chapter, in the final section where its use completes the sequential introduction of the fundamental thought: will to power is the ultimate subject of psychology, the study of the human soul, the science affording privileged access to the fundamental problems.

Having offered his competing interpretation of nature, the philologist adds an indispensable "nevertheless." As different as the will to power view is from the law-abiding view, the will to power interpreter "would end asserting the same about this world as you assert, namely, that it has a 'necessary' and 'calculable' course." The great differences that have been emphasized do not negate the one completely crucial shared feature affirmed at the end: both views assert that a science of nature is possible. The necessary and calculable course of nature, mythologized as law-abidingness in the service of vengeful motives, continues to be studied from the perspective of will to power. According to that perspective, the totality is a field of forces in which "every power at every moment draws its ultimate consequences." This last phrase adds a dimension to the basic view: nothing *governs* nature in a way that would give it an order or a direction from outside of itself; as itself the totality of forces nature is at every moment the total dynamic equilibrium and disequilibrium of those forces.

"Granting that this too is only interpretation"—the invitation to the physicists to indulge their eagerness to accuse the philologist of self-contradiction betrays his own eagerness to trap *them*, to lure them into his own territory, where every view is interpretation: it is "so much the better" that physics view all views and hence its own view as interpretation. But is there no way to adjudicate among interpretations? If not, why prefer tyranny to law-abiding democracy? This section ends without answering such questions, as if the move from the dogmatism of modern mechanistic physics to the openness of competing interpretations were gain enough. But that different interpretations can be judged has been suggested by the previous section which claimed that there are two fountainheads of perspectives, two irreducible dispositions of the human soul, strong and weak. Throughout chapter 1 Nietzsche has set his own thinking within the gains of modern cosmology and evolutionary biology and condemned attempts like Kant's to delay the effect of those gains by sheltering morality from science. If the present section ends by acknowledging that the new view of nature is itself an interpretation, the next section turns to psychology, the study of the human soul, and suggests that the way to judge interpretations may come from an understanding of the human soul, source of interpretations.

Section 23   Section 23 brings chapter 1 to a fitting close. Focusing the will to power teaching on its appalling moral implications, it invites the decent reaction that has been building: stop reading if you can. But counting on the fascination and promise of the initial statements of the will to power teaching, it invites the contrary response as well: gather courage if you can't.

The chapter on the prejudices of the philosophers ends with prejudices that cripple psychology, the study of the human soul: "Moral prejudices and fears have deprived it of the daring necessary to descend to the depths of the soul." Study of the soul's depths is a "morphology and *evolution-doctrine of the will to power*." In the previous section, will to power named the fundamental process of nature as a whole; psychology studies the forms that process takes in its evolutionary articulation in our own species. The unity of the sciences derives from the unity of the subjects of science. The human subject offers science a sophisticated articulation of the primary force, an evolved complex of will to power capable of studying itself.

Nietzsche claims that no one before him has brushed against this view, even in thought — and then calls attention to the difference between the thought and the written. The written is not simply evidence for what has been thought but a symptom of what has been kept silent. In addition to being a student of the soul, Nietzsche is a student of the written who knows that philosophers have dared to think what they have not dared to write. Still, he has found no evidence of the view he has descended to. Instead, he found that moral prejudice penetrated into "the most spiritual world," the world of philosophy, and did great damage. A damaging descent challenges a damaging superficiality. Nietzsche promises "a proper physio-psychology," recognizing that it meets with resistance: "It has the 'heart' against it." Because the loves and hates of the investigator's heart resist the conclusions of his mind, the only course open is the one suggested in an aphorism this section elaborates: "*Bound heart, freed mind.* — If one binds one's heart with hardness and imprisons it, one can give one's mind many liberties" (87).

Three views that meet with the heart's resistance are mentioned, and all three counter the faith in the oppositeness of values, the basic faith of Platonism set out in section 2. The final section of the first chapter balances that opening section by setting forth dangerous maybes entertained by the new genus of philosophers. The three views are increasingly radical in their rejection of the faith in opposite values, but only the third goes as far as Nietzsche's dangerous view: "hate, envy, greed, the lust to rule" are necessary conditions of life and must even be enhanced for life to be enhanced. No attempt is made to soften the shock of this claim, the whole focus being on the nausea the investigator is bound to experience: it will be like seasickness. Seasickness signals the penultimate image of chapter 1, a coming odyssey, a voyage worthy of Odysseus.

Nietzsche's invitation to decline the voyage is followed by the dare to risk it if one has already begun. Because "we sail *away* right over morality," the voyage may even crush "the remnants of our own morality" — the truth seeking that commands this voyage and that was pictured at the beginning of the chapter under another image of self-destructive danger, answering the riddle of the Sphinx. We are at risk in this voyage, "but what do *we* matter!" This favorite refrain of Nietzsche's[44] is the cry of those who may go down with the ship; it measures the voyager against the greatness of the voyage — the self against something far greater than the self. Nietzsche's stirring ending appeals to passions of the heart different from the fears that kept the mind from this voyage. Nietzsche elevates the promise: "Never yet has a *deeper* world of insight opened itself to daring travelers and adventurers."[45] We are in the world of Odysseus, and an odyssey of this magnitude requires that the voyager offer a sacrifice for safe arrival. "It is not the *sacrifizio dell'intelletto*" — the sacrifice Pascal made (46), believing the heart had reasons the mind could not know. "On the contrary!" — it is the sacrifice of the heart demanded by the mind.

The psychologist who offers this sacrifice is no mere supplicant; his sacrifice entitles him to make a demand: "that psychology be acknowledged once again as the Lady of the sciences for whose services and preparation the other sciences exist." "Lady" is *Herrin*, literally, mistress or female master: psychology is Mistress of the Court of the Sciences, the noble Lady to whom the other sciences devote their service. The unity of the sciences arising from the unity underlying their subject matters is a hierarchy of the sciences in the service of their ultimate purpose: human understanding of the human.[46] The risky voyage, if

---

44. " 'What do I matter!' — this sign stands over the door of the thinker of the future" (*D* 547, see *D* 494).

45. On the open seas for the adventurous interpreter, see *GS* 124, 283, 289, 343.

46. Nietzsche's hierarchy of the sciences makes the human sciences the reason for the other sciences, but he does not presume that the human is the reason behind evolution as a whole: "We have placed the human back among the animals. We consider it the stron-

successful, may arrive at a new ordering of human things: the final image of the first chapter pictures science as an aristocracy united in the purpose of its rule, united in serving the Lady of the Sciences, human self-knowledge.

Psychology has a rightful claim to rule the Court of the Sciences, "For psychology is once again the path to the fundamental problems." — *once again*: Nietzsche implies that the sciences were on the path to the fundamental problems once before but were deflected by moral prejudices. The book ahead argues that Platonic dogmatism blocked a path opened by the Greek enlightenment and the philosophers of the tragic age of the Greeks.[47] The end of chapter 1 opens a vista on the monumental historic possibility suggested in the preface: after the long interregnum of Platonic dogmatism, it is philosophy's task to set the sciences once again on the proper path, a path, as Plato knew, of great danger to humanity because it destroys the lie of opposite origins that human life seems to require.

What are the *"fundamental problems"*? They are the problems of truth, judging from chapter 1, the problem of how to win it and the problem of how to live with it after it has been won.

---

gest animal because it is the most cunning: a consequence of that is its spirituality. . . . We oppose the vanity that . . . the human is the great hidden purpose of the evolution of animals. It is by no means the crown of creation; every living kind stands beside it on the same level of perfection" (*A* 14).

47. See *A* 59 for a concise statement of this view of the history of the sciences.

The Free Mind

Chapter 2 is the most important chapter in the book, for it arrives at the point of deepest insight that the first chapter prepared and that all the other chapters take as settled. Its ultimate concern is the possibility of philosophy, successful pursuit of truth who is a woman, plus the merest glimpse of how to live with truth. It argues the possibility of philosophy by demonstrating its actuality. Faced with the skepticism that naturally follows the demise of our dogmatism, it shows that a plausible conclusion can after all be drawn about the "intelligible character" of the world. That conclusion, initially so appalling, assigns the philosopher a responsibility: bring human life, life lived out of values, into accord with truth. In language that even Nietzsche was cautious about using, this chapter indicates that genuine philosophy can flower naturally into religion. The two chapters on philosophy thus lead to the chapter on religion, depth's creation of surfaces or, if a Platonic image may be used, the philosopher's return to rule the cave through shadows and echoes.

Der freie Geist — the subject was not a new one for Nietzsche: from 1878 to 1882 Nietzsche wrote a book a year with the "common goal of erecting *a new image and ideal of the free mind*."[1] That five-year project culminated with the

1. Stated on the back cover of the 1882 edition of *The Gay Science,* which announced that the series on the free mind was now complete.

fourth part of *The Gay Science,* "Sanctus Januarius," in which a new mood of affirmation and promise broke through for one reason alone: the key thoughts of *Thus Spoke Zarathustra* had just overtaken him.[2] When Nietzsche turns explicitly to the free mind in *Beyond Good and Evil* he returns to an old theme enriched by the gains of *Zarathustra.*

Modern free minds must advance past their active skepticism to recognition of the possibility of philosophy. They must learn that the philosopher is different from the rest of humanity, different even from its exceptions (24–26). The philosopher is therefore difficult to understand despite his best efforts at communication (27–29). Difference and difficulty make esotericism unavoidable for the philosopher, though the history of the species, understood comprehensively enough, permits the prevailing form of that esotericism, Platonic moralism, to be abandoned (30–32). After this preparation, chapter 2 centers its central matter, arguing that philosophy can emancipate itself from the remnant of morality still binding it, the salutary epistemological skepticism that helped destroy Platonic dogmatism but that is itself bound by a conviction about the good (33–35). The next sections show how it is possible for the true to win independence from the good and achieve its most fundamental insight—to be is to be will to power (36–38). This insight cannot be a resting place, however, for the new understanding of the true implies its own sense of the good—an unbounded Yes to everything that was and is. Who can avail themselves of the access these sections give to the mind and heart of Nietzschean philosophy? The next sections suggest what is necessary (39–41). Finally, like *Zarathustra, Beyond Good and Evil* indicates that the new view entails responsibility for the whole future of humanity, and chapter 2 ends by introducing the philosophers of the future and their historic task (42–44).

By the end of chapter 2 Nietzsche's fight against the democratic Enlightenment is visible in its essential features. Free-minded skepticism is not the highest form of enlightenment; the philosophers of the future hold views of nature and human nature that claim to be true and claim to be good. The new good opposes the Enlightenment good, which elevates equality and aims to abolish suffering; as the love of nature, the new good establishes an order of rank in accord with nature and understands suffering as nature's inescapable means to high achievement. Chapter 2 prepares chapter 3 — the philosophy of the future generates the religion of the future.

---

2. The single use of "the free mind" in *Zarathustra* (2. "On the Famous Wise") contrasts it with the famous wise. This contrast occurs just before the three songs of part 2, which poetically present the essential discovery of *Zarathustra,* the will to power, the teaching that is then shared with "you who are wisest" ("On Self-Overcoming").

The main structural features of *Beyond Good and Evil* are visible in their unity by the end of chapter 2: clearing away the moral prejudice of past philosophy prepares the skeptical mind for a new insight into nature, and that insight prepares a new affirmation of the whole of nature. This new philosophy and new religion entail a politics and a morality. After chapter 4, an interlude between the greatest tasks and the great tasks, *Beyond Good and Evil* contains five chapters setting out the great tasks of morals and politics dictated by the new philosophy.

The Philosopher's Difference
SECTIONS 24–26

The three opening sections, 24–26, stamp chapter 2 with its defining theme: the philosopher is different. He's a lover of knowledge amid lovers of ignorance (24); any attempt to reduce the difference and distance is bound to fail (25); he's a natural solitary, like all exceptions, but he's an exception among exceptions because he breaks his solitude (26). The three sections are, in turn, cheerful, earnest, and programmatic, and each claims that the philosopher's difference has important consequences for himself and society.

Section 24   The remarkable human propensity for simplification and falsification moves Nietzsche to exclaim, "O *sancta simplicitas!*" and to end every sentence with an exclamation mark. His wonder at simplification and falsification, at human custom, is not a critique, for he ends by acknowledging that the propensity to live within a horizon of custom is dictated by the love of life. But then philosophy, the passion for the subtle and true, must recognize that in some ways it is both profane and antilife. The most spirited and spiritual form of life places in jeopardy the holy simplicity that the love of life generates. It runs an unholy risk.

The opening section of chapter 2 is a cheerful repetition of the theme treated gravely in the opening section of chapter 1, the risk philosophy runs in seeking knowledge when humanity has a natural "will to ignorance" and thrives on ignorance. But the "gay entrance" (25) to chapter 2 refuses the outcome of the tragedy of Oedipus referred to in chapter 1: rather than put out one's eyes at the horror seen, it "puts in one's eyes for the wonder" of simplification and falsification and never puts them out again because the wonders never cease. Philosophy begins in wonder, and part of the wonder is the human will to ignorance. Philosophy of this sort—the desire to know the desire for ignorance—is indelibly associated with Socrates; in turning to the human in wonder Nietzsche repeats the Socratic turn.

The one who keeps his eyes in for the wonders of holy simplification ends up laughing at himself because his drive for knowledge seems to attempt the impossible: language lacks the refinement for the subtle and true, and morality prejudices the whole of language. Philosophy is a comedy driven knowingly to attempt the impossible while knowingly putting at risk life's simplifications and falsifications. But the laugher laughs particularly at science for its part in the will to ignorance: only on the "foundation of ignorance could science rise till now," and "even the best science still wants to keep us in this *simplified* world." The new philosophy will aim to found science on the true, but for now it must retain its gaiety and not succumb to the earnestness so natural to it and publicly demand that simplification and falsification be replaced by the real and the true (25). The gaiety of the first section entails the earnestness of the second, earnest counsel to philosophy not to grow earnest refuting the simplification and falsification natural to humanity—if philosophy insists on the practice of Socrates it risks the fate of Socrates.

Section 25   Linked to the comedy of the opening section is section 25, suggesting—not tragedy but the decay of tragedy, its fall into the satyr play performed in Athens during the early spring *Dionysia* after the morning of tragedies and followed by a comedy that ended those long days of theater. "Around the hero," Nietzsche said, "everything turns to tragedy, around the demigod everything turns to satyr play; and around god everything turns to— what? perhaps to 'world'? — " (150). Why not to comedy, as one would expect from the Athenian Dionysia? But maybe Nietzsche means comedy: comedy creates worlds, simplified, falsified, livable worlds; such worlds *are* comedies and come into being around gods. Perhaps this earnest section can be viewed as itself a comedy, a covert reflection on the divine Plato, a god corrupted by a half-god, the satyr Socrates. For although the examples named are Spinoza and Bruno, it is impossible not to think of Socrates, that "covert suicide" (*HH II AOM* 94) whose public advocacy of the truth led to the most public defense of philosophy and to the most public of all deaths for the sake of the truth. The new philosophers will mimic Socrates in public defense and public martyrdom no more than Plato did; they will shelter philosophy's difference, though not exactly in the way that Plato did—and around them too everything will turn to "world."

The earnest word addresses "the most earnest"—"you philosophers"—and warns them not to martyr themselves on the difference between the truth they know and the simplification and falsification within which humanity lives. Instead of a public defense of the truth before lovers of falsification, Nietzsche counsels truth-lovers to turn aside, to shelter themselves behind masks and refinements permitting them to be mistaken for someone else. Truth is a woman who no more needs the gallantry of knightly defenders than she does the clumsy affection of dogmatic lovers. Addressed to philosophers as counsel, this section seems to indicate how Nietzsche counseled himself, how he handled the problem of truth telling in the truth-lover. He tells of his love in a way that preserves his garden, the garden with the goldwork filigree whose exterior is so engaging that it keeps almost everyone out of its still more entrancing interior.[3]

Nietzsche entertains "a performer's curiosity" at the public performances of philosophers, the "dangerous wish" to see the philosopher in his degeneracy, reduced to a "platform screamer" for the sake of the truth.[4] With the performance of that satyr play, "the long genuine tragedy *is at its end:* assuming that every philosophy in its origins was a long tragedy. — " Not a merely personal tragedy, surely, but heroic recognition of the truth of tragedy over against the comic falsifications in which humanity prefers to live. As insight into the truth of tragedy, philosophy is vulnerable to a specific degeneracy: the demeaning spectacle of the philosopher on the public stage hectoring lovers of simplification and falsification on the falsity of their little comedy.

Section 26   The exceptions to the multitude insist on a fortress of solitude; the exception among the exceptions abandons that fortress to learn the way of the multitude. Just after the earnest counsel to withdraw into solitude, section 26 describes the exceptional solitude of philosophy. Once again it is hard to avoid the conclusion that this is a reflection on Socrates, that exception among Greek philosophical solitaries whose turn to the human things redefined philosophy and initiated its politics. "You must go down," part of Socrates' famous injunction to philosophers in Plato's *Republic* (7.520c), is part of Nietzsche's injunction as well and includes "go inside" to discover both the unexceptional and the exceptional in the exception. And once again Nietzsche requires that the exception among the exceptions do something different from what Socrates did. Instead of entering the marketplace to question and refute the reputed wise, the exceptional knower is to "station his ears" where he can

---

3. In a notebook entry from the time of *BGE* Nietzsche experimented with his garden image: "A garden whose very fencing glitters with gold needs to guard itself against more than thieves and rogues: its worst dangers come from its intrusive admirers who want to break something off everywhere and all too eagerly want to take this and that along with them as a memento. — And don't you even notice, you casual strollers in my garden, that you could never ever *justify* yourselves against those herbs and weeds of mine that tell you right to your face: Get out of here you intruders, you ——— " KSA 11.38 [22].

4. Public insistence on the truth spoils "the innocence and neutrality of the conscience." Like soul, conscience is an old and venerable hypothesis Nietzsche refuses to abandon. He sets out to forge a new conscience steeled under the revaluation of values (203).

hear a certain kind of cynic, a satyr Nietzsche calls him, who speaks badly of human beings without speaking ill of them. The cynic stands higher than the moral man because he is free of indignation, free of the need for vengeance, and free of the need to lie. But the cynic still wants to reduce humanity to hunger, sex, and vanity. The exceptional listener has no such want, wanting instead to preserve the possibility of human nobility; without ever imagining that hunger, sex, and vanity can be wholly transcended, he wants to believe that they can be transformed or spiritualized into the high desire and self-regard of high selves. Though the most difficult and dismaying item in the education of the philosopher is "the study of the average human being," the study that comes closest to refuting life for Zarathustra (Z 2 "On Redemption"), the cynic aids the philosopher in this study in the marketplace.

Nietzsche opens the chapter on the free mind by focusing on the philosopher and his pursuit of the truth about humanity hidden by its simplifications and falsifications. The exceptional character of the philosopher makes it difficult for him to communicate what he comes to understand. Do they *try* to be unclear? Do they do everything possible to be hard to understand?

Why the Philosopher's Tempo Is Hard to Understand
SECTIONS 27–29

Section 27   Does Nietzsche do everything possible to be hard to understand? Employing Sanskrit words almost no one will understand is a pleasant way of saying — No, while suggesting that a lot of work will be required, for such words must be looked up and interpreted, though he will do what he can to help: he translated one of them.[5] Together the three Sanskrit words state the main difficulty: the mind of the philosopher moves at a tempo different from that of the other two kinds of mind. The strange gait of the philosopher's mind makes him inexpungeably foreign; he thinks as the Ganges flows, presto, but not merely presto: he thinks with the relentless swiftness of the sacred river, swift and steady but with "a dialectical rigor and necessity that takes no false step" (213). But being the exception who has studied the tempo of other minds, he finds himself among those who unavoidably, irremediably think as the tortoise creeps, or, in the best case, the translated case, as the frog hops, quick and jerky. The problem of a philosopher's communication, therefore, calls for effort from two sides: *his* side requires the effort of translating his

5. Nietzsche wrote out the Sanskrit words in a notebook, translated each one, and indicated its appropriate tempo: "*gangasrotogati* 'as the stream of the Ganges flows along' = *presto; kurmagati* 'with the gait of a turtle' = *lento; mandeikagati* 'with the gait of a frog' = *staccato*" (KSA 12.3 [18]).

singular experience of thinking as far as possible into ours; *our* side must make the effort of hearing the results of a very different experience. The two sides are perhaps indicated by the sole translation: he *is* making an effort and he's making it for the quick but erratic minds who must steady themselves and be prepared to be instructed in order to understand him at all.[6] When the Sanskrit words are translated and the implicit claim about the philosopher's difference becomes clear, the use of foreign words can be seen to have another function: that difference is a sensitive matter bound to be heard with offense and scandal; it is therefore best that it not be spoken out loud but allowed to be discovered gradually.

Because Nietzsche does not try to be hard to understand but simply is hard to understand, and because he has the good will to try to bridge the gap in gaits separating his experience from that of others, he would be grateful for the complementary good will: the refinement in interpretation necessary to complete the communication of the foreign. Some readers stand at a special disadvantage in this respect, the writer's "good friends," who believe that friendship with the author spares them the labor of understanding and makes it easy for them to pick up his meaning. Is this directed at Rohde and Lou and Rée and Overbeck, warning them not to presume special access to the writings through access to the writer? Written in a book with the ambitions of Nietzsche's books, this warning must have a wider range too and include those made good friends of the writer by the lure of his writings: we're deluded if we suppose that affinity for the writer gives easy access to the writings.[7] By warning us that

6. Nietzsche returns to the problem of tempo in the final section of "We Scholars," the chapter distinguishing the philosopher from scholars and scientists: what a philosopher is "cannot be taught" because it includes experiences unknown to others such as "the genuine philosophical combination of a bold and exuberant spirituality/intellectuality that runs *presto* and a dialectical severity and necessity that takes no false step" (213). *GS* 381, "On the question of being understandable," provides a most valuable series of insights to Nietzsche's problem of communicating across tempos. It gives reasons for not wanting to be understandable — and to whom. More important, it states why he wants to be "understandable to *you*, my friends," despite the difference in tempos, despite what he describes as the two great impediments to his being understood, his "ignorance," the ignorance endemic to philosophy, which looks bad in a time of scientific knowledge, and "the liveliness (*Munterkeit,* cheerfulness, jauntiness) of [his] temperament," which fits him to approach the most elusive quarry of knowledge in the only way appropriate to them.

7. See *HH* II *AOM* 129: "The worst readers of aphorisms are their author's friends if they are intent upon guessing back from the general to the particular instance to which the aphorism owes its origin, for with this pot-peeking they reduce the whole effort of the author to nothing, and thus only deserve it when, instead of a philosophic outlook or

he intends to give us room for misunderstanding in order to laugh at us or cut us off entirely from what he communicates, Nietzsche seems to want to make his friends *un*comfortable, to *dis*comfort us into the effort we could imagine friendship spares us. Consequently, the two following sections seem composed to flow as the stream of the Ganges flows.

Section 28   Not only does a *presto* tempo make some individuals foreign, it makes whole languages foreign. An author who thinks and lives presto and wants to communicate "the most delightful and daring nuances of free, free-minded thought" but has to write in German is obliged to warn his readers about what he's attempting. It's difficult to translate a presto tempo into German, a language not given to presto. Still, because of his "actor-nature," Lessing was able to translate Bayle's French into German. But the tempo of Machiavelli was beyond even Lessing's German. Machiavelli's *Prince* "cannot help presenting the most earnest affairs in an unbridled *allegrissimo*." Nietzsche's prose seems to aim at a Machiavellian presto that escaped even Lessing.[8] Like Machiavelli, Nietzsche seems to have "a malicious performer's sense of what a contradiction he risks — thoughts, long, difficult, hard, dangerous, and a tempo of the gallop and the very best, most mischievous mood." "Finally," Nietzsche turns to the one he named first, Aristophanes, and his reflection on Aristophanes seems to honor him as most foreign in tempo, most untranslatable, and the reflection is itself all presto, all gallop.

There is no higher praise in Nietzsche's vocabulary than his praise for Aristophanes, "that transfiguring, complementary mind": "the complementary human being" is the peak of humanity "in whom the *rest* of existence is justified" (207). Nietzsche's praise of Aristophanes also speaks of justifying: for his sake "one *forgives* the whole of the Hellenic for having existed, provided one has understood in all its depths all that here requires forgiveness and transfiguration." What most requires forgiveness and transfiguration in the Hellenic is Platonism, the dogmatism that came to rule European thought so disastrously. Nietzsche does not leave to inference his cardinal point about forgiving Plato for the sake of Aristophanes, for he moves directly to Plato, citing his hiddenness and "Sphinx-nature" — does Plato harbor a riddle that is life threatening while promising rule to its successful unriddler? A luckily preserved little fact set the unriddler Nietzsche to dreaming about Plato's hiddenness and Sphinx-nature: a copy of Aristophanes was found under the pillow of his deathbed. Always so hidden in life through his masking di-

---

instruction, they gain nothing but, at best — or at worst — the satisfaction of a vulgar curiosity."

8. On Nietzsche's relation to Machiavelli's *Prince,* see *TI* Ancients 2.

alogues, the dying Plato failed to cover his tracks for a presto dreamer like Nietzsche. The little fact transfigures Plato in his relation to Platonism: Plato hid something very different from what he paraded in his dialogues; "no 'Bible,' nothing Egyptian, Pythagorean, Platonic." Foreign moralism could never help a Plato "hold out in life — a Greek life to which he said no." Plato could not have borne his own momentous no to Greek life, the highest form of human life yet achieved according to Nietzsche, without an Aristophanes, who is anything but a no to Greek life. Plato, master of tempos, introduced a foreign tempo into the Hellenic, translating it so successfully that he prepared the eventual takeover of the Hellenic by the foreign, the European by the Asian.[9]

Plato's cure for Platonism was Aristophanes. Knowing what Plato hid under his pillow, the presto dreamer imagines that Plato's "higher swindle" (*TI* Ancients 2), Plato's Platonism, was not what Plato himself held. For the sake of what Plato loved, even his anti-Hellenic swindle of such magnitude and consequence can be forgiven. Is this Nietzsche's ultimate stance toward Plato? — unforgivable Platonism can be forgiven Plato because Plato was Aristophanic? To place this transfiguring suggestion about the author of our dogmatism in a section on the difficulty of translating a presto tempo, to make it in this galloping fashion, suggests that such matters always remain Sphinx-like, riddles to be guessed at. Nietzsche does not handle Plato's swindle as a riddle, for he calls it a swindle right out in the open; but he does handle Plato's hiddenness riddlingly, as the hiddenness of a different tempo that can be pointed to even if it can hardly be believed, a hiddenness of philanthropy and solicitude for others that led him to believe that a swindle spared them worse harms. This section on being misunderstood ends by suggesting a way to penetrate the misunderstood Plato, whose success depended on being misunderstood. Nietzsche, "a complete skeptic about Plato" (*TI* Ancients 2), is not a cynic about Plato and he's certainly not indignant. Plato's disastrous dogmatism seems to have had its origins not in the base but the noble, in his kinship with Aristophanes.[10]

9. Nietzsche is explicit about this historic link in *TI* Ancients 2: "In the great disaster of Christianity, Plato is that ambiguity and fascination, called an 'ideal,' which made it possible for the nobler natures of antiquity to misunderstand themselves and to step on the *bridge* which led to the 'cross.' " See also, letter to Overbeck, 9 Jan. 1887: Speaking of the fate of Greek philosophy in a Christian world, Nietzsche says, "And it's all Plato's fault! He remains the greatest *Malheur* [misfortune] of Europe!"

10. *GS* 359 ends on what seems to be an implicit comparison of Augustine and Plato on Platonism that spares Plato the charge of revenge that Nietzsche levels against Augustine (see also *GS* 372). An important element in Nietzsche's overall evaluation of Plato is the

Section 29   "It is the concern of the fewest to be independent: — it is a prerogative of the strong." But it seems to be a concern of "the most independent man in Europe"[11] to make the independent ways of the fewest known to a larger number, for these sections report on those ways, that tempo, making it as understandable as possible. The chapter on the free mind informs the free minds about the *very* free mind of the philosopher.

This section on independence is not an invitation to it but a warning against it for those who may imagine themselves fit for it.[12] — "but without *having to*." The only italicized word in the section seems to be the crucial word: one who *had to* warns off those who probably don't. He who seeks independence without having to "proves thereby that he is probably not only strong but rash to the point of madness." He places himself in a labyrinth, and of the thousand new dangers thus added to life this is "not the smallest": "No one sees with eyes how and where he loses himself, becomes isolated, and is torn apart piece by piece by some cave-Minotaur of conscience." To be alone in the labyrinth facing a Minotaur is to be in Theseus's place, Theseus the hero who *had to* be there to deliver Athens from the blood sacrifice of its best youth forced on it by conquering strangers from Crete. But to be there without having to is to lack the sword that slays the Minotaur, the first of the aids Ariadne granted Theseus. "Suppose such a one perishes,[13] it happens so far from the comprehension of humanity that they don't feel it and don't feel for him." If he has perished for humanity out of reach of its sympathy, what about his feeling for humanity, this one who entered the labyrinth without having to? " — and he can no longer get back! he can also no longer get back to the compassion for humanity![14] —— " To be unable to get back is to lack Ariadne's second aid, the

---

praise he accords Plato in *TI* (in the context of criticism of Schopenhauer): whereas Schopenhauer "prizes art especially as a savior from 'the focal point of the will,' from sexuality . . . . [n]o less an authority than the divine Plato . . . maintains a different proposition: that all beauty stimulates reproduction. . . . Plato goes further. . . . Philosophy in Plato's style would be better defined as an erotic competition, as a development and internalization of the old competitive gymnastics and of its *prerequisites*. . . . I will also recall . . . to Plato's credit, that all the higher culture and literature of *classical* France also grew on the soil of sexual interest" (Skirmishes 22–23).

11. Letter of Overbeck, 30 April 1884.

12. This section resembles Zarathustra's counsel to potential followers in "On the Way of the Creator," *Z* 1.

13. Perhaps Nietzsche is exploiting the ambiguity of *geht zu Grunde* (a variant of the customary *geht zugrunde,* which Nietzsche often uses): what looks like perishing to others may be the actual getting to the ground of things.

14. *"zum Mitleid der Menschen"* is ambiguous: "to the compassion *for* humanity" sustains the focus of the passage on the actions of the solitary, but the phrase can also

clue she granted Theseus that enabled him to get back out of the labyrinth after slaying the Minotaur. The risk of independence, the experience of the labyrinth, ruins mere adventurers, the rashly brave, in this second way too; their feeling for humanity is irrecoverably destroyed, turned into hatred perhaps, or cynicism.

Obliquely, describing failure, the exception among exceptions claims success for himself, heroic success through Ariadne's aids. And writing a book like this certifies his success, proving that he has not been destroyed by the Minotaurs of conscience and that he has found his way back to compassion for humanity. But it must be a different compassion from the virtue of compassion that defines modern times and that he must oppose (202, 260, 284); it is a compassion or love for humanity that will be the quiet theme of many later sections until finally it appears mythically at the end, where Ariadne herself, giver of indispensable aids to the hero, to one who has to, makes her only direct appearance in the book (295). Yet she appears not with Theseus but with Dionysos, the god who replaced Theseus as her consort in the myth. Will the book indicate how Ariadne's hero became a superhero, a god? At the end of Nietzsche's book, Dionysos himself avows that "under certain circumstances, I love humanity," and with this declaration of love "he alluded to Ariadne, who was present." What does Dionysos' love for Ariadne portend for humanity? The ending of the book puts mythically what the whole book argues: the philosophy of the future aims to enhance humanity out of compassion or love, and it does so in ways that will not at first look like enhancements and with motives that do not sound like love.

The hero of the labyrinth, slaying the Minotaur of conscience, gets back to compassion for humanity; he writes books. What kind of books does he write? Two dashes end this section as they end the next section. This unusual punctuation[15] sets off a singular section: section 30 sounds like a pitiless report from the labyrinth by a survivor of the minotaurs of conscience who got back to a different sort of compassion for humanity.

Philosophers' Esotericism
SECTIONS 30–32

If the philosopher is ineradicably different, an exception among exceptions whose essential experience is incommunicable but who still wants to "get

---

mean "to the compassion *of* humanity," a sense in keeping with the general issue of the context on how the solitary is viewed by others.

15. Two dashes end section 51, but there they are stand-ins for the unsupplied clause that completes the unfinished sentence.

back" or communicate in some sense, how can he? Only esoterically, Nietzsche states in these sections, only in a form that masks or distorts his experience. Esotericism, the theory of masks, has a double rationale: it is dictated by the philosopher's difference and by what he differs from, humanity as a whole. The sections that follow seem to be determined by this dual rationale as Nietzsche speaks first of philosophic esotericism and then of human maturity.

Section 30   Nietzsche's statement on esotericism opens a closed topic that became forgotten as well as closed with the victory of the democratic Enlightenment. The exoteric and the esoteric had been distinguished by all philosophers prior to the Enlightenment: "wherever one believed in an order of rank and *not* in equality and equal rights." The inescapable ground for philosophic esotericism is stated in the first sentence: "Our highest insights must—and should!—sound like follies, possibly like crimes, when they come without permission to the ears of those who are not the kind for them, not predestined for them." The highest insights of the exceptions among the exceptions—those victors in the labyrinth who get back and report their insights—are bound to be misunderstood by the nonexceptions, by almost everyone, and in two precise ways. If the philosopher's insights are not judged folly—if they seem in some way effectual—they will be judged criminal—and should be. Plato's Socrates stated the same point when pressed by Adeimantus on his claim that only the philosopher is fit to rule: the citizen rightly judges the philosopher to be either useless or vicious.[16] Nietzsche states the consequences of this proper judgment in the first words of the next sentence: "The exoteric and the esoteric as one formerly among philosophers distinguished them." Philosophers distinguished exoteric and esoteric because they recognized that it was proper that the genuine philosopher would be ridiculed as mad or persecuted as criminal if he stated his views openly. Nietzsche does not elaborate just how the ubiquity of this threat of ridicule or persecution might guide our study of the history of philosophy—he is not Leo Strauss. Instead, noting that the exoteric/esoteric distinction arose wherever philosophy arose, Nietzsche corrects a misapprehension about it: it "does not so much consist in this" (though it in part then consists in this) "that the exoteric stands outside and from outside, not from inside, views, evaluates, measures, judges." The more essential difference, Nietzsche asserts, is that the exoteric views things from below, the "esoteric, however, *down from above*." The customary understanding suggests that to enter the esoteric all that is needed is permission or instruction and one can walk on in. Nietzsche's correction suggests that the esoteric view is unattainable or inaccessible to anyone who is not the kind for

16. *Republic* 6.487a-e.

it: no one can be carried to the view from the height. Nietzsche's thought about esotericism is itself mad or criminal, radically antidemocratic. And it's a reason he constructed his books as he did—not simply to avoid ridicule or persecution but to invite readers of a certain sort to the labors through which alone his height could be shared.[17]

Nietzsche's brief lesson in esotericism prepares the core thought of section 30, the one particular high insight that may now be suggested to fit listeners even if it will be judged mad or criminal. "There are heights of the soul where, to look out from which, tragedy itself ceases to have a tragic effect." The view from the height does not abolish tragedy, but it does liberate the viewer from the *effect* of tragedy, pity and fear.[18] Nietzsche then puts his crucial claim as a question: "And taking all the woe of the world together, who may dare to decide whether its sight *necessarily* seduces and compels precisely to pity and thus to doubling the woe?" This, it seems to me, is a glimpse into the highest insight afforded by the philosopher's esoteric viewpoint: is the ultimate judgment on the world necessitated by the supposed effects of tragedy? This glimpse is a preview of what will be serially or dramatically arrived at in the book, first as the comprehensive inference about the intelligible character of the world (36–37), then as the ultimate judgment occasioned by that inference (56).

Who may dare to decide? Who is fit to weigh the world in all its woe? Who but the one who has gained the most comprehensive view? Experiencing that view, is he necessarily compelled to pity? Nietzsche, with all due caution, will use theological language to express this claim to an experience high above what is commonly possible. The hero experiences the world as tragedy. But the demigod? And the god?

17. Leo Strauss's essay on *Beyond Good and Evil* does not deal explicitly with this section on esotericism, though his one reference to it suggests that it is a means to tempt some of Nietzsche's readers to his fundamental insight (*Studies in Platonic Political Philosophy* 178). The transcript of one of Strauss's seminars on *Beyond Good and Evil* records this comment on Nietzsche's statement that esotericism "looks *down from above*": "This remark is a very remarkable divination; as far as I know, Nietzsche had no empirical knowledge of these things, except the general tradition that there were these distinctions between exoteric and esoteric teaching" (University of Chicago, Winter semester, 1967, p. 5/11). Strauss had more empirical knowledge of these things than any twentieth-century reader, but is this judgment about Nietzsche correct? Without speaking of details, Nietzsche seems to exhibit empirical knowledge of the esotericism of Plato and Aristophanes, for example.

18. Nietzsche mentions only *Mitleid,* translated in this instance as *pity* rather than *compassion,* in keeping with the customary English terms for the classical or Aristotelian account of the effects of tragedy. On Nietzsche's view of the effects of tragedy as pity and fear, see *BGE* 239; see also *TI* Ancients 5, where Nietzsche challenges Aristotle's view.

How is such a matter decided? Not by what is known but by a disposition toward what can be known. Such judgments are symptoms; they show the germ of life out of which a philosophy grows (6). That a nonpitying comprehensive judgment can be a philosopher's symptom will be shown first in a report on such a judgment (56). That such judgments are the philosopher's responsibility (205) — "a judgment, a Yes and No . . . about life and the value of life" — will distinguish the philosopher from the scholar.

Viewing all the woe of the world together, the section on esotericism suggests, may not preclude celebrating the world as comedy — not because it ends well but solely because of the marvel of the spectacle and of the viewer of the spectacle, reasons for affirmation that will be elaborated only once in this book, in section 56. Brave in the face of the fearful, delivered from necessitous pity, the esoteric view is not only exceptional, but, the book as a whole will suggest, it also gets back to a kind of compassion for humanity. That is, it creates a mold for a possible recasting of exoteric experience that brings it into accord with esoteric experience. This is the philanthropic or gift-giving act that descends from the height, a new philosophy or lust to rule, a new kind of compassion that stoops to rule out of choice (*Z* 3 "On the Three Evils") and prepares new festivals of celebration.

Esotericism in Nietzsche's sense is inexpungeable even from a philosophy that elevates the virtue of honesty. But the exoteric teaching of such an esotericism will not consist of pious fraud; as Nietzsche wrote in a notebook, "We're proud not to have to be liars anymore, or slanderers, or discreditors of life" (*KSA* 13.15 [44]).[19] Nietzsche's exoteric teaching aims to align the exoteric with the esoteric, to allow the open and public to ring with the same sense and sensibility as the inaccessible and exceptional without ever being able to reach its heights. The new exoteric teaching will be a physiodicy and justify the ways of the world to men; it will communicate the view ultimately accessible only from above that all the woe of the world can be viewed together and yet not necessarily evoke pity and fear; it will justify, elevate, divinize the inexorable flow and mortality of things and help to see it as lovable. This new exoteric teaching is bound to come to the ears of those who are not the kind for it as the highest crime. Therefore, part of the task of the philosopher who brings it must be to expose the exoteric lies of previous philosophers, especially the dangerous lies of dogmatic Platonism, revealing them for what they are, pampering tales told to children who need to hear that parental forces punish their

19. After his famous recommendation to "live dangerously!" Nietzsche says to "you knowers": "The age will soon be gone when it was enough for you to live hidden in forests like shy deer" (*GS* 283).

bad acts and reward their good ones. The next two sections address this issue of human maturity; they carry forward the question of esotericism by asking whether the state of humanity still dictates being treated as such children.[20]

Section 31 Nietzsche gives his lesson on esotericism both an individual and a historical dimension in sections 31 and 32: youth's vehemence denies it the subtleties of the exoteric and esoteric appreciated by true maturity. But the vehemence of youth and its long-term cost apply to our whole species: the history of our species can be viewed as the painful passage from youth to maturity, the present age paying the natural price for the youthful vehemence of the dogmatic moral millennia. The speaker who presumes to speak from the heart of the labyrinth and from the pinnacle of the esoteric now presumes to speak from an enlightened human maturity.

Nietzsche is categorical about the immaturity of the categorical: the "art of nuance . . . constitutes the best gain of life. . . . the worst of all tastes [is] the taste for the unconditioned."[21] And he is categorical about maturity: "everything is so arranged" that maturity will pay for the intellectual and spiritual crimes of dogmatic immaturity. One matures out of immaturity immaturely.

---

20. In a stunning book written from the perspective of Nietzsche's genuine enemy, the democratic Enlightenment, written with deadly intent to kill the Nietzsche corps/e, written with blood and fire and astonishing scope, Geoff Waite argues that the crucial leverage *against* Nietzsche is gained by recognizing that he is an esoteric writer (*Nietzsche's Corps/e: Aesthetics, Politics, Prophecy, or, the Spectacular Technoculture of Everyday Life*). The *exoteric* in Nietzsche, according to Waite, consists of all the attractive devices of critique that have been so successful in drawing so many to him, particularly those with progressive or protestant aims against the ruling regime of ideas. But what is the *esoteric* in Nietzsche according to Waite? what do the masks mask? Exactly what Nietzsche says: a tyrannical will to rule, to enslave, to reestablish cruelty and suffering; a demonic teaching to Waite, who believes in no devils but Nietzsche. To arrive at this conclusion Waite must interpret Nietzsche's direct claims about philosophical rule with antipathy, finding malice and mere glee where Nietzsche claims philanthropy, philosophy's love of humanity and consequent love of the whole. In my view, Waite's brilliant book fails only on what matters most, readerly attentiveness to writerly nuance, sensitivity to the grace with which Nietzsche conveys what is best about himself and philosophy. Waite is committed to what Nietzsche hates, and the very gravity of his communism seems to have made Nietzsche's dance seem a travesty, a contemptible playing at play with the future of humanity — its outcome in global equality and well-being — hanging in the balance or, worse, being wrecked by an alleged dancer who captured the imagination of those who should be Waite's allies.

21. Nietzsche again plays with the unconditioned when speaking about maturity in terms of health and sickness: "Objection, infidelity, gay mistrust, a passion for scorn are symptoms of health: everything unconditioned belongs in pathology" (154).

Conscience is the agent by which a supposed maturity punishes youthful enthusiasm as if it were wholly blamable instead of wholly natural. One experiences good conscience itself as a danger, as if it were a dishonesty that hid some still more subtle honesty. Section 31 ends by stepping into another maturity: "—A decade later: and one grasps that all of that was still—youth!" This decade later is a future maturity for free minds: their distinctive unfreedom, the vehemence with which they learned the lesson of dogmatism, binds them to a severe conscience that mistrusts all its faculties. Free-mindedness mistakes for maturity itself the honest skepticism that mistrusts the senses and mistrusts reason out of self-punishment for dogmatic trust. The maturity beyond free-mindedness exercises the art of nuance, attempting to recover from the voluntary blindness that free-mindedness naturally preferred to dogmatic seeing.

Given the connections between sections 30 and 31, perhaps the maturity beyond maturity does more than simply permit youth its natural vehemence in despising and venerating: it may employ youth's vehemence for the ends of true maturity, taking the step already risked by "life's real *Artisten*" —its real performers or high-wire artists. Perhaps exoteric Nietzscheanism can be construed as in part a wisely guided Children's Campaign, a youth movement serving real maturity.[22]

Section 32   The new maturity suggested in section 31 arises in a transition time that could mark an advance in maturity for the whole species. Nietzsche pictures that maturity in a new periodization of human history with three periods—premoral, moral, and extramoral, but the term *extramoral* is provisional, fitting only "at first." The two turning points between the three periods hinge on a single matter: experiments in self-knowledge.

Nietzsche says only one thing about the longest, or premoral, period: "The imperative '*know thyself!*' was still unknown" because the worth of an action was measured by its consequences alone.[23] An experiment with self-knowledge gradually took over "in the past ten thousand years in a few large regions of the earth" as humanity learned to measure the worth of an action by its origins instead of its consequences. This reversal of perspective advanced self-knowledge but introduced the "disastrous new superstition" that the origins of human actions were to be found in intentions. This superstition gained the right to praise, blame, judge, and even philosophize everything on earth. "Today" is a pivotal time in the history of our species, and Nietzsche puts the pivotal point about the pivotal time in the form of a long rhetorical question:

22. As Leo Strauss argued Machiavellianism was: *Thoughts on Machiavelli* 127.
23. On consequences as the initial measure of the value of an actor, see *HH* 39.

—"Isn't it the case" that we must become decisive once again about a reversal and fundamental shift in values? The ground for our shift is the same as the ground for the previous shift: "a self-examination and deepening on the part of humanity."

—"Isn't it the case that we stand on the threshold of a period that, negatively, could at first be characterized as the extramoral?" Ten thousand years of dominance by the moral view force the new view to become visible first as negative, the view of "immoralists" (see also 226).

—Isn't it the case that "at least among us immoralists the suspicion is stirring that precisely in what is *not intentional* in an action lies its decisive value?" What is not intentional is what is given or granted in our passions and dispositions, what has become instinct. Most profoundly, what is not intentional is that basic either-or of dispositions that articulate themselves into the total nuanced variety of human values: the gratitude and love prompted by an overflowing abundance of energy or the revenge against everything that exists prompted by an impoverishment of life (*GS* 370).[24] The human species stands on the threshold of a vast new period of self-knowledge, Nietzsche suggests, in which the instincts that have reigned in the moral period can be supplanted by instincts inclined to interpret nature and history differently, affirmatively.

—Isn't it the case "that all of the intentionalness [of an action], everything in it that can be seen, known, 'conscious,' still belongs to its surface and skin, — which, like every skin, betrays something but *hides* still more?" The immoralist judges that the moral view misreads the skin of intentions and is therefore "a prejudice, a precipitancy, a preliminarity perhaps." Certainly prejudiced and precipitant, the moral view is only "perhaps" a preliminarity because its overcoming can hardly be regarded as inevitable. As a preliminarity, it has "somewhat of the rank of astrology and alchemy" — the moral view is part of the "noble childishness," perhaps "a promise across millennia" (preface), a protoscience of the soul that so disciplined the soul that it could stand to an extramoral science of the soul as astrology stands to astronomy, a soul science that would read what the skin of intention hides.

Section 32, assigning new names to the newly glimpsed phenomena of the moral history of our species, ends by assigning a corrective name to the extramoral stage. The coming stage is *extra* moral only to the morality of intentions, for "the overcoming of morality" is in a certain sense even "the self-

---

24. On the science of the unintentional, see "intelligent sensuality" in *KSA* 13.14 [117] and Ansell-Pearson, *Viroid Life* 120–22. This point seems echoed in what Wallace Stevens saw as basic to the morality of the modern poet: "the morality of the right sensation" (Stevens, *The Necessary Angel* 58).

overcoming of morality: let *that* be the name for this long secret work which has remained reserved for the most subtle and most honest, also the most malicious consciences of today." Today's work is driven by today's conscience, forged to refinement and honesty by the history of conscience. Stalled at a salutary skepticism, the immature conscience of free minds is goaded to aspire to a more self-critical stage beyond the merely extramoral. The new conscience is "the *boshaftesten* conscience" — not a conscience poisoned into malice, judging by everything Nietzsche says about such poison, but a sporting conscience given to mockery and ridicule, a conscience hardened out of its learned tenderness, the ease with which it used to be wounded or the delicacy with which it refused to bite, a conscience eager to make itself and others ashamed at countenancing the stupidity and dishonesty that conscience sheltered till now. The coming work is anything but extra moral in this broadened sense of morality, for it derives an imperative about what ought to be done from its understanding of what humanity has become through its history.

This imperative has implications for the esotericism with which philosophy sheltered itself till now, the compromise with the moral view made most effectively by dogmatic Platonism. Nietzsche's most elaborate and beautiful account of what the end of the moral period portends for philosophy's exoteric strategy is given in *On the Genealogy of Morality* (3.10): the emergency conditions under which philosophy arose may have dictated that it lyingly clothe itself as an ugly caterpillar of moral asceticism spiritually harmonious with the sole acknowledged spiritual authority, priestly asceticism. The maturity beyond the moral period liberates philosophy into open disclosure of its genuine extramoral character; the ugly caterpillar metamorphoses into a beautiful butterfly as philosophy exhibits its mature and entrancing form. The nontragic view from above would then cease to look criminal as it was translated into livable poetry of the whole human comedy for a maturing humanity less in need of deliverance from a life immaturely construed under the effects of tragedy.[25]

It may well be that Nietzsche taught postmodernism its "incredulity toward metanarratives,"[26] but sections like this one make it obvious that Nietzsche composed his own metanarrative, an account of the whole of human history that claimed to be true. Nietzsche refused to surrender the science of history to the petulance of the disappointed, cynics of the possibility of a true narrative of what actually happened. Nietzsche's metanarrative here focuses on what

---

25. For earlier statements of the necessity of esotericism because of the communally dictated lies of morality, see *HH II AOM* 89–90, *WS* 43–44.

26. Lyotard, *The Postmodern Condition*, xxiv, 39; see Cox, *Nietzsche* 1.

humanity believed about itself, with human history now turning on what humanity was gradually forced to see as true about itself. The present age according to this metanarrative may mark a decisive advance in human enlightenment — but only because human history can be seen as a fragment of natural history, which grounds the human in biological, chemical, and physical histories that themselves are part of the most meta of all narratives.

The Central Matter: The Maturation of Philosophy at the End of the Moral Period, Or Can the True Win Independence from the Good and the Good Learn Dependence on the True?
SECTIONS 33–35

Here is the core engagement with the immediate adversary at the end of the moral period, the democratic Enlightenment; here "the *good European* and free, *very* free mind" identifies the central issue in his campaign against the spiritual power whose hegemony dissipates the tensed energies gathered by the centuries-long fight against Platonism. The issue is twofold, knowledge and action: Can the world, in some fundamental way and with a high probability, be known? And if it can, are human beings fit to live in accord with the known world? The issue is the possibility of philosophy: Can there be a valid ontology or insight into the way of all beings? And if there can, is there a morality or humanly devised good and bad that can be aligned with the way of all beings? Chapter 2 has been building to this central issue:

— What is the philosopher? One who finds comedy in the simplification and falsification in which human beings live (24) but who warns against the martyrdom of trying to persuade humanity of the real and true (25), and who instead studies the common man to understand the difference between himself and them (26). The philosopher learns that his mind moves at a different tempo (27), yet aims to communicate across tempos (28) because his victory in the labyrinth enabled him to get back to a certain compassion for humanity (29).

— What is the philosopher *today?* One who betrays what philosophy has always been, esoteric or a view from above that surveys the whole tragedy of human woe without fear and pity (30). One who can survey the whole human past and see the last ten thousand years as a period of youthful vehemence during which humanity judged the whole morally, and who sees as well that the moral period now passes into a more mature skepticism about human judgments that is still not the full maturity of reasonably grounded judgments (31–32).

— What problem does the philosopher face today? The problem of the possibility of knowledge given the erroneousness of the world in which we live, a world of both outer and inner fictions. The central section (34) confronts that problem and traces it to a naive faith that truth will accord with our belief in the good (35).

Section 33   Considering its placement — just after the suggestion of a "self-overcoming of morality" at the end of the moral period, just before the central aphorism presenting the problem of knowledge (34) — this little aphorism on moral reform must be read for its broadest application. What then comes to light is a new imperative imperiled by a new temptation. "There's no help for it": necessity rules this transition. What came to rule in the moral period — "the whole self-renunciation morality" — has become second nature and must be subjected to merciless judgment. That judgment suggests a reversal: the feeling of "for others" and "*not* for oneself" has become the temptation that one must resist because it seduces one away from the imperative of a new "for oneself." The old imperative is the new temptation, the old temptation the new imperative. Temptations tempt through pleasure: the formative power of the morality of the moral period has made self-sacrifice pleasurable. The pleasures of self-sacrifice must now be sacrificed; one must now be hard on oneself by forcing oneself to be for oneself. "Mistrust" of moral judgment prepares the central section: "So let's be cautious!" — *vorsichtig:* foresightful.

Section 34   The central section 34, on deception and the duty of the thinker, suggests the possibility of a mature response to the inevitability of simplification and falsification.

Nietzsche does not doubt the erroneousness of the world in which we believe we live: every philosophical standpoint today, like the standpoint of a Copernicus or Boscovich (12), finds grounds for that conclusion. Nietzsche counters the temptation to assign responsibility for the erroneousness of the world to the world, to some "deceptive principle in the 'essence of things.' " It is better to assign responsibility to us, to "our thinking itself," holding "the 'mind' responsible for the falsity of the world." Such Kantian epistemological caution is laudable, "an honorable way out which every conscious or unconscious *advocatus dei* takes." But to take "this world together with space, time, form, motion to be falsely *inferred*" dictates a further duty that moves Nietzsche beyond Kant: the duty to mistrust "all thinking itself," to expect thinking here too to do "what it's always done," falsify. Such mistrust would cure the innocence that still places thinkers before consciousness asking it *please* to give them honest answers.[27] "Faith in 'immediate certainties' " (see 16) may be

27. See *KSA* 13.11 [113] = *WP* 477: "I maintain the phenomenality of the inner world, too: everything of which we become conscious is arranged, simplified, schematized, interpreted through and through. . . . The 'apparent inner world' is governed by just the same

"a *moral* naiveté that does honor to us philosophers," but such faith is not good enough for a philosopher: we philosophers, Nietzsche says, "should now for once not be '*merely* moral' men." Philosophers must condemn their faith in immediate certainties as stupidity and abandon it.

Chapter 2 has focused on the philosopher's radical difference from the rest of humanity, and here that difference dictates an essential duty regarding the moral: now, at the end of the moral period, the philosopher must exercise suspicion against the vestige of moral faith that imagines that consciousness yields immediate certainties. Such suspicion further separates the philosopher from humanity and invites a judgment against him: "civil life" always regards active mistrust as imprudence, as a sign of "bad character." But uncivil imprudence has now become necessary "among ourselves, beyond the civil world and its Yeses and Nos." Philosophy's historic or Platonic prudence, its civility, its long alliance with the unnuanced immaturity of society's moral vehemence must be abandoned in favor of what society counts imprudence. "Among ourselves" it can be said that the philosopher "has practically a *right* to 'bad character.'" Why? Because the philosopher is "the creature that till now has always been most made a fool of." Always judged a fool, the philosopher has won a virtual right to become a criminal, to draw down on himself the more serious of the two common judgments on the philosopher (30), to become an "immoralist" (32, 226) with a "*duty* to mistrust, to the most malicious cross-eyed squinting up out of every abyss of suspicion."

Having thus himself made the thinker look like something of a fool, an uncivil, imprudent frog squinting up out of a swamp of suspicion, Nietzsche forces a halt to his thought: Forgive me, he says, for "the little joke of this dismal grotesque." The halt to ask forgiveness highlights what has just been said — the now honorable course for the philosopher plunges him into seemingly dishonorable suspicion about the mind's propensity to deceive — and it allows Nietzsche to assert his own peculiar credentials: he's a thinker whose squinting up out of every abyss of suspicion has "long since" taught him "to think differently, to value differently, about deceiving and being deceived." Deceiving and being deceived are not necessarily evils of the mind for which blame must be assigned; deception as such is not to be morally condemned, for deception may be species preserving, even species enhancing — that is what may sound strangest in the new thinking (4). Because deception and being deceived are neither eradicable nor blamable, "I keep at least a few pokes to the ribs (*Rippenstösse*) handy for the blind rage with which the philosophers resist

---

forms and procedures as the 'outer' world." See also *KSA* 13.14 [152] = *WP* 478, and *KSA* 13.15 [90] = *WP* 479.

being deceived. Why *not?*" Why not be deceived? The dutiful philosopher so resistant to being deceived falls into "*blind* rage" against deception, deceiving moral rage driven by the conviction that it ought to be otherwise. Holding deception morally blamable, such unconscious advocates of god blame themselves. A conscious advocate of god, schooled in deceiving and being deceived, Nietzsche holds that they ought not to blame even themselves, for "it is no more than a moral prejudice that truth is worth more than appearance."[28]

Lovers of truth at the end of the moral period must learn to treat their prejudice in a mature manner. In order to be intelligently prejudiced in truth's favor they must know who they are: products of a long history of moral enthusiasms still in the grip of an enthusiasm. And they must know where they are: at the end of the moral period and on the threshold of what will first appear to be extramoral — uncivil and criminal. As rare lovers of a beloved with scant appeal to others, they must learn new approaches to truth that acknowledge the deceptiveness of their own faculties as well as the value of deception for life. Nietzsche asks his reader to admit "this much at least: no life at all would exist if not on the ground of perspectival evaluations and apparentnesses." Such an admission of the perspectival would bring thinkers into alignment with "the fundamental condition of all life" (preface), terminating Platonism's antilife opposition of true and false. "The virtuous enthusiasm and foolishness of some philosophers" wanted "to completely abolish the 'apparent world' " — maybe they even succeeded, Nietzsche implies in this little *Rippenstoss,* those old philosophers who had the luxury of another world to flee to, but "suppose *you* could do that," you free minds who've already abolished that other world, "there would remain at least of your 'truth' nothing left over!" And with that little poke to the ribs Nietzsche accuses the free minds of still being victims of the metaphysical faith in the oppositeness of values (2) with its belief in an essential opposition between true and false. In place of that faith Nietzsche suggests "degrees of apparentness" and "lighter and darker tones of appearance," a nuanced artistry in reading the *Schein* of things without casting it into the shadow of some now-abolished reality. The particulars of what would be required in such artful interpretation of outer and inner appearance — epistemology as philological subtlety in reading the text of nature and human nature — is not further elaborated in this "No-saying book,"

---

28. Nietzsche's thoughts on deceiving and being deceived are carried forward in *GS* 344, "How far we too are still pious," an opening section of the new chapter on the free mind and science; see also *GM* 3.24, in which Nietzsche ends his essay on the ascetic ideal by raising the issue of truth and science.

even though Nietzsche was at this time composing notes on this topic for publication in the *Transvaluation of All Values.*

A little dialogue ends these cautions about deception and administers another poke to the ribs: "Why should the world *of any concern to us*[29] — , not be a fiction?" Fictions should not be a moral problem even for virtuous truth seekers. Neither do fictions force the further inference Nietzsche hears being made: to whomever asks, "But to a fiction belongs an author" — *ein Urheber,* an originating maker responsible for its rising up — "one can roundly reply: *Why?* Perhaps this 'belongs' belongs with the fiction?" Those who have studied sections 17 and 19 will find this answer enough: a trick of grammar makes it seem that the world must have a subject as its author.[30] Putting a simple *Why?* to that seeming necessity renounces faith in grammar, the faith of our nannies who first taught us how to view the world. But if the inference to a subject as author of the world reflects a childish faith, Nietzsche is about to show how responsible method dictates a mature inference about the world drawn on the basis of what is given as real. But first — another little poke to the ribs.

Section 35   Our nannies. Nietzsche can't let this opportunity pass without taking a poke at one of his own nannies: he had gratefully dedicated the earlier version of this book, *Human, All Too Human,* to Voltaire, rushing it into print by May 30, 1878, in order to honor the one hundredth anniversary of Voltaire's death. Voltaire is an Enlightenment nanny now replaced by the mature and cynical Abbé Galiani as the one to listen to on the greatest themes (26), the true and the good, though Galiani too must be replaced by someone beyond mere cynicism. "O Voltaire! O humanity! O nonsense! There's something about the 'truth,' and the *search* for truth; and when a human being goes

---

29. The concreteness of Nietzsche's German inevitably becomes abstract in English: *die Welt, die uns etwas angeht* is a world that impinges on us, goes against us, a world with which we have to do. See also 226. Nietzsche had already used the phrase in a very similar setting at GS 301 when discussing the philosophers as "the contemplatives": it dawns on them that "we alone have created the world *of any concern to man!*" GS 301 expands and helps explain the mythic expression of the same thought in *GS* 300, in which Nietzsche used the myth of Prometheus to depict the philosopher's task of interpretation. It is Prometheus himself who is depicted as taking the step suggested in *BGE* 34: Prometheus first had "to *fancy* that he had *stolen* the light and then pay for that — before he finally discovered that he had created the light *by coveting the light* and that not only man but also God was the work of his own hands and had been mere clay in his hands." See the illuminating reading of *GS* 300–01 by Picht, *Nietzsche* 222–44.

30. See the expansion of this thought in *GM* 1.13.

about it too humanly — 'il ne cherche le vrai que pour faire le bien'[31] — I bet he finds nothing!" The search for the true, the chief theme of the book as indicated by the opening of the preface and the openings of chapters 1 and 2, must sever its ties with Platonism's faith in the harmony of the true and the good, even with the remnant of that faith held by Enlightenment nannies. The little section 35 looks back to the previous section, confirming that it deals with the central philosophical issue of our time, the possibility of a true understanding of the world, and it suggests that this possibility has been thwarted by a prior understanding of the good. This little section also looks forward to the next sections, in which the search for the true is guided solely by a desire for the true and is conducted by a free, very free mind that is not merely moral or in the service of the good. Section 36 fulfills the implicit promise of the central section to show what inferences about the true can be drawn by the most suspicious mind reading the *Schein* of inner and outer worlds. Like the central section, it generates a very brief section attached to it by a dash and internal logic. Section 37 gives voice to an outcry on behalf of the good: enlightened free minds still controlled by the old good register shock at what they have been forced to hear about the true. But to the sons of Voltaire who think they hear something even worse than the Abbé Galiani in the new teaching, Nietzsche offers an edifying suggestion: untethered search for the true opens one's eyes to a new good.

The problem of the true and the good at the center of the new philosophy demonstrates that the issues of Platonism do not die with Platonism. The *advocatus dei* who opposes Platonism opposes the Enlightenment knowing that Plato kept a copy of Aristophanes under his pillow. The central sections point presto to a kinship between agonistic philosophers who mix gravity with levity, philosophers capable of writing both comedy and tragedy. Plato suggests, in the dialogue that was Nietzsche's early favorite, that this is what Socrates told Aristophanes while Aristodemus was dozing, an inattention that cost us an argument we could scarcely have understood anyway, being from a height of the soul where not even tragedy has a tragic effect.

The Mind and Heart of Nietzschean Philosophy
SECTIONS 36–38

As Leo Strauss noted, the pair of sections 34 and 35 are related in form to the pair 36 and 37, the second section of each pair being a reaction to the

31. He seeks the true only to do the good.

first, a "lighthearted" response arising out of a "grave" reflection.[32] Relatedness in form signals relatedness in content. The first pair identified commitment to the good as the inhibiting problem in the search for the true, an inhibition that kept the thinker from the uncivil suspicion required to investigate consciousness. The second pair overcomes that problem by a process of reasoning about the inner world of consciousness that is uninhibited by any prejudice about the good (36); the reaction to that ruthless reasoning shows how the new true is bound to be condemned in the most extreme fashion by the old good.

The four sections treat the themes that lie at the center of Nietzsche's thought, the basic matters of Nietzschean philosophy and Nietzschean religion: can the world be "known"? and can it be lived with as "known"? Philosophy and religion are inseparable from one another; moreover, the presentation of the new philosophy and religion is inseparable from where we stand today. This book, focused on "what is nearest, the age, the around us" (*EH* Books *BGE*), presents these matters of the true and the good in constant awareness of how they will be heard by the free minds to whom they are addressed. And it treats them with amazing brevity, as the experiences of a singularity who thinks as the Ganges flows but whose treatment invites testing and experiment by those bound to treat them slowly and steadily or quickly and jerkily.

Section 36 Here, finally, Nietzsche presents his reasoning on behalf of will to power as the fundamental phenomenon. The need for such reasoning was made acute by the series of claims made in chapter 1 that the subject matters of philosophy, biology, physics, and psychology reach their primordial ground in will to power. Chapter 2 has prepared for this reasoning by setting out the exceptional character of the philosopher and the particular problem faced by philosophy of understanding the true independent of prejudicing notions of the good.

This section repeats in the manner befitting a "No-saying book" the presentation of the reasoning on behalf of will to power first set out in *Zarathustra* (*Z* 2 "On Self-Overcoming"). For after the discovery of will to power in the solitude of the songs of part 2, after seeing that life could be fathomed despite the skepticism of the philosophers that called life unfathomable, Zarathustra called the philosophers together — "you who are wisest" — and invited them to reason with him on the new fundamental hypothesis. The reasoning in *Zarathustra* is similar to that of section 36, but the conclusion is drawn by Life herself — she presents the ultimate truth about herself as the secret she will-

---

32. *Studies in Platonic Political Philosophy* 176–78.

ingly betrayed to the one who crept into her fortress. But if the reasoning of section 36 on behalf of Nietzsche's fundamental insight into will to power can be usefully supplemented by looking back to *Zarathustra,* Nietzsche himself was expecting that his readers should also be prepared to look forward as well: in the months during which he was composing these sections of *Beyond Good and Evil,* Nietzsche was preparing *The Will to Power: An Experiment in a Transvaluation of All Values* as his chief work, and the notes projecting the structure of that book uniformly make will to power its constant, basic theme. *Beyond Good and Evil* is a close look at the things around us, and it belongs to the character of such a book that it look only very economically at the things not evidently around us, the fundamental matter treated in fable in *Zarathustra* and more soberly and extensively in *The Will to Power.*

Section 36 is structured as an experiment, and it sets out both the conditions of the experiment and the constraints on the experimenter. The experimenter freely adopts an unfreedom, submitting himself to "the conscience of *method*" and allowing that conscience to dictate his procedure. The entranceway to the extramoral period of human history is guarded by "a moral of method" that cannot be shirked; the maturing mind is a mind "grown hard in the discipline of science" (230).

The experiment itself takes place within the predicament of philosophy set forth in section 34: it grants that the world of any concern to us is a fiction but refuses to surrender to the total skepticism about the world that would follow from total skepticism about our faculties. Extending suspicion to consciousness itself, the suspicious mind nevertheless employs its faculties to arrive at a probable conclusion about the ultimate character of the world. "Granted that nothing else is 'given' as real except our world of desires and passions," the experimenter wants to determine whether the reality of the nongiven, of what can never be given, can nevertheless be inferred. The eventual conclusion is implied in the first sentence: is it permitted to conclude that the nongiven, the world apart from our desires and passions, "the so-called mechanistic (or 'materialistic') world," is like in kind (*Seines-Gleichen*) to our desires and passions? Given the restricted field of what we can know, is it enough?

A twofold question thus structures section 36: Is the experiment permitted? Can the experiment succeed? Nietzsche's answer will be given serially as a twofold yes, but only after a clarification that separates Nietzsche's view from those of Berkeley and Schopenhauer. Nietzsche does not presume some reality lying behind or under appearance or representation, different from it but ascertainable in its difference through the clue of appearance. Nietzsche states clearly what he does presume: the nongiven reality of the world would have the same "reality-rank" as what *is* given, our affects themselves. But, while

having the same reality-rank, it "has a more primitive form," being less orga-
nized, less articulated: what "branches itself off and organizes itself" into the
articulations of the organic given in us "still lies enclosed in a powerful unity"
in what has not so articulated itself. On this view, nature is of one kind, one
reality-rank, but is a hierarchy of self-organization or self-organized complexity. The organic is a more complex organization of the nonorganic, being
different only in degree of complexity.

Having set aside the "real" worlds of Berkeley and Schopenhauer with the
outline of his own view, Nietzsche can begin to answer his twofold question. Is
the experiment permitted? The experiment is *commanded*. Conscience of
method commands that the experiment with a single kind of causality be
pushed to the extreme limit before assuming several kinds of causality; if the
experiment is successful it will never be necessary to assume several kinds.
Clearly, the belief that everything has a cause is not in question; Nietzsche
stands within the fundamental principle stated by Greek science and basic
to rational procedure as such: out of nothing nothing comes, into nothing
nothing falls. The experiment begins where it must begin, with the kind of
cause we can be acquainted with, will-cause; to experiment with some other
kind of cause would be to begin by assuming several kinds of causality. Ultimately, Nietzsche says, the question is whether we acknowledge the will
"wirklich als wirkend" (really as realizing or effecting). Nietzsche does not
repeat what he has already shown: the sophisticated anatomy of willing that
was his display piece in the first chapter (18–21); "belief in the causality of the
will" is not an idle supposition but presupposes understanding will in all the
complexity already laid out by Nietzsche. Given our experience of ourselves as
willing—given Nietzsche's earlier analysis of willing—"we *must* make the
experiment of positing will-causality hypothetically as the single one." Singleness in the cause implies singleness in the effect: every effect too will necessarily
be a will-effect.

Having answered his first question, Nietzsche turns to the second, Can the
experiment succeed? Success for the purposes of this section, this book, remains undemonstrated: "Granted finally, that there was success in explaining
our entire drive-life as the ordering and articulation of one fundamental form
of will—namely, of the will to power as is *my* principle—" Granting this,
granting what Nietzsche is preparing to show about our entire drive-life in *The
Will to Power*, the whole apparatus for a successful conclusion is in view,
though everything hypothetically granted will have to be kept under "the
police supervision of mistrust" (GS 344). Self-knowledge of the kind specified
would be enough to gain "the right" to a comprehensive conclusion about the
unknowable world. "One would have gained the right to define *all* effective

force univocally as: *will to power.*" This conclusion to the experiment is clarified by the single sentence Nietzsche appends to it: "The world seen from within, the world defined and described according to its 'intelligible character' — it would be precisely 'will to power' and nothing besides. — " The world can never be seen from within. There is no such thing as knowledge of the "intelligible character" of the world. Nevertheless, what we can, in a sense, know from within, our desires and passions, what is intelligible in the processes most accessible to us, permits us in good scientific conscience to draw a hypothetical conclusion about the world as a whole. We can posit an intelligible character to the whole as continuous in kind with that particle of the whole especially accessible to us. The world can be said to have the "necessary" and "calculable" course (22) required by any rational account of it, any physics of its *physis.* Positing this intelligible character to the world provides the only possible foundation for the sciences; naming it will to power names its fundamental quality of expansive force, which articulates itself into all phenomena.

This passage and others like it make it clear that Nietzsche's view takes its place in the family of cosmological and biological reductionisms common to ancient and modern naturalism while respecting the strictures of an inescapable epistemological skepticism. We cannot know the world directly — but we can make probable inferences about it that are consistent with the procedures of our most sophisticated science and that lend that science the powerful reinforcement of a comprehensive perspective and an ultimate explanatory principle. Nietzsche's view, expressed here in great conciseness, shows how philosophy can contribute to the gains of modern science by providing a unifying perspective; it shows that philosophy has a warrant to assume leadership of the sciences, not by teaching physics and biology what to do with their subject matters, but by uniting those subject matters in the comprehensive unity of the fundamental fact.

Section 37 Nietzsche's reasoning has arrived at its highest point and the audience of free minds hears it as it should be heard: as folly or, worse, as crime. But Nietzsche rebuts the criminal charge, suggesting a different way to hear his conclusion. The little dialogue that constitutes section 37 is surely one of the finest moments of *Beyond Good and Evil,* a pivotal moment in which the primordially true is condemned by the old good, which is in turn countered by the suggestion of a new good. Extreme gravity yields to gracious levity on the oldest of charges raised against the philosophers. It is a moment worthy of a thinker who honors Plato for having Aristophanes under his pillow.

The first voice is that of Nietzsche's friends, free minds to whom his reasoning was addressed. But what they say betrays an unfreedom of mind, bondage to the prejudices of our philosophers, the faith of our nannies. At the end of the moral period, the old morality still reigns over the free-minded. They are appalled at Nietzsche's conclusion, but as offspring of the Enlightenment they have no language of their own to express the degree of their horror, so they revert to a language they no longer believe in, the unenlightened language well outfitted with extremes. "What! Doesn't that mean, to speak in the common language, 'God is refuted, but the Devil is not?'" *God*—the free minds revert to the old word for everything high, refined, sacred, good; every solace, everything sweet and beautiful. *Devil*—the free minds revert to the old word for everything base, coarse, profane, evil; every terror, everything bitter and ugly. Haven't you committed the highest crime, making everything sacred demonic, everything demonic sacred?

In response, Nietzsche speaks as a theologian; he does not repudiate their shift from the reasoned to the religious, only their prejudices within the religious: "On the contrary! On the contrary, my friends!" This laconic reversal forces his friends, his natural allies, to think through the core implications of his conclusion on their own, as if the only way to make his own their own was to codiscover it. To think the contrary of what they have stated is a promising beginning, for the exact contrary is that the Devil is refuted but God is not. Pondering the exact contrary will give enlightened, free-minded atheists the savory pleasure of entertaining the ultimate blasphemy to our tradition of divinity. The will to power teaching, a complete immanentism, refutes a transcendent, immutable God, but is that God God? On the contrary, that God must be seen as the Devil, an all-powerful tyrant who put the earth under a curse and assigned it to the Prince of Darkness. The will to power teaching does not refute what the old divinity called the Devil's: the world, the worldly, the love of the world with its incessant change and inexorable mortality, but is that Devil the Devil? On the contrary, what was once seen as the Devil's is vindicated as divine. This crime against our divinity goes far beyond the merely historical judgment that God is dead; it speaks the ultimate ill of the dead so it can't be tastefully spoken though it can be usefully implied. The crime against our divinity reverses the earlier crime against our world.

Nietzsche adds one more helpful correction to this dialogue with his friends on divinity. It begins "Und, zum Teufel auch," which may be translated literally, "And, as to the Devil"; but *zum Teufel* in colloquial German rings of "Go to Hell!" or "goddamn it!": "And, as to the Devil, goddamn it, who compels *you* to speak in the common language?" Who but that old Devil himself, dead but not gone, lingering on for centuries as a shadow on our cave wall as the only language of divinity possible for reduced moderns, free minds liberated into poverty regarding the sacred by the welcome death of the tyrannical God of our Platonic tradition.

In the move from section 36 to section 37, ontology turns to theology and not accidentally: the account of all beings carries implications for the highest beings. This is the first intimation that the chapters on philosophy must be followed by a chapter on religion, the first intimation that the Enlightenment denunciation of religion, a vehement reaction against *our* religion, is not a reasonable response to religion as such. The intimation comes at the fitting moment, in a little dialogue among friends just after Nietzsche has spelled out the reasoning on behalf of the will to power teaching. The dialogue intimates a key facet of Nietzsche's thought: the mind's teaching on the totality of things reasonably generates a response of the heart, a religious response. The initial response to the new account of all beings may well be fear and hate of what seems to refute everything humanity most deeply desires, but that response is itself a relic of the old religion. The dialogue suggests the contrary; gratitude and love may become the genuine human responses to the way the world is. The new philosophy, this dialogue suggests, generates a new religion. That religion differs radically from any Platonism for the people, including the democratic Enlightenment that has captured free minds. It will be a religion aware of its historic place beyond the moral period of humanity with its moral gods and immoral devils; it will be a more mature religion subtly tied to a mature philosophy with a longer view backward and a deeper view inward. It will be a vindication of the gods by a philosophical *advocatus dei* who cannot avoid seeming an *advocatus diaboli*. The chapters on philosophy must therefore be followed by the chapter on religion for the two themes are connected by the deepest logic of mind and heart.

Section 38   The little aphorism that is section 38 is the fitting finale to the series of sections on the comprehensive problem of interpretation. In its laconic complexity, its main point obscured by the force of the example with which it opens, it informs the enlightened free minds of something else they will have to endure in addition to the new interpretation of nature: a new interpretation of history. Nietzsche's revaluation of being and time requires free minds to abandon both their skepticism and their belief in progress.

The theme of this section is not the interpretation of the French Revolution by noble Europeans from all over Europe,[33] for that act of misinterpretation is only the most recent and prominent fragment of a more general misinterpretation that "could" happen: a noble posterity could interpret "the whole of the past" in perhaps the only way that would make the sight of it bearable, thus causing "*the text* [the whole of the past] *to disappear under the interpreta-*

---

33. For how the French Revolution is to be interpreted correctly, see 46 end, and 195.

tion." What could happen happened: "We ourselves were — this noble posterity." We ourselves held the Enlightenment view that history is progress, the view that made the whole labor and suffering of past generations bearable or meaningful because future generations would inhabit a new world created by their labor and suffering. But the Enlightenment's noble misunderstanding of the whole past carried its refutation secreted away within it, for "right now, insofar as we grasp" that *we* are the posterity for the sake of which the whole of the past allegedly labored and suffered, right now, "it's all over" with that view. The democratic Enlightenment relaxed the proper tension of modern times with its complacent view that the whole of the human past can be interpreted as progress toward itself, the end of history. In the brightest brightness of modern times that comforting view must be laid aside: the very posterity on whom nobility was conferred by the forefathers proves noble enough to disown that view; honesty will not permit us to suppose that we are the meaning of history. At the end of history — right now — it's all over with the view that it's all over with us. But the tension restored by the destruction of that comforting view promises a great gain: the text of the past may yet reappear from under the misinterpretation that caused its disappearance. Therefore, in addition to a chapter on religion, this chapter on philosophy will have to be followed by chapters on history, beginning with the natural history of morality.

If Nietzsche stands to the democratic Enlightenment as Pascal stood to Jesuitism, then Nietzsche's *Provincial Letters* reach their apex here: what looked like the great gains of philosophical skepticism in the midst of progressive civilization in fact masked a refusal to face the cruelty of nature and the meaninglessness of history. The Enlightenment was only another Platonism for the people, a dull, blunt one suited for the overthrow of refinement and difference. But if the cruel truth about nature cannot be masked by skepticism, and if the whole of the past cannot be made endurable by misunderstanding it as progress, how can nature and time be endured at all? Modern free minds — Voltaire's children — will have to endure a new teaching on nature and a new teaching on time.

The Free-Minded Philosopher
SECTIONS 39–41

Having touched the deepest truths of nature and history, Nietzsche turns to an essential corollary, how to speak about them.

Section 39   Nietzsche's audience of free minds does not need to be told that "happiness and virtue are no arguments" for they have already abandoned the comforts of "the lovely 'idealists' " in favor of their own relatively comfortless views. But they may need to be told that "making-unhappy and making-evil are, just as little, counterarguments." Nietzsche thus returns to the issue about truth that he had insisted upon since *On the Use and Disadvantages of History for Life*: truth may be deadly; "something may well be true even though it is, at the same time and to the highest degree, harmful and dangerous" — like the truths stated in the previous sections. Truth's character may be such that "the strength of a mind could be measured according to how much of the 'truth' it could just barely stand, more clearly, to what degree it *necessarily* diluted, disguised, sweetened, dulled, falsified it." These claims are stated conditionally, but Nietzsche avows that "no doubt underlies" the fact that for "the discovery of certain *parts* of the truth, the evil and unhappy are more favored." And he adds: "not to speak of the evil who are happy, a species kept under silence by the moralists." Nietzsche speaks of the evil who are happy but almost silently; he speaks of "the strong independent mind and philosopher," while painting "the portrait of the free-minded philosopher." To speak this way means "assuming what comes first anyway, that one does *not* narrow down the concept 'philosopher' to the philosopher who writes books" — which would allow us to include among the free-minded philosophers the most prominent philosopher who did not write books, Socrates; or to the philosopher "who even brings forth *his* philosophy in books" — which would allow us to include the most prominent philosopher who did not bring forth his own philosophy in books but always had others speak, Plato.

Are Socrates and Plato to be counted among the evil and happy free-minded philosophers? Nietzsche's little game fakes complicity with the moralists' conspiracy of silence while helping to break it. What is barely spoken is that the unnamed philosophical moralists, Socrates and Plato, themselves happy and evil, maintained a conspiracy of silence: as moralists they wanted it believed that only the good can be happy; as philosophers they knew that the highest happiness looks evil to the moral. Nietzsche breaks the conspiracy of silence conspiratorially, not quite uttering the truth about genuine philosophers but allowing the evil pleasure of unriddling it to make the reader happy. The next section, on the philosopher's masks, is well introduced by the decipherable riddles of this one.[34]

34. Nietzsche speaks more directly about philosophy and evil when it serves his purpose: "*The evil principle* — Plato gave a resplendent description of how the philosophical thinker must within every existing society count as the paragon of all wickedness, for as

Section 40   Section 40 seems to me to be a lesson in esotericism that every serious reader of Nietzsche, friend and enemy alike, will want to contemplate. It claims that the best things are the most reluctant to display themselves, that shyness and rectitude and pride actively conspire to keep them hidden by flaunting their opposites: they know how to look shameless, so sensitive are they to the shame of self-display. The most telling cleft in Nietzsche's readership may open right here: who is willing to believe what Nietzsche implies about himself here? For what he implies is that there is no way to say what he is: what he is will not permit it because what he is is a goodness so intense that it cannot bear to give witness to itself.

The core claim is put didactically: "It's not the worst things about which one feels the worst shame: there's not just craftiness behind a mask, — there's so much goodness in cunning." Good's cunning is illustrated in the immediately preceding sentences: "There are processes[35] of so delicate a kind that one does well to submerge them under a crassness and make them unidentifiable; there are acts of love and of an extravagant magnanimity after which nothing is more advisable than to take a stick and thrash the eyewitness: that would cloud his memory." Such delicacy extends even to the ultimate witness: "Some understand how to cloud and mishandle their own memory in order to take their revenge on at least this single accessory [to their act]: the sense of shame is so inventive."

Are there any examples of this? "I could think that a human being who had to hide something precious and easily harmed could roll through life rough and round like an old green, heavily banded wine barrel: the fineness of shame would want it so." Who can this rough and round wine barrel be in a section on masking and acting and sheltering the precious? Who but Aristophanes, rollicking offspring of Dionysos, the god who was himself willing to appear a mere drunk? Aristophanic concealment of the most precious "needs speech for silence." It conceals from the nearest and most trusted not only his mortal danger — it does friends the justice of not harming them with what endangered even him; it conceals as well his "recaptured mortal safety" — it conceals its supreme success, that out of mortal danger it won mortal safety; it has not been torn asunder by the Minotaur of conscience, and graciously withholds that there was a Minotaur at all.

---

the critic of all custom he is the opposite of the moral man, and if he does not succeed in becoming the law-giver of new customs, he remains in the memory of human beings as 'the evil principle' " (*D* 496) — and if he succeeds there is no such memory.

35. *Vorgänge* — literally, foregoings, preceedings, things that go before.

But suppose the Aristophanic concealer did *not* want "a mask of himself to wander around in his stead in the hearts and minds of his friends." What is easier to suppose than a desire on the part of the high to be seen for what it is in all its beauty and grace? But even if he did not want a mask, a mask would grow there anyway, a mask not of his own making. Rather a self-made mask that some readers—some Plato, say—could see for a mask and learn to treasure the masked for who he is while keeping him masked, keeping him under his pillow while learning to mask himself. But in the end, the masked does not rue the fact that a mask grows even if he did not want it to: "It is good that it be so." He does not rue what belongs to the character of things. The last sentence therefore reports a fact and not a lament: "Around every deep mind a mask is continuously growing thanks to the false, namely, *shallow* interpretation of every word, every step, every sign of life he gives. — " If every sign of the deep is bound to be shallowed, Nietzsche is trapped—trapped as Aristophanes was trapped, not utterly trapped.

Section 41   Nietzsche assigns the tests one must assign oneself to determine if one is fit for independence and command, and in their ascending difficulty up to "the most dangerous game" they record the tests Nietzsche himself faced. His own record of breaking free from mere loyalty includes shorthand references to not sticking fast to his hopes for Wagner, for modern Germany, for the superior human beings as a whole (this third test being the final test of Zarathustra's independence), for a particular science like the science of philology. The two final tests seem most illuminating for the author of *Beyond Good and Evil*, for they are reciprocal in implicitly claiming that he stuck fast neither to his own breaking away nor to the virtue of generosity: he is neither wholly for himself nor wholly for others. In overcoming the "danger of the flier" Nietzsche again claims to be the bird-spirit that flew to the highest heights but refused to remain there (Z 3 "The Seven Seals," 6,7). But even if he is that returned bird, he has not stuck fast to his own virtue, "the danger of dangers" for a high kind of rich soul, the danger of squandering himself in "hospitality" by welcoming others to his solitary abode. He has not pushed the virtue of liberality to a vice; giving liberally, he conserves himself or preserves what is most his own; he does not indulge in excessive philanthropy but knows how to be for himself (33). The last three sections of "The Free Mind" report on the "philosophers of the future," but the report conforms to the necessities of self-preservation, for Nietzsche deleted the claim made in a draft of section 42: "Insofar as I know them, insofar as I know myself, for I belong to these coming ones."[36]

36. *KSA* 14, *Kommentar* p. 353.

The Versucher — *The Philosophers of the Future*
SECTIONS 42–44

Section 42   In section 42, Nietzsche "baptizes" the new genus of philosophers he is helping bring to birth. The new genus is unlike the genus brought to birth by Plato, for it looks primarily to a future beyond the moral period, not primarily to the preservation of a past morality through pious fraud. Nietzsche withholds the name of the new philosophers till near the end of this short section, emphasizing the riddling quality of a name that is "not undangerous": *Versucher*. The name is rich in implications for there are four senses in which Versucher can be understood.[37] Perhaps the first and always dominant sense must be "experimenters." The new philosophers are inclined to say to every experiment of intellect and spirit, "Let's try it!" (*GS* 51), a spirit of adventure that contrasts with what Plato advised the philosopher to say about innovation: "Let's not."[38]

Perhaps the second sense of Versucher should be as dominant as the first: the new philosophers are "tempters." God's advocate seems to confirm the worry expressed even by his friends that his teaching refutes God but not the devil, for *the* tempter is the Devil himself, the Tempter who dared tempt Jesus (Mt 4:3). God's advocate lets loose upon the world a whole band of devils and says so at their baptismal by outfitting them with a name that flaunts their dangerousness, a name that is itself a temptation (*Versuchung*).

By baptizing them Versucher, Nietzsche also names the philosophers of the future for the failures they will inevitably occasion, for they are "attempters." An attempt may be as likely to fail as to succeed; the work of the new philosophers would not be a Versuch if it were not an experiment risking failure. They risk themselves, "but what do I matter?" (*D* 547). More ominously, they risk others or society as a whole whose necessary simplifications and falsifications have so far followed a morality of good and evil; the "experiment with the truth" that the philosophers of the future run attempts something untried: simplifications and falsifications that accord with the truth or the spirit of the truth.

Finally, even though Nietzsche presents the name as a novelty, *Versucher* has a pedigree he must have enjoyed as an admirer of Montaigne and Emerson: as Georg Picht notes, "The German translation of 'essay' is *Versuch*."[39] The new

---

37. Picht makes *Versucher* one of the key terms of his pathfinding interpretation of Nietzsche. The first part of his study is entitled "The Philosopher as *Versucher* — The Concept of Experimental Philosophy — ." Picht, *Nietzsche* xxi-xxii, 31–131.

38. *Republic* 4.424b.

39. *Nietzsche* 56.

philosophers are essayists or essayers whose natural mode of expression is the essay or aphorism, the mode mastered not only by Montaigne but by his great essayist followers, Bacon and Descartes, and by Emerson, whose essays Nietzsche studied in the German version entitled *Versuche* and which trace their experimental method to Montaigne.[40]

Section 43   "Are they new friends of the 'truth,' these coming philosophers?" How one stands to the truth is the fundamental issue of the book, governing its openings (preface and section 1) and its closing (296). It is the constant issue of chapter 2, which opened with the simplifications and falsifications within which humans live, presented an argument for the fundamental truth, and reflects everywhere on truth seeking and truth telling. The new genus of philosophers does not differ from the old in being lovers of truth; they differ on how they view their beloved. Dogmatists want their truths to be as common as possible; the pride and taste of the philosophers of the future want truth shared only by those who have won the right to it. "My judgment is *my* judgment: not so easily does anyone else have a right to it." This is not a radical relativism with respect to truth itself but with respect to truth seekers and the perspectives of which they are capable, perspectives of high and low where the right to the high must be won. For "it must stand as it now stands and always stood: . . . everything rare for the rare." Truth is less relative than it is rare, rarely attained and sharable only in attainment.

Section 44   The last and longest section of "The Free Mind," section 44 ends the two parts on philosophy by marking off the new genus of philosophers, the philosophers of the future, from what now count as future-directed thinkers, the utopians of the modern revolution. But the section begins by noting that the philosophers of the future are something more than free minds, "higher, greater, and fundamentally other." Because that difference "does not want to be misunderstood and misidentified," identifying it will form the chief theme running through the whole of the rest of the book. The stance of the philosophers of the future toward religion will shock the antireligious ire of Enlightenment free minds, but the importance of that stance singles it out for close connection to philosophy itself (chapter 3). After an interlude of "Epigrams and Interludes," the new genus of philosophers will be identified with respect to where they stand in "The Natural History of Morality"; how they differ from "We Scholars" while arising within the discipline of science and

40. Through Montaigne the term can be applied even to Plato, a "dogmatist" whom Montaigne holds to be a Pyrrhonist "in affirmative form" whose great innovations experimented with philosophical rule through religion; see *Essays* 375–80.

scholarship; how their virtue differs from "Our Virtues" but augments and grounds it; how differently they view the history of European civilization and hence the total history of "Peoples and Fatherlands"; and how consideration of the old question "What Is Noble?" redefines nobility by pointing to them.

But for now, at the end of the chapter on the free mind, Nietzsche has a special obligation to the philosophers of the future. Of course they will be "free, *very* free minds," the little formula Nietzsche repeats from the end of the preface, but Nietzsche has a duty to distinguish them sharply from those who already use *free mind* to designate themselves. To make "the concept 'free mind' " transparent again requires showing that modern free minds are enslaved to the ideals of the democratic Enlightenment.[41] With respect to the eventual appearing of the philosophers of the future, modern free minds are "really and truly closed windows and bolted doors" because they are "*levelers*" rather than advocates of an order of rank; because they locate "the cause of just about *all* human misery and failure" in the structures of the old society, in alterable human convention, rather than in human nature itself; and because "suffering is taken by them as something one must *abolish*," rather than as a necessary condition of human enhancement. Modern free minds are believers in "the green pasture happiness of the herd" without a shepherd, the "autonomous herd" whose hegemony Nietzsche will eventually portray as the alternative to the rule of the philosophers of the future.

Nietzsche belongs among the *Umgekehrten*, those turned in the other direction, the opposites. As an advocate of suffering, of "life, suffering, and the circle" (Z 3 "The Convalescent"), what does *he* think of the human future? Nietzsche speaks directly of what he thinks in a series of statements that make apparent the need for indirection. He thinks that "the plant 'human being' has grown most strongly into the height till now," not under conditions of green pasture happiness but under the "opposite conditions every time." A botanist of humanity, he thinks humanity reaches its peaks only under conditions of need and distress in which "the dangerousness of its situation has grown into something enormous." This must be the ultimate reason for Nietzsche's willingness to risk the great experiment with the truth: in the

---

41. Just how little *free mind* in Nietzsche's sense means what is ordinarily suggested by the English phrase *free spirit* is indicated by his account of the medieval Islamic order of Assassins, "that order of free minds par excellence whose lowest degree lived in an obedience the like of which no order of monks has attained" and whose "uppermost degrees" had "as their *secretum:* 'nothing is true, everything is permitted' " (*GM* 3.24).

midst of an experiment with the false that has captured every vision of the future, an experiment with the truth must be run to win the future for the sake of human enhancement and the very experiment creates the required conditions of duress.

The history of our species shows that enormous danger has enhanced two aspects of humanity: mind and will. Mind, humanity's "strength of invention and strength of alteration," developed under prolonged pressure and compulsion into something "refined and daring." Will intensified itself under such conditions from "life-will" into "power-will." The latter term emends the term used in this sentence in the drafts: *will to power;* "life-will" is itself already a will to power.[42] Will to power as human life-will expands beyond mere survival in ages of greatest danger and ascends to human power-will.

Nietzsche further thinks that "hardness, violence, slavery, danger in the alley and in the heart, hiddenness, stoicism, the art of the tempter, and devilry of every kind, that everything fearsome, tyrannical, predatorlike and snakelike in human beings serve as much for the enhancement of the species 'human being' as its opposite does." And he adds, "We don't even say enough when we say that much." Like the end of chapter 1, the end of chapter 2 states that the unsettling things it says stop short of unsettling things it might have said, promising again that the voyage ahead into what the mind dictates will be costly to the heart. The chapter that began by acknowledging the necessity of the simplifications and falsifications within which human beings live ends by declaring truths that modern human beings regard as demonic. "Is it any wonder that we free minds are not exactly the most communicative minds? That we do not want to betray in every respect *from what* a mind can make itself free and *to what* it will then perhaps be driven?" But Nietzsche has already betrayed a lot simply by using the "dangerous formula 'beyond good and evil' " as his title.[43] Why do that if he's cautious about what he communicates? Presumably because it's imperative to protect the free, *very* free mind from being misidentified with its opposite, which calls itself the *free mind* in all the languages of Europe.

To call attention to a voluntary limit is to provoke its trespass, and Nietzsche ends chapter 2 as he ended chapter 1, with a temptation, an invitation to adventure, a full-page marvel of a sentence that must be counted among the

---

42. See *KSA* 11.37 [8]; 34 [176] is a particularly interesting forerunner of section 44 because it moves directly from some of the thoughts of 44 to formulations of the "philosophy of Dionysos" later used in section 295.

43. See *GM* 1.7 on the "dangerous title" as a "dangerous slogan."

most beautiful in the book and that is addressed at its end to "you who are coming up," the philosophers of the future whom the tempter aims to engender. "It is certainly not an overstatement to say that no one has ever spoken so greatly and so nobly of what a philosopher is as Nietzsche,"[44] and in this sentence Nietzsche describes his experience as a free-minded philosopher who is also something more, the something more that the rest of the book will intimate.

44. Strauss, *The Rebirth of Classical Political Rationalism* 40.

3

Das Religiöse Wesen

Why does a chapter on religion follow the two chapters on philosophy? The chapters on philosophy indicate why: every successful philosophy acknowledges the simplification and falsification within which humanity lives, and it accommodates itself to that fact, as Platonism so successfully did. To be livable by more than a few rare minds, philosophy must create a world in its own image; "as soon as any philosophy begins to believe in itself . . . it can do no other" (9). Nietzsche's philosophy surely believes in itself, in its successful wooing of truth who is a woman, and in its historic necessity as a public teaching amid the ruins of Platonism. The chapter on religion shows how Nietzschean religion rises naturally out of Nietzschean philosophy and how it possesses a historic as well as a logical rationale.

Chapter 3 has a roughly historical cast. It looks first at the past of our religion, Christianity, setting it off from its Greek and Hebrew predecessors. It centers on the present, the religious crisis of our time in the atheism and nihilism that arise naturally out of the reasonable fight against Christianity. It moves then to the future of religion or the religion of the future and what must be done to establish it. Throughout, the perspective is that of the philosopher, a solitary viewer in the first section, a solitary actor in the last.

The eighteen sections of chapter 3 develop an underlying argument: philosophy must rule religion, reason rule belief. The chapter opens on the inescapable singularity of the philosopher's view of religion and on its chief theme, the conflict between faith and reason (45–46). What is basic to Christianity contrasts radically with what was basic to its now almost inaccessible Greek predecessor, Homeric religion (47–49). Christianity also contrasts radically with its Hebrew predecessor (50–52). At the center of the religious issue today lies the crisis of atheism and nihilism, consequences of modern philosophy's attack on the Christian God and its assassination of the old soul concept (53–54). But out of that pessimism an affirmation arises by an inexorable historical logic; that affirmation permits a glimpse of a new ideal, linked logically to the new teaching on the intelligible character of the world (55–57). If religion is to be brought under the care of philosophy it is necessary to know what religions are good for (58–60). A mission with respect to religion therefore falls to philosophy, a cultural task of the first magnitude that follows from knowing the goal in the postmodern, post-Platonic, postmoral world (61–62).

Perhaps the most alien of all the lessons Nietzsche sets out for post-Christian free minds concerns the power and utility of religion. Whether schooled primarily by the Enlightenment's demonizing of religion as benighted superstition or by Hegel's *Aufhebung* of religion as a museum piece that once aided humanity's ascent to wisdom, modern minds have been freed into irreligion ignorant of religion's power and good. Nietzsche's chapter on religion aims to win over modern minds to a new appreciation of religion.[1] More than that, it aims to prepare them for something far more peculiar, the actual return of Dionysos and Ariadne, Homeric or trans-Homeric divinities who return at the end of Nietzsche's book.

The Philosopher's Understanding of Faith and Reason
SECTIONS 45–46

Section 45   "The love of truth" — the pleasant little joke that ends section 45, the opening section of the chapter on religion, indicates (as do all the other chapter openings so far) that the key issue is the love of truth. When loosed into the field of religion, however, the passion for truth surfaces as something else: "A curiosity of my kind remains after all the most agreeable of all vices." The vice of uncovering truth in religion must therefore learn

---

1. Nietzsche's principle seems to me to be stated exactly by Francis Bacon: "It is true that a little philosophy inclineth man's mind to atheism; but depth in philosophy bringeth men's minds about to religion" (*Essays or Counsels Civil and Moral,* "Of Atheism"). This does not say that the deepest philosophers become religious believers, only that their minds are brought about to religion, turned to the indispensability of religion, as Bacon's was.

religious speech — "Forgive me," it says, correcting its candor and making its vice a virtue, "I wanted to say that the love of truth has its reward in heaven and even on earth." But the chapter on religion will not remain this virtuous; another "I wanted to say" appears at the end of its final section and instead of masking vice, it states Nietzsche's vice even more viciously.

The first section on religion indicates just what the task is and who must perform it. Love of truth applied to the religious *Wesen* studies "the human soul and its limits," the whole range of heights, depths, and distances reached by the human soul "*so far* and its yet unattained possibilities." The focus of philosophy's inquiry into religion is not "the things aloft" and "the things under the earth," what Greek philosophy was accused of investigating in its vice of rational inquiry into the gods and the ultimate fate of the human soul. The meaning of the title of chapter 3, *Das religiöse Wesen,* is thus indicated by the first words of the first section: the religious *essence* is to be sought in the religious *being,* not in its objects of religious longing or religious dread.[2] As Leo Strauss notes, the title of chapter 3 declares Nietzsche's break with Platonism: "The third chapter is entitled 'Das religiöse Wesen'; it is not entitled 'Das Wesen der Religion,' one of the reasons for this being that the essence of religion, that which is common to all religions, is not or should not be of any concern to us."[3]

Nietzsche depicts the soul as a fascinating domain, "the predestined hunting ground for a born psychologist and friend of the 'great hunt.'" It is also immense, "a primeval forest," and its investigator wishes he had a few hundred well-trained hounds to send into the forest to gather his game. "But who would do me this service?" The chapter on religion begins with a warning that the philosopher has to do the essential work himself. The limits of scholarship and science — to be set out in "We Scholars" — preclude it from capturing the ultimate quarry in the field of religion, for in that field the lover of truth must transcend the heights, depths, and distances of the soul achieved in religion so far and view them from above — and such transcendence is extremely rare. The student of religion must understand "what sort of history the problem of *knowledge and conscience* [Wissen und Gewissen] has had till now in the soul of the *homines religiosi.*" This problem shadows the whole chapter as the

2. The third chapter of *Beyond Good and Evil* thus improves on the title of the third chapter of *Human, All Too Human,* "*Das religiöse Leben.*" *Wesen* is a useful term for an anti-Platonic philosopher: its primary meaning, essence or nature, makes it serviceable for Platonism's search for form or essence, but it also means an individual being or creature or person; the very title therefore suggests that the religious essence is to be found in the religious being.

3. *Studies in Platonic Political Philosophy* 176.

relation between reason and faith. Nietzsche's example confirms the rarity of the fit investigator: to succeed, "an individual must perhaps himself be as deep, as wounded, as monstrous as the intellectual conscience of Pascal was." And he would still need to transcend Pascal's experience, viewing it from above, from "that vaulting sky of clear malicious spirituality" into which Zarathustra claimed to fly in one of his most important speeches (*Z* 3 "Before Sunrise"). Pascal is named in both the opening and closing sections of this chapter, and it is Pascal's *sacrifizio dell'intelletto* (229) that serves Nietzsche later as the greatest example of Christian spirituality, its supreme sacrifice of the mind for reasons of the heart. Expressing his love for Pascal, one of his underworld judges (*HH* II *AOM* 408), Nietzsche calls him "the most instructive victim of Christianity" (*EH* Clever 3). If one must transcend the experiences of a Pascal and view it from above, "one has *a lot* to do" in the field of religion for one must do it alone.[4]

The problem of knowledge and conscience, *Wissen* and *Gewissen,* is prominent throughout the chapter and is carried forward into later chapters as part of the task for the new philosopher: he must forge a new conscience on the basis of new knowledge, a *good Gewissen* for *Wissen* and *Wissenschaft.* Hardness of conscience is a Christian attainment not to be abandoned but transformed into post-Christian conscience, intellectual conscience or the vice by which the mind rules the heart.

Section 46   The height and depth achieved in the Christian soul of a Pascal points the solitary investigator back to one of the greatest events in our spiritual history, the Christian capture of classical culture, an event that modern taste has made difficult to recover. Other solitary investigators of the human soul drew conclusions about this event similar to Nietzsche's; Machiavelli, Montaigne, Bacon, Descartes, Hobbes, Spinoza, Rousseau, all held that Christianity's victory over classical culture in the Roman Empire cost European civilization what was best in it. The first half of the chapter on religion attempts to make the real meaning of Christianity's historic victory visible again; only then can the future of religion be considered in the second half.

Pascal is important in part because he signals individually what was characteristic of early Christianity generally: the suicide of reason in the name of faith where reason is still powerful. "Faith" — the emphatic first word of the dense, veering, opening sentence — stands as a virtual title over all the main concepts of section 46. *Faith* and *reason* are the primary terms but prominent as well are *sacrifice, cruelty,* and *suffering,* deeply ambiguous terms that become

4. On Pascal, see also *D* 46, 63–64, 68, 79, 86, 91, 192, 481, 549; *GM* 3.17; *TI* Skirmishes 9.

important items in what Nietzsche himself advocates — but as dictates of reason, not of faith. The warfare of Christian faith against reason within the individual soul occurred on a world historical scale in Christianity's fight against Rome. Rome was Christianity's adversary both intellectually and politically: Rome was "a skeptical and southerly-free-minded world" formed intellectually by the centuries-long fight among the philosophical schools, a fight that granted reason the right to adjudicate; and Rome was an empire that provided a political "education in tolerance" through Roman policy toward alien religions within the empire.

Christian faith demanded sacrifice — it is a rung on "the ladder of religious cruelty" whose history Nietzsche summarizes in a later section (55). Christian faith sacrificed reason, but it also sacrificed other aspects of human achievement made possible by reason and elevated by Greeks and Romans: freedom, pride, and self-confidence of mind. In place of human self-regard, Christian faith demanded enslavement, self-ridicule, self-mutilation. Nietzsche thus maintains the perspective that Herodotus says the Greeks always maintained on their wars with Asia: they were wars between free human beings and slaves. In Rome's war with Christianity, slaves of "the Great King" have become slaves to God prepared to sacrifice all aspects of rational humanity to gain God's favor.[5] Christian victory over Rome is Asia's belated victory over Greece, a victory Nietzsche ascribes in part to Greek betrayal: Plato's public adoption of the perspective of the "deep Orient," the moral view of nature and time.

The cruelty of Christian faith is exercised by "an overripened, multiple, and multiply spoiled conscience." This conscience, inner commandments working on behalf of faith to kill reason, is spoiled or pampered (*verwöhnt*) because it is a conscience without conscience, an unconscionable conscience: Nietzsche said, "Hooray for physics!" because physics or rational inquiry into nature places a conscience over conscience (*GS* 335), replacing a pampered conscience with one "hardened in the discipline of science" (230). Conscience ruled by reason is also cruel, demanding its own sacrifices as Nietzsche emphasizes in his basic lesson on *Geist* (229–30), and when the time comes for Nietzsche to define the transvaluation of values he makes part of its task the steeling of a new conscience (203).

Modern humanity, no longer guided by the taste of classical antiquity, lives

---

5. Montaigne too regarded the Christian God as the ultimate tyrant who turned all his adherents into slaves, and he made that the theme of each of the central essays in the three books of the *Essays*. See *GM* 1.16: " 'Rome against Judea, Judea against Rome': — so far there has been no greater event than *this* battle, *this* formulation of the problem, *this* mortally hostile contradiction."

within an intellectual and spiritual world dictated by Christian taste; it can no longer feel reason's hurt at "the height of absurdity" represented by the core of Christian faith, nor is it able to experience revulsion at "the horrible superlative" that most offended classical taste, "God on the Cross." Nietzsche's sentences build to a phrase he was planning to make prominent as one of his identifying phrases: the victory of Christianity is a "transvaluation of all classical values." The back cover of *Beyond Good and Evil* announced a new book in four parts, *The Will to Power: An Experiment in a Transvaluation of All Values.* That projected book exists only in its first part, *The Antichrist,* but there the themes of this section are greatly expanded, culminating in the victory of Christianity over Rome (A 58–60).[6] Nietzsche's transvaluation occurs within a setting created by Christianity's successful transvaluation of classical values, an "inversion"[7] Nietzsche attempts to invert, restoring classical taste, "noble taste," with its skepticism, free-mindedness, and tolerance, its "roman 'catholicity,'" its "enlightenment," its rational estimation of the relation between reason and faith.

Nietzsche's contrast between Christian faith and Roman "noble and light tolerance" employs categories elaborated in greater detail elsewhere, such as slave and master moralities (260 and *GM,* First Treatise) and the passion of revenge (Z 2 "On the Tarantulas," "On Redemption"). The conflict between slave and master became spiritual, Nietzsche claims, and focused on how to deal with human suffering, the whole theater of human woe on which the philosopher comes to have an unpitying view (30).[8] The master outraged the slave by his indifference to faith and his freedom from faith based on a schooled indifference to suffering. "'Enlightenment' outrages" and moves the outraged to take revenge. Nietzsche employs the categories of immaturity (31) to explain the outrage: youthful vehemence, a taste for the unconditioned, love and hate without nuance. Christian faith was a revolt against "the greatest gain of life," the maturity of nuanced civility that had learned a noble

6. Nietzsche there emphasized that Rome successfully carried forward for centuries the science of the Greeks; it is the Christian transvaluation of the Greek enlightenment that especially draws Nietzsche's blame: "The whole labor of the ancient world *in vain:* I have no word to express my feelings about something so tremendous" (A 59).

7. *Umkehren;* Nietzsche uses this term later to say that "the Jews brought about the miraculous feat of an *Umkehrung* of values" (195).

8. "Christianity, which springs from a Jewish root and is understandable only as growth on this soil, represents the *countermovement* to every morality of breeding, of race, of privilege" (*TI* Improvers 4). Nietzsche is there speaking of the law of Mani, which he had just studied and which "completes his ideas on religion in the most remarkable way" (letter to Köselitz, 31 May 1888).

stance toward human suffering. The attitude toward suffering is the hinge that distinguishes classical taste from Christian taste: to Christian taste, classical taste seemed "to *deny* suffering," to act as if it were not necessary for God on the Cross to redeem it. This Roman/Christian warfare over the meaning of human suffering is a great episode in a wider conflict that carries into the present. The modern conscience, heir to Christian conscience, is also a pampered conscience, trained to view the meaning of history as humanity's abolition of suffering. Nietzsche's moral teaching rises against the modern conscience and its effort to abolish suffering; it necessarily advocates suffering as the indispensable precondition of human achievement. The defense of such a seemingly indefensible view requires the recovery of a past still broader than the conflict between Rome and Judea, the recovery of the whole natural history of morality, a recovery that sets the program for the whole second division of Nietzsche's book.[9]

Christian Religion and Greek Forbears
SECTIONS 47–49

Sections 47–49 deal with "the religious neurosis" and "religious childishness" before turning to the religion of a "very noble kind of human being." Taken together they point to great differences among religions and suggest a perspective on Christianity's triumph over Rome.

Section 47   How can one interpret the phenomenon of religious conversion? Nietzsche insists that great caution is necessary in interpreting the "religious neurosis,"[10] the "miracle" of transformation from sinner to saint. He almost orders the interpreter "to look away, *to go away*" from this questionable phenomenon, which even the philosophers have counted the most interesting. Nietzsche himself has not gone away from the problem, for the final sentences suggest how an interpretation can be ventured if the transformation is viewed with a sufficiently artful philology of the soul, a proper physiopsychology.

If one asks not about the cause of the neurosis but about what causes it to be so interesting even to philosophers, an answer can be given "without any doubt at all." The saint fascinates because of an inexplicable "appearance of miracle" about him, "namely, the *immediate succession of opposites*" he

9. Suffering is the key theme of the chapter "Our Virtues."

10. Nietzsche's suggestion that *die religiöse Neurose* and *das religiöse Wesen* are synonymous, that religion simply is neurosis, is belied soon enough with the appearance of the religion of a noble kind of human (49).

seems to embody; conversion in an instant from "bad man" to "good man" seems to bespeak the presence of something supernatural. "The previous psychology suffered shipwreck at this point," but the problem is soluble by a psychology free of "the faith in opposite values" (2) that kept previous psychology from the depths (23). If explanation is freed from moral categories, the appearance of miraculous transformation of something into its opposite disappears: the opposites inhere not in the thing but in the interpreter's categories. The saint is a natural phenomenon if an extreme one; the individual miracles of Christianity no more need a supernatural explanation than does the historical miracle of its victory over Rome. "—What? 'Miracle' only a mistake of interpretation? A lack of philology? — " Philology, the art of interpretation, is as necessary for reading the text of "the human soul and its limits" (45) as for reading the text of nature (22).

Section 48   Nietzsche now turns from Christian faith to post-Christian unbelief, from *Glaube* to *Unglaube*. As in section 46, he divides Europe into southern civility and northern barbarism, but now he himself, not Luther or Cromwell, is the northern barbarian, and as such he finds himself in "antipodal" opposition to the southern, "voluptuous" unbelief of French skepticism, particularly Renan's.[11] In a draft of section 48 Nietzsche explicitly called the French skepticism he describes "French free-mindedness," "the whole French war of Enlightenment."[12] Post-Christian unbelief as expressed in the most modern French Enlightenment thinkers is a religion of religion, a belief in belief, and Nietzsche quotes Renan to indicate his opposition to this form of post-Christian piety. The most modern of ostensibly free-minded moderns are Nietzsche's polar opposites, who stand truth on her head.[13] "How distinguished to have one's own antipodes." What is antipodal in Renan is similar to what Nietzsche objected to in Voltaire (35), the belief that one comes nearest the truth only through the guidance of the good.[14] "The religious childishness

11. The characteristics of northern and southern are described more elaborately in chapter 8, "Peoples and Fatherlands." Extreme northerliness belongs to the "hyperboreans," occupants of the land of Apollo beyond Boreas, the north wind; to open the *Antichrist,* which was to open *"The Will to Power,"* Nietzsche says, "We are the hyperboreans . . . we know the road, we found the exit out of millennia of labyrinth" (*A* 1). See also Zarathustra's imagery of northerliness in ice and clarity, *Z* 3 "On the Mount of Olives," a speech on reserve in speaking. Wallace Stevens shared Nietzsche's sense of what was possible for extreme northerliness as attested by "The Snow Man."

12. *KSA* 14, *Kommentar,* p. 354.

13. For standing truth on its head, see also preface and 44; antipodes also appear in 44.

14. On Renan, see *TI* Skirmishes 2.

par excellence" is the belief that "man is closest to the truth when he is most religious." The antipodal view would be that the true is least accessible when one is held by a conviction about the good.

Section 49   After considering the religious neurosis and religious childishness in Christian and post-Christian forms, Nietzsche turns to "the religiousness of the ancient Greeks," Homeric or pre-Platonic Greeks. His account of Christianity will continue in the following two sections but only after this brief glance at Greek religion, for the glance serves Nietzsche's account of Christianity: one of the prerequisites of Christianity's success in Rome is traceable to an event in the history of Greek religion. Nietzsche distills his view of the one great turning point in Western spiritual history into two sentences. The first: "What astounds about the religiousness of the old Greeks is the unrestrained fullness of gratitude that streams out of it: it is a very noble kind of human being that stands before nature and before life *this way!*" The old Greeks are the Greeks born out of Homer, the educator of Greece who, "like the wisest, knew the secret of all life" (*Z* 2 "On the Tarantulas"), and who taught the highest civilization yet achieved to stand before nature and life in gratitude.[15]

The second sentence describes the event in Greek history that was to have immeasurable consequences for the whole of European humanity: " — Later, when the mob came to predominate in Greece, *fear* took over in religion too; and Christianity prepared itself. — " No preparation was as important for Christianity as the shift in Greek religion under the democracy from a noble gratitude to popular fear, and in Nietzsche's view no one was more responsible for the ultimate success of this shift to popular religion than Plato. The crisis of Homeric religion evoked from Plato the effort to replace Homeric gods with moral gods and the Homeric mortal soul with an immortal one. Noble old Greeks stood gratefully before nature and life; Platonic Greeks knelt before gods who decided the destiny of their immortal souls. "Plato versus Homer: that is the complete, the genuine antagonism" (*GM* 3.25). This is not the antagonism of philosophy versus religion but, in the public sphere, the antagonism of two religions. Homeric religion, arising from gratitude, was a noble stance toward nature and life, one that generated the highest artistic and intellectual achievements of humanity so far. Platonic religion, grounded in

15. On the nobility of Greek religion, see *HH* 111; on Homer's irreligion, see *HH* 125 and *GS* 302. On religion as a form of gratitude, see *KSA* 13.17 [4 §1]. *CW* "Epilogue" states that "the essence of great art is gratitude." Nietzsche's view of Greek religion is elaborated in "The Dionysian World View" (*KSA* 1. pp. 553–77); on the Homeric gods, see esp. pp. 559–66.

fears, was a slavish subjection to invented supernatural powers and led eventually to the capture of European humanity by an Asian religion of total human abnegation before a sovereign, redeeming deity.[16]

Nietzsche, the northern barbarian, seems bent on engendering a new seriousness about religion in post-Christian Europe. The view being set out points to antipodal attitudes among religions and to religion itself as a power by means of which the greatest, most inventive poets generate whole worlds of culture.

Christian Religion and Hebrew Forbears
SECTIONS 50–52

Section 50   Section 50 seems to follow the downward trajectory in Western religion passing through Plato, a move from noble to base, from a grateful human stance before nature and life to fear and eventually to Christian "passion for God," the need for a redeeming power from beyond nature and life. What was prepared by Platonism is exhibited in the three types of passion for God that Nietzsche describes. The first returns to the distinction between a European north and south (46) and to the northern crudeness introduced into Christianity by Protestantism. The second returns to the distinction between Europe and Asia (46) and to the religious slavishness before God introduced into Europe by Christianity.[17] The third (with three examples) locates the passion for God in sublimated sexuality, a transformation of natural passions that frequently led to the proclamation of sainthood, the subject of the next section.

Section 51   Why did the most powerful bow down before the saint? In this setting Nietzsche's question must concern, in part, the bafflement with which Roman power confronted the new phenomenon of Christian passion for God. Opening with "Till now," section 51 ends on a question the powerful did not know how to pose. "The powerful of the world learned a new fear" before the ascetic saint, "they sensed a new power, a strange, as yet unconquered enemy."

16. "In the great disaster of Christianity, Plato is that ambiguity and fascination, called an 'ideal,' which made it possible for the nobler natures of antiquity to misunderstand themselves and to step on the *bridge* that led to the 'cross'" (*TI* Ancients 2). *GM* 2.23 expands considerably on *BGE* 49 and does so after a lengthy discussion of Christianity in the preceding sections.

17. Luther and Augustine, Protestantism and the Roman Church, are again treated serially one year later in the fifth book of *The Gay Science* (358, 359). Those much lengthier discussions argue that Protestantism is a decline away from the subtlety of the Roman Church and that Augustine, a father of the Roman Church, is to be understood as a teacher of revenge in contrast to Plato, whose Platonism is not founded on revenge.

Roman power measured the new power by what it understood of itself, but that understanding was deficient, lacking the proper physiopsychology to plumb either itself or the new phenomenon. Nietzsche names his own ultimate explanatory principle for the only time in this chapter to point to a more adequate way to interpret what moved both warring parties: "It was the 'will to power' that made [the worldly powerful] stop before the saint." "They had to ask him —— " Lacking a psychology of their own will to power, they failed to understand the more spiritual forms the will to power could take. The new psychology "as morphology and evolution-doctrine of the will to power" (23) implicitly promises to explain the fateful civilizational encounter that caused the mastering empire that ruled the European world to fall to the slavishly otherworldly.

Section 52   Like the look back at pre-Christian Greeks (49), section 52's look back at pre-Christian Hebrews judges Christianity. The Jewish "book of divine justice" that Christians call the Old Testament is accorded the highest praise: there are in it "human beings, things, and speeches in so great a style that the Greek and Indian writings have nothing to place beside it." As with Homer, its greatness refutes the Christian notion of progress that has captured Europe. Implicitly opposing Aquinas's judgment that in matters of taste there is no disputation, Nietzsche argues that taste measures the "book of grace" against the book of divine justice.[18] To have glued the New Testament to the Old Testament to make a Bible is perhaps the greatest " 'sin against the spirit' that literary Europe has on its conscience" — Nietzsche's accusation of injustice against Christianity quotes the book of grace against itself, employing the strongest curse Jesus could utter, the curse on the sin for which there is no forgiveness (Mt. 12:31).[19]

This is the last section to treat Christianity itself. The next sections turn from Christian forbears to post-Christian descendants and assess the cost to religion of almost two millennia of Christian rule. Only after this brief look at post-Christian atheism and nihilism (53–54) does the possibility of a religion of the future appear (55–57).

The Central Issue of Religion in Our Time
SECTIONS 53–54

Chapter 3 centers the key religious issue of our time: it pairs at its center sections on God and the soul, the *death* of God and the *assassination* of the

18. The difference between justice and grace will be a distinguishing feature of master and slave moralities (261, 265).

19. On the Old Testament and Christianity, see *D* 84, "The philology of Christianity."

soul (53–54). Each is introduced with a question, and each deals with one of the great contemporary consequences of the successful modern fight against Platonism. Just as Nietzsche refused to renounce the soul, "one of the most ancient and venerable hypotheses" (12), he refuses to renounce the gods—the crisis of religion in our time is a local or Christian-Platonic event and need not signal the end of what is great in religion, what is represented by Homer and the Hebrew Bible.

Section 53 The Christian doctrine of God is responsible for the disaster of modern atheism. "Why atheism today?" Nietzsche's answer reports the results of "numerous conversations, inquiring and listening": the answers given are not his but those of his contemporaries. The mood of this report on "the greatest recent event" (*GS* 343) lacks completely the sense of terror present in the madman's famous speech—"we have killed him, you and I" (*GS* 125).[20] Instead, Nietzsche reports the profoundly sober reasons for the atheism of his contemporaries in an attitude of amusement, as if he himself were merely an interested observer of the event. " 'The father' in God is thoroughly refuted, ditto the 'judge' or 'rewarder.' "[21] The intellectual conscience hardened by modern science seems to find the Christian God unbelievable and intolerable. Similarly refuted is the notion of God's free will, his capacity to act in the world: he "does not hear,—and even if he heard he wouldn't know how to help"—how to break into the unbreakable chain of natural causes. But "worst of all," concludes this litany of God's reported failings, the Christian God can't seem to speak clearly: "Is he unclear?" What purported to be revelation is a philological disaster that falls apart at the slightest touch of the philological conscience and casts doubt on its source.[22]

After listing these "causes of the decline of European theism," Nietzsche

---

20. On "The madman" (*GS* 125) see Pippin, "Nietzsche and the Melancholy of Modernity." Pippin argues that it is wrong to interpret the madman as the flamboyant spokesman of Nietzsche's understanding of the event "God is dead." Instead, the madman is to be viewed as *mad* both in his conception of the death of God—that we are responsible for a murder bound to haunt us—and in his manner of communicating it—not only to mild atheists but to believers in the midst of their worship. Nietzsche understands the event differently: not as a murder but as a coming to our senses that subtracts belief from what is unworthy of belief. And Nietzsche communicates the event differently: not screaming accusations and prophesying insurmountable melancholy or malaise, but with comparative restraint about an event that was bound to happen and that, even though it presages a period of nihilism, gives reason for good cheer and exhilaration (see *GS* 343).

21. This part of the report echoes the conversation of the "old, saddened, dried-up nightwatchmen" overheard by Zarathustra in "On Apostates" (*Z* 3).

22. On philology and revelation, see *GS* 358, *A* 52.

speaks for himself, focusing on another aspect of his investigation of the modern religious problem: "It appears to me that in fact the religious instinct is growing powerfully." Nietzsche had called the religious *Wesen* the religious *Neurose* (47), but it seems to be something far deeper and better than mental disorder, for the religious instinct, "that is to say, the god-forming instinct" (*KSA* 13.17 [4, §5]), can take healthy as well as neurotic forms. As an instinct that now "refuses with deep mistrust precisely the theistic satisfaction," the religious instinct is a human drive capable of being cruel to itself, depriving itself of the only satisfaction that seems available to it. The act of intellectual conscience that killed off the Christian God leaves humanity with no satisfaction for its instinct for gratitude and justice, healthy religious sentiments expressed nobly by pre-Christian Greeks and Hebrews; it leaves humanity no satisfaction for its instinct to love and dedicate itself to something infinitely greater than itself. Nietzsche's response to the cultural disaster caused by the death of God will not be intimated until two more elements of the post-Christian situation have been set forth in the next two sections.[23]

Section 54   From the modern attack on the Christian God Nietzsche moves to the modern attack on the Christian soul, and again the overcoming of the Christian view supplies an opening for affirmative possibilities: what initially looks like the demise of the religious becomes a new grounding for it. "What then is the whole of modern philosophy doing fundamentally?" By framing the opening question this way Nietzsche implies that modern philosophy's refutation of the Christian God (53) is merely corollary to its fundamental deed, its reassessment of the human in its attack on the old soul concept. The whole of modern philosophy is engaged in a political act, the revolutionary overthrow of the ruling concept of Christian Europe: "an assassination of the old soul concept . . . that is, an assassination of the fundamental presupposition of Christian doctrine." Philosophical assassins carried out their deed under the cover of a critique of the subject-predicate concept, and Nietzsche traces the deadly conspiracy to Descartes, presumably to *Les passions de l'âme*, the book that sets forth the first modern account of soul as an epiphenomenon of the machinery of the human body.[24] When Nietzsche emphasizes that modern

---

23. For an excellent account of Nietzsche's analysis of Christianity's consequences for religion, see Ronald Beiner, "George Grant, Nietzsche, and the Problem of a Post-Christian Theism." Beiner's account relies primarily on notes selected for *The Will to Power,* but it arrives at conclusions similar to those suggested in *BGE.* See also Tyler Roberts, *Contesting Spirit: Nietzsche, Affirmation, Religion,* for an evaluation of what is affirmative in Nietzsche's view of religion.

24. Nietzsche says that modern philosophy carried out its assassination "more in

philosophy is *anti-Christian* he adds immediately that it is "in no way anti-religious," stating again what he had emphasized in the previous section: the modern attack on the core of the Christian religion is not an attack on religion itself.

Modern philosophy's aggression against Christianity takes the form of "an epistemological skepticism," a rethinking of the "I" that liberates it from a trap of grammar, the superstition Nietzsche referred to earlier (preface, 17, 34) that he here says was believed "once upon a time" — the view that a subject must preexist the actions and properties predicated of it. Then, with "admirable toughness and cunning," modern philosophy experimented with the opposite possibility, namely, that actions conditioned or even produced the subject. Kant is the other modern philosopher named in section 54, and if Nietzsche had earlier criticized Kant for the use to which he put ignorance of the self (11), he is here much more affirmative about that ignorance: "The possibility of a *merely apparent existence* of the subject, that is, the 'soul,' may not always have remained strange to [Kant]" — even Kant, despite aiming to keep the old soul concept believable by making it unknowable, may have glimpsed the possibility that the soul has only a *Scheinexistenz,* that it is precisely its appearances and not some reality underlying them.

Having made this general claim about modern European philosophy from Descartes to Kant, Nietzsche concludes his final sentence in a telling way for a chapter on religion. The whole of modern European philosophy with respect to the soul, or the I, moves toward a thought that was already reached by Vedanta philosophy and that made it "a tremendous power on earth." Deliverance of European philosophy from Christian capture advances it to a view won millennia earlier by non-European philosophy, a philosophy that was so

---

defiance of [Descartes] than on the basis of his precedent," perhaps implying what he stated explicitly in *A* 14, that Descartes *excepted* human beings from the physiology that made animals machines. In fact, Descartes did not except human beings, he merely appeared to — as befits an assassin as accomplished as Descartes. Did Nietzsche read Descartes skeptically enough? The first edition of *HH* quoted — "In Place of a Preface" — Descartes' famous statement (in the central paragraph of the *Discourse*) reviewing the occupations of men and choosing to stay with the one he had already chosen, philosophy, because the intense pleasure it afforded made nothing else of any value. Nevertheless, Nietzsche's few statements about Descartes in his books and notebooks lead one to conclude that he did not read Descartes skeptically enough to see in him one of his great predecessors in doubting the metaphysicians' faith in opposite values, for instance (*BGE* 2), or in not making the human animal an exception to the mechanics of the universe. For a reading of Descartes that aligns him closely with Nietzsche, see Lampert, *Nietzsche and Modern Times* 145–271.

far from being antireligious that it became a tremendous power on earth through a religion compatible with its philosophic insight. *On the Genealogy of Morality* supplements this mention of Vedanta philosophy. At the end of his extended argument about the ascetic ideal in Western philosophy, Nietzsche states that the most modern spirit carries forward the very kernel of that ideal in its will to truth, which takes one form only today: honest atheism (*GM* 3.27). He then adds a parenthetical remark that "should prove something": "(The same evolutionary course in India, completely independent of ours . . . : the same ideal forcing the same conclusion; the decisive point reached five centuries before the point from which Europeans reckon time, with Buddha, more exactly, already with the Sankhya philosophy, which was then popularized by Buddha and made into a religion.)"[25] What this proves is that there is an inherent logic in Western spiritual history that forces atheism on it as a consequence of its will to truth, a human virtue inexorably at work in human thinking whether Eastern or Western. But that very logic points beyond the present atheism or nihilism to a postnihilistic possibility in which religion is generated by philosophy, a religion spiritually harmonious with philosophy. *On the Genealogy of Morality* does not take the step that *Beyond Good and Evil* does; that is, it does not indicate the core of the religion of the European future as the next sections of *Beyond Good and Evil* do.[26] As these sections show, Nietzsche did not take the way of his friend Paul Deussen and the few other Europeans who followed Schopenhauer out of the European fiction of its spiritual progress and back to an earlier Eastern philosophical perspective. The religion of the future for the philosophers of the future lies in a different direction, the direction whose trajectory is mapped in the next three sections.

The Religion of the Future
SECTIONS 55–57

The religion of the future arises naturally out of the philosophy of the future. It appears as a new ideal glimpsed in the very depths of modern nihilism and pessimism by a philosopher, an investigator whose primary goal is not

25. In a letter accompanying a copy of *BGE* (20 Sept. 1886) that Nietzsche sent to his friend Paul Deussen ("Europe's first real *expert* on Indian philosophy" *GM* 3.17), Nietzsche told Deussen that he wished he had more information on Sankhya philosophy that would make it as clear as Deussen's book, *The System of the Vedanta,* had made Vedanta philosophy.

26. The limited character of *GM* is illuminated by this lack: it supplements *BGE* only on selected points. *GM* indicates its limitations by pointing to *Zarathustra* at the end of its central essay (2.25).

to edify or promulgate a new ideal but to understand: the philosopher of the future glimpses the religion of the future "without really meaning to do so" (56). For while Nietzsche is true to Hegel's edict that "philosophy must beware of wanting to be edifying,"[27] he too shows that philosophy is of necessity edifying, consequentially edifying: a new sense of the good arises out of what philosophy does want, to possess the true.

Only in the chapter on religion and only once and without naming it does *Beyond Good and Evil* touch the teaching with which Nietzsche wished to be identified: "I, the teacher of the eternal return" (*TI* Ancients 5). In sections 55–57, therefore, the essential argument on philosophy and religion reaches its most important conclusion. The five sections that follow these three and end chapter 3 look to the consequences of the completed argument: how can the new religion natural to experimental philosophy begin to make its way in the world? The one who first glimpsed the new ideal must show his irreligious modern readers what religions are good for and how the new religion differs from the prevailing ones.

Section 55 Something far more comprehensive and powerful than anti-Christian ire lies behind the modern sacrifice of the Christian God and assassination of the Christian soul: a profound force in the human soul demands sacrifice. *Sacrifice* is heard seven times in this short paragraph as Nietzsche describes the three most important rungs on the ladder of religious cruelty. First is the premoral sacrifice of human beings; second, the moral sacrifice of "one's instincts, one's 'nature'" to antinatural, supernatural gods. The final cruelty sacrifices those gods themselves and the comforts they promised. This final sacrifice is a "paradoxical mystery" because it sacrifices the very things for the sake of which humanity's other sacrifices were made. It seems the last possible sacrifice, the sacrifice of everything worth sacrificing for, nihilistic sacrifice.

Nietzsche's presentation of the final cruelty asks, "Did one not have to sacrifice once and for all, everything comforting, holy, healing, all hope, all belief in hidden harmony, in future blessedness and future justice?" His formulation focuses on beliefs that made life on earth bearable, but the question is asked again with an added element: "Did one not have to sacrifice God himself and, out of cruelty against oneself, worship the stone, stupidity, gravity, fate, the nothing?" The sacrifice of God does not end worship; it is demanded by a different worship, itself a form of self-punishment. The questions are meant to be answered affirmatively, as shown by the indicative sentence that ends the section: "To sacrifice God for the nothing—this paradoxical mystery of the

27. *Phänomenologie des Geistes* 14.

final cruelty remained reserved for the generation now coming up." Nietzsche does not name the necessity at work in this final, paradoxical step of religious cruelty, but the book has made clear that the one force powerful enough to impel such self-punishment is conscience, now the intellectual conscience or the love of truth that demands its reward, the sacrifice of untruthful views of nature with which humanity comforted itself till now.

Nietzsche was just beginning to analyze this culminating sacrifice as "European nihilism," described in the preface as the "need and distress" dawning on the most wakeful. And if "we all already know something of this," Nietzsche seems to know something more: "perhaps also the arrow, the task, who knows? the *goal*." These sections display Nietzsche's understanding of the task and goal facing the philosopher of the future. For the only time in the book, and in the midst of a developing argument about the state of European religion, Nietzsche touches the teaching that *Thus Spoke Zarathustra* had been written to introduce.

Section 56   Given its placement and theme, section 56 is one of the most important in the book.[28] It consists of a single sentence with a final, one-line question about divinity. Its first half begins, "Whoever . . ." and its second half, "that one. . . ." — whoever pursues the experiences described in the first half of the sentence "may perhaps" undergo the experience described in the second. That these are Nietzsche's experiences is stated at the beginning: the "Whoever" is said to be "like me." Nietzsche seems unwilling to identify what drove him in his investigations into the deepest pessimism — "some riddlesome longing or other" — but he makes it clear that he was not driven by a longing to discover some new ideal, for he came across it "without really meaning to do so." In the crucial section in the chapter on religion this little qualification is necessary: Nietzsche is not in the first instance a teacher of religion; he was not moved primarily by the need for the edifying. The riddlesome longing that did drive him must surely be identified with the longing that governs the whole book, the philosopher's will to truth with which the preface and each of the first three chapters began, *riddlesome* partly because its satisfaction costs human beings everything that was thought to be comforting or high till now. The crucial insight into the religion of the future is gained by a philosopher, not by one of the *homines religiosi* whose will to truth is incidental to his passion for God.

The first half of the section reports Nietzsche's effort "to think pessimism

28. Among the subtitles Nietzsche projected for *BGE* was *Prelude to a Philosophy of Eternal Return*, KSA 11.26 [325] Summer-Fall 1884. See other titles at KSA 11.27 [58,80,82], 29 [40], 34 [191].

through to its depths," pessimism thus serving to link section 56 to 55 as the specific form of "the worship of the nothing" that carried Nietzsche to the thought of eternal return. *Pessimism* is not a prominent word in *Beyond Good and Evil,*[29] but Nietzsche here assigns an important task to the riddlesome longing to think pessimism to its depths: to "redeem" pessimism from "the half-Christian, half-German narrowness and simplicity with which it finally presented itself to our century," to separate pessimism from the moralism of Schopenhauer.[30] That effort of thought required a new kind of seeing not limited by "the spell and delusion of morality," a seeing from the perspective of "an Asiatic and supra-Asiatic eye." The eye confined neither to European nor to Asiatic perspectives is ultimately the eye of Nietzsche's Zarathustra, who transcended the moral view of being and time introduced by the historic Asiatic, Zarathustra. The supra-Asiatic eye also views from a perspective beyond the Buddha and beyond Vedanta philosophy (preface, 54). Aware of itself as transmoral, as occurring at the end of the ten-thousand-year moral period of human experience (32), it surpasses any historical precedent in its pessimism. The experience of thinking pessimism through to its depths is "beyond good and evil," but as Nietzsche emphasized in the final sentence of the first treatise of *On the Genealogy of Morality,* " 'beyond good and evil' . . . this means at the very least *not* 'beyond good and bad' " (*GM* 1.17). While not guided by good and evil or by good and bad, guided by love of truth "even if it be bad [*schlimm*]" (Z 2 "On Self-Overcoming"), the thinker of section 56 arrives at the fundamental good of a new good and bad.

In *Beyond Good and Evil* the thought of eternal return is an insight achieved by the one who thinks pessimism to the depths: that one "may just thereby . . . have opened his eyes to the opposite ideal" — opposite to the ideal of self-denial

---

29. *Pessimism* is also used in sections 59, 208, 225, and 254.

30. Nietzsche's effort to think pessimism through to its depth continued after the completion of *BGE.* A few months later, *pessimism* appears in the alternate title added to the second edition of *The Birth of Tragedy: Or Hellenism and Pessimism,* and it is referred to in the first section of the new preface: "Is pessimism *necessarily* a sign of decline, decay, degeneration, weary and weak instincts — as it once was in India and now is, to all appearances, among us, 'modern' men and Europeans? Is there a pessimism of *strength?* An intellectual predilection for the hard, gruesome, evil, problematic aspect of existence, prompted by well-being, by overflowing health, by the *fullness* of existence? Is it perhaps possible to suffer precisely from overfullness?" That the answer to these questions is Yes is indicated in the new book then added to *The Gay Science,* where *pessimism* describes Nietzsche's own view, "an altogether different kind of pessimism, a classical type. . . . I call this pessimism of the future — for it's coming! I see it coming! — Dionysian pessimism" (*GS* 370).

and world-denial taken even further than Schopenhauer or Buddhism had taken it. Before presenting the new ideal, Nietzsche describes the person capable of thinking it as an ideal: "the most high-spirited, most alive, most world-affirming human being." What this saint of affirmation and not of denial affirms Nietzsche presents in two stages, "not only . . . but also," a high affirmation capped by a still higher affirmation. The one who affirms the new ideal "has not only come to terms with and learned to get along with whatever was and is" — to learn this is to learn "reconciliation" (*Versöhnung*), the word used in *Zarathustra* for this stage of affirmation (Z 2 "On Redemption"), or "*amor fati*," the words used for it in *The Gay Science* at the opening of the fourth book (276), the book that closes with Nietzsche's first announcement of eternal return. "To come to terms with and learn to get along with everything that was and is" means no longer to take revenge on the world or seek deliverance from the world — a high achievement of affirmation given the pervasive rule of revenge in the teachings of the moral period as Nietzsche understands them. But the opposite ideal goes beyond even that high affirmation and "wants to have it again, *exactly as it was and is,* out into all eternity, shouting insatiably *da capo*." Nothing in this formulation suggests that the most world-affirming human being has just discovered a new fact about the world. Instead, the formulation describes a passionate desire or disposition and an ideal in accord with that disposition. What is discovered in glimpsing the opposite ideal is the highest or ultimate way to satisfy a passion for world affirmation. The highest ideal for a world-affirming human being is that the world as it is eternally return just as it is.

The one who insatiably shouts da capo to everything that was and is employs a musical direction identical to the title of the song Zarathustra taught the superior men, *Noch ein Mal!* (Once More!) (Z 4 "The Nightwanderer's Song"), the song of eternal return that begins, "Oh Mensch! Gieb Acht!" There is a logic or ground to this vehement "Once More!" and Nietzsche completes his sole presentation of eternal return in *Beyond Good and Evil* by displaying that ground and its cycling or circling quality. The one who embodies the new ideal shouts da capo "not only to himself but to the whole play and spectacle" — the ultimate affirmation is self-affirmation *and* affirmation of the whole. Nietzsche answers the implied question of why the ideal of affirmation takes this form: it is "not only to a spectacle," — not even this greatest of spectacles, the totality of beings in their " 'necessary' and 'calculable' course" (22) — "but fundamentally [*im Grunde*] to him who needs precisely this spectacle — and who makes it necessary: because again and again he needs himself — and makes himself necessary — —" The affirmation is ultimately of the most affirmable thing in the whole affirmable spectacle, the human spectator of the spectacle. But to shout da capo to oneself as the human or rational viewer of the whole of things entails shouting da capo to the whole of which the viewer is a self-conscious fragment.

But why put the highest affirmation so emphatically in the language of necessity? Nietzsche emphasizes necessity by using two phrases twice: *nötig hat* (has necessary or needs) and *nötig macht* (makes necessary). This is not a physical or cosmic necessity but a lover's necessity, erotic necessity. What the lover needs as lover is the beloved, and what the beloved needs as beloved is the lover. The highest pitch of the lover's passion desires the eternal return of both beloved and lover. The lover "has precisely this spectacle as necessary — and makes it necessary." To *have* it as necessary is the lover's recognition of his need of the beloved. To *make* this spectacle necessary can hardly be to cause it or to inflate himself into thinking he caused it; rather, it must be to make the spectacle necessary *as beloved,* to acknowledge its indispensability, to avow, to shout, It's you, you I want and want eternally as you are. The lover's love of the beloved is itself necessitous, though not stemming from a lack: "because he always has himself as necessary — and makes himself necessary" — not as his own self-caused cause, a fundamental absurdity (15, 21) that can have no place in a logic of love. A chance consequence of everything that was and is, the lover of what was and is makes himself necessary as a lover; he crowns his being by loving it, by expressing the most exuberant gratitude for it — and gratitude for *it* entails gratitude for the whole to which it owes its being. Affirmation of self circles into affirmation of the whole as its source, which circles into affirmation of the self: da capo to the whole piece.[31]

What Nietzsche has described is a lover's *ideal,* what the most world-affirming human being would, more than anything, love to be the case. As a lover of life, he wants his life once more — in *Zarathustra,* "Once More!" is the song one sings at death (Z 4 "The Nightwanderer's Song," 1). To want this life once more entails wanting once more the whole spectacle that made his life possible, the life of a lover of truth. Humanity's highest possible affirmation affirms the world in its generation of its rational viewer consciously loving what he views. What is ultimately affirmable about the world by the lover of

31. GM comes closest to this affirmation of *BGE* 56 at the end of its central treatise. Speaking of the erection of a new ideal as a lover's task, Nietzsche introduces one who *"must one day come,"* "the *redeeming* human of the great love and contempt. . . . This human of the future who will redeem us from the previous ideal" as well as from the nihilism that grew out of it (24). But after describing this future human redeemer Nietzsche ends by pointing back to *Zarathustra* (GM 2.25). See also what Nietzsche says toward the end of the third treatise: "Where is the opposing will that might express an *opposing ideal?*" (GM 3.23).

truth is the intelligible character of the world, its purposeless will to power; love of truth grows into love of the true, or, as the plot of *Zarathustra* presents it, love of Wild Wisdom is transfigured into love of Life.

The compact lover's formula of needing the self and the beloved and making the self and the beloved necessary is the closest this No-saying book comes to the Yes-saying of *Thus Spoke Zarathustra*. To expand on the formulaic expression of the new ideal, one must do what Nietzsche expected the reader of *Beyond Good and Evil* to do, follow its investigations of the near into the investigations of the far in *Zarathustra*. "Before Sunrise" (*Z* 3), perhaps the most revealing of all of Zarathustra's speeches because it provides the ground for the teaching of eternal return, illuminates the new ideal as an act of conferring necessity. Addressing the open sky, Zarathustra exults in the rule of "Lord Chance," transcendent rule over the apparent rule of any rational, teleological, or mechanical necessity, any conception of "compulsion, goal, or guilt" that clouds the sky with "human constructs of domination" (*KSA* 13.11 [99]). The rule of the absence of rule frees Zarathustra's hands to confer a human blessing on everything under the open sky, an "immense unbounded yes and amen" that desires the eternal return of the whole stupendous array of accident, innocence, chance, and playfulness, an affirmation that understands itself as letting things be what they are, the affirmation of a lover making the beloved necessary as it is.

This peak section, 56, is not permitted to end on the peak. Instead, as with so many of the crucial sections of *Beyond Good and Evil*, Nietzsche gives his audience their say just after he's had his. " — — What? And this wouldn't be — *circulus vitiosus deus?*" Wouldn't this supposed ideal actually be a vicious circle made god?[32] This reaction seems to be the fitting variant of the reaction Nietzsche heard from his friends when he drew the conclusion that the world is will to power and nothing besides: God is refuted and the devil not (36–37). Now that Nietzsche has drawn the conclusion that the new ideal affirms the eternal return of the world as it is, it seems that his friends again react in religious language to suggest that he has made the demonic divine, turning the vicious cycle of meaningless forming and dissipating, dying and rising, into something divine.[33] At the end of the section affirming eternal return, as at the

32. All three Latin words are nominatives and many translations are possible: A vicious circle made god. God is a vicious circle. The circle is a vicious god. A vicious god is a circle. The first seems most appropriate in the setting.

33. This was the actual reaction of Augustine to the Greek teaching of eternal return — it was the highest crime because it made salvation or deliverance from the curse of earthly existence impermanent (Augustine, *The City of God* xii.13–15). This was also the reac-

end of the section arguing on behalf of will to power, Nietzsche acknowledges that his most important teachings will be heard as the embodiments of evil. Unspoken but almost heard at the end of section 56 is Nietzsche's theological response to this response: "On the contrary. On the contrary, my friends."

Beyond Good and Evil touches eternal return only once. It does so in the chapter on religion at the precise point at which Nietzsche's history of European religion has entered the spiritual present of the death of God, the assassination of the Christian soul, and their consequence of nihilism. The following sections help clarify just why the affirmation of eternal return belongs here in the history of religion (57), and just what religions in general are good for and therefore what a new religion would be good for (58–62). It can already be said that eternal return belongs in the chapter on religion and not in the previous chapters because it is not itself philosophy, it falls outside of what can be known. But it follows directly from philosophy, from what the new philosophy infers as the intelligible character of the world. As the new ideal, eternal return arises logically as the fitting ideal of the philosopher for whom the world is will to power and nothing besides. The textual connection between the end of section 56 and the end of sections 36–37 thus suggests a connection in content: speaking as a theologian to those whose theology is still tyrannized by the now dead God, the philosopher who has concluded that the world is will to power and nothing besides offers a glimpse of the new ideal made possible by that conclusion. The new ideal, like the ontological conclusion out of which it arises, at first seems demonic, a vicious circle, because of what the old God demonized. Eternal return stands to will to power as religion stands to philosophy; the highest value arises out of the fundamental fact by a logic of love. The new ideal differs from the Platonic or moral ideal: it celebrates and amplifies what is true rather than masking the truth behind a moral lie contradicting it. Eternal return is the ideal at the core of the new, earth-affirming religion; as with Homeric religion (49), an abundance of gratitude streams out of it. As an ideal it is a more abstract version of what will be depicted mythically or in the language of divinity with the appearance of Dionysos and Ariadne at the end of the book (295).

Eternal return is not presented in *Beyond Good and Evil* as a fact about the world, ascertainable or otherwise. This is consistent with Nietzsche's presentation of eternal return in *Zarathustra*. Zarathustra's *animals* claim to know

---

tion of the honest atheist Schopenhauer, whose pessimism was still moral and half-Christian in judging existence a curse (see *The World as Will and Representation*, sections 54, 59); Zarathustra banishes the Schopenhauerian dwarf with the thought of eternal return (Z 3 "On the Vision and the Riddle").

eternal return, and they live it as its believers (*Z* 3 "The Convalescent"). At the crucial moment in his own dance with Life (*Z*.3 "The Other Dance Song"), Zarathustra whispers something in Life's ear. We are not told what he whispers, but it must be a declaration of love that persuades Life entirely because when she hears it she consents to the marriage whose song then ends part 3. Zarathustra must whisper in Life's ear what is described in *Beyond Good and Evil* 56, that he so loves life that he desires its eternal return. Life replies to what Zarathustra whispers, "No one knows that." No one can know that the world eternally returns. One can, however, be so well disposed toward the world one knows that one would desire above everything else that the world eternally return exactly as it is. Eternal return is a desire of the heart consistent with the dictates of the mind.[34]

Section 57   In a quieter, more settled mood that views from a distance the impassioned affirmation of section 56, section 57 takes a long historical perspective on what was glimpsed by the thinker of that section. As a result of new "spiritual sight and insight" by "the eye of the mind," "the distance and, as it were, the space around . . . a person grow: his world becomes deeper, ever new stars, ever new riddles and images come into sight for him." Such an expansion of experience leads to a series of three events each prefaced by a *perhaps*. The spatial imagery becomes temporal, for the whole past and future of humanity begin to look different to someone with vision of this sort. This little section thus reflects on the consequences of the teaching of eternal return for human history, picturing it as human maturing that links it to the maturing described in chapter 2 as the end of the moral period of human history (31–32).

For one who has glimpsed the new ideal, the deepest earnestness of the past comes to sight as "perhaps" simply the occasion for the play of the mind; everything on which the mind exercised its acuteness and gravity could be seen as "something for kids and big kids," something to grow out of. The second *perhaps* singles out the two items on which big kids exercised themselves most till now, "the concepts 'God' and 'sin,'" "the most solemn concepts around which the most strife and suffering have occurred": perhaps they "will one day appear no more important than a child's toy and a child's pain appear to an old man." The final *perhaps* completes the sentence, bringing this thought on the whole of human spiritual history to its culmination: "And perhaps then 'the

34. A forerunner of section 56 addressed to "my friends" and reporting what he has busied himself with for years gives a much more personal account of the discovery and logic of eternal return (*KSA* 11.34 [204]). It contains many of the elements of section 56 but pits them directly against "the most annihilating and life-hostile of all thoughts, God" in a contest of opposing views and opposing dispositions. This opposition seems to be a forerunner of the next section, which in its final form is far less polemical, far more poetical and serene.

old man' will again have need of another toy and another pain, — still child enough, an eternal child!" Looking backward with understanding at the childish toys of the human spiritual past, the viewer is an old man; looking forward, he becomes a so-called old man, a child, an eternal child in need of playthings.[35]

There is no end to human play with human suffering, though every particular play, every particular way of conceiving and explaining that suffering comes to an end. We now stand at a momentous end in the history of human explanations of human suffering, the end of the moral period that could be a maturing into a new beginning as the eternal child turns to new riddles and images. The deepening of human experience marked by the final rung on the ladder of religious cruelty and by insight into the opposite ideal replaces the childish old riddles of God and sin with new riddles of eternal return, the new toy and new pain. The ideal of self-denial that generated the riddles of God and sin gives way to the ideal of self-affirmation and world affirmation that generates the riddles and images of eternal return: the eternal child cannot live without ideals that simplify and falsify.[36]

Humanity cannot live without religion. But the new religion differs in the decisive respect from moral religion: moved by the will to affirm rather than deny, it abandons as childish the deepest concepts of past religion and moves to the affirmations of *amor fati* and eternal return. The new religion will also be *held* differently from the old religion: it knows itself to be play. It is childlike enough to play but not childish enough to suppose that its riddles and images define the nature of things. It knows the limits of human knowledge while inferring that the world seen from the inside would be will to power and nothing besides. This discovery by the human mind no longer evokes shock and fear from the human heart, but rather an impassioned "da capo," the shout of a lover who glimpses his true beloved and can imagine nothing more desirable than that the beloved return eternally just as it was and is.

What Religions Are Good For
SECTIONS 58–60

The theme that brings this chapter to an end brings all three chapters on philosophy and religion to their proper end. That theme is anticipated in the

---

35. Pastor Nietzsche's son presumably has one of the pivotal themes of Lutheran theology in mind when he speaks of "the old man" putting off God and sin; see Romans 6:6–7; Ephesians 4:22–24; Colossians 3:9–10.

36. See *BGE* 94: "Maturity in a man: that means to have found again the seriousness one had as a child, at play." See also the beautiful reflection on "Seriousness at Play," *HH* 638.

preface: here and now, in the midst of a dying Platonism that so disastrously prepared the religion that has given religion a bad name, it is necessary to understand religion as profoundly as Plato did and act as decisively as Plato did, though in an anti-Platonic way. It is necessary for religion once again to pass into the care of philosophy, for the philosopher once again to use religion as a means of education and nurture, as an instrument for the spiritual cultivation of a new sort of human being loyal to nature and the natural. First, however, it is necessary to understand what religions are good for.

Section 58   In much of modern Europe religion is treated with indifference. The "genuine religious life" needs leisure to be properly tended, and modern times are marked by "industriousness" and its combination of "business and pleasure." Moving from the broad to the narrow with respect to modern indifference to religion, section 58 deals primarily with the inability of modern scholars to take religion seriously, the scholars the philosopher could not employ in the great hunt for the heights and depths of the human soul (45). Modern scholars, in contrast to earlier ones,[37] "no longer know what religions are good for." What they're good for will be the chief theme of the remaining sections on religion, sections that aim to educate indifferent scholars on the indispensability of religion and make them employable on behalf of the new religion.

The section ends on a contrast of faiths that insults the scholars: modern scholars adhere to a naive faith that blinds them to the importance and subtlety of other faiths while blinding them to their own perspective *as* a faith. Their indifference to religion is a product of their own inferior religion, which employs the scholar as the "diligent and quick head-worker and hand-worker of 'ideas,' of 'modern ideas.' "

Section 59   Section 59 follows naturally from the previous section as a corrective to modern superficiality about religion, but it follows as well from section 56, expanding the conclusions of the one who has thought pessimism through to its depths: "Whoever has seen deeply into the world can surely guess what wisdom there is in the fact that human beings are superficial." Depth recognizes the need for surfaces, for simplification and falsification (24), for masks (40) — and recognizes that "it is good that it is so." This section wins its proper gravity when viewed from the perspective of the preface: for philosophy to rule religion, it was necessary that Platonism become various Platonisms for the people. Plato's profound gaze into the depth of the world led to the inventions of Platonic religion, concepts of god and sin Plato himself

---

37. See *GS* 358: "the degeneration of the modern scholar . . . his lack of reverence, shame, and depth."

could not have believed in, based on hopes and fears Plato himself could not have shared. As a reflection on Platonic religion, our variant of moral religion, this section prepares the action on which the chapter ends: Plato is the prototype of the philosopher who knew what religions are good for and did not shy away from using religion in "his project of cultivation and education" (61) — and philosophy must again think and act on the scale of a Plato.

Behind Platonic religion lies Platonic wisdom: this section argues that fear is the emotion that made superficiality necessary, fear having turned Greek religion from the Homeric to the Platonic and prepared the way for Christianity (49). "One finds here and there a passionate and overdone worship of 'pure forms,' among philosophers as among artists." Can this apply to Plato, inventor of the pure forms, of "the pure mind and the good in itself"? If Plato stands to his inventions as Homer stood to his, the answer is No, for Nietzsche marveled at Homer's audacity in inventing gods he could not have believed in himself because he was their inventor.[38] "Let no one doubt that whoever stands that much in *need* of the cult of surfaces has at one time made a calamitous reach *beneath* them." Plato did not need a cult of surfaces in Nietzsche's view; Plato was not one of the "burnt children" described in the next sentence. A few months after completing *Beyond Good and Evil,* Nietzsche argued that philosophical idealism is based on fear of the senses, but he made an exception of Plato: Plato's idealism was the prudence of a prudent Socratic, a healthy caution that feared for the overpowering senses of his contemporaries; Platonic wisdom about superficiality is based on fear of what is possible for others (*GS* 372). Like all philosophers, Plato viewed things esoterically, looking down from above. It is not Plato but *homines religiosi* like Augustine, the most influential religious Platonist, that this section describes.

Charging modern scholars with blindness to the gravity of religion, Nietzsche seems bent on conveying religion's power, the indelible imprint it made on our culture through its most powerful agents. They are "born artists who can still find the pleasure of life only in the intention to *falsify* its image (as it were in a long-winded revenge on life)" — terms Nietzsche used later to describe Augustine (*GS* 359). "One could include the *homines religiosi* among the artists as their *highest* rank." At the start of the chapter (45) Nietzsche claimed that it was necessary for the philosopher to transcend in understanding the heights, depths, and distances achieved by the *homines religiosi.* Here, to understand them means to see their motive as revenge on life and their

---

38. "*Irreligiousness of artists.* — Homer is so much at home among his gods, and as a poet takes such pleasure in them, that he at any rate must have been profoundly irreligious" (*HH* 125; see also *GS* 302).

achievement as the creation of worlds that became the places of habitation for whole populations. Scholars must learn what religions are good for because religions have created the worlds that housed humanity, and it created them out of profoundly suspect motives.

Nietzsche turns explicitly to our religion and the world its artists made. Fear, the passion that took over Greek religion and is basic to Platonic religion, played the fundamental role: "It is the deep suspicious fear of an unhealable pessimism that compels whole millennia to hold on with their teeth to a religious interpretation of existence." Fearlessness before that pessimism led Nietzsche to glimpse the ideal of life-affirmation, the ideal opposite to the one that ruled the two Platonic millennia of European history now coming to an end. That fear sprang from an "instinct which senses that one might get hold of the truth *too early*, before humanity has become strong enough, hard enough, artist enough." Humanity's becoming strong, hard, and artist enough for the truth suggests that the highest art — religion — can have a basis different from the fear basic to our religion, that it can be based on an instinct that senses that it is no longer too early for humanity to get hold of the truth. Humanity's readiness for the truth is the pivotal issue in this history of religion. Nietzsche, critic of the Enlightenment dream of progress, suggests nevertheless that progress for our species is both possible and actual at the end of the moral period. Progress in religion can generate an art of surfaces that does not falsify by making otherworldly but says to everything that was and is: Be eternally what you are. A basis for religion other than fear has already been exhibited by the gratitude of pre-Platonic Greek religion and the justice of extra-Platonic Hebrew religion. The section began by avowing the wisdom in the superficiality of humanity: it culminates in suggesting a new ground for a wisdom of surfaces.

The final thoughts of this section concern "piety, the 'life in God,' considered from this viewpoint" — not the viewpoint of enlightened modern scholars amused that religion can still interest some people, but a viewpoint that sees wisdom in this art of surfaces and appreciates its world-creating power. From this viewpoint, piety appears as "the finest and final offspring of the *fear* of the truth." Our Platonism for the people practiced a virtue that is the opposite of the truth-seeking virtue of philosophy; such piety is "the will to the inversion of truth, to untruth at any price." Fear of the truth, of an unhealable pessimism truth would cause, spurs the highest artistic inversion of the truth, a whole civilization dedicated to "life in God." This charge against piety's falsifying art does not arise from antireligious ire: "Perhaps there has been no stronger means till now to beautify the human itself than piety: it can turn the human into so much art, surface, play of colors, goodness that his sight no longer makes one suffer. — " This judgment prepares the following section on one aspect of that beautifying piety, the love of the human for the sake of God.

Section 60 "Till now" — repeating this phrase from the previous section, section 60, too, looks back at our Platonism for the people, focusing "piety, the 'life in God' " (59) on its human consequences: "To love the human *for the sake of God.*" This virtuous love is the great invention of the artist whose inversion of the truth has had the greatest impact on our culture. Nietzsche calls this love "the noblest feeling till now" and praises its unnamed first advocate as "the one who has flown highest so far."[39] But these two phrases are balanced by phrases to which they are joined: it is also "the oddest feeling till now," and its first advocate is "the one who has lost his way most beautifully so far." This noble, high-flown, beautiful piety deserves honor in a study of religion attentive to religion's power and place in our culture, but its extreme oddness must also be fully appreciated and its founder seen as having erred profoundly.

To love the human for God's sake inverts the truth, basing a love of what we are on an immense falsehood, a God invented by the fear of an unhealable pessimism. This section blends gratitude with clarity: our religious past has nobility, sublimity, and beauty but is essentially perverse; its way of love posits an unnatural and antinatural divinity that falsifies more than any other way.[40] Our religion taught that apart from God, love of the human would be "just one more stupidity and animality" — our religion is based on a deep misanthropy, on self-contempt and self-hatred; only its long detour through a supernatural, loving God could make the human lovable.

Can the human be loved on other grounds? Is there a basis for genuine philanthropy? The religion suggested by the new ideal needs no antinatural detour in its love of the human. The most high-spirited, alive, and world-affirming human being loves himself and loves the world in the most exuberant way imaginable. Self-love of this sort is an important theme in *Zarathustra,* a

39. Walter Kaufmann suggests in a note to his translation that this unnamed first is Moses because Moses said that his own stumbling tongue required a substitute speaker (Ex 4:10). But it is more likely that Jesus is meant: the description of the founder is consistent with the portrait of Jesus in Z 4 "On the Voluntary Beggar," and in A 27–41, the love described is characteristic of the Christian tradition of otherworldliness, and the chapter's emphasis on our religion seems to dictate that the critique so far offered be accompanied by an account of the reason for its power.

40. Section 198 refers again to "the love of God and of the human for God's sake." There the theme is "morality as timidity": such timidity permitted the passions to be expressed only under strict religious control, the passion of love being permitted only in sanctified forms.

self-love that is very far from modern humanism, love of the generalized human that is itself a Christian relic (*Z* 3 "On the Three Evils"). The love of the human expressed in *Zarathustra* is a love of what humans can aspire to and attain; ultimately, it is a love of the human for the sake of philosophy, for the sake of human openness to the truth of things.

What Is to Be Done? Philosophy's Rule over Religion
SECTIONS 61–62

The chapter on religion ends with a pair of sections devoted to the relation between philosophy and religion, a political relation, a contest for rule that Nietzsche aims to set on its proper footing again: after "eighteen centuries," philosophy must bring sovereign religion under its sway. For philosophy to rule religion means it must rule the beliefs that rule action. Religion becomes philosophy's primary political tool: the beliefs that move human beings to action are brought into accord with what philosophy now sees to be necessary; naturalized religion complements world-affirming philosophy. This is the "great politics" (*EH* Destiny 1), the answer to Zarathustra's question, "Who shall be lord of the earth? Who will say 'Thus shall you run, you rivers great and small!' " (*Z* 4 "The Nightwanderer's Song" 4). It is Platonic politics, the return to the cave to rule through the only means available, rule over opinion.

Religion is far too important to leave to the religious. The chapter on religion therefore ends on an action that brings the first three chapters to their proper conclusion, the action by which a philosopher of the future sets out to rule the religion of the future. The first three chapters are a completed whole because they set forth the theory and practice of the new philosophy. It is fitting that an interlude follow the decisive action at the end of this chapter.

Section 61   Section 61 opens by defining the philosopher's essential action, and it does so ironically: "The philosopher as *we* understand him, we free minds —, as the human being of the most comprehensive responsibility who has the whole development of the human on his conscience." We free minds understand that the philosopher is not free. Having broken free of every demand to stick fast on the ascent and descent to insight, he binds himself by a conscience he forged for himself: responsibility for the future of our species. The philosopher loves not only the truth but the species that pursues the truth, and he is compelled to act in order to enhance humanity. This statement of the grounds of the philosopher's essential action serves as the undefended premise for the argument: the responsible philosophical actor uses religion in his cultivating and educating tasks. Knowing what religions are good for, he employs them for ends that are fully persuasive to him alone. Achievement of those ends depends upon his ability to persuade others to act to achieve complementary ends. Using religion means providing believable reasons for pursuing ends whose genuine worthiness only he can know.

The chapter on religion implements the policy set out at its end. Nietzsche, knowing what religions are good for, looks back over the past of religion from a perspective different from that of advanced moderns; so far from being left behind by modern progress, religion is the instrument of genuine progress. The difference among religions puts our Platonic religion in a decidedly bad light; but glimpsing a new ideal opposite to the ideal of Platonic religion lays a ground for new actions. What are the cultivating and educating uses of the new world-affirming ideal? The final sections of the chapter on religion invite the reader to consider how Nietzsche came to understand and implement his own responsibility.[41]

The philosopher with responsibility for the human future seeks a "selecting, cultivating influence, as much destroying as creative and formative." What religions are good for can be pictured in a horticultural image, for cultivation is basic to culture: the philosopher influences through a selection process that both forms and destroys, breeding and weeding the plants under its care. Successful use of religion for such influence depends on knowing the kinds of human beings "that can be placed under its spell and protection." Plato, the prototype of the philosopher who exercised influence with the help of religion, maintained that the philosopher must discern the various kinds of soul and the forms of discourse persuasive to each.[42] Nietzsche follows Plato by describing three kinds of human being and the ways in which religion is useful to each. Behind all three stands a fourth, religion's ultimate user, the thinker, who employs religion consciously for his own ends.

The distinctions among human beings described in this section are based on a more fundamental division into two kinds, ruler and ruled, or the commanding and the obeying.[43] For the natural commanders, "religion is one means

---

41. In *HH* Nietzsche described "the immense task for the great minds of the next century:" humanity must set for itself ecumenical goals embracing the whole earth, the first requirement for such goals being knowledge of the preconditions of culture as a scientific standard for such goals. *BGE* dares to take on the task assigned to the best minds of the next century by *HH*. The discoveries chronicled in *Z* seem to have assigned Nietzsche the responsibility he once thought he could leave to future thinkers, and which Zarathustra too, in part 1, also left to future thinkers, to some future superman, before seeing that the responsibility was his.

42. *Phaedrus* 269c-272b.

43. This is also Machiavelli's basic division, *Prince* ch. 18. See Rahe, *Republics Ancient*

more to overcome opposition, to be able to rule." As in Plato's noble and necessary lie,[44] religion is "a bond that binds rulers and subjects together, and betrays and delivers over to the [rulers] the conscience of the [ruled], their most hidden and most inward, that which would most like to escape obedience." Plato stressed the desirability of the ruler's believing that he rules by grace and not by force and guile. Nietzsche first stresses that the ruled must be believers for the bond to hold; religion can control their inwardness only if they are inwardly bound by it. But he then moves to what rules those rulers. Speaking of "a few singular natures," he describes a "high spirituality"[45] that reserves for itself "only the most subtle form of rule." These singular natures use religion in a singular way: religion gives them peace and purity; that is, religion is the pious shelter behind which they pursue their more refined intellectual tasks. More than that, however, religion is the instrument whereby they rule the rulers. Using the Brahmins, Hinduism's highest caste, as his example, Nietzsche describes how "they gave themselves the power to name the kings of the people while they kept themselves and felt themselves apart and outside, as human beings of higher and supraroyal tasks." The more-than-kingly rule by ruling kings. They are Plato's philosopher-kings.[46]

From the uses of religion for the rulers of rulers Nietzsche turns back to its uses for the ruled, dealing first with a small fraction of the ruled, the rising classes aspiring to rule. But it is the largest group of the ruled to which Nietzsche devotes most attention, "the great majority" that found Christianity and Buddhism so useful. The rest of this section and the whole of the final section are devoted to this use of religion because it is here that Nietzsche finds the decisive reason for action by the responsible philosopher. Religion is the opiate of the people, the heart of a heartless world. Nietzsche does not share Marx's outrage at this fact, but because the opiate takes a variety of forms, Nietzsche is even more outraged at the Christian religion than Marx is: the Christian opiate poisoned the civilization that gave rise to science and philosophy. Section 61 deals with the utility of opiates, section 62 with the special dangers of the Christian opiate.

Nietzsche lists five ways in which religion is useful to ordinary human beings, and each reconciles to a situation that cannot be fundamentally altered

---

and Modern vol. 2, for a brilliant account of this twofold division in Machiavelli and his great early modern followers, pp. 35, 46, 57, 150, 191.

44. *Republic* 2.414c-415d.

45. Compare the high spirituality of *BGE* 219; 201 speaks of a high, independent spirituality.

46. *A* 57 describes philosophical rule in India and in Plato in greater detail.

for the better. The power of imagination and belief to transfigure a hard lot is an indispensable power, though some forms of that power are worse than the condition they remedy. This generally positive assessment of religion by a philosopher who has glimpsed a new ideal confirms the possibility already suggested: religion, with its consoling, transfiguring, sanctifying, and justifying powers, might be brought into accord with an affirmative view of things. Nietzsche has praised religion as art, even the highest art. Because the philosopher's reasons for gratitude and celebration can be persuasive only to the few for whom life is thought, the upshot of the whole chapter on religion is clear: out of the new philosophy arises a new, transfiguring art cognizant of the uses of art.

This section ends by honoring the art through which Christianity and Buddhism taught reconciliation to the lowliest. "Perhaps" what is most worthy of praise in Christianity is that it is a superstition that permitted the mass of humanity to think well of itself and find contentment in its hard lot; Nietzsche is so far from the Enlightenment that he can praise Christianity for its millennia-long power to deceive. Still, "that's all over now" (GS 357); the Christian God is dead, the Christian soul assassinated, and post-Christian European civilization is poised on the edge of an abyss of nihilism. In the end, what most characterizes the sovereign religion of Christianity for the philosopher is not its usefulness but its "uncanny dangerousness," to which Nietzsche turns in the final section.

Section 62   Nietzsche ends the chapter on religion with a "total accounting" of sovereign religion, a last judgment that details what to be grateful for, what to blame, and, finally, what must be done. The last judgment grounds the action on which all three chapters on philosophy and religion end, an act that aims to reestablish wise rule over horizon-forming belief.

"It always costs dearly and terribly when religions reign *not* as means of cultivation and education in the hands of the philosopher, but reign for themselves, reign *sovereign*." Two fundamental alternatives vie for the cultivation and education of humanity. When religions reign sovereign, they are "themselves the final goal." When philosophy is sovereign, religion is one "means among other means" to the goal philosophy sets. Humans are an animal species with the unique character of being "the *not-yet-determined animal*." Alone among animal species, humanity determines itself in part by cultural means, the force of its beliefs on its actions. It belongs to the nature of humanity to be formed in part by custom, to live a construal of itself into which every malleable offspring is hardened by nurture and education. The malleability of the human to malleable custom makes the human species the *always* not-yet-determined animal. At the present historic moment—

postmodern, post-Christian, post-Platonic, postmoral—the philosopher's task is still what Nietzsche defined it as being in *Richard Wagner in Bayreuth* (3), before he gained clarity about what exactly must be done: "The most vital of questions for philosophy appears to be to what extent the character of the world is unalterable: so as, once this question has been answered, to set about *improving that part of it recognized as alterable* with the most ruthless courage."

The question of the final section on religion and philosophy is precisely focused: how did the two great religions, Christianity and Buddhism, respond to nature's indifferent production of high and low? Nietzsche answers, "They seek to preserve, to hold firm in life, whatever lets itself be held." Nietzsche's final measure of religion invokes the difference between preserving and enhancing; he takes as his standard the view that life is will to power and nothing besides and that to bring human beliefs into accord with nature requires releasing the human into contest and striving, into agonistic enhancement. Not only did sovereign religion side with preservation, it did so in the most extreme political way: it fought to make its view the only view permitted to exist. Sovereign religion exercised the lust to rule, spiritual will to power; it was imperial and tyrannical, ruling out every other view of life—in *The Gay Science* (143) Nietzsche called this the great danger of monotheism, "perhaps the greatest danger that has yet confronted humanity," the danger fostered by Plato's invention of the pure mind and the good in itself.[47]

Nietzsche's "total accounting" recognizes that sovereign religion practiced a "protecting and preserving solicitude," but this solicitude "preserved too much of *what ought to perish*." In its cultivating task it selected for preservation what ought to have been weeded. Still, "we have inestimable benefits to thank them for; and who is rich enough in gratitude not to become impoverished in the face of everything which, for example, 'the spiritual human beings' of Christianity have done for Europe till now!" Despite this gratitude that can never be adequately expressed, the total accounting must ask how sovereign religion made it possible for the spiritual human beings to perform these great deeds of humanitarian service. Nietzsche answers: only through a transvaluation of values that stood all valuations on their head, an inversion of values that brought the actually highest lowest, made the actually best worst, and loved humanity only for God's sake. The Christian inversion of values demonized natural values, aiming to "break the strong, contaminate the great hopes, cast suspicion on joy in the beautiful, break down everything that rules itself, everything manly, conquering, lusting to rule, all instincts characteristic of the

47. On the danger of monotheism, see Roberts, *Contesting Spirit* 57–61.

highest and best-turned-out type of human being, break it down into unsureness, agony of conscience, self-destruction." The sovereign Church set itself the mission of inverting "the whole love of the earthly and of mastery over the earth . . . into hatred against the earth and the earthly." Through these values sovereign religion practiced its own form of destruction, weeding out what was naturally superior or strong, what ought to have been cultivated. Nietzsche's final accounting of sovereign religion implicitly appeals to both nature and history, to the existence of a natural order of rank and to the spiritual warfare actually conducted by Christianity against Hellenized Rome. With its mix of gratitude and blame, Nietzsche's judgment implies that the great social achievements of Christian solicitude could well be performed by nonsovereign religion, a religion capable of charity without the inversion of values effected by sovereign religion, a religion grounded in philosophy that aims in the first instance not at preserving what ought to perish but at enhancing what can surpass.

The final sentences of the chapter on religion, the culmination of all three chapters on philosophy and religion, picture a philosophical spectator viewing this great event in our spiritual history, the Christian transvaluation of earth-loving values. How should he act? Like an Epicurean? "Suppose one was able to look out over the amazingly painful and in equal parts coarse and refined comedy of European Christendom with the mocking and uninvolved eyes of an Epicurean god" — suppose one was able to look out over European Christendom with the same serene composure with which Epicurus himself watched the sun set on Hellenic civilization (*GS* 45) — "I believe, one would find no end at all to amazement and laughter, for doesn't it appear that a single will has ruled over Europe for eighteen centuries, the will to make out of humanity a *sublime deformed birth?*" The comedy of European history since the rise of Christianity would be endlessly entertaining to a philosophical viewer bent on *ataraxia,* a knower without care, content to share a spectator's pleasure with the few of his kind while watching the shipwreck of our whole civilization from the safety of his divine outpost on the margins between worlds.

Being an Epicurean god is not possible for Nietzsche; he has "opposite desires," the desires of a contemplative man so charmed by the great spectacle of these "tremendous struggles and transitions" that he "must take part and fight" (*BT* 15). By becoming an actor in the great drama of civilization, Nietzsche follows Epicurus's rival, Plato. But Nietzsche is a Platonic actor who can't be the butt of Epicurus's venomous joke (*BGE* 9), he's no *Dionysiokolax,* he doesn't invent a dogmatism to flatter the tyrant. If such a philosophical actor, "no longer Epicurean, but rather with some divine hammer in his hand, stepped up to this almost deliberate degeneration and atrophy of humanity represented by the Christian European (Pascal, for example), would he not have to cry out in fury, in pity, in horror[?]" Pascal stands at the beginning and end of the chapter on religion: to survey the spiritual experience of a Pascal from above (45) is to be horrified at what the Christian teaching can do to the highest human types, breaking down the nobility of their intellectual conscience and replacing it with guilt and surrender to the antinatural. Gratitude for Christianity's solicitude for the needy is outbalanced by hatred of what it does to a Pascal.

What the horrified philosopher cries out takes two forms, a direct speech to the Christian artists who formed the Christian view of humanity and what Nietzsche "meant to say" with that speech. The philosopher first addresses sovereign religion as one maker to another: "You fools, you presumptuous pitying fools, what have you done! Was that work for your hands! How you've bungled and botched my most beautiful stone! What have *you* taken upon yourselves!"[48] The hammer in the philosopher's hand is the sculptor's hammer, the tool of the rarest artists fit to work the stone of the not-yet-determined animal into its most beautiful shapes.

"I meant to say" — the final section of the chapter on religion ends as its first section ended, with Nietzsche explaining what he meant; but now all jesting accommodation to piety is past, for he speaks as directly as he will in the *Antichrist:* "Christianity has been the most calamitous kind of presumption yet." Presumption or arrogance (*Selbst-Überhebung*) marks both parties of artists, for each presumes a right to sculpt humanity. What would grant such a right? Nietzsche's final sentence lists three qualities the Christian sculptors lacked, the absence of which deprived them of the right to sculpt humanity. By inference, possession of these qualities grants the right, and they are clearly qualities Nietzsche claims. The Christian sculptors of European humanity were "not high and hard enough to have any right as artists to fashion *humanity . . .* not strong and farsighted enough to *allow,* with a sublime self-conquest, the foreground-law of the thousand-fold failure and perishing to rule . . . not noble enough to see the abysmally different order of rank and chasm of rank between human and human." The three verbs describe an action, an allowing, and a seeing; the action is based on the allowing, which in turn is based on

48. Nietzsche knows where he is: in a world in which Christianity now lacks the institutional power to effect its will; he can be far more open in his attack on Christianity than could philosophers like Bacon and Descartes, who shared Nietzsche's view of Christianity and set in place the cultural project to curb its power: "It's not their love of humanity but the impotence of their love of humanity that keeps the Christians of today from — burning us" (*BGE* 104).

seeing. Read in the affirmative as what grants a right to fashion humanity, Nietzsche's statement asserts that the artistic action that fashions humanity must accord with nature and be grounded in insight.

The artistic fashioning of humanity is the action that makes religion the highest art. Humanity, Zarathustra's thousand peoples, is determined by formative, founding actions that create the spiritual and intellectual worlds within which peoples live. Who is high and hard enough for that? Only someone capable of an allowing or letting be, "strong and farsighted enough" not to intervene in a fundamental process of nature but instead "to let the foreground-law of the thousand-fold failure and perishing rule." Allowing this law to rule allows nature in all its cruelty and indifference to rule; sovereign religion disallows that law, preserving too much of what ought to perish. If strength and farsightedness — "sublime self-conquest" — are lacking in the face of nature's evident inhumanity, elevation of the rule of the unnatural or antinatural seems natural. Why call this the foreground law? Perhaps because the sheer evidentness of nature's wastefulness — its generation of stupendous superfluity — covers over something less evident about nature but eventually accessible to its philosophical viewer — the third quality in Nietzsche's list.

Who could allow the foreground law of nature to rule? Only someone noble enough to see the chasm of rank separating human and human. Here again is the cardinal theme of *Beyond Good and Evil,* recognition of philosophy as the apex of human spiritedness and intellect, an achievement of nature that grants the philosopher the responsibility to rule. Philosophy rules by a kind of natural right, fashioning humanity out of a wisdom that permits the foreground law of nature's cruelty and indifference because it has seen the background of that foreground, which Nietzsche will later describe: " 'nature' as it is, in its whole wasteful and *indifferent* magnificence, which appalls, but is noble" (188). The nobility of nature, of the world seen as will to power and nothing besides, draws from the philosopher the highest possible affirmation. Love of truth becomes love of the true. At the end of the chapter on religion, while defining what was lacking in the religious artists who fashioned Western humanity by fashioning its world-denying ideal, Nietzsche defines what qualifies the philosophic artist to fashion humanity by fashioning the opposite ideal. The teaching of eternal return, the new highest ideal, is an instrument of cultivation wielded by a philosopher who knows what religions are good for. Eternal return appeared first in Nietzsche's writings as *"the greatest weight"* (*GS* 341), the thought that, as it takes command over one, either crushes or transforms, destroys or enhances. That first appearance of the thought of eternal return prepared the appearance of Zarathustra himself (*GS* 342), and it is in *Thus Spoke Zarathustra* that the thought of eternal return is exhibited in its cultivating function: it crushes the spirit of gravity that moves all teachers of revenge, and it transforms and exhilarates the opposite spirit of affirmation. Eternal return is the severest of teachings, for it allows what ought to perish to perish, what cannot bear the eternal return of life as will to power and nothing besides.

The argument of the first three chapters of *Beyond Good and Evil* is Nietzsche's fundamental argument, the argument that moves from philosophy to political philosophy and that is displayed mythically in *Thus Spoke Zarathustra:* the rational must rule the irrational, the natural the unnatural. This has been philosophy's fundamental argument since it first developed a public case for itself, since it first took to the stage. Since Plato, philosophy has acted rationally on its own behalf, it has developed a political philosophy. In Nietzsche, philosophy becomes openly what it has been covertly since Plato. It risks what Platonism held to be *impolitic* because it judges that Platonic concessions to what is antitruth and antilife invited the catastrophe of Western spiritual history, the fashioning of humanity by sovereign religion.

The fundamental argument is complete, but *Beyond Good and Evil* does not stop. It continues with themes of morals and politics that display both the possibility of genuine philosophy and the necessity of its public task. To help define the genuine philosopher or the complementary human being (207), Nietzsche shows how "The Natural History of Morality" has evolved a crisis for philosophy; how the natural kin of the philosopher, "We Scholars," differ from the philosopher but are indispensable instruments of philosophy; how "Our Virtues" serve philosophy; how the current conditions of the "Peoples and Fatherlands" of European civilization compel philosophic action; and how answering the question "What Is Noble?" gives precision to a new human ideal.

4

Epigrams and Interludes

Chapter 4 consists of 125 brief aphorisms, two of which repeat the number of the preceding one (65, 73). Fully 100 of the 125 items were lifted with no change, or minor changes, from a single notebook whose 445 or so brief entries were composed in the summer and fall of 1882, more than three years before Nietzsche wrote *Beyond Good and Evil* during the winter and spring of 1886.[1] In the early summer of 1882 Nietzsche had just completed *The Gay Science* and was preparing to write *Zarathustra*. Moreover, he was actively cultivating the highest hopes for Lou von Salomé, thinking he had found at last a fit follower for his thought. Some of the aphorisms seem to have been composed with her in mind, some even in her presence, during the nearly two weeks they spent together in Tautenburg in August 1882.[2]

1. See *KSA* 14 *Kommentar*, pp. 355–58. The notebook is *KSA* 10.3 = manuscript source Z I 1. An additional 11 items were taken from other notebooks of 1882 and 1883; only 14 of the 125 sections lack a manuscript source from 1882 (84, 87, 110, 115, 124, 127, 131, 134, 142, 144, 145, 146, 153, 177). Nietzsche added titles to the notebook from which he took most of the entries: "On the High Seas: An Aphorism-book," "Silent Sayings: An Aphorism-book," " 'Beyond Good and Evil.' Aphorism-book." One hundred thirty of the entries in this notebook were used in *Zarathustra*.

2. See the contemporary notebook *KSA* 10.1 [10]. Nietzsche and Lou first met at Saint Peter's in Rome in April 1882 and had brief but significant encounters in May

These aphorisms present a rich variety of sayings in such forms as parable (124), riddles (140), quotes (142); some are witty little jokes (101, 104, 121, 157, 168, 172), some are sobering insights into human foibles (68, 158, 185), some are elevating claims about humanity (119, 122); some explain their obscure point (105, 119, 129), others leave it at dark questions (80, 81, 150); some are little dialogues (83, 185), some are direct addresses (174), some are placed within quotation marks (113, 183, see 103, 140), some are even personal (151); some bear titles in italics (83, 87, 140, 165), some bear titles without italics (71, 99, 103). The chief or most frequent theme seems to be knowledge or the knower; other frequent themes have Nietzsche speaking as a theologian (65, 66, 67, 80, 101, 121, 129, 141, 150, 152, 164), and reflecting on woman and man (84, 85, 86, 114, 115, 127, 131, 137, 144, 145, 147, 148). As these numbers indicate, the chapter does not appear to be arranged by its explicit themes.

Perhaps the chief significance of the aphorisms lies in their collective presence as an interlude between the two chief divisions of the book; they force a pause or many pauses, dividing the chapters on philosophy and religion from those on morals and politics. Taken individually, their charm lies in their isolated immediacy, their power to stand alone and through their insight and candor force wry reflection on the reader or quiet amusement or, often, a countering thought, a rebuttal to their unconditionality, a less cynical riposte, a more cynical riposte. Most need no explanation and would be burdened or labored by comment.

In their rich variety these aphorisms often shed instant illumination on points developed at greater length in other chapters. Conversely, the consistent and coherent perspective developed in the other chapters provides a framework within which the variety of these aphorisms can be appreciated as something more than a swarm of insights, as the sparkle and snap attendant to an artist's comprehensive vision of nature and human nature.

Besides their individual insight and pleasure, does the assemblage itself possess any "rhyme or reason" — any poetic or rational principle — "in [its] selection and sequence"?[3] There seems to be a meaningful opening and closing and perhaps even a center; the theme of all three appears to be the knower. There

---

climbing the *monte sacro* near Orta and in the Löwengarten in Lucerne. See Binyon, *Frau Lou* 52–80.

3. Strauss, *Studies in Platonic Political Philosophy* 181–82. Strauss's own suggestions of order seem particularly helpful on the opening aphorisms and on the chief theme of the knower; his main structural suggestion is also decidedly whimsical, based on inaccurate counting that allows him to center the theme of nature.

are also other clear groupings (65[2ⁿᵈ]-67, 84–86,) and pairs (104–05, 109–10, 114–15, 144–45, 152–53, 164–65) that raise the question of an overall order. I will deal briefly with some of the groupings that seem significant to me because they contribute to the theme of the knower — but the readings offered are meant to supplement, not replace, the pithy, pungent character the aphorisms possess in their singularity.[4]

The Knower

Sections 63–66   The chapter opens as the book did in its preface and first section: on the search for knowledge, or on the question of why have knowledge at all? (230) The true knowledge seeker is not a teacher from the ground up, one who seeks knowledge for the sake of students (63); neither does he seek knowledge for its own sake (64). Passing in this way beyond the final snare of morality, the knowledge seeker passes through shame (65), experiencing ultimately, perhaps, even the shame (or modesty) of a god among men, inclined to depreciate himself, to let himself be robbed, lied to, and exploited (66). The true knower, inclined to a shelter that masks his true rank, exists among humans as something less than either the teacher or the moral human being while actually being far more.

Are sections 63–66 bound together this way? Seeing such a binding depends upon having gained the perspective on the knower and on divinity that is suggested by the sustained argument of the book. The suspicion of a connection here derives from the suspicion of connections there, and although the suspicions mount they always fall short of conviction, for such convictions would belong in pathology (154), convictions being "more dangerous enemies of truth than lies" (*HH* 483).[5] Both in his aphorisms and in their arrangement Nietzsche practices the advice he passed on privately to Lou Salomé at the time

---

4. The impression that there seems to be no tight sequencing tying all 125 sections to some structured architectonic seems indirectly confirmed by Nietzsche's practice in assembling these aphorisms from his existing notebooks: the eight sections 155–62, for instance, retain the sequence they had in the original notebook while omitting all the intervening sections, almost all of which had been used in *Zarathustra* or elsewhere in *BGE;* in *KSA* 10.3 these aphorisms are numbers 140, 159, 174, 176, 185, 191, 193, 202.

5. Nietzsche later reassessed this famous judgment: "Long ago I posed the problem whether convictions are not more dangerous than lies as enemies of truth (*Human, All Too Human* 483). Now I'd like to pose the decisive question: Is there any antithesis at all between a lie and a conviction?" (*A* 55). Nietzsche then suggests that the lie is one of the embryonic forms of conviction, where *lie* means "wishing *not* to see something one does see; wishing not to see something *as* one sees it."

he was composing them: "It's neither courteous nor clever to take away the reader's easiest objections in advance. It's very courteous and *very clever* to leave it to the reader to sound out on his own the ultimate quintessence of our wisdom" (*KSA* 10.1 [1, 109 §10]).

Why repeat number 65? Is it just a little mistake? Then the repetition of 73 and of 237 would also be mistakes. But Nietzsche was extremely careful with the last stages of his manuscript and book preparation, stating in a letter to Lou Salomé that it is here that "the final decision on the text requires the most scrupulous 'listening' to word and text. Sculptors call this work of finishing, '*ad unguem*' " (9 July 1882) — an application of cosmetics that could well include numbers.[6] Could the repetition of number 65 indicate a connection between the two, perhaps suggesting that they state the same thing? Or could it (also?) be a bridge between the two 65s and 66, the first 65 and 66 both dealing with shame, the second 65 and 66 both speaking theologically? Or could it (also?) be meant to reserve number 66 for the culminating thought on the knower and divinity, 66 being a significant mystical number as 3 × 22 and also a number for completion based on the number of books in the Bible?

Section 66, as the culminating thought of the opening series on the knower, suggests something even more radical than the theological thought that almost ends the book, the thought that the gods, too, philosophize, for here Nietzsche suggests that the true seeker after knowledge — driven neither by a need for pupils nor by the morality of knowledge for its own sake and prepared to take on shame — is a god among men. This may well be the core of Nietzsche's theology, what he divines of the divine: he finds most estimable what humanity as a whole depreciates, robs, lies to, and exploits. Philosophy would then be the divine activity not because it mirrors what the gods do but because to philosophize is to be a god — and to be taken as a devil. On this reading, section 67 may also belong to the opening theme as a further reflection on divinity: monotheism is barbarism, even misanthropy, lavishing on a single God what would be better spent on a plurality or on humanity.[7]

The very end of the chapter consists of a small bundle of sections closing the

6. Nietzsche played with numbers in composing *Zarathustra,* contriving each of the first three parts to have twenty-two chapters, part 3 having twenty-two in an oblique way that suggests that the total of sixty-six chapters is a meaningful repetition of the Bible. See Lampert, *Nietzsche's Teaching* 240–41. See also *GM,* in which section 13 in all three treatises begins "Let us return," all three section 12's having dealt with fundamental matters somewhat tangential to the themes of the three treatises.

7. See *HH* 129: "*Forbidden generosity.* There is not enough love and goodness in the world to permit us to give any of it away to imaginary beings."

chapter on the theme of the knower. But the precise aspect of the knower taken up at the end of the chapter is the same as what ends the book: What is noble? Or how does the knower stand to the noble and to the rest of humanity? And humanity to him?

Section 185 and preceding   Has any human being ever answered the question of why he dislikes someone by admitting he's not up to him? The pungency of the ending depends upon answering No, there's something about humanity that refuses to acknowledge the humanly high — the humanly high having just been demonstrated in an explosion of insights on the deepest themes. But on reflection the answer could also include a Yes: a whole social order, the Greek city, once chose to admit that and to institute the practice of ostracism to be rid of the most dislikable, the intolerably superior,[8] the noble man who stands in everybody's way (Z 1 "The Tree on the Mountainside"). The final section can be read as a comment on the fate of the most noble, the intrepid knower who pursues a higher selfishness,[9] the philosopher. Such a knower holds views that are beyond the common good and evil, but the high-spiritedness of his "goodness [*Güte*] is taken as malice [*Bosheit*]" (184) — the common good and evil misjudges the highest as low, the most noble as base. The antepenultimate section (183) — without overriding or replacing the sharp poignancy of the quoted statement for any intimate to whom it is addressed — perhaps also suggests something wider, in keeping with the theme of the knower and how the knower long sheltered his superiority and superior view: in the long history of moral lying by the "improvers of humanity" the right to lie was understood as given (*TI* Improvers 5). But now, perhaps, the lying ways of the wise so shake the rest of humanity that they are not able to find them believable any longer. The now-unbelievable knower, the unrecognizably noble, may be unbearable in other ways too, for instance, in the unrequitability of favors that poisons the recipient of any intimacy they may offer (182) — intimacies that would include the gift of sharing what is most true and perhaps least known or least welcome. The noble knower finds himself in a double bind: the unrequitable intimacies of his truths poison their recipient, while the lies he might be inclined to indulge in to avoid being poisonous have justifiably shaken the confidence of the lied to.

If opening and ending admit of interpretations that focus on the knower, what about the center? — for the central section of the book falls in this chapter. (Any attempt to find an exact center must be sobered, if not refuted, by Nietzsche's last-minute decision to instruct the printer to remove the unnum-

8. *Homer's Wettkampf, KSA* 1. 788–89.
9. See *D* 552, *The ideal selfishness.*

bered epigraph of this chapter, place it at the very end of the book, and assign it a number—the book thus has 296 instead of 295 sections.[10] Further complicating matters are the duplicated numbers 65, 73, and 237. Section 150 is thus the center only if the three additional sections are added to the 296 and if the fact that two of the added sections appear before 150 is ignored. Still, even if it is the center only whimsically, 150 is central to the issue of the knower.)

Section 150   "Around the hero everything turns to tragedy, around the demigod everything turns to satyr play; and around god everything turns to— what? perhaps to 'world'?—" *World* seems to amplify the expected answer, *comedy:*[11] for a god, for that height of soul, even tragedy ceases to have a tragic effect (30); for a god, given "seriousness in play" with respect to the human (*HH* 628), everything could hardly turn to the farce of satyr play; gods who philosophize (*BGE* 295) indulge the "Olympian vice" of laughter, "*golden* laughter" with no tinge of malice (294). Not only does everything— *Alles*—turn to the seriousness of comedy from the god's viewpoint, but the god's viewpoint makes *Alles* a world—a mere everything worlds for a god, coheres and becomes meaningful as comedy. The ultimate knower knows the making of worlds or makes a world or enjoys a world.[12]

But is even the divine knower a *knower?* Omniscience was flattery paid to the gods by Platonism. In Nietzsche's view, however, because even the gods philosophize, they too could say with him, "Whoever revealed to us the essence of the world would disappoint us all most unpleasantly" (*HH* 29). But if the world is will to power and nothing besides, its alluring fascination can never be fixed in the permanently contemplatable; even if its essence can in some way be said to be known or named, that very name *will to power* declares that the gods are not condemned to boredom.

The Knower and Self-Knowledge

If the limits on knowledge continually lure the lover of knowledge onward, what about self-knowledge, that key issue of Socratic and Platonic philosophy that Nietzsche himself sees as crucial (23, 36)? Nietzsche speaks of it in oracular fashion (80): "A matter that becomes clear ceases to be of concern to us.—What did that god mean who counseled: 'Know thyself'! Does

10. See letter to Naumann, 13 June 1886.

11. See above, on section 25.

12. It seems significant if not modest that 150 is followed by perhaps the most personal of all the aphorisms in this chapter, the only one addressed directly to Nietzsche's friends. The final, personalizing clause ("—right, my friends?") was added to the original found in the notebook of 1882; see *KSA* 10.3 [1§146].

that say perhaps, 'Cease to be of concern to yourself! Become objective!' — And Socrates? — And the 'scientific man'? — " This echo of *The Birth of Tragedy,* aligning once again Apollo, Socrates, and the scientific man who developed from Socratism, seems to need the next aphorism to aid its unriddling: "It's terrible to die of thirst in the sea. Must you then likewise so salt your truth that it no longer even — quenches thirst?" To become objective in order to "know" oneself is to salt a sweetwater sea of inexhaustible fascination. For Apollo to counsel "Know thyself!" is not necessarily to say, "Become objective, cease to be of concern to yourself." And Socrates himself may not be guilty of misinterpreting the Delphic saying — sections 190–91 interpret the Platonic Socrates as a Homeric monster and Socrates himself as subtle and cunning, as knowing himself in a more than objective way that points to the impossibility of complete self-knowledge, to an unsalted sea that can quench thirst but never fully and never be drunk dry.

The Knower and the Gods

"The wise man as astronomer. — As long as you still feel the stars as an 'Above-you' you still lack the view of the knower" (71). This diminishment of what Kant still felt is also a slight against the heavenly gods as knowers; some of Nietzsche's best jokes in this chapter are directed against the most powerful of these gods, the God of the Bible who had, as Nietzsche says, "a hellish fear of science," of human knowledge (A 48). "It was subtle of God to learn Greek when he wanted to become an author, — and not to learn it better" (121). It was subtle of God to learn koiné, or common Greek, to spread the Christian message to the masses of the Mediterranean world; to learn it better, though, would be to move up to Attic Greek, the Greek of Sophocles, Aristophanes, Thucydides, and Plato. To really learn Greek would be to gain a perspective above that of the God who learned only koiné. Included in that perspective would be a clear understanding that for a subtle Asian god to learn Greek cost Europe not only Greek science: "Christianity gave Eros poison to drink: — he did not die of it but degenerated — into a vice" (168).

Nietzsche's theological barbs against God take a different, more blasphemous form in two little pairs of sections. As a knower with many abstract truths to teach, Nietzsche must charm or seduce the senses to them (128), and he turns immediately to an instance of such seduction (129): "The devil has the widest perspectives for God, therefore he holds himself so far away from him: — the devil namely as the oldest friend of wisdom." The devil holds himself in Hell as far away from Heaven as possible — but if that Hell is the place of wisdom's oldest friend, what would that make Heaven? *God* and *devil* are useful terms to seduce the senses to an abstract truth of wisdom: wisdom's greatest friend and wisdom's greatest enemy can be nicely pictured in the theological language of devil and God if the usual associations are inverted. Nietzsche returns to this little blasphemy later, varying the image: " 'Where the tree of knowledge stands, there is always Paradise': thus speak the oldest and the youngest serpents" (152). The youngest serpent thus speaks his alliance with the oldest serpent on the true paradise: eating the fruit God forbid, the fruit of the tree of knowledge of good and evil. And the next section — directly linked by its naming the fruit of the tree of knowledge — suggests the serpent's motive: "Whatever is done out of love always happens beyond good and evil" (153): offering the fruit of the tree of knowledge of good and evil is itself an act of love that may transport its recipient too beyond good and evil, to paradise, as far away as possible from God, on whom wisdom gives the broadest per-spectives. In offering humanity the fruit of the tree of knowledge, perhaps the newest serpent too offers it first to Eve, as Nietzsche suggests when he brings his thoughts on woman and man to a close at the end of the chapter "Our Virtues," though he uses a different name for the primal woman he means to tempt to knowledge of good and evil, Europa (239).

"The Pious of Knowledge"

Nietzsche is remarkably didactic about knowers of a certain kind in one of the longest sections in chapter 4, drawing out his point quite explicitly even though he had already suggested it often enough in the chapter "The Free Mind": "To the free mind, to the 'pious of knowledge' — the *pia fraus* goes more against his taste (against his 'piety') than the *impia fraus*" (105). Free minds are bound by their own piety, which commands them to oppose the fraudulence of traditional piety. This has an important consequence, as Nietz-sche explains:[13] "Hence his deep lack of understanding for the Church, as belongs to the type 'free mind,' — as *its* unfreedom."[14] As the chapter on reli-gion showed, Nietzsche's own very free mind does not share this lack of

13. Unlike most of the sections in chapter 4, this one underwent considerable expan-sion and alteration from the original version; *KSA* 10.3 [1 §378] stated simply, "To the knower the *pia fraus* is still more against the taste than the *impia fraus*."

14. See *HH* 110: "During the period of the Enlightenment people did not do justice to the significance of religion, there's no doubt about that." See *GM* 1.9, in which the free mind adds an epilogue to Nietzsche's critique of Christianity and ends by admitting, "Who among us would be a free mind if the Church didn't exist? The Church repels us, *not* its poison . . . Apart from the Church, we too love the poison."

understanding; he is freed to impiety about knowledge itself, recognizing and accepting the limited way in which it can be persuasive or livable.

Taking all Nietzsche's little remarks about the knower together, it's no wonder he can joke about a new incarnation — a new descent into body — of God: "Today a knower may well feel like God become animal" (101). He may well *not* feel like that in himself, though others could think he should feel like that because of the insight and candor of remarks like this one.

* * * *

As interludes, as *Zwischenspiele,* these aphorisms are not the *Spiel* itself; the play itself is accessible in the chapters separated by these pleasant interludes. Nietzsche's book, like his thought, is not reducible to its myriad insights — it is not "a mishmash of a hundred disparate paradoxes and heterodoxes."[15] Instead, as Nietzsche was at pains to inform the first intelligent popularizer of his thought, the hundred insights arise from "a long logic of a wholly determinate philosophical sensibility," or, as Nietzsche explained in a later letter, "everything hangs together, one is necessary and doesn't know it; but all of it must be seen as I've seen it in order to be believed."[16] And even though "one doesn't love one's knowledge enough any more as soon as one shares it" (160), judging from *Beyond Good and Evil,* Nietzsche devised a way to share his knowledge and keep it lovable to him.

15. Letter to Brandes, 8 January 1888.
16. Letter to Brandes, 4 May 1888.

5

On the Natural History of Morality

The question concerning the origin of moral values is a question of the first rank for me because it is crucial for the whole future of humanity.

— *EH* Books D 2.

After the interlude of "Epigrams and Interludes" *Beyond Good and Evil* turns from the greatest themes, philosophy and religion, to the great themes of morals and politics, practice or action on the broadest scale — morals being the judgments on good and bad that lie behind human action, politics in this context being the implementation of a new good and bad to overthrow an old one. Nietzsche does not simply survey morals and politics from the new philosophical perspective — he enters them as domains for conquest by the knowing actor, the philosopher, who performs the decisive deeds. The final five chapters of *Beyond Good and Evil* present a reasoned case for a new morality served by a new politics:

Given the whole history of good and bad, what must be done now to secure a human future that enhances the human species? — The philosopher must effect a turn from the autonomy of the modern herd to the rule of the philosophers of the future ("On the Natural History of Morality," chapter 5).

How can the philosopher rule? — By ruling authoritative opinion in alliance with science and scholarship and by means of a transvaluation of values that creates new values ("We Scholars," chapter 6).

What will those values be? — Natural values grounded in the kind of mind granted to a thinker and artist, values which forge virtues that initially look like vices because they seem to advocate suffering ("Our Virtues," chapter 7).

How could such values take root in modern Europe? — Through a good Europeanism aware of its inheritance from Greeks, Hebrews, and Romans, aware of the history of modern European values, and prepared to found or father a global people on the principles of a universalism based on philosophy ("Peoples and Fatherlands," chapter 8).

How can global humanity be transformed into a culturally unified people whose order of rank supplies models to admire and emulate? — By public acknowledgment of a nobility whose claim to respect is securely founded in wisdom, in the freedom it wins to think and act in ways that are at least heroic and that poets could celebrate as divine ("What Is Noble?" chapter 9).

Directing the whole majestic sweep of these five chapters is the rigorous pursuit of the single question with which the book began, that most dangerous of all questions: What is the *value* of the will to truth? "Given that we want truth: *Why wouldn't we rather have* untruth? And uncertainty? Even ignorance?" (*BGE* 1). This was the question the young Nietzsche defined for himself in *The Use and Disadvantages of History for Life,* in which he first raised the issue of "true but deadly" teachings (*UD* 9). Even then Nietzsche contrasted himself with Plato, advocate of "the mighty *necessary* lie" securing society against deadly truth (*UD* 10). Platonism is still the key opponent in the last five chapters of *Beyond Good and Evil,* the view that for society as a whole the value of truth is far outweighed by the value of edifying untruth. Because the ultimate opponent is a pampering Platonism, the argument of these five chapters — an argument for the value of truth — reaches its critical point in "Our Virtues" over the issue of suffering: How can the new teaching defend itself in the face of the suffering its truthfulness inflicts? Isn't it simply an advocacy of cruelty that proves its advocate demonic? The defense appeals to nature as its foundation and to poetry as its instrument — not the poetry of noble lying but the poetry of beautifying truth. The morals and politics of the last five chapters of *Beyond Good and Evil* are the morals and politics of truthfulness, of the seamless fabric of loving truth and living with it.

In the preface to *On the Genealogy of Morality* Nietzsche said that the natural history of morality was the problem he'd studied longest and knew best, the problem for the sake of which all his other studies were undertaken until finally he gained the comprehensive view within which alone the natural history of morality could be adequately treated (*GM* Preface 2). Chapter 5 of *Beyond Good and Evil* is an installment in that lifelong study. It shows how an understanding of the history of morality forces one to act on behalf of the human future. Its eighteen sections form a coherent essay presenting the chief points of Nietzsche's history of morality: the natural types of morality, ultimately reducible to two; the rootedness of those two types in human nature and in nature as a whole; the origins of our particular morality in Platonic philosophy and biblical religion; the natural history of our Platonic civilization as the gradual victory of one type of morality over the other. These points gather into an argument for action: the present moment in moral history, with the human future it is likely to generate, necessitate a *turn* on behalf of the moral type now threatened with eclipse, a turn both natural and rational. Chapter 5 thus expands the sketch of moral history given in chapter 2: the end of the ten-thousand-year moral period of humanity will at first look "extramoral" (32) but in fact it is only beyond good and evil, not beyond good and bad. It is good, or in accord with nature and reason, to turn against a morality that is bad because it threatens the human future. Chapter 5 ends by stating a hope radically different from the hope of the progressive societies that developed out of European Christianity, a hope for new philosophers as agents of the great turn in morality.

Forbidden Knowledge
SECTION 186

" 'Where the tree of knowledge stands is always Paradise,' so say the most ancient and most recent serpents" (152). The most recent serpent not only tempts his reader to eat the fruit of the tree of knowledge, but also aims to make the most ancient forbidden knowledge of good and evil an open science that will ground society's good and bad.

Nietzsche follows Francis Bacon in making natural history basic to science. The method he sets out for the advancement of the science of morality, which is now deficient or nonextant, is strikingly Baconian. It is "a natural and experimental history"[1] that begins with the extensive gathering of data, moves to the conceptual ordering of the immense field of subtle value-feelings and value-distinctions that "live, grow, produce, and perish," "perhaps" performs experiments that would make vivid the more frequent and recurring forms of this living crystallization, and concludes with a typology or taxonomy of morals like Bacon's descriptions of natural kinds.

By setting this task as "enticing" work for scholars, Nietzsche recommends for morality what he regarded as impossible for religion (45): he can send the hundred hounds into this dark forest to gather up his game because it does not

---

1. All three terms are Bacon's: see "A Natural and Experimental History," *New Organon* 297. How well did Nietzsche know Bacon? See Lampert, "Nietzsche and Bacon."

presuppose the highest experiences as a measure of what is examined.[2] Still, for the tasks of description in the field of morality, "the finest hands and senses can hardly be fine enough." The new science of morality replaces what philosophers have till now tried to do with morality. Instead of viewing morality as a problem, they took it as given and labored to provide a foundation or rationale (*Begründung*) for it. The "ultimate ground" of this philosophical grounding of morality amounted to "a kind of denial that . . . morality *ought* ever be considered a problem" — a moral prohibition against treating morality as a problem.[3]

Did Nietzsche really suppose that all philosophers had been ignorant of morality as a problem? He makes clear a few sections later that he knows that Socrates and Plato were perfectly aware of morality as a problem, so aware that they forbid others to treat it as a problem. Fearing the consequences of treating morality as a problem, they prudently attempted to outfit morality with a publicly satisfying foundation and rationale. Nietzsche treats in the open what Platonic philosophy chose to veil: many sections in this chapter will be contributions to the problem of esotericism, the philosophers' moral masking of the view from the height down into morality.

Nietzsche's example of a refined moral sentiment examined by an unrefined moral science is Schopenhauer's statement of what he took to be the fundamental proposition of all moralists: "Hurt no one; rather, help all as much as you can." Schopenhauer is the exemplary modern pessimist, the honest atheist who believed he opposed the Platonic and biblical traditions. A genuine science of morality will have to be more pessimistic and more knowledgeable than Schopenhauer's; it will be based on a philosophy that is not under the spell and delusion of morality (56). In the context of Schopenhauer's inadequate pessimism, a pessimism whose flute playing, whose moral whistling, kept him from the depths of pessimism, Nietzsche mentions will to power. This reference to the fundamental phenomenon at the very beginning of the chapter on moral phenomena can hardly be casual; it points to the methodological key to understanding and classifying moral phenomena, *derivative*

2. The first treatise of *GM* ends with a call for a series of essay contests on the history of the development of moral concepts.

3. "My demand on philosophers is well-known: that they place themselves *beyond* good and evil, that they put the illusion of moral judgments *beneath* them. This demand follows from an insight that was formulated for the first time by me: *that there are no moral facts at all.*" These are the opening words of the chapter "The 'Improvers' of Humanity" in *TI,* a chapter that sets out the immoral means by which humanity has been made moral till now.

events of valuation whose ultimate source in the essence of the world must be appreciated if they are to be understood.

In making morality an open problem, Nietzsche treats it the way all problems are treated by Nietzschean science, as part of "a world whose essence is will to power." The science of morality derives its principles from the fundamental science, the philological science of nature as a whole, which views the foundation as not simply irrational but as a process with "a 'necessary' and 'calculable' course" (22). What Nietzsche once referred to vaguely as "a chemistry of concepts" (*HH* 1) is now secured in the more precise formulations of will to power. The natural history of morality will trace the evolving configurations of human will to power as exercises of moral commandments that kept psychology from the depths (23). Nietzsche's straightforward claim about "the essence of the world" demonstrates just how definitive the conclusion in section 36 is for his investigations: having shown the reasoning on behalf of viewing the world as will to power, the conclusion of that reasoning can be used as a premise about the essence of the world that helps solve hitherto unsolvable problems in understanding human social behavior.[4]

Morality first comes into view as a problem through a comparison of many moralities. Examination of that manyness begins in the next section and does not dissipate into mere variety, for the varieties arrange themselves into variants of the two fundamental moralities of a world whose essence is will to power: moralities of obedience and moralities of command. The main features

4. A similar procedure is followed by the great French Nietzschean Georges Bataille. In *The Accursed Share*, vol. 1, without mentioning either Nietzsche or will to power, Bataille examines the implications of what he calls a "general economy" (cf. *BGE* 23) that "may hold the key to all the problems posed by every discipline concerned with the movement of energy on the earth" (10). The issue is "the general problem of nature" (13) or of "excess energy translated into the effervescence of life" (10). Dealing with this fundamental issue requires "thinking on a level with a play of forces that runs counter to ordinary calculations"; according to that way of thinking, "*it is not necessity but its contrary, 'luxury,' that presents living matter and mankind with their fundamental problems*" (12). The problem is excess, surplus energy, superfluity, superabundance — will to power. To appreciate Bataille's Nietzscheanism it is necessary to see Nietzsche as Bataille saw him, an ontologist whose comprehensive view of nature includes the explanatory principles that make human history interpretable because they make human behavior interpretable as natural, as in keeping with the constituent features of the totality of beings. Bataille's great project of understanding in *The Accursed Share* is identical to the one set out in *BGE* on the identical foundation. Even Bataille's strategy as a writer is derived from Nietzsche: "The announcement of a vast project is always its betrayal. No one can say without being comical that he is getting ready to overturn things. He must overturn, and that is all" (10).

of the morality of obedience appear gradually (187–95); the moralities of command appear later and ascend to the height (196–203). True to its "extra-moral" character, Nietzsche's analysis does not locate the key to morality in the superstition of intention (32) but in the two basic dispositions given in human will to power, the disposition to preservation or enhancement.[5]

Nature and Morality

SECTIONS 187–89

Section 187   Initially section 187 seems to set out an indiscriminate list of many moralities. But as a contribution to a science of morality it may in fact classify moralities in two ways. First, it culminates in a generalization that maintains that in one sense at least, moralities are of one kind: "Moralities are also only a sign language of the affects." Because moral claims display the character of the claimant, the science of morality will depend upon a psychology of the affects, passions, and drives and their manner of indulgence or expression, and it will exercise the basic art, the philological art of interpretation, to read a deceptive sign language that masks its source and aim. So little is morality simply given as an irreducible phenomenon. Second, the seemingly haphazard list is a series of pairs each of which may exhibit the basic duality of the affects that becomes explicit in the final pair: there are moralities of command and moralities of obedience. The typology called for in section 186 seems to be suggested in section 187: as sign languages of the affects, moralities ultimately fall into only two types, and those two types express what is deepest and defining in human beings, commanding and obeying. As with section 186, the example that names a philosopher seems particularly important as exemplary of what Nietzsche opposes: Kant's morality of the categorical imperative takes morality as simply given, and as a morality of obedience exercises an imperialism prohibiting any other kind of morality.

Section 188   This defining section states directly the indispensable role of morality for the enhancement of the human species. Its broad generalizations do not shy away from defining what is "natural" about morality and what is "essential" to the flourishing of the human species. It culminates in giving words to "the moral imperative of nature," and in doing so indulges a playful little oddity typical of Nietzsche's care for the quiet details of his writerly art: every other use of the word *nature* puts it in quotation marks as if to suggest that "nature" is always only some tyrannizing interpretation of nature, but

5. See *GS* 370, "What is romanticism?" for Nietzsche's account of his deepening understanding of these dispositions.

this last use drops the quotation marks as if to claim a special status for the interpretation that accords with will to power.

Nietzsche's general claim is that "every morality is a piece of tyranny against 'nature,' also against 'reason,' " and the whole section argues that such tyranny is natural and reasonable. This is not paradoxical in a world whose essence is will to power (186) for human phenomena naturally exemplify the contest and conflict basic to things. Whatever humans have achieved of "freedom, subtlety, boldness, dance, and masterly certainty" owes itself to the human power to tyrannize itself and "the probability is not at all slight that precisely this is 'nature' and 'natural.' " What would be unnatural and unreasonable in a world whose essence is will to power is a morality that opposes tyranny as such and replaces it with *laisser aller* — Nietzsche's argument in this section is polemical, opposing modern moralities that declare every kind of tyranny impermissible. The whole of chapter 5 as a natural history of morality moves toward the endorsement of a particular morality or tyranny and will demand even a kind of slavery: the polemic of this section is characteristic of the whole chapter in endorsing a morality bound to sound immoral from the modern perspective.

Nietzsche even repeats himself on his unwelcome main point: "The essential, 'in heaven and on earth' as it appears, is, to say it again, that there be *obedience* over a long period and in a single direction." With such obedience there eventually appears something "for whose sake it is worthwhile to live on earth, for example, virtue, art, music, dance, reason, spiritedness." In keeping with its polemical character against modern prejudice, this section then singles out our particular historical tyranny against nature and reason, Christianity, in order to praise it for the singular achievement its obedience made possible: "This tyranny, this caprice, this strict and grandiose stupidity has *educated*" the European mind and spirit.

In the midst of his expression of gratitude for Christian hardness, Nietzsche makes a parenthetical but crucial statement about nature: "Here as everywhere 'nature' shows itself as it is, in its whole wasteful and *indifferent* magnificence, which appalls but is noble." "How *could* you live in accord with this indifference," Nietzsche had asked the noble Stoics in his first description of nature and his first naming of will to power (9). That question is the deepest question of the new morality: How *can* humanity live in accord with noble nature in its appalling magnificence? How *can* humanity bring its self-tyrannizing obedience into accord with what it knows to be true of nature? As the book moves to morals and politics, the basic issue of these domains becomes apparent: the new philosophy implies a new morality whose imperatives accord with nature. Like all moralities, it will be a piece of tyranny against "nature," also against "reason." As such it will be natural: as itself a kind of tyranny it will be in keeping with the world whose essence is will to power. And it will be reasonable: it will be capable of demonstrating its historic rationale at this point in our natural history of morality as a turn from modern morality to a view that accords with nature. While looking extramoral or immoral, it will in fact be a consciously created morality based on knowledge of nature.

Nietzsche states "the moral imperative of nature" as "Thou shalt obey, someone and for a long time: *else* you will perish and lose the last respect for yourself." Nature's noncategorical imperative is addressed not to the individual but to "peoples, races, ages, classes, but before all the whole animal 'human,' *the* human." Section 188 thus alludes to the global character of the new obedience, the project Zarathustra described when speaking of the thousand goals, the thousand obediences, which created the thousand peoples so far: the thousand and first goal yokes humanity together, providing humanity as a whole with the unifying obedience that will define anew the difficult, the rare, and the sacred (Z 1 "On the thousand goals and one").

If every morality is natural in "planting the need for limited horizons" and in "teaching the *narrowing of perspective* — in a certain sense teaching stupidity as a condition of life and growth" — what happens to the love of truth that is the core of philosophy and the chief theme of the book? Nietzsche always acknowledged that in some sense philosophy looks unnatural and antilife in its drive to open all horizons, to fly into the horizonless as Zarathustra aimed to do, to increase perspectives until one can revel in our new infinite of infinite perspectives (*GS* 374). Just how the new obedience or the new horizon can accord with philosophy as the passion to transcend all horizons is a chief theme of subsequent chapters.

Section 189   "There must be fasts of many kinds" — section 189 extends the theme of the moral tyranny of nature and reason. Through the precepts of "the lawgivers" the drives learn "to cower and cast themselves down" but also "to *purify* and *sharpen* themselves," fitting themselves through sublimation for tasks that seem contrary to their nature. From its "higher vantage point," this section looks out over whole generations and ages of "moral fanaticism" in "philosophical sects" and in "the most Christian period of Europe." It seems to prepare for the next sections, on Socrates and Plato, the lawgivers whose thinking lies behind these events of moral fanaticism.

The Socratic-Platonic Turn: Our Great Event in the Natural History of Morality
SECTIONS 190–91

Sections 190 and 191 separate at a single line of Greek verse set off at the end of the first, "a jest, Homeric at that," a marvelous little adjustment to a line of Homer, a presto capture of the problem pursued by both sections, the problem of Socrates or what Nietzsche here calls the problem of "the morality of Plato." The first section deals with Socratism and how "the most daring or rash of all interpreters," Plato, treated Socratic moralism. After the Homeric riddle, the second section unriddles Socratism and Plato's formulation of it.

But what are two sections on Socrates and Plato doing in the chapter on the natural history of morality? The answer, left implicit, is that they deal with the decisive event in the history of Western morality, the Socratic turn, the turn to morals and politics within Greek philosophy that transformed the Greek achievement. More particularly, these sections deal with the Socratic turn as advanced by the morality of Plato in his invention of Platonism, the pure mind and the good in itself. In *The Birth of Tragedy*, Nietzsche called Socrates "the one turning point and vortex of so-called world history" (*BT* 15). These sections express Nietzsche's mature understanding of that turning point — how the rabble gained the upper hand in Greece (49) and turned Greece away from the Homeric or genuinely Hellenic toward something alien, an imported or "Asian" moral view that prepared the way for Christianity and eventually for modern ideas. The Homeric jest, a kind of riddle about a monster, suggests that unriddling the Platonic Socrates frees us from its power over us and perhaps prepares a turn back to what was represented in the Homeric.

Sections 190 and 191 can be fruitfully entered only if one recognizes the distance between Nietzsche's Socrates and Plato and the Socrates and Plato of mainstream modern scholarship: Nietzsche is aware of the uses of pious fraud and of the full range of the philosopher's ambition. These two matters — what a genuine philosopher is and the esotericism those philosophers employed — plus Nietzsche's own presto style in speaking of his quarrel with Socrates and Plato make these two sections particularly rich while particularly resistant to decipherment.[6]

---

6. The problem of Socrates occupied Nietzsche from the beginning to the end of his career. The basic statement remains *The Birth of Tragedy* (esp. 11–17), though that statement must be read in the light of later corrections. The most direct correction is the preface written "sixteen years later," "Experiment with a Self-Criticism," which focuses on the problem of Socrates as the problem of science (1) and blames in particular Socratic moralism (4). Further corrections are found in the review of *BT* in *EH*, and "The Problem of Socrates" in *TI*. See also *GS* 340: the antepenultimate section of the first edition of *GS*, entitled "The dying Socrates," this section brings to an end a series of sections dealing with the present moment in human history; it prepares the final two sections which introduce eternal return and Zarathustra. Socrates, that turning point in human history who offered a new ideal, must be overcome: "We must overcome even the Greeks!" even Socrates, and Zarathustra attempts to do that. The image presented by "the dying Soc-

Section 190 Nietzsche treats Socratism and Platonism as in part at least philosophic masks or hiding places, assuming here what he had stated earlier, that all philosophers prior to the age of Enlightenment sheltered their true opinions behind exoteric masks (30, see also 289). The reasoning Nietzsche presents as typifying Socratism identifies good with useful and agreeable and bad with stupid—the reasoning of the rabble, Nietzsche says, a moralizing on the basis of the consequences of an action, a primitive stage of moral reasoning (32). Such Socratism "does not really belong to Plato" himself but is "merely present in his philosophy." Plato "was really too noble" for Socratism. This emphasis on Plato's nobility appears to leave Socrates holding the view of the rabble, but the next section indicates that Socrates himself "privately and secretly" did not hold the view that reasons can ultimately direct the instincts, and in a concluding section to this chapter Nietzsche states that the utilitarian view was only "what that famous old serpent promised to teach" about good and evil, not what he himself "knew" (202)—Socrates too was a philosopher who made a popular view serve his own purposes.

In order to show how "Plato did all he could to interpret something refined and noble into the proposition of his teacher," Nietzsche pictures a composer picking up "a popular tune from the streets in order to vary it into the infinite and impossible." Plato's daring composition, Platonism, added the infinite and impossible to Socratism's utilitarianism, added an ontology, a mythology, and a theology that secured Socratism in a transcendence ostensibly accessible to intellect. Nietzsche is more blunt about Plato's inventive variations on Socratism in the preface, calling it "the worst, most durable, most dangerous of all errors"; later in this chapter, when Nietzsche gives the reasons behind the historic triumph of "morality as fearfulness," Platonism is counted among the attempts to tame the passions that "smell . . . of the other world" and that Nietzsche describes as "prudence, prudence, prudence mixed with stupidity, stupidity, stupidity" (198). The natural history of morality traces the moral disaster of the present back to the prudence of the most rash of all interpreters,

---

rates" is basic to Nietzsche's reflections on Socrates from *BT* (13, 15) to *TI*. Nietzsche admired "the courage and wisdom of Socrates in everything he did, said—and did not say" (*GS* 340), but he did not seem to admire what Socrates said in his last words in Plato's *Phaedo,* concluding that they betrayed the judgment that for Socrates, too, life is a disease. Perhaps Nietzsche misinterpreted those words by a great talker who was "equally great in silence"; perhaps they sustain to the end Socrates' talk about an immortal soul that kept silent the real healing for which he owed a cock to Asclepius, the healing of the soul of the crucial listener cured of the misology and misanthropy that can result if philosophy is pursued by souls incapable of bearing the deadly truth philosophy uncovers.

prudence that proved imprudent in giving morality what could look like a rational foundation.

Nietzsche calling Plato the most rash of all interpreters? Is this a joke? Only the continued reign of Platonism could make it seem so. Plato rashly tied philosophy itself to what he knew was a lie, the rashness of his act consisting of turning truth on her head and denying perspectivity (preface). Plato is guilty not of revenge, but of recklessness, of introducing a monotone "good in itself" that the vengeful could turn into an instrument of moral terror. Nietzsche judges that it is not reckless to make that singular event in the history of our morality available again.[7]

The Homeric jest that is the pivot of these two sections changes the nouns in Homer's description of the mythic monster, the Chimaira, "in front lion in back serpent and in the middle female-goat" (*Iliad* 6.181). The Platonic Socrates is "in front Plato in back Plato and in the middle Chimaira" — Plato embroidered a shelter of his own invention to enclose a Socrates who was already a Homeric monster. "Plato's hiddenness and Sphinx-nature" (28) led him to guard his master, the relatively unguarded Socrates, with a Plato-like front and rear, part of the successful theatrics so envied by Epicurus (7), part of the strategy of making philosophy palatable to tyrants. In the preface, Nietzsche acted like a physician bent on diagnosing the disease that "the most beautiful growth of antiquity" contracted from Socrates, corrupter of Athenian youth. In the present section, Nietzsche pictures the Platonic Socrates as a riddle to be guessed at, and in the next section he makes his own guess at "the person of Socrates," Socrates without Plato in front and back, Socrates as a Homeric monster.

Section 191 The break between the two sections on Socratism and Platonism permits Nietzsche to do what he frequently does: approach the same thought from a new perspective, far afield from the core already opened. "The

---

7. Leo Strauss makes matters clear with regard to Platonism without spelling everything out: with regard to deadly truth "Nietzsche could choose one of two ways: he could insist on the strictly esoteric character of the theoretical analysis of life — that is, restore the Platonic notion of the noble delusion — or else he could deny the possibility of theory proper and so conceive of thought as essentially subservient to, or dependent on, life or fate" (*Natural Right and History* 25–26). Strauss says only what Nietzsche's "successors" chose: the second option. Strauss chose not to spell out the fact that he himself chose to restore Platonism or what he chose to call Platonic political philosophy, in part the necessity of salutary lying. Strauss recognized that Nietzsche chose neither the noble delusion nor sophism but instead a third possibility, the dangerous way of openly questioning the value of truth in order to test its alleged deadliness and ultimately to conduct the experiment of making its deadliness livable.

old theological problem of 'faith' and 'reason,'" a problem that has long seemed a Christian problem, is actually a moral problem that appeared first in "the person of Socrates" and divided "the intellectual world long before the rise of Christianity," divided it along the line drawn by the Platonic strategy for philosophy, placing on one side those who followed "Socrates and his disease of moralizing," and on the other those who carried forward "the height attained in the disposition of a Democritus, Hippocrates, and Thucydides [which] was not attained a second time" (*KSA* 11.36 [11]), but to which Epicurus was heir and which grew victorious: "Every respectable mind in the Roman Empire was an Epicurean" (*A* 58). To understand the moral issue that now seems theological and Christian, it is necessary to peer into its historical roots in philosophy and into the debates in Greece and Rome about the politics of philosophy.[8]

The old theological problem of faith and knowledge is "more clearly" the problem "of instinct and reason — therefore the problem whether, with regard to the evaluation of the worth of things, instinct deserves more authority than rationality, which wants to know how to evaluate and to behave according to reasons [or grounds, *Gründe*], according to a 'Why?', according to usefulness and utility." How did Socrates himself stand toward this great issue of instinct and reason? In keeping with "the taste of his talent — that of a superior dialectician," Socrates' stance was nuanced and included a *zunächst* and a *zuletzt*. These two terms seem to be used here not in their more usual temporal sense of *at first* and *finally* but in the less usual, *apparently* and *ultimately,* for Nietzsche is not charting Socrates' intellectual biography from at first to finally — he even says that what Socrates did *zunächst* he did "his life long." Instead, Nietzsche indicates that Socrates gave an open appearance that protected a hidden reality the great dialectician kept "in silence and secret." Apparently, and his whole life long, Socrates sided with reason, laughing "at the clumsy inability of his noble Athenians, who were humans of instinct like all noble humans and could never give an adequate account of the reasons for their behavior." Ultimately, however, in silence and secret, Socrates laughed at himself too because "his refined conscience and self-interrogation" enabled him to find the same difficulty and inability in himself. Socrates was an exception among the Greek philosophical exceptions, the first philosopher to suspend

8. Nietzsche's anti-Platonism reevaluates the sophists but does not place Protagoras or Gorgias or Hippias at the peak: In Thucydides "the *culture of the sophists,* which means the *culture of realists,* reaches its perfect expression: this invaluable movement in the midst of the Socratic schools' moralistic and idealistic swindle that was breaking out on every side" (*TI* Ancients 2).

his solitude in order to study the average man and the average man in himself (26). Socrates, examining himself and others, learned the difference between himself and others, learned the necessity of esotericism. The Socratism set forth in the previous section is no more to be identified with Socrates' true views than Platonism is with Plato's.

"But for what end, he encouraged himself, detach oneself therefore from the instincts!" For no end at all: Socrates' insight into the limits of reason in himself and others allowed him to see that reason is no ground for detaching oneself from the instincts; he saw that his own reasoning was in the service of his own instincts. Lacking an end for detaching oneself from the instincts, Socrates made a place for both: "One must help provide justification" for both instincts and reason, "one must follow the instincts but persuade the reason to assist them therein with good grounds." This conclusion regarding Socrates' way to Socratism leads Nietzsche to an additional conclusion: "This was the real *falseness* of that great, secret-rich ironic" — Socrates did not own up to his insight into himself; he permitted the false impression to be drawn that he gave reason primacy over instinct. Socrates "brought his conscience" — a subtle conscience — "to the point of giving itself to be satisfied with a kind of self-trickery: at bottom [*im Grunde*] he had seen through to the irrational in moral judgment." Socrates did not fool himself, he fooled others about himself; his was the falseness of a great esoteric, an ironist who sheltered his view from above by hiding it in a view from below. The Chimaira that the Platonic infinite and impossible sheltered was an esoteric thinker who had penetrated the irrational in moral judgment and brought his conscience around to the point of enduring a lie, *giving* itself as satisfied with self-trickery, acting as if he didn't know what he in fact knew, as if he supposed that reason ruled the instincts. The rational tradition in Western morality traces itself back to Socrates, back to a great ironist who had no faith in opposite values, in the opposite origins of reason and instinct, an ironist who knew that the moral lacked rational grounds but who found reasons to act as if it had rational grounds.[9]

9. For reason as the instinctual in Socrates, see Nietzsche's view of Socrates' *daimonion* in BT 13. Nietzsche's early reflection on Socrates states that "the Platonic dialogues do not permit us to view [Socrates] solely as a negative force" (*BT* 14). The positive is the impassioned scientific pursuit of knowledge, albeit under the delusion that science can fully understand being and even correct it (15); such a pursuit warded off practical pessimism, acted as a goad to life, and inspired noble youth. In addition to these positive matters, Nietzsche suggested the possibility of an advance on Socrates, an "artistic Socrates," a "music-making Socrates" (15, 17), who would combine Socrates' instinctive dialectical power with what he most notably lacked, music or the Dionysian. In the

Having treated the Socratic turn as the willingness to endure the moral lie,[10] Nietzsche moves abruptly to Plato, a dash introducing the single sinuous sentence that sets out Plato's fateful extension of the Socratic turn. Plato, the most beautiful growth of antiquity, possessed "the greatest strength that a philosopher till now has had to expend!" Plato, the noble young Athenian, interpreted Socrates' falseness with the greatest rashness, transforming it into something refined. Plato's interpretation of the Socratic turn created that monster the Platonic Socrates; this great event in the natural history of morality transformed Greek religion and unknowingly prepared the way for Christianity (49).

"—Plato, in such things more innocent and without the craftiness of the plebeian, wanted with the expenditure of all his strength . . . to prove to himself that reason and instinct of themselves tend toward One Goal, toward the Good, toward 'God.'" Reason and instinct invented the "worst, most durable, most dangerous of all errors" and set "all theologians and philosophers on the same track," creating the dogmatism that ruled European thought. The conclusion of Nietzsche's sentence is an arresting statement about the rationalist tradition in Western morality: "That means, in matters of morality till now, instinct, or as the Christians name it, 'faith,' or as I name it, 'the herd,' has triumphed." Instinct prevailed in the rational tradition of morality. Nietzsche of course is an advocate of the primacy of instinct over reason, over intention as he earlier argued (32)—"reason is merely an instrument," he says at the end of this section. But the instincts that came to triumph through Platonism are the instincts of the "herd"—only one kind of instinct; the typology of morality that this and subsequent chapters develop isolates two types of morality based on two types of instinct, two ways in which the essence of the world, will to power, expresses itself in what is primary in humans. Just what the triumph of base instincts means historically forms the culminating argument of this chapter, an argument anticipated here by Nietzsche's use of one of its central terms, *herd*: the Socratic turn ultimately made possible the modern "autonomy of the herd" (202), the condition that makes necessary a new turn, the turn to the rule of the philosophers of the future (203). The Socratic turn necessitates the Nietzschean turn, each being a

---

preface added to the 1886 second edition of *BT* Nietzsche asked, "I wonder if the reader understands what task I was already daring to undertake with this book" (6); he does not identify that task but it is presumably the advance on Socrates that Nietzsche assigned to Zarathustra, his own task, mistakenly assigned to Wagner in *BT*.

   10. See Plato, *Republic* 7.537e-40a, on the need for philosophers to endure the moral lie.

philosophical turn to the human and eventually to a politics on behalf of philosophy. The observer of the natural history of morality is forced by what he observes to take part and fight.

Nietzsche's natural history of morality, his consideration of the fate of the instincts in the still-incomplete history of the human animal, carries out what the preface hinted at: it puts Socrates on trial again. Did Socrates deserve his hemlock? Looking back from the depth of the modern, judging on ultimate consequences, Nietzsche implies that Socrates did deserve his hemlock, not for the corruption of the many Pheidippideses, as Aristophanes argued, not even for the corruption of the few Critiases or Alcibiadeses, as Athens believed in convicting him, but for the corruption of Plato, the rash defender of Socrates whose defense prepared the way for the triumph of base instincts over noble instincts by putting reason at *their* disposal.[11]

Did Nietzsche understand Plato adequately? He understood that Plato wrote esoterically and that Platonism was an instrument of philosophical rule, but did he fully plumb the "seclusion and Sphinx-nature" (28) of that "monster of pride and sovereignty" (*GS* 351)? He absolved Plato of revenge, the moral motive of the indignant, and discerned a philanthropic impetus to his claim to possess wisdom (*GS* 359). Still, Nietzsche's judgment against Plato for inventing Platonism is marked by two condemnations. The first is Nietzsche's judgment as a historian. Plutarch judged that Plato's Platonism saved Greek science and philosophy from the persecution of the superstitious,[12] but Nietzsche judges the cure worse than the disorder, suggesting that the moralism of the Socratics was a strategy for philosophy less desirable than that of Democritus, Epicurus, or Lucretius. Second is Nietzsche's judgment as a physician: Platonism seems to testify to a sickness in its inventor because of its antitruth, antilife character (preface). But this suggestion seems definitively countered by a remarkable statement composed a few months later that has the appearance of the physician's final diagnosis: summarizing his critique of idealism Nietzsche says, "All idealism to date was something like a sickness, unless it was, as it was in Plato's case, the caution of an overrich and dangerous health, the fear of *overpowerful* senses, the prudence of a prudent Socratic" (*GS* 372). Caution, not of sickness but of a very special health, lay behind Plato's idealism, "the great health" on which Nietzsche ends his book a few sections later (*GS* 382). Fear, but not a fear that his own senses would overpower his judgment, lay behind Plato's idealism: the section opened referring to Odysseus's act of stopping the ears of his friends to spare them the irresist-

11. See "The Problem of Socrates," *TI.*
12. See "The Life of Nicias" 23.5.

ible temptation of the Sirens' song, a temptation to which Odysseus kept his own ears open while having himself tied to the mast. Finally, Plato's idealism is the *Klugheit,* the prudence and cleverness, of a Socratic, a superprudence that wrapped the already prudent Socrates in a still more sheltering riddle.

Plato can be absolved of revenge, but he cannot be absolved of being rash in employing the disease of moralism as an antidote, and he cannot be absolved of being too successful. His rash strategy for defending philosophy by tying it to the infinite and impossible has now put philosophy itself at risk. Rash Plato leads to rash Nietzsche: he says out loud that the gods too philosophize. But if the gods quarrel, Nietzsche seems to judge that it serves his end in the quarrel to make that fact available again: wisdom is served by having the Greek quarrel of the wise become more visible.

Lying and Dreaming
SECTIONS 192–93

The two sections on the role of Socrates and Plato in the natural history of our morality lead to two sections on more general lessons learned from that science, arresting lessons about lying and dreaming that seem to reflect back on Socratism and Platonism.

Section 192   The science of the natural history of morality allows one to bring morality to a vast domain of human awareness where it has been lacking: "all 'knowledge and cognition.' " It can do so because this science, like the history of any science, provides a "clue for understanding the oldest and most common processes" of knowledge. In those processes, a *"lack of mistrust"* is present earliest when the senses are most directly under the influence of the affects; impressions formed under that lack of mistrust exercise continuing force, conditioning all later perception.[13] The natural history of morality therefore counsels a new morality of mistrust in which mistrust is unnatural because the very senses have been naturally trusting and inventive instruments prone to transform everything perceived into the already familiar.[14] Any novel

---

13. The consequences of this lack of mistrust for mature rationality were well known to Descartes; see *Discourse on the Method,* Discourse 2, end of first paragraph.

14. The philosopher's "duty to suspicion," which civil life measures as imprudent and as a "sign of 'bad character' " (34), thus receives an additional rationale from the history of morality. Graham Parkes inserts section 192 into his extended analysis of "The Fabric(ation) of Experience" as set out in *Dawn of Day* and in unpublished notes from 1881. The result is an illuminating account of Nietzsche's view of "the contribution of phantasy to the constitution of experience" (*Composing the Soul* 301, see 289–305).

view must contend with this natural conservatism built into the senses; it requires "more strength, more 'morality' " than the views it contests.

The new morality of mistrust draws a general conclusion from its understanding of the inertial power of the familiar: "We are from the ground up, from time immemorial — *accustomed to lying.*" This conclusion of the new morality may sound immoral, so Nietzsche restates it more virtuously: "One is much more an artist than one knows." Such lying, such artistry, covers a far broader expanse than the conscious lying Socrates and Plato permitted themselves on behalf of the moral decency of the multitude. The morality of science, its subtlety, mistrust, and patience, brings morality to the received moralities whose lying, artful basis in all perception and cognition it comes to understand.

Section 193   The remnants of early sensations are not the only cognitions that help condition conscious experience: so too do dreams. What is experienced in habitual dreams, Nietzsche claims, "spoon feeds" the wakeful mind even in its brightest moments, giving it its sense of happiness and what to aspire to. This general claim is augmented by an example that elaborates it and helps make it persuasive: the dream experience of flying colors the waking sense of happiness or what is found fulfilling.[15] Perhaps this example must be viewed as part of the general argument of the context, the primacy of the historically formed unconscious over a merely instrumental reason, and perhaps even as part of the particular focus of the context, the turn in the natural history of morality effected by the rationalism of Socrates and Plato. Platonism's dream of happiness in *Aufschwung,* in uplift, in transcendence of the earthly and mortal, colored all of waking life, imprisoning reason in a dream of reason's supposed transcendence and capacity to apprehend the transcendent, "the pure mind and the good in itself," the dream from which we are only now awakening. What happens in the dark goes on in the light: Nietzsche counters the Platonic dream with a different dream. Out of the dark, out of dreaming, out of the stupidity of healthy instincts arises a new waking experience with the most acute reasoning attendant to it, day wisdom in defense of deeper night wisdom, in the image from *Zarathustra* (Z 3 "On the Three Evils").

15. The published version alters the final version in the notebooks in one significant way: the impersonal "someone" replaces "I," leaving it to inference that the experience is Nietzsche's own (*KSA 14 Kommentar,* pp. 358–59). Flying, breaking free of gravity, is a primary image in *Zarathustra,* basic to Zarathustra's contest with his devil and arch-enemy, the spirit of gravity.

Love and the Instinct to Possess: *The Origins of Our Morality*
SECTIONS 194–95

"From which it follows. . . . ." Following these last words of section 194 is section 195: Nietzsche placed at the center of his central chapter a pair of sections linked by a line of reasoning. That reasoning forms a most appropriate center to *Beyond Good and Evil* because it suggests a quiet inference left up to us, a move from a meditation on love (194) to a decisive event in the natural history of good and evil (195): in a world whose essence is will to power (186), an understanding of human passion leads to a reasonable interpretation of our accidental past and prepares, perhaps, the necessary means for taking in hand the future of humanity (203). Nietzsche's typology of morality aims to exhibit the fundamental differences among human beings, and here (194) he turns to something that exhibits that difference even more than do the thousand tablets of good and evil that humans have produced: the difference displayed by what humans count as really having or possessing a good. Nietzsche's phenomenology of having develops a theme central to a view that takes the essence of the world to be will to power: how human will to power expresses itself in the fundamental relations of possession. The final example, parents possessing their children, ends with the words, "From which it follows. . . . . ," and the next section begins with "The Jews"—the Jews founded "the slave revolt in morality," and their way of possessing their children in strict loyalty to the way of the fathers enabled them to carry forward that "inversion" of good and evil. At the center of the chapter on the natural history of morality, having already dealt with the crucial event in philosophy that led to the moral present (190–91), Nietzsche deals with the corresponding event in religion.

Section 194   In a speech setting out a chief argument of his teaching, Zarathustra emphasized the importance of the thousand tablets of good and evil: their variety helps one understand the differences among human beings and what lies behind those differences (Z 1 "On the thousand goals and one"). Here, after restating the importance of those tablets, Nietzsche claims that the difference among human beings is shown "even more" in what counts "as really *having* and *possessing* a good." Here is a basic matter in the natural history of morality, a psychology of possession or how the will to power expresses itself in basic human relationships. Nietzsche gives four examples of what it means to possess, examples with four different objects of possession— a woman, a people, recipients of help, and children. The four examples deal with four kinds of love, though Nietzsche uses that word only in the first example.

In all four examples Nietzsche speaks only of the perspective of the possessor. But his treatment is fragmentary in another respect as well, for it grows
less complete as it moves from the first example to the fourth: the first gives
three different kinds of possession, the second only two, and the third and
fourth only one. The kinds of possession described in the first cases involve
refinements in knowledge on the part of the possessor or lover, refinements in
the desire to know or to be known. It is odd in a section whose chief point is
the different ways of possessing a good that instead of indicating different
ways for the final two examples, only the crasser or more ignorant form of
possession is discussed. But the section ends, "From which it follows. . . . ." —
the final words and ellipse seem to invite the reader schooled in the refinements of the first two examples to supply them for the third and fourth.
Those refinements in knowledge and self-knowledge applied to philanthropic
love and parental love touch some of Nietzsche's central and most delicate
thoughts, shy thoughts left to the reader to entertain.

With respect to a man's possession of a woman, Nietzsche describes three
kinds of "thirst in possession," beginning with "more modest" men content
with the use of the body and sexual favors as the sign of possession. A more
suspicious and demanding thirst to possess requires not only that the woman
give herself, "but also that for him she leave what she has or would like to
have." But "mistrust and *Habenwollen* [wanting to have]" turn in a different
direction in the third and most demanding kind, which requires abandoning
any misconstrual of what he is; such love requires that the beloved know the
lover "fundamentally, even abysmally [*gründlich, ja abgründlich*]"; the lover
"risks letting himself be fathomed," "risks allowing the riddle of himself to be
guessed." What really counts as having or possessing in this case depends upon
knowledge and self-knowledge, on being loved "as much for his devilry and
hidden insatiability as for his goodness, patience, and spiritedness." This is a
fragment of the great mystery of male and female love that Nietzsche often
placed at the center of his reflections on nature. That it is only a fragment — if a
key fragment — is evident from the central section of book 5 of *The Gay
Science* (363), composed a few months later. Male love, *Habenwollen,* is more
fully analyzed there as a problem because it lacks what Nietzsche found characteristic of female love, loyalty to the beloved; the problem of male love is
that it comes to an end with the possession of what it pursued, it lets the
beloved fall when it thinks there is nothing new to possess. There too, however, Nietzsche speaks of a "more refined and more suspicious thirst for possession," presenting it as the solution to the problem of male love. In *Zarathustra* the fragments of male and female love had been presented in their

unity; the question of fathomability and "hidden insatiability" had been dealt with as the solution to love's continuance, and the connections between will to power, possession, and male and female love given full poetic display.[16] *Beyond Good and Evil* puts the issue of male and female at the center of the central chapter and relates it to the chief theme of the chapter, an account of the natural history of morality that isolates the principal historical shifts in the history of morality and their grounds in the essence of the world.[17]

Nietzsche's second example deals with a ruler's possession of a people, and the difference he draws between two types of ruler employs the same scale of refinement in the "thirst for possession" as the first example. It omits the crasser sorts of physical rule and begins with the "higher Cagliostro- and Catiline-arts" — arts of rule pleased to employ all manner of deception in the interests of rule — and moves to an art of rule irritated by deception, by ruling from behind a mask, seeking instead to rule through knowledge of what it is. This requires of the ruler that "I first know myself!" Rule based on self-knowledge seems to be philosophic rule, wise rule based on an understanding of the human.

The first two examples suggest that the desire for self-knowledge turns possession into something given voluntarily as choiceworthy for itself. The final two examples say nothing about such maturity in possession; they lack the scale of refinement displayed in the first two examples. The third example concerns "helpful and charitable people." "The bestowing virtue" is the name Zarathustra at first chose to describe what was most his own (Z 1 "On the Bestowing Virtue"), but he later retracted that name and replaced it with "lust to rule" (Z 3 "On the Three Evils"), a name that serves to link the second and third examples of possession or love in this section. The example of the philanthropic remains at an unrefined level on the part of the bestower who is ignorant of the drive for possession in his apparent philanthropy.

The final example too remains at this crasser level: parental possession of children, in which parents "involuntarily make out of the child something similar to themselves." "From which it follows. . . . ." that a more refined parental desire for possession of their offspring would result in voluntariness or self-knowledge and the desire to be known: higher forms of parental love would learn to let go or let be; they would learn to allow the child to become

16. See especially the dance songs of parts 2 and 3 and the chapters surrounding them. See also Lampert, *Nietzsche and Modern Times* 376–87.

17. Nietzsche placed further reflections on male and female at the end of "Our Virtues" (231–39).

what it is, to alter and flower as itself. And such letting go could itself result in a more successful possession, dictated by the sentiment of gratitude in the beloved permitted by love to become itself.

In a world whose essence is will to power, love, rule, bestowing, and raising offspring are all understandable as forms of possession that may be less or more refined, refinement consisting of self-knowledge and the desire to be known as what one is by what one possesses. The fundamental human relationships can be transfigured through such refinement without contradicting their impetus and source in will to power and without fictionalizing the source through the invention of opposite values or supposedly non-will-to-power sources. The natural history of morality identifies these fundamental processes present in human relationships in both their basis and their transfiguration in order to gain a more adequate perspective on human history. The next section points to a major turning point in the natural history of morality, and the verbal link between "From which it follows . . . . ." and "The Jews" indicates a conceptual link between the parental example and the people defined by loyalty to the fathers and forefathers. The lowest form of parental possession, involuntary demand dictating involuntary adherence, is a kind of slavery, to use the word Nietzsche borrows from Tacitus.[18]

Section 195   Nietzsche stands with Tacitus and the whole of the ancient world in judging the Jews to be "a people 'born to slavery,' " the roots of that slavery being found in the parental instinct to possess their children by making them like themselves. But Nietzsche is a late ancient who views the history of the Jews from the perspective of late-modern times, a privileged perspective opening up for inspection a longer stretch of the natural history of morality. From that perspective, "the significance of the Jewish people" is that "with them begins the *slave revolt in morality*," a revolt that can now be seen to have been faithfully advanced by Christianity (*GM* 1.7) and the French Revolution (46). The center of chapter 5 thus deals with the psychological and historical origins of what is now becoming global; modern morality finds its psychological origins in an unsophisticated form of possession and its historical origins in slave morality. "Ni dieu ni maître" is the outcome of a circuitous but calculable route beginning with subjection to God the Father.

Nietzsche expresses gratitude for the *Umkehrung*, the transposing or rever-

---

18. The five-period ellipse that ends this section is also used in this chapter to end section 202, where it clearly ties 202 to 203. Nietzsche used such an ellipse frequently as terminal punctuation: preface, 3, 11, 87, 108, 172, 205, 214, 239, 252, 271, 292; he used a terminal four-period ellipse at 62, 211, 213, 227, 230, 277, 278; and a terminal three-period ellipse at 236, 245, 295.

sal in values, successfully brought to pass by the Jews: "Thanks to it life on earth received a new and dangerous attraction for a couple of millennia." Nietzsche's own *Umwertung aller Werte*, the transvaluation of all values, aims to bring to pass a similarly monumental shift; in moving beyond good and evil it in part restores the good and bad that the slave revolt in morality eclipsed, a morality of nobility, and it implies an advance to a more refined form of possession based on self-knowledge.[19]

The Inferential Science of Morality Applied to the Morality of Fearfulness
SECTIONS 196–98

Section 196 The second half of chapter 5 probes the grounds of the prevailing morality, a "morality of fearfulness." At its head stands a parable on the method to be employed, an inferential method of moving from the seen to the unseeable. The parable likens the new science of the soul to the science of astronomy; its phenomena have trajectories less certain than those of stars and comets, but it claims the status of a science whose inferences can be tested. It is the science that studies the fundamental phenomenon as articulated in human moral values, the risky science promised at the end of chapter 1, psychology as the doctrine of the evolution of the will to power (23). The "psychologist of morality" will infer the presence of many "dark bodies" obscured by the light of the sun or ideal. Though "we will never see them" these dark realities can be identified by an astronomy of the soul as the most powerful forces affecting what is held high or valued. But because "the whole starscript" of moral ideals is a "sign language of the affects" that has permitted much to remain in silence, a proper physio-psychology brings to speech the unspoken or unspeakable reality behind the ideals and identifies it as the morality natural to a certain type of human.

Section 197 Following his parable on inference, Nietzsche infers the invisible reasons behind the judgment made by "almost all moralists" against a special class of human beings, *Raubmenschen*, a play on *Raubtier*, "predatory animal" or "beast of prey." His inference opens the way into the chief theme of the second half of chapter 5: nature generates in our species rare individuals who depart from the norm and are treated by our dominant morality with suspicion. What can be inferred about the reasons for this suspicion? The present section suggests an answer that is expanded in the following section

---

19. *GM* 1.7–10 refers back to this section of *BGE* and expands its historical claim, noting that "we no longer see" the slave revolt in morality "because it has been successful" (7).

and whose consequences are traced in the sections following that until finally chapter 5 ends by indicating how these rare cases can be treated differently by a philosophy of the future.

At issue is nothing less than a proper understanding of human nature. Almost all moralists till now have interpreted the most healthy either as sick or as suffering some inner torment. Why though? What moved almost all moralists to misinterpret what moved the rare growths? Nietzsche's answer keeps to the metaphor of global geography that enlivens this section: "For the benefit of the 'moderate zones'? For the benefit of the moderate humans? The 'moral'? The mediocre?" This inferred dark body—the highest were cast into suspicion in order to spare the moral and mediocre—contributes to "the chapter 'Morality as Fearfulness.'" How? It suggests (and the next section makes this clearer) that moralists led by Plato have not feared for themselves but feared for the moderate and moral and out of prudence aligned moral philosophy with their common and natural fear of the exceptional growths. Where has this prudence landed us? The rest of the chapter will outline that. What is to be done? The chapter will end on that.

Nietzsche's example of a *Raubmensch* is Cesare Borgia. Placed so prominently at the opening of Nietzsche's consideration of morality as fearfulness, this fearful example seems to flaunt Nietzsche's own lack of fear and his willingness to encourage fear and hate of himself. This attitude aligns him with the philosopher responsible for making Cesare Borgia prominent, Machiavelli, an exception to almost all moralists in not aligning himself with the common fear and hatred of the Raubmenschen, a philosopher who dared to court the label "teacher" of evil. But Cesare Borgia is no more the outstanding example for Nietzsche than he was for Machiavelli, who showed him to be a tool of his father, each being tools of Machiavelli—Nietzsche's list of examples will move up to Alcibiades and Caesar (200), themselves ambiguous lions in the midst of their cultures, and peak with the new philosophers, "there is no choice" (203).[20] This section also begins to display Nietzsche's agreement with Machiavelli on the basic matter developed in the second half of chapter 5: there are, Machiavelli said, "two diverse humors to be found in every city," "two diverse appetites," and they are exhibited in turn in "the people" and in "the great," the ruled and the ruler: "The people desire neither to be commanded nor oppressed by the great, and the great desire to command and oppress the people."[21] For Nietzsche as for Machiavelli, the greatest among

20. On Cesare Borgia, see *TI* Skirmishes 37 and *A* 61.
21. *The Prince*, chap. 9.

the great must know how to use the two humors, and, it seems, such use entails acquiring the reputation for being a teacher of evil.

Section 198   The second contribution to the chapter "Morality as Fearfulness," section 198 is a page-long single sentence that achieves its rhetorical peak at its center before moving to the five examples that illustrate its central claim. "All these moralities" advocated by "almost all moralists so far" (197) address the individual person as an inhabitant of "the temperate zones," (197) promising him "happiness, as it's called." What can be inferred about these moralities is that they are "counsels for behavior in relation to the degree of *dangerousness* in which the individual person lives with himself." "These recipes against [the] passions" aim to temper the passions "so far as they have the will to power and would like to play the master" — they presume to administer a cure to the essence of the world (187) as it expresses itself in the human animal. The dark body inferred beside all these moralities is fear in the temperate classes of nature itself.

The section is partly a critique of unconditional generalizing in morality, and it indulges in its own unconditional generalizing in summarizing all these moralities, repeatedly beginning its thoughts with "all these moralities." All of them are unreasonable because "they generalize where generalizing may not be done" — not all humans fall into the temperate zones, living for the sake of what is called happiness. All of them speak unconditionally and take themselves unconditionally — all belong in pathology (154) as symptoms of immaturity, failure to make the greatest gain of life, the art of nuance (31). All of this is, "measured intellectually, of little worth and not by a long shot 'science,' to say nothing of 'wisdom.'" If neither scientific nor wise, what have all the prevailing moralities been? — "All of that is, to say it once more and to say it three times more, prudence, prudence, prudence mixed with stupidity, stupidity, stupidity." Plato's strategy for philosophy mixed sophisticated prudence with popular stupidity and called itself the safe way on Socrates' dying day (*Phaedo* 100d-e). But excessive prudence in the name of safety proved a rash miscalculation because it led to universal generalizations about our species that now threaten the very possibility of rare growths.

The Timid Morality of Herd Animals
SECTIONS 199–201

Section 199   Section 199 contributes to a typology of morality by beginning the demonstration of why one of the only two possible types has come to predominate in Europe and why action must consequently be taken on behalf of the other type, the rare tropical growths of section 197. The reason is found in the natural history of the human species, more particularly in the specieswide development of conscience. Nietzsche sets out that history in a series of brief conclusions he will later expand into the second treatise of *On the Genealogy of Morality*. Throughout human prehistory and history, the obeying many far outnumbered the commanding few; obedience was therefore practiced and nurtured best and longest; therefore, "one may fairly assume that on the average now in everyone the need [for obedience] is inborn as a kind of *formal conscience*." That conscience commands, "Thou shalt unconditionally do something or other, unconditionally permit something or other," content being provided for this merely formal commandment by some parent-like entity. "The strange limitedness of human development" can be accounted for by the fact that "the herd instinct of obedience" is inherited at the cost of "the art of commanding."

That look backward into causes prepares a look into their present consequences and into the future of a species with this tendency to obedience. "The commanders and independent ones" will either be entirely lacking or fall prey to the inner sickness of a bad conscience that they must trick into conformity in order to command at all. The obeying many will take themselves to be "the sole permitted kind of human being" whose properties are "the real human virtues," and Nietzsche lists eight virtues, ending with compassion. The unconditional demands of conscience presage the unconditional victory of the obedient. This section thus prepares the final major argument of chapter 5: the future sway of the autonomous herd lays the grounds that make reasonable the turn to the rule of the philosophers of the future.

Section 200   Placed between two sections that speak at length of the human herd and the morality of fearfulness, section 200 emphasizes the exceptions. Nietzsche argues that the ground for a morality of fearfulness is especially fertile during "ages of dissolution," late cultures like the culture of modern times in which the inheritances of many races are mixed. But the main point of the section seems to come in its second half: times of dissolution also prove fertile for the appearance of great exceptions whose morality differs from that of the average, the other moral type.[22] The makeup of the exceptions is precisely described, beginning with what seems basic, "the opposition and war in such a nature works like one life-charm and life-thrill *more*." Such an affirmative, warlike nature may find "opposed to its powerful and irreconcilable drives, a real mastery and refinement in making war with oneself, or self-

---

22. Section 200 thus repeats the structure of section 199, which ended with the appearance of Napoleon, the exceptional commander in an age of the obedient.

mastery and self-trickery" — warlikeness turned inward and commanding mastery over its powerful drives. Such qualities of self-command in times of dissolution can lead to the appearance of "those riddlesome human beings predisposed to victory and to seduction, whose most beautiful expression is Alcibiades and Caesar." These restless, warloving exceptions are unlike the majority in not taking rest or peace to be ultimate either in themselves or in their times. Their passion for victory and their powers of seduction combine to move their troubled times to exploits that seem contrary to the disposition of the great majority. Because Nietzsche also lists among such exceptions the Hohenstaufen German emperor Friedrich the Second and Leonardo da Vinci, he seems to indicate that the two separate periods of renaissance in the Christian West were also times that generated such contrasting types.

Leo Strauss comments acutely on placing Alcibiades alongside Caesar: Nietzsche "could not have shown his freedom from the herd morality more tellingly than by mentioning in one breath Caesar and Alcibiades. Caesar could be said to have performed a great, historic function for Rome and have dedicated himself to that function — to have been, as it were, a functionary of Roman history, but for Alcibiades Athens was no more than the pedestal, exchangeable if need be with Sparta or Persia, for his own glory or greatness."[23] Nietzsche's freedom separates him from almost all moralists who prudently saw to the well-being of the great majority. Nietzsche looks instead to the well-being of the few Alcibiadeses and Caesars.

Alcibiades is the most flamboyant figure in Thucydides, his anti-Periclean strategy setting Athens on a renewed course of imperial conquest that Thucydides makes his reader believe could have succeeded had Alcibiades been granted freedom to lead it.[24] Alcibiades is also a major figure in Plato's dialogues: no one except Socrates is named more often. Plato's Socrates, expert in erotic matters, is shown pursuing no one more ardently than Alcibiades — Socrates can tell Callicles that he has two loves, "philosophy and Alcibiades, son of Clinias" (*Gorgias* 481d). Plato shows Socrates pursuing Alcibiades just before he began his political career (*Protagoras, Alcibiades I, II*), and he allows Alcibiades himself to say why Socrates failed to win him (*Symposium*). Plato also makes it apparent that behind the trial and execution of Socrates lay the Athenian suspicion that Socrates corrupted Alcibiades, and he makes

23. *Studies in Platonic Political Philosophy* 184.

24. In an earlier draft of this section Nietzsche referred to one of the ages of dissolution as "the Athens of Pericles" and did not mention Alcibiades by name; by naming Alcibiades, the final version assumes that his love of victory and his capacity for seduction enabled him to succeed in an age in which the vast majority sought only rest.

every effort to refute that suspicion. Nietzsche raises the suspicion that Socrates corrupted not the beautiful Alcibiades but "the most beautiful growth of antiquity," Plato himself. In this chapter, Nietzsche has argued that Socrates' corruption led Plato to make the prudent compromises with stupidity that contributed to the eventual autonomy of the herd. He has thus gradually made it clear why the errors of the corrupted Plato mentioned in the preface can be said to be "the worst, most durable, and most dangerous of all errors": encouraging the tendency to seek rest already present in the great majority, Plato's dogmatism contributed powerfully to a universalizing morality that threatens the appearance of any other type of human being besides the restful average.

Socrates' corruption of Plato and his failure with corrupt Alcibiades suggest the aspirations of the corrupter Nietzsche. A turbulent exception arising in an age of more serious dissolution than any other, charmed by life to war rather than peace, and trained to self-mastery by his warlike, commanding nature, Nietzsche aims to corrupt all philosophers of the future and put them on the same track, a track that recognizes that the essence of the world is will to power. Nietzsche therefore refuses to compromise with stupidity for the sake of the great majority and sides instead with the few Alcibiadeses, giving heart to the restless rather than to those in need of rest. "What shall we do about Alcibiades?" asks Dionysos in Aristophanes' *Frogs.* Aeschylus, who wins the prize for wise counsel, answers, "It is best not to rear a lion in the city. But if one is reared, the city must submit to its ways." Nietzsche disagrees with the first part of Aeschylus's counsel: it is now necessary and desirable to raise the lions in our midst; but he agrees with the second part.

Section 201   Nietzsche summarizes in section 201 the conclusions of his natural history of fearfulness, tracing the conditions of its rise and dominance and outlining its threat of ultimate success in contemporary Europe. In Nietzsche's account, fearfulness created moral values in two great stages. First, human communities had to achieve a level of settled security over against their neighbors, who were always their enemies. The first stage was therefore based on "fear of the neighbor" and dictated a morality of doing good to friends or community members and harm to enemies or neighbors. The characteristic practices basic to "neighbor love" that would later be baptized virtues were all present — "considerateness, compassion, fairness, mildness, reciprocity of assistance" — but they were all still "extramoral." Nietzsche's example for this stage comes from "the best period of the Romans," the period prior to Christianity; compassion was practiced but not as a virtue, and it ranked lower than what did count as virtue, action that "served the well-being of the whole," the whole of Rome. What had to be cultivated under these conditions and esteemed as virtue included "passion for adventure, foolhardiness, vengefulness, craftiness, rapacity, and the lust to rule," matters which then bore more favorable labels. Indispensable to a community fearing external danger, these traits were cultivated in the exceptions rich in these "virtues," allowing them to flourish in a setting that needed their exceptionalness.

In the second stage, under more settled conditions, "the opposite drives and inclinations receive moral honors." "Fear once again becomes the mother of morality" but a very different fear, fear of the exceptions themselves, who had once been needed and hence praised and nurtured. No longer necessary, the exceptions no longer needed to be tolerated. "High, independent spirituality, the will to stand alone, even powerful rationality are now experienced as a danger"; the drives that move the exceptions "are branded as immoral and abandoned to slander," especially the slander of being evil. As Nietzsche describes this trajectory of society, peaceful conditions are finally reached under which all forms of severity, including severity in justice, begin to disturb the conscience. The penultimate step in the morality of fearfulness is a fear of punishment. The final step would be taken if all danger, all basis for fear, could be abolished; then the morality of fearfulness would have abolished itself, for "whoever reaches his ideal transcends it by reaching it" (73).

Nietzsche's final sentences apply this result to modern Europe: "Whoever tests the conscience of modern Europe" will discover the imperative of "herd fearfulness": "We want that at some time or other there be nothing *more to fear!*" "Some time or other — the will and way *to that point* is everywhere in Europe today called 'Progress.'" This genealogy of fearfulness sets the task for the student of conscience: the advocate of the exceptions, of the only other moral type, must become the advocate of severity; against the morals of our climate Nietzsche must become a teacher of evil. Equipped with a new conscience for the whole future of humanity, he is driven to the actions set out in the final two sections of this chapter.

Two Faiths
SECTIONS 202–03

"Let's say it again immediately, what we've already said a hundred times, because ears today are not well disposed to such truths — to *our* truths" (202). "May I say this out loud, you free minds?" (203). The final two sections of chapter 5, numbers 202 and 203, emphasize the almost unspeakable character of what they have to say and they give the reason why it's almost unspeakable: we're immersed in a uniform moral dogmatism, and any view from outside is bound to be misheard and bound to wound. That moral dogmatism persuades us that we're wiser than Socrates (202): we know with certainty what Socrates knew he did not know, "what good and evil is." Knowing he did not know it, "that famous old serpent promised to teach it." Nietzsche thus makes clear that Socrates veiled his knowledge of his ignorance, practicing the standard philosophic esotericism. Opening with these references to the unspeakable and to Socrates' veiled speech, these two sections advertise their rashness, their refusal of the esoteric caution of past philosophers. They say for the hundredth time what we're insulted to hear — that we're an animal species at a plottable point in an evolutionary trajectory. And they ask permission to say the impermissible out loud — we stand in need of the exceptions, rare teachers who will forge a new conscience for the whole of our species. These sections may be un-Socratically rash, but they're still the work of a serpent; they promise new knowledge of our good and evil taught by one acutely aware of the limitations of human knowledge.

Section 202   Nietzsche knows it's insulting to count the human among the animals, and he knows it will be accounted to him almost as guilt that he constantly uses the expressions "herd" and "herd instinct" in relation to modern ideas. Why knowingly insult and make himself seem guilty of a crime? Because he "can do no other for precisely here lies our new insight." The insulting, criminal-sounding insight sees the moral condition of modern humanity: uniform modern "knowledge" of good and evil is dictated by "the instinct of the herd animal man," and the victory of this instinct eclipses and controls all other instincts, homogenizing them into uniformity. Nietzsche risks criminal speech because a moral imperialism threatens to dominate or eliminate the aspect of human diversity that is of fundamental worth, the scale of high and low, lofty and base, which can reach up to "high independent spirituality, the will to stand alone, the great reason" (201). Forced to speak by the crisis in the natural history of morality, Nietzsche speaks in italics: "*Morality in Europe today is herd animal morality.*" Why, in Heidegger's words, did "Nietzsche, one of the quietest and shiest of men . . . endure the agony of having to scream"?[25] Heidegger's answer fits Nietzsche's argument in this section: what counts as progress in a culture committed above all to the progressive is in fact decay of a very precise sort, decay into the tyranny of an instinct for comfort and ease. The section treats this crisis as a great event in the history of Western spirituality, one that demands action be taken, action that begins in speech.

In the rest of this section and in the final section, Nietzsche speaks his unwelcome message in the rhetoric of religion. The historic crisis in morality

25. *Was heisst Denken?* (Tübingen: Max Niemeyer Verlag, 1962), 19 (English trans., 48).

can be depicted as a conflict between two faiths, a monotheism and a polytheism; the conflict in morality is spiritual warfare, the One God, living or dead, and the uniform mass he serves are pitted against many gods and the many nobles they serve. "One kind of human morality" proclaims, "I am morality itself, and nothing besides is morality!" thereby ruling immoral all other possible moralities, above all, "*higher* moralities" whose memory it seeks to efface or defame. A basic point in Nietzsche's spiritual history of the West is touched here: the modern "*democratic* movement has come into the inheritance of the Christian movement" — modern secular society is the ungrateful heir of a parent it disavows as its spiritual opposite. For Nietzsche, modern ideas and Christianity are morally uniform, each representing the same basic instinct and each moving toward the One, the sole permissible good and evil. Each is a Platonism for the people, each gives witness to the disaster of the Platonic compromise. Christianity pampered and flattered "the most sublime herd animal needs" — it promised almost everything to almost everyone for almost nothing — and prepared the way for the pampering and flattering of the modern democratic movement.

That democratic movement of "progress" (the final word of the previous section that prepares this section) consists of many parties; but just as that movement gave the false appearance of a radical break with its Christian ancestor, it gives the false appearance of meaningful moral diversity. The rest of the section is devoted to a demolition of that appearance, a demonstration of the moral uniformity of the opposite extremes of modern moral ideas: "anarchist dogs" appear to be the opposite of "peacefully diligent democrats and revolution-ideologues" and those who call themselves socialists. "In truth," Nietzsche says, the seemingly diverse are "at one" — and *at one* is repeated eight times in a list of eight items of uniformity on what really counts. At the end of the chapter on the natural history of morality, a chief theme of the preface comes into focus: Nietzsche opposes the democratic Enlightenment partly because of its politics of moral uniformity, the entrenchment of the morality that has been gathering strength under two millennia of Platonism. The natural trajectory of the present threatens to fulfill itself in the rule of the "final humans" (Z Prologue), what Nietzsche here calls "the *autonomous* herd." The eight items on Nietzsche's list, each important in its singularity, share a quality that becomes evident with the central pair: they are tenets of a new religion, the secular heir to Christianity, a Platonism for the people that dispenses with gods because it must dispense with the very idea of superior beings. Modern atheism — that "second and more refined atheism" of section 22, in which Nietzsche first used the phrase repeated here in the first item, ni dieu ni maître — is a full-fledged religion of humanity in which all become as gods knowing good and evil; good themselves, any deviation from themselves becomes evil. The central pair of tenets speak of the new "religion of compassion" as moved by a "deadly hatred of suffering," an "inability to be able to *allow* suffering." This new religion, this "pampering" that is heir to Christian pampering, has a *faith* — "faith in the morality of *shared* compassion as morality *an sich,* the peak, the *attained* peak of humanity." It interprets itself as the sole *hope* for the future, as *consolation* in the present, and as *absolution* from the guilt of the past. It even has a *redeemer,* the only redeemer possible for it, the community itself. Following this summation of the tenets of modern faith, the next section begins, "We, the we who are of another faith." The final section on the natural history of morality states the tenets of this different faith — its hope, absolution, consolation, and redeemer — and it culminates, as it must, in a call to action: spiritual warfare between faiths.

Section 203 Where do the we who are of another faith place their hopes? In something so radical it can be justified only by the extremity of what it fears or what the democratic Enlightenment means. Plato is again on Nietzsche's mind. The we who are of another faith do not regard the democratic movement as Plato did in the *Republic,* as a decayed form of "political organization" in a perpetual cycle of aristocracy, timocracy, oligarchy, democracy, and tyranny. Instead, it is now a decayed form of the human itself, whose victory would be the end of history, a tyranny of democracy that would rule out renewed cyclings of higher forms of political organization. The hope of the other faith is therefore invested in the most radical, "in *new philosophers,* there's no other choice." The chapter looking backward to the natural history of morality ends by looking forward to the two possibilities for the future, completion of Platonic morality or the appearance of new philosophers who will embody and teach a new morality. The not-yet-determined animal species stands at a crisis point in its natural history.

The need for new philosophers had first been announced in the final sections of the two chapters on philosophy, in which they were baptized "tempters" (42), labeled "philosophers of the future," and described briefly in their difference from previous philosophers (43) and from free minds commonly understood (44). The end of the chapter on religion emphasized their responsibility for religion (61–62). Now, at the end of the chapter on the natural history of morality, they appear as the sole hope for the preservation of humanity in face of the threat represented by the outcome of Platonic morality. New philosophers differ from old philosophers who were set on "the same track" by Plato (191): they will "tie the knot that forces the will of millennia onto *new* tracks." The new philosophers share the greatness of Platonic ambition — they will be strong enough "to transvalue, to reverse, 'eternal values,'" Platonic values —

but they are anti-Platonic in what they legislate and anti-Platonic in teaching "humanity the future of humanity as its own will, as dependent on a human will." Nietzsche too hopes for an end of history, of "the gruesome rule of nonsense and chance that has been called 'history' till now." Nietzsche too looks to the future, but what he anticipates is "a new kind of philosopher and commander in whose image everything that has existed on earth of hidden, fearsome, and benevolent spirits will be seen as pale and dwarfed." "Hidden, fearsome, benevolent" — these three complementary words stand for the genuine philosopher: necessarily hidden at a height inaccessible to others, causing fear as different and mysterious, but necessarily benevolent or philanthropic as desiring the future well-being of the species. As Leo Strauss argued, Nietzsche is not preparing *a* change to new values, he is preparing *the* change from the rule of chance to the rule of the philosophers of the future.[26]

"It is the image of such leaders that floats before *our* eyes" — and Nietzsche must ask permission before uttering the sentence that sketches out this image: "Am I permitted to say this out loud, you free minds?" After the long sentence that says it out loud Nietzsche adds: "Do you know any of this, you free minds?" That Nietzsche's genuine audience would find impermissible and know little about what he most hopes for — *that* is the emergency compelling Nietzsche to an openness about philosophy that previous philosophers were spared. For the impermissible that he speaks turns out to be, who he is and what his task is: his sentence described his own task in relation to the genesis, maturing, and special task of the new philosophers. He is the founding teacher of the new genus of philosophers; he stands to them as Plato stood to the Platonists. His task, as he described it, has three components that he calls *"our genuine cares."* First, the conditions which one must in part create and in part exploit to make the *genesis* of the new philosophers possible. Second, the maturing that follows this genesis: the probable ways and tests by which a soul would *grow* into such a height and force that it would feel the compulsion for the tasks of the new philosopher — the growth into philosophy, the dual insight into the world as will to power and its affirmation, is at the same time growth into responsibility, a stooping to rule after the achievement of insight. Third, therefore, is "a transvaluation of values," the great creative task with respect to values that the new philosophers must undertake. That transvaluation does more than generate new values, it generates resolve: "under [its] pressure and hammer a conscience would be steeled, a heart transformed into bronze." The steeling of a new conscience creates a resolute inner commander

---

26. Unpublished transcript of a seminar on Nietzsche, University of Chicago, Winter semester, 1967, p. 8/13.

wholly detached from its initial formation as the voice of God or the fore-fathers, attached instead to the mind's knowledge of the duties arising at the end of the moral period. A steeled conscience is allied with a heart hardened by the mind to the responsibility of warfare against the morality of compassion.

A fourth genuine care repeats Nietzsche's first three cares of generating, maturing, and hardening but in the mode of failure: the care "that they may fail to appear or that they may turn out badly or degenerate." These profound cares, unknown even to advanced moderns, lead Nietzsche to a final matter, what the person with these cares sees or comprehends: possessing "the rare eye" for the total danger that humanity itself is degenerating, he sees "with incomparable alarm" what has happened to humanity, alarm heightened by the fact that "not even a finger of God" takes part as a player in the future of humanity. At the same time he "grasps, yes, with a single glance" what might yet be made of humanity. This mix of alarm and promise leads up to the final word of the chapter: "a new *task! . . . .*" That task has just been defined but more needs to be said: the ellipse following the final word opens the four additional chapters, aids to help modern free minds see and embrace the almost unspeakable great new task.

The "Prelude to a Philosophy of the Future" thus becomes a prelude to the philosophers of the future as each of the subsequent chapters addresses the task or responsibility of the new philosopher. Chapter 6, ironically titled "We Scholars," defines how the acts of the "genuine philosopher" stand to those of philosophers as commonly understood, "philosophical laborers" (211). Chapter 7, ambiguously titled "Our Virtues," contrasts the virtues of modern intellectuals with the virtue of the new philosopher and argues the essential point that his virtue requires advocacy of cruelty and suffering. Chapter 8, "Peoples and Fatherlands," shows what role the new philosopher, the "good European," must play in the politics of the future of European civilization. Chapter 9, "What Is Noble?" gathers the political task into the elaboration of a single word, *noble*— the word that names what is most abhorrent to modern ideas but that is nevertheless recoverable for the new ideal.

For a comparable sense of historical crisis and the need for decisive philo-sophical action it is perhaps necessary to study Plato's *Phaedo*.[27] On his dying day, Socrates described the necessity that drove him very early in his life to become Socratic or a defender of the "safe way" of the ideas: he recognized that misology and misanthropy threatened philosophy (89d-91c). Socrates' study of the human, of the common man, led him to recognize a natural hatred

---

27. One might also study the rationale of another philosophic revolutionary, Francis Bacon: see *An Advertisement Touching a Holy War*, Lampert ed.

of the rational because it deprived humanity of its fondest hopes and a natural hatred of the human because it fell short of what it could dream. Socrates' knowledge of the human led him to invent a new strategy for philosophy.[28] The ultimate fate of that strategy requires a philosophical act with the same gracious character and the same ambitious end—the *phil*ology and *philan*thropy of a philosopher.

Nietzsche asks, like Wallace Stevens,

> How did we come to think that autumn
> Was the veritable season?

Learning the answer, the largest of answers, through heroic investigation of the natural history of morality, Nietzsche, again like Wallace Stevens, composes the essential poem, "God is Good. It is a Beautiful Night,"

> Squeezing the reddest fragrance from the stump
> Of summer.[29]

28. See Peter Ahrensdorf, *The Death of Socrates and the Life of Philosophy*, 129–48. See also David Bolotin, "The Life of Philosophy and the Immortality of the Soul: An Introduction to Plato's *Phaedo*."

29. The quotations from Stevens come from the final poem of *Parts of a World* ("Examination of the Hero in a Time of War") and the opening poem of his next book, *Transport to Summer* ("God is Good. It is a Beautiful Night"), *The Collected Poems of Wallace Stevens*.

6

We Scholars

I've thought about the conditions for the existence of the wise man from childhood on, and I don't want to keep silent about my happy conviction that he is now possible *again in Europe—perhaps just for a short time.*

—*KSA* 11.26 [75]

Chapter 5 ended on the hope of those few who are not of the democratic faith, hope in new philosophers capable of rule through a transvaluation of values. Chapter 6 defines those philosophers and shows not only why they must be distinguished from the scientist and scholar, but why and how science and scholarship must become the fitting instruments of their rule.

This is the most essaylike of the nine chapters of *Beyond Good and Evil*. Consisting of a mere ten sections, the shortest over a page long, it argues, from many sides, one principal point that highlights the irony of its title: "We Scholars" is written by a philosopher in order to school scholars in the natural sovereignty of philosophy. The argument does not invite scholars and scientists to become philosophers or even to aspire to it. Instead, it attempts to persuade them to recognize the possibility of the philosopher—of the wise man—and to grant the philosopher both his preeminence and his responsibility. Beginning with the contemporary eclipse of philosophy (204) and the modern impediments to philosophy (205), it describes philosophy as a natural but rare growth bound to inspire envy (206). While honoring the objective spirit of science (207), its desirable skepticism (208–09) and the achievements of its critical temper (210), the argument peaks with a definition of the "genuine philosopher" (211), his singular responsibility (212) and the uniqueness of his experience (213).

Nietzsche's aim in this chapter is political: to fashion a belief about philosophy that will allow it to rule the spiritual ruler of modern times. The political aim employs political means: chapter 6 is an exercise in persuasion addressed to the pride of the proud; practitioners of the supremacy of science are forced to acknowledge realms of experience transcendent to their own. How could such persuasion possibly succeed? Only by forcing scholar/scientists to see that the philosopher is a superior knower who evidently knows their nature and grounds (204–06), knows their highest achievements as truly high but as meaningfully transcendable (207–10), and knows those transcendent experiences themselves and their incumbent responsibilities (211–13). The needed allies can be recruited to volunteer only by one who demonstrably knows their natures and appeals to their natures. Nietzsche is a recruiter who conscripts his volunteers.

Philosophy and Science: A Question of Rule
SECTION 204

Nietzsche runs the risk of revealing personal wounds. But the merely personal wounds incurred by a philosopher typify the wounds incurred by philosophy itself in our time: its eclipse by science threatens the disappearance of the very possibility of philosophy. Therefore, at the cost of appearing shameless, Nietzsche steps forward to oppose "an unseemly and dangerous displacement of rank" between science and philosophy. Because the experiences of genuine philosophy are open to "the fewest" (213), to step forward on behalf of the rule of philosophy over science means at best to create a belief in philosophy where currently there is only a wholly understandable unbelief in philosophy, "*unbelief* in the responsibility to rule and the rulership of philosophy."[1]

The problem lies with the "declaration of independence," the "emancipation" proclamation of the scientist from philosophy. This political revolution

1. Robert Eden asks, What's the risk? And answers, Giving the strategic advantage to opponents by reminding them of their power to do damage (*Political Leadership and Nihilism* 79). Eden's account of chapter 6 provides keen illumination of Nietzsche's philosophical politics even though it judges those politics to be ultimately nihilistic.

in the spiritual realm is a highly refined aspect of the modern revolution generally, part of the politics whose rallying cry is "Freedom from all masters!" the ultimate Master being God himself.[2] Nietzsche describes the displacement in rank between science and philosophy as a second act that opened "after science with the happiest success rid itself of theology, whose 'handmaid' it had been for all too long." Victorious science, now "in full exuberance and ignorance," aims to fashion laws for philosophy and "for once to play the 'master'—what am I saying! the *philosopher.*" Science aims to give laws to the lawgiver.

Viewed this way, the modern revolutionary displacement of philosophy by science is an unforeseen consequence of the great politics of Plato. Nietzsche's view of the spiritual history of the West again focuses on Platonism and its spiritual consequences: a once-successful strategy for philosophy now threatens the erasure of philosophy. The Socratic turn away from Greek natural science and other gains of the Greek enlightenment, the defensive alignment of Socratic philosophy with pious fraud, now draws the philosopher Nietzsche out into the open for a new kind of fight on behalf of the existence of philosophy. If the fate of the philosopher Socrates taught Plato the need to shelter philosophy—the least conventional human enterprise—in the conventional, the fate of Platonic philosophy taught Nietzsche to publicize philosophy's unconventionality, to make its transcendence of the conventional believable to those who thought *they* practiced the highest spiritual and intellectual tasks.

Nietzsche's memory teems with the naive misconceptions scientists hold about philosophy, and he offers a sample of six. The final item states the most frequent source among young scholars: youthful discipleship to a philosopher leaves but one conviction after discipleship ends—belief in that philosopher's destructive critiques of competing philosophers. Philosophers' attacks on other philosophers lead nonphilosophers to unbelief in philosophy.[3] But what about Nietzsche's attack on the prejudices of philosophers? Doesn't it contribute to the discrediting of philosophy itself? What Nietzsche calls his final item generates a comprehensive consideration about modern philosophy: it lacks "the whole type of a Heraclitus, Plato, Empedocles . . . kingly and magnificent hermits of the spirit." Plato is placed out of chronological order between the

2. Section 22 similarly tied modern physics to the modern spiritual politics of atheism: "Neither God nor master!"

3. See Eden, *Political Leadership and Nihilism* 81: Nietzsche adopts the principle that the responsibility for misgovernment in science must lie with philosophy; the dissolution of philosophy must lie with its omissions or mistakes.

two philosophers of the tragic age of the Greeks whom Nietzsche admired most, two whose philosophical kingship was usurped and obliterated by Plato's rule. Absence of this type in modern philosophy has most damaged the respect for philosophy gained in premodern times. The name *philosopher* is now claimed by those who represent in word and deed "*unbelief* in the ruling task and rulership of philosophy." Nietzsche's attack on the prejudices of philosophers stakes a claim to a difference in type: it stems from a thinker who belongs to the type of a Heraclitus, Plato, Empedocles and who aims to rule.

What a "Real Philosopher" Aspires To
SECTION 205

How do a Heraclitus, Plato, or Empedocles become what they are? Nietzsche's preliminary sketch of the rungs of philosophical aspiration includes a brief statement of the very highest aspiration, the philosopher's right to a judgment about the whole of life. Here at the beginning of chapter 6 Nietzsche sets that aspiration into the context of dangers threatening it, dangers that usually destroy this rarest of growths before it can mature.[4] For the philosopher is a natural growth — a fruit that may ripen — and its dangers are just as natural.

The first danger is represented by "the scope and the tower-building of the sciences": they have grown so immense that they forestall the growth of the philosopher, a growth upward to a different height that commands a view all around and a view downward. Or they force him to arrive too late at that summit so that "his view, his comprehensive value judgment" is weakened. Or the potential philosopher is held down by the sensitivity of his own "intellectual conscience," which fears becoming "a great actor . . . and pied piper of minds . . . a tempter." This issue of the actor, expressed briefly here, touches the basic issue behind all of Nietzsche's reflections on Nietzsche contra Wagner, the issue expressed most graphically in *Zarathustra* part 4: The old sorcerer is a great actor who is mere actor; his contest with Zarathustra for leadership of the superior human beings is a dramatic contest between the mere actor and the philosophic actor, the actor who has not lost respect for himself as knower — Zarathustra, the actor whose *Schauspiel* is based not on the desire for immortal glory but on knowledge and philanthropy of the sort this chapter will elaborate. Even if the problem of becoming mere actor were not a question of the intellectual conscience, it would still be "a question of taste" — a higher and more refined standard than conscience. Distaste holds

4. See *KSA* 11.26 [47] entitled "The Way to Wisdom"; the following note [48] develops the same theme in three similar steps.

the philosopher back from what could taste like the ultimate loss of self-respect, the need to become a pied piper of minds. How to honor taste and still be a pied piper of minds is part of the problem addressed in "What Is Noble?" That final chapter culminates — the whole book culminates — in divinizing the philosophical pied piper, the tempter Dionysos.

If conscience and taste double the difficulty of becoming a philosopher, the difficulty is doubled again by the greatest of all difficulties: that the philosopher "would demand of himself a judgment, a Yes or No, not about the sciences but about life and the value of life." The philosopher "learns reluctantly to believe that he has a right or even a duty to this judgment, and that only on the basis of the most comprehensive — perhaps most disturbing, most destructive — experiences and often hesitatingly, doubtfully, mutely, must he seek his way to this right and this belief." This is a more formal statement of the experience Nietzsche described in section 56, the transfiguring experience of insight into the new ideal in the very midst of the most world-denying of all possible ways of thinking. The most difficult right a philosopher finds conferred on himself is the right of supreme judge about life and the value of life, the breathtaking right Nietzsche reflected on from the beginning of his authorship (*UD* 7) and depicted most graphically in Zarathustra.[5]

From this supreme right or duty Nietzsche plunges directly to the popular view of the philosopher — and "all popular opinions" about the philosopher "are false" (213). The false view is recognizably a Platonism for the people, for it respects philosophy as the greatest exercise of moderation, of ascetic discipline of the passions. Correcting this false view, Nietzsche addresses an aside to "my friends" for the only time in chapter 6 — "so it seems to *us*, my friends?" It *won't* seem so to them, as Nietzsche knows perfectly well — the aim of chapter 6 is to correct their sharing of the popular misjudgment.[6] As is known to the philosopher alone, "The real philosopher lives 'unphilosophically' and

5. See for instance Zarathustra's dream of weighing the world at the beginning of "On the Three Evils" (*Z* 3). In *TI* (Socrates 2) the exercise of this right is seen as a symptom of the deepest drive in the wise, and Nietzsche adds, "One absolutely must reach out and try to grasp this astounding *finesse, that the value of life cannot be assessed.*" The present passage makes clear that this statement must not be read as saying that the philosopher must refrain from the ultimate judgment — it does not spare the philosopher the display of his symptoms. See also *BGE* 30; the ultimate judgment from the philosopher's height concerns the assessment of suffering: does the sum total of suffering necessitate judging the world in fear and pity?

6. Here as elsewhere, when Nietzsche addresses his friends he refrains from saying that "as yet I *know* of no friends" (*GM* 3.27).

'unwisely,' above all *imprudently*." To live *above all* imprudently reverses
Platonic caution, making the philosopher the most rash of dangerous ex-
plorers.[7] The real philosopher "feels the burden and duty of a hundred attempts and temptations of life." Such experiments with life mean that "he risks
himself constantly, he plays *the* wicked game." To play *the* wicked game is to
make oneself an actor in that highest of all games, a knowing actor who has
been forced to believe that he has a right to a judgment about the worth of life.
Like Heraclitus, Plato, Empedocles, he ascends to a belief in philosophy that
includes the need to act as judge. Chapter 6 develops the argument that shows
just what those actions are and why they are necessary in the present age of
science.

Envy and Admiration
SECTION 206

The insulting rhetoric of section 206 — directed against its proper
reader — portrays the "scholar, the scientific average man" in what he lacks
when contrasted with the genius, "a being who either *begets* or *bears*." To take
these words of procreation "in their highest range" is to understand them as the
creativity natural to the philosophic genius, the genuine philosopher, whose
begetting or bearing creates values (211). Scholars neither father nor mother;
they have something of the old virgin about them; their self-understanding is
not founded on "the two most valuable functions of humanity" but on respectability instead. However, if we "look more closely" at the scientific human
being, we find that respectability itself is founded on envy, a passion that, like
all passions, has its virtues and its diseases.

The virtues and diseases of scholarly virginity are those of a "non-noble type
of human being." Three negations describe that type, "not ruling, not authoritative, and also not self-sufficient," negations that emphasize the need to be
ruled. Nietzsche lists four virtues of the scholarly type, all qualities of an
industrious and obedient herd animal that Nietzsche can state much more

---

7. When making a similar point about the public face of philosophy in *GS* book 5
(351), Nietzsche speaks of "the great *passion* of the seeker after knowledge who lives and
must live continually in the thundercloud of the highest problems and the heaviest responsibilities." The end of the section invokes Plato and makes it clear that the inventor
of the public image of the philosopher as the most moderate of men inhabited that
thundercloud. Leo Strauss's lifework — itself an exercise in recovering the possibility of
philosophy — has shown how Plato's dialogues must be read as acts of moderate speech
veiling the most immoderate thoughts.

directly than Francis Bacon ever dared to do when he first described the virtues of the scientific workers necessary to the success of Baconian science.[8] The qualities culminate in an instinct that is further elaborated in four precise requirements of the scientific/scholarly type. All but the first (itself a demand for a piece of independence by the essentially dependent) are demands for recognition that have their basis in an "inner *mistrust*" that must always be overcome and that can only be overcome externally, by assurances of worth conferred by others of one's own kind.

Corresponding to the virtues are diseases to which the scientific type is prone. Nietzsche names three, descending to the "worst and most dangerous," and each deals comparatively with the scientist in contrast to the philosopher. First, "he is rich in petty envy," which expresses itself particularly against the envied who occupies an unreachable height, the philosopher: he "has lynx eyes for what is base in those natures to whose heights he cannot ascend." Second, he is friendly and dependable, "but still, only like the individual who lets himself stride but not *stream*." Here too, the moving passion seems to be envy, for Nietzsche expands the contrast between striding and streaming: in the face of "the human being of powerful streaming" — one whose gait is like the flow of the Ganges perhaps (27) — he "grows colder and more closed," external signs of inwardly controlled envy. But the worst and most dangerous disease of the scholar comes from an instinctual awareness of the middling rank of the scholarly/scientific type. In describing it, Nietzsche returns to another set of old virgins, alluded to in the preface, Jesuits who tried to unbend the tensed bow of modern intellectual and spiritual aspiration. The scholar/scientist's "instinct for the mediocrity of his type" is like "that Jesuitism of mediocrity that labors instinctively at the annihilation of the uncommon human being" — a form of active envy based in self-hatred, an instinctive defense of the middle range, one's own kind, that brings down what stands higher. Nietzsche elaborates his image from the preface: such Jesuitism "seeks to break every tensed bow or — much rather! — untense it." It does so with subtlety and cunning: "Untense considerately, of course, with solicitous hand —, *untense* with friendly compassion: that is the genuine art of Jesuitism which has always known how to ingratiate itself as the religion of compassion." The Jesuit effort to untense the bow of modern times, one of the great events of modern spiritual history, failed because of the deadly writings of the solitary Pascal. The spirit of

8. Bacon's analysis of the fable of Daedalus presents an account of the scientist similar to Nietzsche's, particularly in its emphasis on the passion of envy, a manipulable passion, Bacon argues, the key passion for the establishment of a scientific society; see Lampert, *Nietzsche and Modern Times* 34–38.

Jesuitism, revived by science's envious passion to rule philosophy, is again opposed by a solitary writer. *Beyond Good and Evil* stands to the Jesuitical in science as the *Provincial Letters* stood to the Jesuits, but Nietzsche's spiritual war is more fundamental, for he is a philosopher daring to speak out on behalf of the highest, philosophy, not a religious thinker speaking out on behalf of Christianity.

As Robert Eden argued, the insults of this section must be calculated acts: "Nietzsche is deliberately unjust in order to create a bond — initially a bond of enmity — between the philosopher and a certain atypical class of scholars."⁹ The exceptions among the scholars will be goaded into self-reflection, allowing envy to be surpassed by admiration for something that stands higher than even the proudest achievements of the scholar/scientist. For Nietzsche's appeal is ultimately an appeal to virtue, a non-Jesuitical virtue of the middling that is capable of acknowledging virtue superior to its own. The next four sections deal with the characteristic virtues of the scholar/scientist: objectivity (207), skepticism (208–09), and criticism (210); each is lauded though each is deficient, and the indication of the deficiencies begins to define the philosopher and his right to rule. The high, opened to a new perspective on itself from the viewpoint of the highest, is implicitly invited to enter the service of the highest. The argument begun here concerning a rank order of virtues forms the core of the next chapter, "Our Virtues," in which the virtue of the philosopher claims to give measure and order to the virtue of the scholar/scientist.¹⁰

The Objective Mind and the Complementary Human Being
SECTION 207

Listen carefully to section 207, section 208 says, and you'll hear that the philosopher who there criticizes the scientific/scholarly mind is no skeptic. Nietzsche has long since made it obvious that he's no skeptic regarding nature as a whole — to be is to be will to power. In section 207 he "gives it to be understood" that he's also not a *practical* skeptic, for he has a clear strategy for

9. *Political Leadership and Nihilism* 83. Eden also detects a reasonable shift in Nietzsche's rhetoric in the second half of chapter 6: "Earlier, Nietzsche tried to wound and challenge the pride of the nobler scholar; toward the end of his argument he attempts to win over such men by showing them tasks of a difficulty 'in whose service every subtle pride, every tough will can certainly find satisfaction'" (88).

10. Eden's perceptive analysis of Nietzsche's rhetorical strategy founders, it seems to me, on his failure to appreciate Nietzsche's philosophical virtue. The fundamental element of Nietzsche's appeal ends up being nothing more than "great criminality and moral nihilism" (*Political Leadership and Nihilism* 86).

what must be done. Unlike the objective mind, "the complementary human being" (the name here given to the philosopher) has "grounds for taking sides between good and evil"; knowing those grounds and knowing as a consequence what must be done, he sets out to make the scientist the philosopher's ally for philosophy's ends. The proper order of rank between philosophy and science establishes an alliance in which the scientist is the instrument of the philosopher. Nietzsche pictures this alliance in the image Plato used to express the alliance he himself forged between the philosopher and the poet, the alliance that settled the ancient quarrel between them: the poet mirrors the whole of nature and as a mirror is useful to the user par excellence, to the god, as Plato says in his first description of the relationship of user and used, to the philosopher, as Plato indicates in his second description of it.[11] The scholar/scientist aims to mirror nature as it is, Nietzsche says, and in his mirroring serves as an instrument or tool in the hands of someone who does more than mirror. The description of the objective mind thus serves as an opportunity to describe by contrast that ruling someone, that complementary human being.

Gratitude for the "*objective* mind" leads Nietzsche to an exclamation: "And who has not already been sick to death of everything subjective and of his own accursed ipsissimosity!" But gratitude for the welcome flight into objectivity should not lead us to elevate objectivity unduly: such "de-selfing, depersonalizing of the mind" should not be celebrated "as an end in itself, as redemption, as transfiguration." There does exist, however, that which should be celebrated as each of these three things and the section culminates in a description of that individual. The objective mind, the ideal scholar, is itself a rare achievement, a natural growth in which "the scientific instinct for once blossoms and blooms to completeness" amid the thousand failures and half-failures. This rare growth sacrifices itself for the end of knowledge, the end of mirroring some fact or facts about the world, as the paradigm scientist in *Zarathustra* 4 does — "Conscientiousness Himself," who sacrifices himself for knowledge of the leech's brain.[12] The passion to have no other passion but

11. *Republic* 10.596d-e, 597b,e. See Strauss, *The City and Man* 136; Strauss's account brings out the latent radicalism of Plato's politics for philosophy and poetry according to which poetry becomes ministerial to philosophy. Strauss introduces Nietzsche at this point in order to explain the relation between philosophy and poetry: "The poets were always the valet of some morality," now the morality legislated by the founding philosopher.

12. The respect due Conscientiousness Himself is lost in most interpretations of part 4, as is his defense of science and of Zarathustra's teaching as compatible with science. Instead, interpreters seem bent on flying into the net of deconstructive cunning woven by

mirroring costs the objective mind the customary passions; as pure reflector he loses familiarity with himself as person — an experience similar to what Socrates described as the loss he experienced in his early passion for the investigation of the causes of all things (*Phaedo* 96d-e). The great failure of objectivity is its loss of aptitude for subjectivity, accursed though it be. "Know thyself" is lost in the subject's turn to the objective, and such a loss is fatal if psychology is the path to the fundamental problems (23).

The "cheerful totalism" of the objective mind, willingness to treat everything in the same objective way, makes him a stranger to the familiar things of family and person and to the naturally primary passions of love and hate. Only in his cheerful totalism "is he still 'nature' and 'natural,'" the quotation marks signaling an altered nature, an unnatural natural that views everything in abstraction from love and hate. A little jest focuses what Nietzsche thinks remains of the natural passions in the objective mind: don't undervalue that *almost* in the objective mind's statement "I have contempt for *almost* nothing" — his one contempt is self-contempt, the single cheerless exception violating the cheerful totalism that refuses to make judgments of value. In a book entitled *Beyond Good and Evil* perhaps the decisive thing about the objective mind is said last, just before the contrast with the philosopher: "He's no model man; he leads no one forward, nor does he follow anyone; he places himself at altogether too great a distance to have grounds for taking sides between good and evil." Adequate grounds for taking sides between good and evil await the appearance of the complementary human being who takes responsibility for a new affirmation and negation, a judgment on the whole of life (205). This great contrast in the power to judge is elaborated in the next chapter, "Our Virtues," in which a "lack of measure" is said to characterize free minds and turn them into half-barbarians; it is the virtue of the philosopher that makes them civil by teaching them a new measure.

To confuse the objective mind with the philosopher betrays the lack of a criterion of rank, of any standard of ruler and ruled capable of distinguishing the highest from the high. For the philosopher is a ruler, "a Caesarian generator and violent force of culture." To such a Caesar of culture the objective mind is "an instrument, something of a slave, if certainly also the most sublime type of slave, in himself however Nothing, — *almost* nothing!" Given the analysis of slavery in the coming chapters, the objective spirit as "the most sublime type of slave" is something of extremely high rank, almost escaping the com-

---

the old sorcerer, thus duplicating the failure of the superior men to appreciate the alliance between Zarathustra and science. See Lampert, *Nietzsche's Teaching* 301–03.

mon lot of servitude to which our species is confined, as near to freedom as it is possible to get without actually reaching that rarest of states, the freedom that confers the right to judge and the responsibility to rule. Only because the perspective adopted in this section is that of the highest can the achievement of the objective mind be presented as limited and subjected to jests.

The limits of the objective mind afford Nietzsche an opportunity to define the philosopher as one who possesses what the objective mind lacks: the "complementary human being" is a "goal," a "way out and up," "one in whom the *rest* of existence justifies itself";[13] he is an "ending" and still more "a beginning, a begetting and first cause," he is something "tough, powerful, resting in himself, wanting to be master." The ruling character of the genuine philosopher first appears in contrast with his instruments of rule, the highest servants of modern science, whom he presses into his service. No one capable of making such statements about a possibility beyond the modern ideal of science/ scholarship could possibly be called a skeptic. His statements claim a knowledge both of human nature and of what must be done in an age of the rule of science to enhance human nature.[14]

Skepticism and Knowing What to Do
SECTIONS 208–09

The two central sections of chapter 6, numbers 208 and 209, deal serially with two kinds of skepticism, the skeptical virtue of scientist/scholars and a "different and stronger kind of skepticism" whose "audacious manliness" knows what must be done. Nietzsche speaks of the second kind of skepticism in a parable about a certain *Fridericianismus* capable of historic acts for great ends (209). It's a pleasant parable in which our Friedrich, who knows what must be done, contrasts himself, surely, with scientists/scholars, whose skepticism leaves them in principled ignorance about what must be

13. See section 28 and what the complementary man, Aristophanes, justifies.

14. Compare the complementary human being with what is said of the "high spirituality/intellectuality" in section 219. See also the "sovereign individual" of *GM* 2.2, who is the result of a long process and the justification of that process: he has "become free . . . this lord of the *free* will, this sovereign." Free for what? For "the extraordinary privilege of *responsibility* [that] has sunk into his lowest depths and become instinct, the dominant instinct: — what will he call it, this dominant instinct . . . ? But there's no doubt: this sovereign human being calls it his *conscience*. . . ." "His conscience?" Nietzsche says on behalf of the incredulous to begin the next section, thus launching his treatise into the origins and history of what can culminate in the complementary human being or the genuine philosopher, the human being of the highest responsibility.

done. Central to the argument of the chapter on the philosopher and science is this intimation that there are knowable grounds for historic action in the present. Nietzsche describes the connection between knowledge and action as knowledge of what to dream. The great politics of the philosopher who understands the relation of philosophy and science depends on teaching skeptics how to arm themselves with hope.

Section 208   The nonskeptical philosopher — whose voice we are instructed to hear in the previous section — now explains why he appears so ominous to skeptical contemporaries, intellectual "security police" who view nonskepticism as an explosive threatening their world: the morality of fearfulness embraced by modern skepticism cannot welcome a new knowledge of Yes! and No! that inevitably leads to decisive, negating action.

In the dialogue that animates this section, skepticism comes to speech in order to prohibit open speech on underground matters. Not knowing quite what to fear in the rumblings of a general earthquake, the fearful skeptic commands a general quiet: Yes and No go against his morality. He takes Montaigne and Socrates as his skeptical models. But this is a misuse of the history of philosophy for they were genuine philosophers who feigned ignorance in order to shelter the public from unsettling knowledge, in Socrates' case, or to liberate it from false knowledge, in Montaigne's. Today's fearful skeptic falls short of his great and daring strategic models; he does not *feign* ignorance in the ultimate service of knowledge but defends genuine ignorance for its utility as a calming device. His spirit runs counter to the will to truth that drives the opening section of the book, for it comforts itself with reasons *not* to pursue the threatening riddles posed by the questions of the origin and value of truth.

Finding himself addressed by a skepticism in need of security, Nietzsche inquires into its origins: it is "weakness of nerve and sickliness" arising from a cultural breakup of the settled and secure. In such revolutionary times "everything is unrest, disturbance, doubt, experiment"; what is lacking is "balance, a center of gravity, perpendicular security." To skeptics lacking a sense of measure, skeptics whose skepticism is a palliative against the turbulence of the times, Nietzsche offers a fitting measure in the next chapter, "Our Virtues," though never perpendicular security and without ever becoming a dogmatist.

Nietzsche claims that it is the will that is most deeply sick and decadent among moderns; "they doubt the 'freedom of the will' even in their dreams." To be unable even to dream of a free will, a will informed by knowledge of the world and the times, is to find philosophy impossible. *Beyond Good and Evil* aims to make imaginable again the possibility of a free, *very* free mind, and it does so by displaying how the freed mind overcomes the epistemological and practical skepticisms of modern times. Chapter 2 argued that the philosopher, the very free mind, can reasonably surmount epistemological skepticism and draw a plausible inference about the way of all beings; chapter 6 and the chapters that follow argue that the philosopher can surmount practical skepticism and plot a reasonable course for a revolutionary philosophical politics for "our Europe of today," a Europe experiencing a crisis in the natural history of morality.

In this section Nietzsche presents a sketch of the spiritual politics of contemporary Europe for which he can merely vouch — a more detailed argument concerning Europe awaits chapter 8, "Peoples and Fatherlands." For now, Nietzsche introduces a chief issue of that chapter by describing skepticism as a paralysis of will and as an especially French phenomenon. By contrast, there is a German strength of will expanded in the parable of the next section and elaborated as German philosophy in chapter 8. That strength of will knows what to wish, and Nietzsche ends this section on that wish, the dangerous contrary to the skepticism of contemporary European culture, the philosophical politics that will occupy him in its many facets for the rest of the book. It is Nietzsche's wish that Europe grow menacing again, possessed by a single will, "a long, fearsome will of its own which would be able to cast its goals millennia hence." To set such long-term goals for European culture — the scientific, experimental culture originating in Greece, carried forward in Rome and early modern Europe, now lapsed into skeptical inaction — would require as its means "a new ruling caste over Europe."

The philosopher not disarmed into observer status by the present state of Western civilization, the philosopher who harbors a new wish for the global future of Western civilization, prepares for his parable of Fridericianismus by making that wish emphatic: "The next century will bring the fight for the dominion of the earth — the *compulsion* to great politics." Great politics is demanded by the times. Will an empirical, experimental, scientific, universalist culture with roots in Europe come to unify the whole globe or will it be eclipsed by new barbarisms energized by a different vision of humanity's destiny? Fridericianismus or Nietzscheanism depends upon the spiritual caste of scholars and scientists recognizing the epistemological and practical limits on its legitimate skepticism. Philosophy must rule science because without this alliance Europe's decisive contribution to humanity could be lost — the practical issue of philosophy's rule over science forms the very center of chapter 6, with spiritual dominion over the whole globe at stake. What Nietzsche wishes for is a philosophical imperialism of a kind recognizable in the writings of the greatest philosophical solitaries, in Plato's dialogues and in early modern European philosophers like Bacon and Descartes, imperialism whose aspirations become visible again in the writings of a Friedrich who took his meals at the Hotel Alpenrose and polished his thoughts in a room at the Durisch house.

Section 209   The themes of skepticism and an age at war continue uninterruptedly into section 209, a parable of contemporary practical skepticism. In the parable, skepticism appears first as something to be feared, a "spider," a "great bloodsucker," source of the "incurable misery of a heart no longer hard enough for evil or for good" — the skepticism old Friedrich Wilhelm the First feared his son had fallen prey to, "the atheism, the esprit, the pleasurable frivolity of clever Frenchmen." But skepticism appears next in the form it actually took in his son, the skepticism of the greatest Prussian ruler, Friedrich the Great, a "more dangerous and harder new type of skepticism," "the skepticism of audacious manliness that is most akin to the genius for war and conquest." Such skepticism "gives the mind dangerous freedom but binds the heart severely"; such skepticism is "the *German* form of skepticism." Rather than falling prey to sophisticated Frenchmen, German skepticism succeeded in bringing "Europe under the hegemony of the German mind." This German victory over Europe did not come through Friedrich the Great himself but through a form of skepticism that shared his audacious manliness, "a more advanced *Fridericianismus* ascended into the most spiritual." Nietzsche attributes this German victory over Europe to "the unconquerably strong and tough manly character of the great German philologists and critical historians" — "artists of destruction and dissolution."

It's high time to enjoy this parable of Nietzscheanism as yet another pleasant device by which the philosopher Friedrich introduced himself to the world. "We scholars" are called upon to exercise a minimum of interpretive finesse to appreciate the audacious modesty of a nonskeptical philosopher who has the whole future of humanity on his conscience. Friedrich Wilhelm Nietzsche lays claim to a tradition of manly skepticism well prepared to act and to act on the basis of something far firmer than a mere will to will, mere *Entschlossenheit* — prepared to act on the basis of its understanding of nature and history. The sections following this parable focus on the philosopher as historical actor, the genuine philosopher forced by his insight into the responsibility of action.[15]

---

15. Georg Picht treats sections 209, 210, 211 as a sequence in which each section deals with one aspect of justice as expressed in a sentence from Nietzsche's notebooks: "*Justice* as the building, separating, annihilating way of thinking, out of value judgments: *the*

The Nietzschean Philosophers of the Future
SECTION 210

The key issue of chapter 6 becomes overt in section 210: Who are these philosophers of the future whose rank is such that they naturally rule science and scholarship? What are "they themselves"? and what can we call them? They will have the audacious manly skepticism just described in the parable, but — annoyingly enough — they can't be called skeptics. Can they be called critics? The answer is ultimately No, but Nietzsche supplies that answer only after showing how much more fitting *critic* is than *skeptic* as a name for the philosopher of the future. If skeptical but not skeptics, critical but not critics, what is their defining quality? The answer is withheld until the next section: creators of value. The argumentative unity of chapter 6 builds toward that announcement by preparing it as their truly defining quality, one that transcends other important but still limited qualities.

But Nietzsche had already supplied a name, as he reminds his reader: he dared baptize them *Versucher* in section 42. While not retracting this name, with its suggestions of Experimenter, Tempter, Attempter, Essayer, he acknowledges its limitations and links it to "audacious skeptic" and "critic," the other fitting if limited names suggested in the present context. As "people of experiment" they will risk that most dangerous of experiments, revealing the order of rank that stations the philosopher at the peak.

Nietzsche argues that *critic* is a more fitting name than *skeptic* because the philosopher of the future will possess knowledge that a skeptic must deny, including knowledge of the hard things that must be done. In a categorical sentence — "There is no doubt" — that fits nicely in a refusal of skepticism, Nietzsche lists five "grave and by no means unproblematic qualities" that distinguish the critic from the skeptic and that the philosopher of the future will be "least permitted to dispense with": "certainty of value standards, con-

---

highest representative of life itself" (*KSA* 11.26 [484]). Heidegger had given this note great prominence in his slanderous misrepresentation of Nietzsche's view of justice (*Nietzsche II* 198; English trans., 4:144). In a chapter entitled "Justice as the Essence of the 'Philosophy of the Future'" (*Nietzsche* 122–31), Picht argues that "annihilating" is depicted in the skepticism of 209, "separating" in the criticism of 210, and "building" in the creation of values of 211. Picht's discussion is part of a developing argument that is moving toward one of its peaks in the notion of "The Philosopher as Legislator" (*Nietzsche* 226–38). Part of the great value of Picht's work is its demonstration that justice in Nietzsche is in fact understandable as "the highest representation of life itself," the translation into conscious human values of the way of all beings. See also the chapter "Truth and Justice" (*Nietzsche* 94–122).

scious implementation of a unity of method, crafty courage, the ability to stand alone, the ability to take responsibility." Chapter 7 will emphasize the first two qualities, making it clear that it is precisely our virtues that deprive us of the certainty of value standards and a unity of method, leaving us as half-barbarians needing a new principle of measure.

As remarkable and worthy of reflection as these five qualities of the critic are, they are still not enough, and Nietzsche adds acts of negation that distinguish critics from skeptics (208) with their fear of No: "Yes, they entitle themselves to *pleasure* in no-saying and dismemberment and a certain calm cruelty that knows how to wield the knife surely and subtly, even if the heart bleeds." Fundamental to the hard mind of the critic is its stance toward truth: it "gets involved with" truth not because truth pleases or elevates or inspires; its smile at such naiveté turns gradually to genuine disgust. This stance toward hard truth dictates that critics lack any intention to reconcile "Christian feelings" with "classical taste" — the spurious reconciliation peddled by Christian and modern interpreters that masks Jerusalem's capture of Athens. Nietzsche's description of the philosopher of the future as critic ends on a capital point: the uncompromising hardness of mind practiced by such critics concerns truthtelling as well as truth seeking. Wanting to be seen for what they are, they will not tolerate exoteric masks for the hard truths their minds pursue. They will not be inward critics and outward conformists. On the contrary, the philosophers of the future, while demanding of themselves "critical discipline and every habit which leads to cleanliness and severity in matters of the mind," will wear this discipline and habit as their kind of adornment and decoration, their *jewelry*. Having abandoned the uncleanliness of Platonic esotericism, they flaunt what the Platonic philosopher aimed above all to hide, the cruel hardness of the truth.

Critics inwardly and outwardly, the philosophers of the future still do not want to be called critics. Why not? Because "it seems to them no small disgrace done to philosophy when one decrees . . . 'Philosophy itself is criticism and critical science — and nothing besides!'" Philosophy has been disgraced by being limited in this Kantian way to one of its essential functions; more tellingly, philosophy has come to be ruled by science because of that limitation, because it has been deprived of its truly defining activity. "Critics are instruments of the philosopher"; if philosophy were properly understood, criticism too would be seen to be ministerial to philosophy, useful for its service and advancement.

If the philosophers of the future who are to rule science cannot be called skeptics or critics, what can they be called?

Genuine Philosophers — Creators of Value
SECTION 211

It is certainly not an overstatement to say that no one has ever spoken so greatly and so nobly of what a philosopher is as Nietzsche.

— Leo Strauss[16]

The chapter on philosophy's right to rule science peaks in section 211 as Nietzsche finally reaches the defining trait of the genuine philosopher: while in his own way an objective scientist, a skeptic, and a critic, the genuine philosopher is one thing more, a creator of values and as such "*a commander and legislator.*" He is of the type of a Heraclitus, Plato, Empedocles (204); he is what Plato argued in the *Republic* a philosopher could be, a wise man fit to rule by his understanding of nature and human nature and actually ruling through speakers ministerial to himself, ruling through persuasive poetry.

His chapter-long argument fully articulated except for its ultimate point, Nietzsche can begin that point dogmatically: "I insist." Nietzsche insists on calling a stop to the confounding of science and philosophy. The distinction between the two is given new wording in this section, but the concept has been present throughout the book: the "genuine philosopher" is that rarest of beings whose will to truth drives him to discover the "intelligible character" of the world and to glimpse the ideal appropriate to it; "the philosophical laborers" are the scientist/scholars of philosophy. What Nietzsche insists on is strict justice with respect to these two kinds: "Precisely here one should be rigorous about giving 'to each his own' " — justice demands that the genuine philosopher be given what is due him. Confounding the difference between science and philosophy is unjust, giving "that one too much, this one much too little." Nietzsche does not insist on a rigid vocabulary: philosophers are simply the philosophers or the real philosophers or the genuine philosophers. But justice dictates that nonphilosophers, even if they spend their lives on philosophy, even if they are rare geniuses who attain the rank of a Kant or a Hegel, not be called philosophers but "philosophical laborers" or "scientific human beings." The difference is, in part, understood politically, in terms of rule — the philosopher ascends to a position that turns the scientists into his servants. Ultimately, however, the difference must be understood in terms of what the philosopher *is:* his right to rule is granted by his wisdom.

The education of the philosopher, his upbringing and rearing, may require that he himself have stood on all the steps on which the scientific laborers of

16. *The Rebirth of Classical Political Rationalism* 40.

philosophy necessarily remain standing. The list of steps begins with a "perhaps" that governs all eleven items on the list, and it ends by adding "and almost everything." The list begins with the high stage of critic set out in the previous section; it moves fittingly to the stage dissected in the preceding sections, skeptic (208–09), proceeds through terms that reverberate with discussions elsewhere in *Beyond Good and Evil* and in *Zarathustra*, and ends with " 'free mind,' " the special audience of the book, the so-called free mind. The list of steps on which the philosopher does not remain standing is followed by the reason for taking such steps: each step, like the necessary step beyond it, is taken for the sake of something other than the step itself, it is taken in order to "run the entire circumference of human values and value-feelings." Nietzsche adds a second reason: "in order to *be able* to look with multiple eyes and consciences from the height into every distance, from the depth up to every height, from the corner into every expanse." The philosopher's education and rearing are driven by a passion to experience and know the whole of things from every conceivable angle.

As grand and inclusive as Nietzsche's description of the philosopher's passion for knowledge may be, it is followed by a *but*, which relegates everything said so far to the status of precondition for what truly defines the philosopher: his task. "But all these are only preconditions of his task: this task itself wants something different — it demands that he *create values*." For the philosopher as Nietzsche conceives him, insight, though initially the end of all his passion, cannot be a resting point. What the philosopher comes to see impels him to act as it equips him to act. It is clear from this and other descriptions of the philosopher that the philosopher does not begin with this task; it falls to him unasked as a consequence of what he does begin with, the will to truth. That passion ultimately carries him to reaches of insight the very possession of which dictates action. Insight confers responsibility, transforming its most passionate pursuer into an actor. Philosophy generates political philosophy, action on behalf of philosophy, of the rational.[17] As unfamiliar as this description of the philosopher as an actor who creates values may appear, it is the description of the philosopher put forward guardedly but with monumental effect by Plato. Plato argued that the end of knowledge is contemplation, but Plato wrote the dialogues that created the values of our civilization, and that did not happen inadvertently. In Plato's description of the philosopher's ascent, a point is reached at which the philosopher hears the imperative issued

17. An earlier version of section 211 made philosophical action more explicit by naming as exemplars Plato and Mohammed, *KSA* 11. 38 [13].

by Socrates: "You must go down!"[18] That imperative beautifully mimics the first word of the *Republic:* "Down I went." The *Republic* itself is an act of political philosophy, of value creation, by a genuine philosopher. It is not only Glaucon and Adeimantus who will never be the same after spending that night in the Piraeus with Socrates.

Having announced the task of the philosopher, Nietzsche returns to the philosophical laborer and does so in order to contrast the singular task of the philosopher with the highest possible work of philosophical labor. The "noble models" of philosophical laborers are astounding: Kant and Hegel. By taking the very greatest of modern German "philosophers" as exemplary philosophical laborers Nietzsche makes his claim about the rarity and unique purpose of the genuine philosopher both emphatic and unforgettable. How do Kant and Hegel stand to value creation? They remain within preexisting "value-*positings,* value-creations that have become dominant and have long been named 'truths'"—they remain within the value-positings of Christianized Platonism, pressing the facticity of these evaluations, the great mass of their givenness, into understandable, meaningful, livable formulas. They look to the past, they "*overpower* the whole of the past," abbreviating and making manageable or meaningful all that has happened. Philosophical labor is "an immense and wonderful task in whose service every subtle pride, every tough will can certainly satisfy itself." No sarcasm or irony infects Nietzsche's elevation of the high task of philosophy as science. It could seem the highest of all possible human tasks, except for what Nietzsche claims for the genuine philosopher.

From philosophical labor in its most ambitious and successful achievements Nietzsche turns again to the genuine philosopher. The term *eigentlich* cannot imply that the philosophical laborer is ungenuine or inauthentic, a fake or a fraud, only that he is not a philosopher at all in the strict sense but a scientist of philosophy. The statement that follows the elevated description of philosophical labor is the most emphatic in the book, two lines of italics. And the description of the genuine philosopher builds toward a rhetorical peak, the only use of *will to power* in chapter 6, a use that echoes the first use of will to power in the book (9), making it clear that that statement was no criticism of philosophy but the fitting name for the ultimate achievement of philosophy. "*Genuine philosophers, however, are commanders and legislators.*" The commanding and legislating that create values cannot be mere self-legislation; it has nothing to do with the modern notion of autonomy that counsels one to invent one's own values and character—a perfectly ridiculous notion according to Nietz-

18. *Republic* 7.520c.

sche, the teacher of *amor fati,* a merely modern idea, the typically American fiction, Nietzsche thought, according to which each of us is free to make ourselves whatever we fancy — mere existentialism, the ultimate modern idea (GS 356).[19]

Commanders and legislators must be understood here in its full Platonic pedigree as philosophical rulers who legislate for a whole age, the philosophical ruler as understood and embodied by Platonic philosophers of the rank of Alfarabi or Bacon, or as understood and cautiously made accessible by the great twentieth-century student of Platonic political philosophy, Leo Strauss. Nietzsche makes his thought perfectly clear without reciting its pedigree; genuine philosophers say, "Let it be thus!" Just what *it* means in this little formulation is explained by what follows: "They first determine the Where To? and For What? of humanity." This explanation makes it obvious that "Let it be thus!" in no way implies that everything is malleable to human will. Genuine philosophers are not the commanders and legislators of nature, they are not magicians. This is section 211 of Nietzsche's book: he has long since made it clear that nature, *physis,* is what it is and is in some basic way accessible in its intelligible character to the human mind, accessible as what it unalterably is: will to power. As legislators of the Where To? and For What? of humanity, philosophers of the future legislate the values human beings live by, the values that horizon and house whole peoples and ultimately the people humanity. In the next section Nietzsche gives content to his open adverbs *Wohin?* and *Wozu?* and the lovely simplicity of his words conveys the true extent of the genuine philosopher's task: the genuine philosopher says, *Wir müssen dorthin* — We have to go *that* way. Nietzsche, walker of mountain paths, employs the language of hikers in the mountains and makes the scope of value creation clear in his words: the genuine philosopher addresses his whole age and says, We have to go that way, a different way, an untrod way. This is also the imagery of *Zarathustra* in the crucial speech that presents the will to power teaching to "you who are wisest" (Z. 2 "On Self-Overcoming"): humanity is a process always already under way on a path, always already streaming in a direction set by its values. The genuine philosopher is commissioned, on the basis of insight alone, to create the values that shepherd and direct humanity.[20]

19. Retail Nietzscheanism is bent on misreading the clear exclusivity of Nietzsche's claims. Meetings of the academic Nietzsche societies consist of whole rooms of genuine philosophers. Each higher than Kant and Hegel? Each a Caesar of knowledge?

20. The intended but never completed third part of the four parts of Picht's Nietzsche lectures was entitled "The Inversion (*Umkehrung*) of Metaphysics in Nietzsche's Transvaluation of All Values — The Philosopher as Legislator." Unfortunately only a fragmen-

Nietzsche focuses the difference between philosophical laborers and genuine philosophers on their different orientations toward time. Philosophical laborers overpower the past, genuine philosophers reach with a creative hand to the future. This differentiation allows a precise definition of philosophers of the future: they are creators of the human future who employ the work of "all philosophical laborers, all overpowerers of the past." For their creative task with respect to the future, "everything that was and is serves them as means, as instrument, as hammer." Nietzsche does not say that the whole of the past lies at the disposal of the philosopher of the future, malleable under his hammer into whatever shape might please him; rather, he says that the whole of the human past becomes serviceable as the means for hammering the human future into a desirable shape. Given the human past, our natural and unnatural past as *Beyond Good and Evil* makes it visible, the philosopher of the future sets out to redirect the forward flow of humanity.

Nietzsche's final sentence before turning to questions lays bare in stages the inner content of the knowing of genuine philosophers: "Their 'knowing' is *creating*, their creating is a giving of laws, their will to truth is—*will to power*." "Will to truth" are the first words of the first section of the book, words that depict a heroic task for all potential Oedipuses about the origin and value of the will to truth. The dangerous truth is that the will to truth is the most spiritual will to power. That is its origin. What is its value? Ultimately its value seems to be its power to create value, to proclaim that this is worth more than that, to create value on the basis of a judgment it dares to make about the whole of life (205), and to create values that accord with life itself as most valuable.

As the truth about the genuine philosopher comes into the open, it is evident that the description is not an invitation; nobody is being told to do anything except understand a cardinal truth. The description of the genuine philosopher reports an experience bound to remain inaccessible to virtually all readers. The report is given not in order to create a new aspiration but to create a new recognition, namely, that philosophy is possible as both insight and deed. As the truth about the genuine philosopher comes into the open, the argument of chapter 6 is completed: the confounding of science and philosophy will no

---

tary preview was completed (*Nietzsche* 226–38). Its first subsection is entitled "Nietzsche and Plato — The Philosopher as Legislator and Poet of Life," and it contains an illuminating reflection on two noteworthy sections of *GS* that present this great theme poetically, the first on Prometheus (*GS* 300), the second on "The contemplatives" (*GS* 301). As Picht shows, both parties learn their light-giving, law-giving powers only gradually, and only against Zeus, against constituted authority.

longer be possible if philosophy is properly understood. The high and indispensable tasks of science will be given their due; the different and even higher tasks of philosophy will be given their due. Justice will be done to both science and philosophy. And justice will be done to humanity itself: our species generates wise exemplars of such sovereignty that they can be fit mentors and guides.

Three questions bring section 211 to an appropriate end, questions that call scholarship and science to consider the past, present, and future of philosophy as part of the past, present, and future of our civilization. The rule of the philosopher of the type of Heraclitus, Plato, Empedocles, the reestablishment of the legislative preeminence of wisdom, could perhaps become actual in an age ruled by the virtues of objective observation, skepticism, and criticism. For the exercise of these very virtues forces the virtuous to acknowledge virtues that transcend these virtues without abrogating them.

The Philosopher of the Future Today
SECTION 212

Section 212 answers all three questions that end section 211 by stating what the philosopher has been "in all times" and "every time" and must be in "this time," "our time." The philosopher is defined by a task, the "hard, unwanted, inescapable task" of enhancing humanity, a task requiring that the philosopher be the "bad conscience" of his time. In our time, the philosopher is the bad conscience of the age of equality; his task is to do what *Beyond Good and Evil* is doing, make visible the very inequality that philosophers in other times labored to keep invisible or barely visible behind a dissembling mask of irony. The future of philosophy in our time depends upon the philosopher taking the "untrod way" that dares to display the human order of rank by bringing the philosopher into the open.

The task of the philosopher is to apply "the knife vivisectionally to the very *virtues of their time*" — as Nietzsche does in the next chapter, "Our Virtues." Applying that knife, "they betrayed what their own secret was: to know a *new* greatness of humanity, a new untrodden way to its enhancement." What secret, untrodden way of greatness would a legislative philosopher take in "a world of 'modern ideas'"? Nietzsche's answer locates greatness in qualities that belong to the philosopher himself. Necessity dictates that in this time of fragmented specialists, greatness be found in range and multiplicity, in a philosopher's "wholeness in manifoldness" and in how far he "could extend his responsibility." In this time of "weakness of will," greatness is located in "strength of will, hardness, capacity for long-term decisions."

Before moving to the final features of greatness Nietzsche cites two historical precedents indicating that he measures the philosopher's untimely acts
today against the untimely acts of philosophers in the past. The two exemplary
ages are the sixteenth century, or the beginning of modern times, and the time
of Socrates, or the beginning of the Platonic age. In the "wildest waters and
stormfloods of selfishness" of the sixteenth century, the frenzy and turbulence
of Europe-wide religious wars, the philosopher Montaigne said, "We have to
go *that* way," a calming way that followed the ideal of a "dumb, renunciatory,
humble, selfless humanity"[21] — a way that became the modern way and now
has to be remedied. The time of Socrates, on the other hand, was marked by
"fatigued instincts," by "conservative old-Athenians who let themselves go,"
falling into mere pleasures "while still mouthing the splendid old words to
which they had no right." "Perhaps" — and this *perhaps* ranges over the whole
of what that most questionable phenomenon Socrates introduced — perhaps
what that post-Homeric, post-Marathon time needed to achieve greatness of
soul was what it drew from Socrates: irony. Socratic irony cut into his own
flesh, but it cut into the flesh of the noble as well, for it "spoke with a glance
that was understandable enough." Nietzsche invents a speech for Socrates'
understandable glance: "Don't dissemble in front of me! Here — we're equal!"
Socrates let old nobles know the act was up, but he replaced the old act with a
new act: the speech of Socrates' glance is ironic, it is dissembling speech prohibiting the old dissembling. For Socrates to claim equality with old nobles is
to dissemble his superiority to them; against a decayed inequality, he claims
equality fully aware, as a philosopher must be aware, of his own superior
rank.

"Today, conversely" — today no old nobility rules as in the time of Socrates,
nor does turbulence rule as in early modern times. Today is ruled by claims to
"equality of rights," claims that are the ultimate consequence of Socrates'
ironic claim to equality and of the modern ideal of humble humanity advanced
by Montaigne to tame the turbulence brought on by the Wars of Religion.
Today, as a consequence of the legislative acts of previous philosophers, the

21. Other statements about Montaigne indicate Nietzsche's judgment about his philosophical legislation: "What the lone individual Montaigne signifies in the turbulence of
the Reformation-spirit — a coming-to-rest-within-oneself, a peaceable being-for-oneself
and exhaling — and certainly that is how his best reader, Shakespeare, experienced
him — " (*RWB* 3); "Montaigne . . . this freest and mightiest of souls . . . . I would side with
him if the task were to make oneself at home in the world" (*SE* 2) — which in our times
cannot be the task. Montaigne and Socrates were also brought together in section 208,
where their ironic statements about knowledge serve as models for contemporary skeptics. On Montaigne in section 212, see Eden, *Political Leadership and Nihilism* 60–62.

philosopher finds himself in a time of general war against everything "rare, strange, privileged, the higher humans, the higher souls, the higher duty, the higher responsibility, the creative fullness of power and masterfulness" — a war against philosophy. On the model of previous philosophical actors, the philosopher today points to a new way to greatness: "What belongs to the concept 'great' is being-noble, wanting-to-be-for-oneself, being-able-to-be-other, standing-alone, and having-to-live-on-one's-own-resources." This is a list of hyphenated words because no single words have had to be invented for the strange, private self-concept of the philosopher. These are the words with which the philosopher "betrays something of his own ideal"; they betray the ideal that has always moved the philosopher, a Montaigne or a Socrates, whatever ironic speech they found it necessary to invent about themselves. It is the ideal of the free, very free mind that extends its responsibility to long-term decisions aimed at the enhancement of humanity.

The task assigned the philosopher in our time to betray his own ideal ends the ironic reserve that kept the philosopher's difference tactfully sheltered. He even makes a speech betraying his ideal, a speech that mirrors the ironic speech supplied to Socrates' glance and says what is now necessary. The speech is not simply what the philosopher says about his ideal but what he *stellt auf* — what he posits, what he sets out as traps are set out, what he deploys as a strategy is deployed. It is a speech on the great by a value-creating philosopher who says to his age, "Let greatness now be seen *this* way!": "He shall be greatest who can be loneliest, most concealed, most different, the human being beyond good and evil, the master of his virtues, the overrich in will; this shall be called *greatness:* just as varied as whole, just as broad as deep." In the age of science and the age of equality "we have to go *that* way," the way of the highest human exemplar, of the celebration of inequality as it has existed in our species in the most spirited thinkers.

But a question asked at the end of section 211 has to be repeated after this betrayal of the private ideal of the philosopher in all times: "Is greatness today — *possible?*" The reason for repeating the question about the possibility of the philosopher today is made apparent in the first sentence of the final section of the chapter.

What a Philosopher Is
SECTION 213

"What a philosopher is, that's hard to learn because it can't be taught: one must 'know' it, out of experience — or one should have the pride *not* to know it." Chapter 6 ends as it began, on experience, the singular experience of the philosopher, but by now it's clear that not all experience is bad experience. The showing of wounds — showing the injustice done the philosopher — has given way to the showing of health and privilege, the single example in this section again being the essential example, the privilege of thinking as the Ganges flows. Chapter 6 ends with its chief argumentative aim — its aim of persuading the scholar/scientist of the difference of the philosopher — focused on the decisive matter, pride: the success of the argument depends upon a quality in its audience, pride powerful enough to acknowledge something higher than itself and in that acknowledgment grant its right to supremacy. Objectivity, skepticism, and criticism operate unrefuted within a broader horizon supplied by wisdom, by experience that cannot be duplicated but whose claims can be weighed.

The philosopher Nietzsche knows where he stands: within a world of decayed Baconianism that has lost all memory of its origins in philosophy, in the rapidity, brevity, and rigor of Francis Bacon's thought, and in the political program set in motion by the philosopher Bacon, the rule of science over society. Nietzsche's political program bears close affinity to Bacon's, for it too aims to cement an alliance between philosophy and science. Nietzsche's alliance is with scholar/scientists generated by the Baconian project but now severed from their origins by the oblivion of genuine philosophy. To show a philosopher's wounds to those who regard philosophy as impossible is to moralize (204), to appeal to justice (211, 213): chapter 6 begins, peaks, and ends on an appeal to give things their due. The appeal can be affective only to those already disposed by their scientific bent to give things their due, investigators of nature disposed to respect and honor that on which they lavish their life energy. Nietzsche's rhetoric measures the souls of its audience and entrusts itself to necessity: objectivity, skepticism, and criticism dictate that scholar/scientists assent to a superior wisdom that accords with their criteria however much its experience transcends what can be attained by objectivity, skepticism, and criticism. Pride appeals to pride and pride rules.

The final section is not a summary of the preceding argument but a repetition of its essential point, the difference in the experience of thinking that separates philosophy and science, and a repetition of the consequence of that difference, philosophy's responsibility to rule. "All popular opinions" about philosophers and philosophical states "are false," but Nietzsche corrects only one such false opinion, the crucial error about philosophical thought. Philosophical thought is marked, Nietzsche reports, by a "copresence," a *Beieinander,* that "most thinkers and scholars" do not experience and therefore view as contradictory: "a bold lively spirituality that runs *presto*" and "a dialectical rigor and necessity that takes no false step." The copresence of rapidity and exactitude, *presto* and rigor, is not further explained, perhaps because it is exemplified everywhere in *Beyond Good and Evil* and discussed in sections 27–28. Instead, Nietzsche emphasizes its unbelievability: to speak of such experience in the presence of most thinkers and scholars is to speak of something "unworthy of belief." This is the key rhetorical problem of chapter 6: communicating a different experience of thinking to those whose lives are dedicated to thought, the authoritative thought of science. Nietzsche's explanation of the difference implicitly invokes his ontology of will to power with its twofold character of need or superabundance. For most, "every necessity is need" and not the streaming dialectical necessity Nietzsche reports as a kind of overflow of superabundance. Most thinkers and scholars experience thinking as a kind of subjection or obeying: a "painstaking, even humiliating having-to-follow and to-be-forced." Thinking itself counts for them "as something slow, hesitant, almost as tribulation" — experience that renders Nietzsche's claims about philosophical thinking unbelievable.[22] In a notebook from the time of *Beyond Good and Evil* Nietzsche wrote, "Abstract thinking is for many a tribulation, — for me, on good days, it's feast and frenzy" (*KSA* 11.34 [130]) — "something light, divine, closely related to dance and high-spiritedness," in the words of *Beyond Good and Evil*.[23] The authority of scientific thinking in a scientific age seems to stand as a greater danger to philosophy than other forms of thinking, for Nietzsche maintains that the philosopher's experience of necessity in thought can be more easily appreciated by artists, who seem to have "a finer sense of smell" in such matters.

The essay that is chapter 6 comes to a majestic end with a philosopher's authoritative speech about philosophy. Nothing as personal as showing wounds, nothing as urgent as moralizing brings this chapter to its culmination. Nietzsche ends on assertions wholly at odds with the current masks that have grown up around him as merely skeptical and critical or merely willful and nihilistic, assertions wholly in keeping with the high points reached at other well-prepared moments in this book. The philosopher claims a right to spiritual

22. Nietzsche made the same point in a joke in *GS* (231): "*The 'thorough'*: those who are slow to know suppose slowness is the essence of knowledge."

23. When bringing his thoughts on gay science to a new and fitting conclusion that ends his whole series of books on the free mind, Nietzsche again pictured the rapidity, brevity, and rigor characteristic of philosophical thinking while distinguishing it from the methodical procedures of science ("On being understandable," *GS* 381). Nietzsche there avows that he makes every effort to be understandable to scientific minds with a very different experience of thought. See also Nietzsche's claim to inspiration with respect to *Zarathustra*, inspiration that those "with an ounce of superstition" would call "revelation" (*EH* Books *Z* 3).

rule over a science the rules society, and he grounds that right in the ultimate court of appeal, nothing less than "the primordial law of things," a law that cannot be abrogated though modern ideas can act as if it does not hold. The ultimate ground for philosophy's right to rule is given in nature and human nature.[24]

Nietzsche expresses the accord of human nature and nature very concisely: "Ultimately there is a rank order of the soul's states with which the rank order of the problems accords." This natural accord of mind and nature generates philosophy's exclusivity: "The highest problems force back without mercy everyone who dares approach them without being predestined to their solution by the height and power of his spirituality." The highest problems, the problems of truth and the value of truth, are the domain of the philosopher, the thinker who combines presto with dialectical severity. Nietzsche even repeats this one example of the philosopher's difference, speaking of "the bold, light, delicate gait and course of his thought," but he does so in order to state once again that something additional is "above all" necessary for the genuine philosopher. As chapter 6 has led us to expect, what is above all necessary is the creation of values, the act that stands to philosophical thinking as its politics or legislation.

Nietzsche's final sentence employs an old language to gather the great themes of this chapter into a final statement: "right . . . virtue . . . responsibility . . . justice . . . love." These words, rethought, reminted, enter Nietzsche's language as the essential words of a philosopher subject to the primordial law of things and therefore required to act. Chapter 6 thus comes to its end on a claim about nature and a claim about right, "a *right* to philosophy" conferred solely by a long heritage that grants the philosopher or squanders on him the necessary virtues and toward which he learns responsibility.

The final sentence ends with another of those great lists with which Nietzsche favors his slow readers, seven items belonging to the "great responsibilities" of the philosopher. The list centers the virtue of justice, "great justice" that accords with the primordial law of things and that Nietzsche will define in "Our Virtues" (219). But as a list of responsibilities it ends unexpectedly, not on an action but on a passion generated by thought. If the slow eye of the philosopher "rarely admires, rarely looks up, rarely loves . . . ," it admires, looks up to, and loves only what is rare or rarest. At the very end of the chapter defining the philosopher and his necessary actions today, Nietzsche pictures

---

24. Eden judges this "a playful note," a merely rhetorical effort on Nietzsche's part to secure the difference between the philosopher and the scientist with "the appearance of an order of nature" (*Political Leadership and Nihilism* 92–93).

him looking up to the truly high as a lover. Eros has been, from Plato onward, a defining feature of the philosopher, love that is consequent upon glimpsing the whole, love that turns the privileged viewer into one who can claim to know nothing except the things of Eros. The philosopher's judgment on the whole is a lover's judgment. That love is, today, no longer expressible in a myth of permanent ideas accessible to purified mind; it is expressible as the opposite ideal, the ideal of a thinker who wants what was and is repeated to all eternity.

7

Our Virtues

Like the *we* of "We Scholars," the *our* of "Our Virtues" is ambiguous: in each case, the first person plural encloses the difference of the singular philosopher within the features of his broader audience; but in each case, the argument of the chapter gradually isolates the philosopher's difference while showing what the difference implies for his broader audience. *Our* virtues narrow from the virtues of normal moderns — compassion and the historical sense — to the virtue of free-minded moderns — honesty — to the virtue of the singular philosopher. That virtue is able to ground honesty in what is given by nature, two kinds of mind, "the basic will of the mind," which seeks comfort and ease, and the contrary will of the knower's mind, which seeks truth despite danger and tension (229–30). To understand the two kinds of mind is to understand why there must be implacable conflict between the virtues of moderns generally and the virtue of the seeker after knowledge, why they brand him an immoralist, why he puts them at risk. The conflict hinges on the question of suffering. Modern virtue aims to abolish suffering, the virtue of the knower seems to inflict suffering through its insistence on the value of truth. *Beyond Good and Evil* attains one of its greatest summits when the argument of "Our Virtues" climaxes as a case for cruelty, the cruelty of truth telling, the cruelty of the new philosopher who knows why he refuses Platonism, the philosophy whose noble lying aligned philosophy with the basic will of the mind to be comforted and at ease.

Grandsons of the Christian Pigtail, Sons of Anti-Christian Ire
SECTIONS 214–17

Section 214 The opening to chapter 7, customarily cheerful and intricate, reaches back to our distant forbears in virtue, to our Christian "grandfathers" and our modern "fathers" (216). We do not inherit our grandfathers' Christian virtue; on the contrary, our virtues are anti-Christian because they're compatible with our secret inclinations and our hottest needs, which Nietzsche lists as curiosity, an art of disguise, and cruelty of mind and senses. But in searching our labyrinths for our virtues, we encounter just what it is that we retain from our grandfathers: a pigtail of good conscience pinned to the back of our heads. The search in our labyrinths, Nietzsche suggests, will cost us that good conscience, depriving us of this aspect too of our inheritance. The opening section seems to promise that the movement of chapter 7 — its pursuit of curiosity, disguise, and cruelty — gradually robs free minds of the good conscience of their virtue, unsettling it or replacing it with the uneasy or bad conscience the philosopher causes (212).[1]

Sections 215–17 The three short sections 215–17 appear to be probes in search of our virtues; together they point to moral progress too moral to parade itself as progress in the age of progress. We have made moral progress beyond our grandfathers, Nietzsche claims, and also beyond our fathers — Enlightenment thinkers who grew ashamed first of religious posturing and then of antireligious ire. Our virtues are practiced with modesty and a concealment of goodness that prohibits ostentation in virtuous formulas. Taste rules: our fathers could not abide religious posturing; we cannot abide moral posturing. If our taste forbids covering up our immoralism, refusing to lie about it, then our virtues cannot include the moderate virtue of the old esotericism, mutually sheltering ourselves and others from deadly truths. Chapter 7 moves gradually to the problems presented by the cruelty of our virtue of honesty.

The Norm at War with High Spirituality
SECTIONS 218–21

Section 218 commands a task: "Study the philosophy of the 'norm' in its fight against the 'exception.'" Sections 219–21 initiate that study, vivisecting the norm to clarify the exception in its difference. A constant high-spiritedness runs through these sections, a gaiety and jauntiness flaunted by an exception in

1. The opening motto of book 5 of *GS* makes a similar promise based on the knowledge to be gained in the book. The opening section of the preface to *GM* contains a similar invitation to "men of knowledge" to "know ourselves," the implication again being that the knowledge gained entails a loss of innocence.

a risky, high-stakes contest that it seems impossible he can win but that he acts as if he cannot possibly lose.

Section 218   The most acute study of the soul these days, Nietzsche observes, is focused on less than the highest themes and conducted by less than the highest investigators. Since this bourgeois investigation of the bourgeois "is getting boring," Nietzsche recommends a change of focus for our amusement: consider instead "the subtle, involved, Jesuitical craftiness" with which the norm reacts to "the higher spirits and their tasks." This craftiness—an instinct—is a thousand times more subtle than the understanding of its victims, the higher spirits themselves. The study of the common man, already recommended as a necessary study for the philosopher (26), now focuses on the norm's instinctual reaction to the higher. Nietzsche's recommendation becomes a command to study philosophy: "Study, you psychologists, the philosophy of the 'norm' or 'rule' [*Regel*] in the fight with the 'exception.'" The philosophical fight between the norm and the exception is the comprehensive spiritual warfare already outlined in chapter 5, warfare that is now a contest between the autonomous herd and the rule of the philosophers of the future. How can the exception hope to win such a war against the instincts, a war on behalf of cruelty? Chapter 7 moves toward an answer to these questions.

Section 219   Nietzsche himself performs the commanded study of the philosophy of the norm. A concise statement of his teaching on the virtue of justice results: rooted in instinct, justice can be seen, at one extreme of the philosophy of the norm, as "spiritualized malice"; at the other extreme of the philosophy of the exception, justice can be seen as the "spiritualization" of an instinct to give all things their due. This section also provides an initial lesson on *Geist* and *Geistigkeit,* spirit and spirituality or mind and intellectuality, that prepares the basic lesson toward which this chapter moves, a lesson on spirit/mind that grounds philosophy itself in one of the two natural and competing dispositions of spirit/mind (229–31).

Nietzsche's study of the philosophy of the norm at war with the exception focuses on "moral judgments and condemnations" (*Urteilen und Verurteilen*) and finds three basic uses for them. First, they are the "favorite revenge" that "the spiritually/intellectually limited" employ against "those who are less so." Though it is here merely named, such revenge is the primary passion isolated by Zarathustra in the preachers of equality (*Z* 2 "On the Tarantulas") and analyzed as *ressentiment* in Nietzsche's next book (*GM* esp. 1.10–17). Second, moral judgments are "a kind of compensation for having been ill-favored by nature" and are directed in blame against the whole of nature. Finally, moral judgments are "an opportunity to acquire spirit and *become* refined:— malice spiritualized." Morality thus serves as a weapon against the other, as a consolation against nature as a whole, and as a device of self-improvement. Basic to such uses is a standard before which unequals appear as equals: the morality of revenge on humanity and nature generates an enforcing God before whom all humans are equal.

The section turns immediately to the resulting rhetorical problem: How to communicate the hard truth of an order of rank in the face of instinctually grounded moral judgments supernaturally reinforced? Nietzsche could say that "a high spirituality/intellectuality is beyond comparison with any kind of solidity and respectability of a merely moral human being." But to tell the truth that way "would make them enraged: — and I'll guard against doing that." Instead of purposely enraging the indignant, whose rage has already caused storms of revenge against humans, nature, and divinity, Nietzsche chooses a way of stating his "proposition" that flatters the norm. He describes three components of "a high spirituality/intellectuality"[2] in a way that emphasizes its necessary connection to morality. The first and second state that it is the ultimate outgrowth and synthesis of moral qualities, the result of progress in cultivation and refinement. The third states the highest claim of such *Geistigkeit* in terms of the virtue of justice and defines its task: "High spirituality/intellectuality is the spiritualization of justice and of that gracious severity which knows that it is commissioned to maintain the *order of rank* in the world among the things themselves — and not only among human beings."[3]

By what would this spirituality know itself commissioned? When Nietzsche addresses this issue later, the best answer he can give is: by nature itself (230–31). The highest natures are commissioned by nature to maintain the natural order of rank in the world. The great task is maintaining or conserving a rank order threatened with abolition by the moral. The context focuses rank order on the spirituality/intellectuality among human beings, and the maintaining of that rank order seems to be the primary task. But the description of the task is a report on what Nietzsche would say to the merely moral, and at the highest point what he would say does not in fact put the focus on humanity. Instead, it even downplays the human order of rank, making the philosopher's task of maintaining apply in the first instance to the order of rank among "the things themselves." This section had claimed that the revenge of the moral led to a teaching on nature that condemned nature for its neglect of the norm. To maintain the order of rank among things seems to require a vindication of

2. Compare the description of high spirituality/intellectuality in section 61.

3. Georg Picht views such justice as "the essence of the 'philosophers of the future'" (*Nietzsche* 94–131). Nietzsche expressed this view early: "All that exists is just and unjust and in both equally justified" (*BT* 9).

nature against this moral condemnation. Ultimately the revenge of the moral generated a monotheistic teaching on the gods before whose sovereign God all mere humans stand equal and nature itself is condemned as fallen. To maintain the order of rank among things themselves seems to require not only a vindication of nature but a vindication of the gods against the moral God who banished them and whose supremacy grounded the unnatural and unjust moral teaching of human equality. Nietzsche had promised that the study of the norm in its fight with the exception would yield "a theatrical spectacle good enough for gods and godly maliciousness!" (218). It is the spectacle of the creation of gods to serve human purposes. That spectacle continues: a teaching on the gods is entailed by the commission to maintain the order of rank among the things; the moral, supraphilosophical gods or God of Platonism die, replaced by philosophizing gods, gods less humane than humans but well disposed toward humanity, wanting to enhance it by making it "stronger, more evil, more profound; also more beautiful" (295).

Section 220   Nietzsche stays obedient to his command to "study the philosophy of the 'norm' in its fight with the 'exception,' " as that study now turns to the chief question of the book, the pursuit of truth. How is this pursuit understood by the norm and by the exception?

The common man, driven by his interests, can see no interest in the pursuit of truth and therefore calls it, with the encouragement of some philosophers, disinterested.[4] Every higher nature, driven by his interests, recognizes the falsity of that way of designating his pursuit of the truth, for here the naked truth is easy to come by: "The 'disinterested' action is a *very* interesting and interested action assuming. . . . ." — assuming that one has a more comprehensive and refined notion of interests than the common man, that one knows there are different kinds of souls with different kinds of interests.

To the first counterexample raised by the common man — "And love?" — Nietzsche responds rudely, "What? Even an action done out of love is supposed to be 'unegoistic'? But you fools — !" "Whatever is done out of love occurs beyond good and evil" (153). Love of *truth* is the ultimate concern of this section — and of the whole book, as indicated by its openings (preface, 1, 24, 45, 63, 186, 214). The pursuit of Truth herself by the highest lovers, the philosophers, is decidedly egoistic or driven by the most intense passion,

---

4. The section takes the philosophical laborer Kant to be the representative of the common man on the matter of interests. The common man's response to the lover of truth becomes an important theme of Plato's *Republic* when Adeimantus speaks up on his behalf to oppose Socrates' scandalous notion that the lover of truth should rule (*Republic* 6.487ff.)

though philosophers have chosen to cover up the interested, passionate character of their enterprise. As to the second supposed counterexample — "And the praise of sacrificers?" — Nietzsche responds that genuine sacrifice is always interested, it always gives up something for the sake of something it does not give up — like the sacrifice of the heart for the unsacrificed mind (23).

Nietzsche's dialogic display of the truth about love and sacrifice as deeply interested and interesting comes to a sudden end with a warning: "But this is a realm of question and answer in which a choosier mind does not like to linger." Why not, given that he dwells daily within this love and sacrifice? Perhaps because he does not like to be questioned about his most private passion or to be forced to give answers to the disinterested. Why not give answers? Because "in the end, [Truth] is a woman; one should not violate her." The philosopher who pursues truth knowing her to be a woman *tells* the truth knowing her to be a woman, for he has just shared Truth's own response to this questioning and answering on love and sacrifice: "Truth already finds it very much necessary to suppress her yawns when she has to answer." Truth yawns. But pursuit of the naked truth about Truth can no more be boring or disinterested to Truth herself than it is to her impassioned pursuer. She cannot be bored by such questioning — she's violated by it. How to forestall such violation? Artfully, in keeping with her nature. Feigning boredom, she avoids violation; feigning disinterest, she masks her deepest interests. And her lover is her accomplice, reporting only her apparent disinterest in their interest. Still, her secrets cannot remain the private possession of the one who wins them: just after Zarathustra won the deepest secret of Life herself he calls together "you who are wisest" to invite them to pursue that secret and share it themselves (Z 2 "On Self-Overcoming"). Truth is to be shared but only among lovers. No dogmatist in pursuit of the woman truth, he's no dogmatist in relating her secrets.

Section 221　Section 221 carries forward the question of self-interest with Nietzsche still in the theater. He allows "a moralistic pedant and dealer in trifles" to mount his stage and state morally his most important teaching on virtue. And then he takes the stage himself to defend his character against the laughers in his audience. Like Aristophanes, Nietzsche aims to win the laughers, and, like Aristophanes, he aims even more to win the thoughtful among the laughers who linger in order to understand their own laughter.

Nietzsche's moralistic pedant opens with a nice joke at the expense of someone supposedly free of self-interest. But then he says, "Enough" — enough of joking — and takes to moralizing. His moral is nothing other than Nietzsche's own main point in this chapter: selflessness in someone made to command is no virtue but the waste of a virtue. Nietzsche's view is expressed exactly in his pedant's generalization: "Every unegoistic morality that takes itself to be un-conditional and addresses everyman not only sins against taste, it is a provocation to sins of omission, one temptation *more* under the mask of philanthropy." The temptation of the morality of selflessness is for the rare to deny his rarity, to suppress his difference, philanthropically wasting on others what he should devote to himself.[5] The moral preacher of Nietzscheanism with his vocabulary of sin and temptation speaks in imperatives and italics: "One must compel moralities above all to bow before the *order of rank*." He appeals to conscience: "One must force their presumption onto their conscience." He forces morality on the moralities: they must agree that "it is *immoral* to say, 'What is right for one is fit for the other.' "

The author and director of the comedy takes the stage to comment helpfully on the likely reaction to this scene: we laugh at a moralistic critic of moralities. But if the pedant deserves to be laughed at, he deserves not only to be laughed at, for what he says is true, however odd it be that *he* says it. His author defends him: "One should not be too right if one wants to have the laughers on *his own* side; a tiny grain of wrong even belongs to good taste." Wanting the laughers on his side and exercising good taste, Nietzsche can commit the wrong of moralistic pedantry. He's part of the comedy and he knows it, but that only strengthens his hold on the thoughtful laughers.

Our Virtues as Normal Moderns
SECTIONS 222–25

Nietzsche's psychological study of the norm in modern times continues with a section on *Mitleid*, or compassion, the dominant virtue of modern times. Its chief point is made in a pun: opening with *Mitleiden*, it ends by separating the elements of this noun into the verb *mit leiden* — modern compassion is based in perceived suffering that wants to be assuaged by being universally shared. This claim is examined in a series of sections that culminate by clarifying the basic motive behind modern virtue: "*to abolish suffering*" (225).[6] Opponents of modern virtue can then be properly labeled — "*We immoralists!*" — and understood: they are advocates of the most immoral, advocates of suffering (226).

---

5. On the virtue of selfishness, see *D* 552 "*Ideal selfishness*" and *TI* Skirmishes 33: "*The natural value of egoism.* — The value of selfishness is equivalent to the physiological value of the one who has it."

6. In *GS* 333, "*The will to suffer and those who feel compassion*," Nietzsche remarks that the religion of compassion perhaps has another religion as its mother: "the religion of comfortableness."

Section 222   Psychologists who listen carefully will hear, Nietzsche claims, that compassion is "the only religion preached nowadays." Further, they will hear that the preaching of compassion is founded in self-contempt. In its economy, this section simply assumes what is examined at length elsewhere: modern virtue is the secular heir of Christianity; self-contempt is the fundamental motive behind such pessimistic or world-denying teachings; an ideal opposite to world-denial can be founded on the self-affirmation of different selves.

Section 223   Section 223 is the first of two sections on the historical sense.[7] Its opening scene takes place in the fitting room with Nietzsche mocking the modern European for desperate acts of costuming, covering the reality of the impoverished modern self with costumes from earlier times that were not aware that they were costumes, times so unself-conscious that they were what they wore. But all the efforts of present-day costuming to cover its reality end in despair: "Nothing really fits," "Nothing's really *me*."

"The historical spirit" or "the historical mind," however, turns this despair to advantage and opens the next act because the propensity to costume leads to the *study* of costume, ultimately the study of "moralities, articles of faith, tastes in the arts, and religions," custom as costume. Ours is the first age to understand the principles and ground of costuming or cosmetics, how our species dressed itself up to flatter itself and mask its faults. With that understanding there arises the possibility of the Great Carnival of costumes. The model European public festival, the mix of pagan and Christian festivity called Karnival, Fasching, mardi gras, serves as the model comedy but is no longer followed by Ash Wednesday or Lent.

Section 224   The carnival of costuming highlights the lack of a costume of our own. So mere laughter is not enough, and the second section on the historical sense shows why: our historical sense exhibits our lack of measure, our inability to judge high and low. The historical sense contrasts with "noble taste," which is characteristically narrow, proud of its own, and suspicious of the foreign, closed therefore to the best, to Homer, for instance. In this way Nietzsche prepares the crucial question: Is there a nobility that can provide the

---

7. In his account of the structure of this chapter Leo Strauss notes that "the discussion of the historical sense (aph. 223–24) is surrounded by a discussion of compassion (aph. 222 and 225): the historical sense mediates in a manner between the plebeian morality which boasts of its compassion with those who have been neglected by nature (aph. 219) and which is bent on the abolition of all suffering, and the opposite morality which goes together with awareness of the great things man owes to suffering (aph. 225)" (Strauss, *Studies in Platonic Political Philosophy* 188). The opposite morality, dependent in this mediating way on the historical sense, is the morality of "*we immoralists.*"

historical sense with measure, that can civilize half-barbarians by providing a measure neither arbitrary nor dogmatic?

This section of "Our Virtues" makes the historical sense "our great virtue," where *our* means "we modern humans." Three sections later Nietzsche speaks of honesty as "*our* virtue, the only one left to us" but *our* in that case means "we free minds," the smaller subset of moderns to whom Nietzsche makes his special appeal. In the section 224 that appeal takes the form of an invitation to admit something about ourselves, to own up to a particular aspect of our identity as moderns: we can own as our own[8] our singular capacity for costuming; but at the same time we must own as our own a half-barbarism lacking a measure of costumes.

Nietzsche defines the historical sense only briefly and parenthetically at the beginning because the whole section, a highly polished essay, gradually composes a complete definition as the preconditions and components of the historical sense are displayed and its virtues and vices described. The initial definition is a concise lesson in the study of costuming. It describes an acquired skill with two aspects: the historical sense is a capacity to guess quickly the rank order of value-estimates by which a people, a society, an individual lived, and a "divinatory instinct" for the relation of the authority of the values to the authority of the operative forces. This interpretive skill is a "sixth sense," a psychological seeing or hearing that reads the hierarchy of values in terms of the operative forces underlying them in the psyche.

The historical sense is a historic acquisition, an indirect consequence of the democratic revolutions in Europe, which cost Europe its nobility, as the French example shows.[9] The democratic revolution was not altogether a loss, Nietzsche admits, for "the mind saw its advantage in this" (as section 223 had already noted in describing a different advantage). The adaptive advantage here traced is our half-barbarian openness to other cultures, to the alien. The historical sense opened modern European culture to the great gains of awareness and appreciation of other cultures. But it did so democratically, lacking any measure of the relative value of cultures. Consequently, although it enabled Europe to recover Homer, it had no measure of the nobility of Homer or of other noble cultures.

---

8. The verbs *sich eingestehen, sich zugestehen,* and *sich gestehen* give the section the tone of an appeal to self-confession.

9. The next chapter articulates this theme of European history in more detail, placing great emphasis on its historical accuracy and the need to recognize it: clarity about the history of European nobility is a precondition of establishing a new nobility. See especially section 253.

What is noble? Nietzsche's praise of modern virtue, its openness to the foreign, requires a corresponding critique of noble vice: its prideful attachment to its own makes it unreceptive to what is not its own, to "the best things in the world" if they are not its own and cannot be made its booty. Conversely, praise of noble virtue requires a critique of modern vice. Calling the historical sense "our great virtue," Nietzsche displays the vice of our virtue: it "perhaps stands in a necessary opposition to *good* taste, at least to the very best taste." The very best taste is then described lyrically in a passage reminiscent of *Zarathustra:* "We're able only poorly, only hesitantly, only under compulsion to reproduce in ourselves the small, short, highest strokes of luck and transfigurations of human life as they here and there singly blaze up: those moments and wonders where a great force voluntarily stood still before the measureless and unlimited — , where one enjoyed an overflow of subtle pleasure in sudden restraint and petrification, in standing firm and establishing oneself on a ground that went on quaking."

Nietzsche's final injunction is to own as our own that "*measure* is alien to us." The use of *alien* (*fremd*) is nicely ironic: we to whom the alien is familiar find measure itself alien. "Like a rider on a forward flying steed, we let the reins fall before the infinite, we modern men, we half-barbarians — and are there in *our* blessedness only where we are most — *in danger.*"[10] Nietzsche himself, the *Versucher,* fully shares this modernity, epitomizing its drive forward into danger. Yet refusing to rein in before the danger of the infinite must be made consonant with a certain kind of measure; half-barbarism must be turned civil by being taught nobility. Can half-barbarians be taught measure by the human being with a high spirituality?

Section 225   After two sections on the historical sense, "our great virtue," Nietzsche returns to the ruling virtue of modern times, compassion, and delivers a lecture that borders on hectoring. He seems to deserve being laughed at for acting like his moralistic pedant and preaching morality to moralists, a fitting compassion preached to advocates of a dangerous compassion. *We* address *you* through the whole section, *we* reducing to Nietzsche alone, *you* being the teachers of modern compassion. The issue is suffering: *you* want to "abolish suffering" whereas "it seems *we* would rather have it higher and worse than ever!" Cruelty or the advocacy of suffering thus becomes explicit as the central issue of "Our Virtues."[11]

---

10. Nietzsche used this imagery again in the fifth book of *GS* 374–75.

11. The indispensability of this theme is made palpable by the culmination of the third treatise of *GM* (3.28), in which the meaning of suffering — "*To what end* suffering?" — is seen as basic to the whole history of the human interpretation of itself. Nietzsche explains

At the beginning and end Nietzsche criticizes *your* "foreground-thinking and naïveté," *you* who take pleasure and pain to be primary though they are only "secondary-states and side effects." Taking pleasure and pain as ultimate makes the replacement of pain by pleasure the highest good; virtue, action on behalf of the good, is thus reducible to the abolition of suffering. Nietzsche does not name the fundamental phenomenon when pressing his claim about the secondary character of pleasure and pain; instead, he appeals to the experience of "*form-giving* energies and an artist's conscience" — but readers will know that this is the will to power as expressed in its most spiritual form in the philosopher.

Ways of thinking that measure the value of things according to pleasure and pain look down with compassion on those who suffer. A way of thinking conscious of form-giving energies and an artist's conscience looks down with compassion on such compassion. This contest of compassions is a contest of goals. The goal of abolishing suffering seems merely an end (*Ende*), a termination of the history of the species in the "final humans." What should be done with great tension? Should its pain be dissipated in moderate pleasures or should it be used to shoot for distant goals? The advocate of tension, the seeming advocate of making suffering worse, lectures the teachers of modern compassion: "Don't you know" the lesson of history that all the enhancements of our species have come from "the discipline of suffering"? "Do you understand" the lesson of human nature that humanity unites creature and creator? — the creature in humanity having to be "formed, broken, forged, torn, burnt, made incandescent, purified" by the creator, by "form-giving energies." "Don't you grasp" that *our* compassion is compassion for *you*, for the teachers of the worst of all pamperings and weaknesses?[12]

"So it's compassion against compassion!" But one of the competing compassions thinks more deeply than the other: there are higher problems than the problem of pleasure and pain, and "every philosophy that stops with them is a naïveté." Modern compassion, based on a naive philosophy of pleasure and pain, can aim no higher than the abolition of pain. The competing compassion of a form-giving creator views the world as will to power and nothing besides and aims at the enhancement of the species, at what can be achieved only through suffering.

---

the opposition that ends *EH* — "*Dionysos versus the Crucified*" — as an opposition regarding "the meaning of suffering" (*KSA* 13.14[89]). *TI* ends on a similar note regarding Christianity and the Dionysian. See also *GM* 2.19–20, an expansion of *D* 18 on one aspect of cruelty, its pleasure.

12. See section 293 on the compassion appropriate to a *Herr*. See also sections 62 and 203 on the "indescribable anxiety" experienced by the opponent of modern compassion.

Suffering has now become the pivotal issue of "Our Virtues." Our mixed inheritance from Christian grandfathers and anti-Christian fathers unites on the goal of abolishing suffering. To advocate suffering against that inheritance is to lose the pigtail of good conscience and appear immoral (226). If honesty demands that advocacy, honesty will seem mere devilry (227). The comforting if boring moral teachings that prevail (228) condemn the cruelty of the advocate of suffering as a return to animality (229). A lesson in spirit or mind is thus required to show that cruelty belongs to our very nature as knowers (230). And if it belongs to "the basic will of the mind" to condemn the cruelty of the knower as a crime, the defense against that charge is that the drive to knowledge belongs to our species as an unteachable given (231).

Immoral Honesty
SECTIONS 226–27

The only section in this chapter with a title,[13] the thirteenth section is paired at the center of the chapter with the section on honesty.[14] "Immoralists" whose virtue is honesty fight the war of values, "compassion against compassion," announced in the previous section.[15]

Section 226   The world of concern to Nietzsche is a far deeper world than the world of concern to the *you* of the previous section, who measure the value of things by pleasure and pain. You, however, represent the dominant moralities of hedonism or pessimism, utilitarianism or eudaimonism; therefore, in turning to *our* morality we might as well call ourselves, "*We immoralists!*" for we can't avoid appearing so to you.

"The world of any concern to us" — that phrase had occurred in section 34, the central section of chapter 2, and led to section 36, the argument that the world seen from the inside is will to power and nothing besides. The world of concern to *us* therefore extends to the world as such, the world as it is, not

13. Such italicized titles had been used for every section of *HH, D,* and *GS.* The only other titled sections in *BGE* are 83, 87, 140, 165, 274, and 294.

14. From 214 to 239 should be twenty-six sections, but there are two section 237's, or twenty-seven sections, in the seventh chapter. Either the center falls between two sets of thirteen or two sets of thirteen center the fourteenth section, 227.

15. On "immoral," see *D* 103: "I don't deny what goes without saying — assuming I'm no fool — that many actions called immoral [*unsittlich*] are to be avoided and opposed and likewise that many called moral [*sittlich*] are to be done and encouraged — but I mean: the former like the latter *for other reasons than till now.*" Nietzsche explains his use of the term *immoralist* in *EH* Destiny 2, 4–6. He defined the term *immoralist* in a letter to Carl Fuchs (29 July 1888): "an *Immoralist* (the highest form, till now, of "intellectual rectitude," which is *permitted* to treat morality as illusion, after it has itself become *instinct* and *inevitability*)."

simply the world of pleasure and pain. That world of concern to us is "almost invisible and inaudible," out of reach of those whose philosophy stops with the naïveté that pleasure and pain are fundamental. Nietzsche immediately defines the world of concern to him as the world of subtle commanding, subtle obeying, the characteristic terms he employs when explaining will to power as the way of all beings. If this world is "well defended against clumsy observers and familiar curiosity," it leaves its own defenders defenseless against the moral; the ontological foundations of the new moral teaching banish its advocates from the world of the moral.

In this world of subtle commanding and obeying, *we* are commanded: Nietzsche presents himself as passive to forces that command him — he's "been spun into a strict yarn and shirt of duties and *can't* get out of it." "We're men of duty, we, too." It is true that "sometimes, we dance in our 'chains' " — Nietzsche seems, in his books, almost always to dance in his chains — but more often, he says, "it is no less true" that "we're impatient with all the secret hardness of our fate," our *Geschick*, what is granted or given to us. The free, very free mind finds itself bound to a duty it cannot evade. It is tethered, but not to the pleasures and pains that bind most minds; it is tethered to duty commanded by what the mind glimpses of the world of concern to us, the world as it is. The duty that falls to the freest mind has been defined in "Our Virtues" as the spiritualization of justice, the gracious severity "which knows itself commissioned to maintain the order of rank in the world, among things themselves — and not only among humans" (219). That duty remains a "secret hardness" because the ground of its imperative cannot be made plausible; instead, that dutiful mind must seem perversely free, immorally choosing a destructive task.

Nietzsche ends his meditation on the fated solitude of the philosopher by saying, "But we can do what we like: fools and appearances will say against us, 'These are men *without* duty' — we'll always have fools and appearances against us!" Condemnation of the philosopher is unavoidable, given that his imperative is pronounced by an oracle inaudible to others. Does Nietzsche's judgment that his trial will end in conviction prove that he failed to consider the philosophic strategy developed by Plato and Xenophon from the trial and death of Socrates? Their prudent way of noble lying sheltered philosophic immorality in the very virtue it analyzed as limited and limiting, necessary and desirable for you but not a reasonable restraint on us. Did the Socratics develop a timeless strategy for philosophical revolutionaries that Nietzsche failed to attend to?[16] On the contrary, Nietzsche maintains that the natural history of morality commands an end to the Socratic strategy of noble lying,

16. For an authoritative guide to Xenophon's presentation of this strategy, see Leo Strauss, *Xenophon's Socratic Discourse: An Interpretation of the Oeconomicus.*

not because of strictures against lying but because morality itself has become a threat to the natural. The next section, on honesty, the one virtue left to free minds, claims that it is no longer fitting to do what Plato did, mix prudence, prudence, prudence with stupidity, stupidity, stupidity (197) for reasons that will soon be made clear (228–31). But the next section also argues that it is not fitting to be stupidly honest. Instead, honesty, while reasonably forbidding the "immoral" to compromise with moral stupidity, does not preclude prudence on its own behalf; it commands artfulness, ministerial art in the service of the transmoral, nature as it is.

Section 227 "Our Virtues" states that "*our* virtue," the only one left to us free minds, is *Redlichkeit*—honesty or, more exactly, probity, steadiness in honesty understood as intellectual honesty.[17] The root of *Redlichkeit* is *reden* and focusing on the root implies candor in speech, frankness, the *parrhesia* that was the famous virtue of the Athenians. Nietzsche can even offer a kind of prayer on behalf of our virtue: "May its brightness remain spread out like a golden blue mocking evening light over this aging culture and its musty murky earnestness"—this earnest age is honest in its way, may its honesty be made transparent by the evening light of a bright golden blue honesty.

The section is dramatically conversational, Nietzsche addressing free minds and finding himself addressed by the earnest. The conversation ends in counsel because our virtue may become our vice if not constantly kept awake by our "devilishness." The evening character of our culture suggests that Redlichkeit is the one virtue left to free minds because it is the one that can be publicly claimed, *the* surviving virtue of a Christian culture whose adherence to honesty cost it all its tenets but this one. While surviving in the godless heirs of God, it can flourish only if constantly "worked on," driven by more primary forces or whatever remains in us of devilishness. Nietzsche lists five aspects of such devilishness, virtues now considered vices, vicious-appearing virtues that supplement our one publicly admissible virtue:

— "our disgust with the clumsy and inexact," with any form of vagueness that refuses to be hardened in the discipline of science (230);

17. In a subtle analysis that sets out the subtleties of Nietzsche's historical account of *Redlichkeit* and *reden* in GS 110–11, Alan White ("The Youngest Virtue") shows why it is unfitting to translate *Redlichkeit* as *honesty,* or *probity,* or any other word without rethinking the content of those words. Nietzsche had the same problem with Redlichkeit: he gives an old word new content. A summary definition cannot wholly capture that newness, but White speaks of the *redlich,* the honest, as "those who are aware of the perpetual possibility of seeing and naming differently" and of taking delight in such "looking and talking." The context White gives for his illuminating discussion is fittingly Nietzschean: can life, which cannot be trusted (to be definitively this or that), nevertheless be loved?

— "our *'nitimur in vetitum'* — striving for the forbidden," Ovid's praise for defiance of the authority of moral forbidders, a fitting motto for immoralists;[18]

— "our adventurer-courage," the philosophical courage of experimenters, a virtue that is a vice in settled societies, as Plato's Socrates acknowledged when he defined *"political* courage" as the tenacity to hold fast to what had been dyed into one;[19]

— "our crafty and choosy curiosity," not the "comfortable curiosity" of the preceding section, which strands one at the naive level of pleasure and pain;

— "our subtlest, most disguised, most spiritual will to power and world-overcoming which passionately soars and swarms over all realms of the future." *Will to power,* used here for the only time in this chapter, tops the list of aids for our honesty, an ascending list of condemned devils to keep our virtue vigorous. "The most spiritual will to power" is philosophy (9). If philosophy is to come to the aid of honesty, if we are to aid our virtue with this devil, then honesty is conscious of its deepest ground, "the world of concern to *us,"* the world "in which *we* have our fear and our love" (226). Our virtue is conscious of being grounded in nature, its kind of mind is a gift of nature (230).

Our virtue of Redlichkeit is therefore by no means our deepest or greatest virtue, only our sole publicly defensible one in an earnestly honest age, our only godly virtue. But even our one sanctified virtue will be denied us, as shown by the little drama that now breaks into this conversation among free minds. Nietzsche had ended his list of aids for our virtue by speaking once again as a theologian: "Let us come to the aid of our 'god' with all our 'devils!'" Such radical theologizing invites misunderstanding: "It's probable that we'll be misunderstood and mistaken for others: What does that matter! They'll say: 'Their "honesty" — that's their devilishness and nothing else!' — What does that matter!"[20] Custodians of the official theology, whose moral teaching is based on the superficiality of pleasure and pain, are bound to trace even our god to a devil. Nietzsche does not directly answer the slanderers of our god, preferring instead to examine the slandered. If we're honest we'll grant that the moralistic slanderers are right. Our virtue *is* driven by a devil if we take the view ("to speak in the popular language") that the will to power

18. Ovid, *Amores* 3.4.17. Nietzsche makes "We strive for the forbidden" a conqueror's motto in *EH* (preface 3) that replaces an old conqueror's motto: "In this sign my philosophy will conquer one day, for what has been forbidden so far as a matter of principle has always been — truth alone." According to Eusebius, the sign of the cross was given to the Roman emperor Constantine with the words, "In this sign conquer" (*Life of the Blessed Emperor Constantine* 28–32).

19. *Republic* 4.429b-430c.

20. Nietzsche employs "the proverb of Zarathustra that runs: *'was liegt daran!'"* (Z 4 "The Nightwanderer's Song," 1).

teaching means that "God is refuted but the devil is not" (37). Nietzsche responds to his opponent's theologizing with a deeper, historicizing theology: "Weren't all gods till now such holy-grown, rebaptized devils?" The birth and death of gods is a cultural process in which old gods can be expected to oppose new gods in the most effective way open to them. But even if demonization is an old story, could it be true in our case? The questioning inspired by the slander turns inward as honesty takes its natural, self-reflexive course: "And what do we know ultimately about ourselves?[21] And how the spirits that lead us want to be *named?*" Can we honestly say that what leads us is divine rather than demonic? Nietzsche clearly wants to practice "the one sort of honesty" that "has been alien to all founders of religion and their like: They've never made their experiences a matter of conscience for knowledge" (*GS* 319).

"Let's take care," Nietzsche says, that our honesty not become "our vanity, our finery and pomp, our limit, our stupidity" — which it would if we failed to keep our honesty honest with such foundational questions, thinking we knew ourselves when we did not. "Let's take care," Nietzsche says again, "that we don't ultimately become saints and bores out of honesty!" This warning supplies a playful link to the next section, a treatment of how useful the boring has been for morality and how dangerous it would be for morality if it became interesting. Daring to make morality interesting, Nietzsche says, "Is life not a hundred times too short — to get bored in it? One would really have to believe in eternal life in order to. . . . ." To what? — to do with our virtue what Plato did with virtue: "Plato is boring" (*TI* Ancients 2), Plato tied virtue dishonestly to the eternal, the ultimate boring. Let's stay interested and dangerously interesting by always calling our virtue to account. Let's not fall prey to the eternalizing boring, to monotonotheism, whose heirs we are. Let's push on into the transmoral, questioning what's involuntary in our honesty, recognizing that "the decisive value of an action lies in what is *unintentional* in it" (32).

Our Cruel Task
SECTIONS 228–31

If modern virtue is the exercise of compassion aimed at abolishing suffering, then the worst vice to the modern is cruelty, the imposition of suffering. Nietzsche is most clearly an immoralist because he advocates suffering. The argument of this chapter here reaches its critical point: our immoral virtue, honesty, ultimately philosophy itself, is a form of spiritualized cruelty (229). Philosophy must face the fact that it is contrary to the basic will of the mind, the

---

21. "We're unknown to ourselves, we knowers" — thus begins Nietzsche's next book (*GM* preface 1), another attempt to be honest about what most deeply moves the inquirer who inquires into what he judges to be the demonic motive of others.

natural disposition of most minds; yet philosophy is itself grounded in a natural disposition of mind, a cruel disposition, even an insane one (230). Philosophy's recovery of the natural in humanity is therefore a gift of nature (231).

Section 228   No wonder Nietzsche opens section 228 by asking for forgiveness: the immoralist proves that his honesty is his devilry by daring to give an entertaining account of the boring in morality. Nietzsche finds that "all moral philosophy till now has been boring and belongs among the sleeping pills." His own task, "wakefulness itself" (preface), has discovered that "it matters a lot[22] that as few people as possible think about morality" — as many as possible should act morally unthinkingly. "It therefore matters a *whole* lot that morality not become interesting some day." Ignoring his own decade-long efforts, Nietzsche adds, "Not to worry! It stands now as it always stood: I don't see anyone in Europe who has a concept of the fact (or *owns up to it*) that reflection on morality could become dangerous, capturing, seductive, that *calamity* could be present in it."

The moral opiate this section makes interesting is English utilitarianism.[23] One reason for singling out this contemporary moral philosophy is indicated in chapter 8: the modern moral ideas that have captured Europe are English ideas, and the war against them has been the task of German philosophy. The broader reason seems to be a kind of inevitability in their becoming interesting: the trajectory of nihilism dictates that "Christian" morality cannot long survive the death of God (*TI* Skirmishes 5). This section offers an immoral definition of *Moralist:* so far from being a puritan defender of morality, "isn't a *Moralist . . .* a thinker who takes morality to be questionable, to be worthy of a question mark? Shouldn't moralizing — be immoral?" The final question with its precise ambiguity expects an affirmative answer in both the moral and immoral senses of *moralizing*. The wicked tone of this section, including the fine jabs in English words — surprising in a writer not fluent in English[24] — allows Nietzsche to argue like his moralistic pedant (221) while remaining immoral.

22. Given the other links between 227 and 228, "Es liegt viel daran" and "Es liegt *sehr* viel daran" (in the next sentence) could well echo Zarathustra's proverb, "Was liegt daran?" repeated twice near the end of 227. Devilry in morality leads to a whole new understanding of what matters morally.

23. This section is greatly expanded in the First Treatise of *GM*. Nietzsche's little joke about utilitarians helps make them interesting: "You utilitarians, you too love everything useful only as a *vehicle* of your inclinations, — you too really find the squeak of its wheels unbearable?" (174).

24. For instance, Nietzsche puns on the English word *cant* and connects it with "*moral Tartuffery*" to suggest the link with Kant.

Section 229   Cruelty, Nietzsche argues, belongs to our very nature as an animal species and needs to be enhanced if our species is to be enhanced. But our age, like "every late age," prides itself on having tamed the "wild cruel animal" in humanity. Advocating cruelty in an age of compassion violates "the collusion of centuries" to keep silent about the truth of the human animal. Nietzsche is aware of the risk he runs in refusing to honor such exoteric silence; when he lets "one such truth slip out of me," he lets it slip defiantly: "Let others capture it again and give it so much 'milk of the pious ways of thinking' that it lie quiet and forgotten in its old corner." The truth Nietzsche lets slip he declares "my principle": "Almost everything that we call 'higher culture' rests on the spiritualization and deepening of *cruelty*." If this is true, a teaching on virtue that aims to abolish suffering threatens the very sources of human achievement.[25]

To understand the cultural value of cruelty it is necessary to abandon the old psychology with its faith in opposite values and invoke the new psychology, which recognizes only drives and passions and their spiritualization. The old psychology conceived cruelty as the suffering of others. The new psychology uncovers an element of enjoyment in one's own suffering, in self-denial or even in self-mutilation and especially in the self-cruelty of "the Pascalian *sacrifizio dell'intelletto*." "Finally," leaving behind the achievements of religious cruelty (sacrificing the mind, the only source of knowledge, for the heart, the source of comfort and consolation) and moving upward, Nietzsche turns to the achievements of philosophic cruelty, those of "the knower" or "the seeker after knowledge," *der Erkennende:*[26] "Finally, consider that even the seeker after knowledge, in that he forces his mind to know *against* the inclination of his mind and often enough against the wishes of his heart — namely to say No where it would like to affirm, love, worship — prevails [or rules, *waltet*] as the artist and transfigurer of cruelty." The highest artistry of cruelty is knowledge; it cruelly seeks the truth even when the mind is most inclined to love untruth. Once again the value of the will to truth, the most persistent theme of the book, becomes the focus. The final sentence concludes, "indeed, every taking-deeply, taking-fundamentally is a violation [a rape, *Vergewaltigung*], a wanting to inflict pain on the basic will of the mind which unceasingly wants appearances and surfaces — in every wanting to know there is already a drop

25. See *GM* 2.6: "In *Beyond Good and Evil* 229 (and even earlier in *Dawn of Day* 18, 77, 113), I pointed with a cautious finger to the ever-growing spiritualization and 'deification' of cruelty that runs through the entire history of higher culture (and in a significant sense even constitutes it)."

26. On *Erkennende,* see Clark and Swenson, eds., *GM*, end note to 1.1, 119–20.

of cruelty." Mind violates mind: philosophy is cruelty exercised against one's own basic inclination.[27] This claim of the cruelty of knowledge is so important to a proper understanding of virtue that Nietzsche cannot allow it to stand unexplained: "Permit me a clarification," he says at the opening of the next section, the great climax toward which the whole argument of "Our Virtues" has been moving. The clarification expands the one truth Nietzsche let slip against the centuries-long collusion to keep silent, a truth about cruelty: knowledge is cruel to our affirmative and loving instincts, it deprives them of what they think they cannot live without.

The centuries-long collusion to keep silent includes Platonism's defensive strategy for philosophy, its concession to the basic will of the mind permitting it its comforting toys. "Our Virtues" peaks with Nietzsche's anti-Platonic strategy for philosophy, his "letting slip" the cruel truth kept silent by Platonism. Once let slip can others secret it back to its old corner again by feeding it "milk of the pious way of thinking"? Not under the evening sky of honesty, not at the end of the moral period with its hope for the appearance of experimental tempter philosophers of the future. What Nietzsche lets slip is cruelly unforgettable.

Section 230   Nietzsche's clarification of the basic will of the mind exists to explain the knower and his cruelty. It offers an account of knowing that is grounded in ontology, the way of all beings. It is ultimately a defense of the virtue of the cruel philosopher: philosophy is the pinnacle of naturalness that affirms the whole of nature, including what it recognizes as the natural antinaturalness of the basic will of the mind.

The clarification moves through three main stages: First, the basic will of the mind is a drive to mastery through a kind of knowledge. Second, a will to ignorance is an only apparently opposed drive, being in fact a subtle modification of the basic will of the mind. Third, the will of the knower genuinely opposes the basic will of the mind. Having arrived at this irreconcilable opposition, Nietzsche shows — in "Our Virtues" — why the knower must refuse the cosmetic of virtuous names for the inclination of his mind, and in some of the most memorable and important sentences in the book explains the task that falls to the knower. But the solid sanity of the basic will of the mind can still raise a reasonable question about the "insane task" of the knower. The section ends with that question unanswered, for the answer is found in the

27. The movement of thought is similar to that found in sections 55–56, where "religious cruelty" includes the cruelty of the knower; but here Nietzsche does not even intimate what is emphasized there: the passion to affirm, love, and adore can be reinstated by the mind but only in application to what the cruel mind has glimpsed of the world as it is.

next section with its ultimate appeal to nature itself. The defense of cruelty, a defense of philosophy, ends in an appeal to nature.

"That commanding something that is called by the people '*der Geist*'" — mind, spirit, with an echo of *ghost* — is defined ontologically by Nietzsche as a mode of the will to power, though the term is not used. The mind "wills to be master in itself and around itself and to feel itself as master." Intrinsic to its commanding is its way of knowing: "the will from multiplicity to simplicity, a binding, taming, lusting-to-rule, truly mastering will."[28] This basic will of the mind is shared with "all that lives, grows, and multiplies." Continuous in kind with all of life, the basic will of the mind is fundamentally a drive not to self-preservation but to enhancement and expansion — mind evolved as a mastering device. The strength of the mind to appropriate the foreign, to take it into itself, displays itself in a "powerful inclination to make the new like the old, to simplify the many-fold, to overlook or push away the completely contradictory" and generally to falsify the whole world of experiences to the degree that it facilitates mastery over it. The "intention" of the mind in its basic activity is "to the incorporation of new 'experiences,' the lining up of new things along old lines, — that is, to growth or more precisely to the *feeling* of growth, the feeling of increased strength." The basic will of the mind thus incorporates by misrepresenting in a way that facilitates mastery; in other places (e.g., 268 and GS 354) Nietzsche describes the natural history of this misrepresenting as a process of natural selection that "physiology and the history of animals" now enable us to begin to comprehend. Nietzsche's evolutionary psychology and biology seem as prescient for those sciences as does his energy model for physics.

Nietzsche then considers "an apparently opposite drive of the mind" that in fact serves the same will to mastery but does so through deception and self-deception. He distills into twenty lines and three classes the fruits of decades of investigation into the human propensity to simplification and falsification. What the basic will of the mind cannot digest it pushes away or denies, what it cannot master by incorporation it masters by refusal, by a will to ignorance. Nietzsche adds two significant subcategories to the deceptive forms of mastering, more sophisticated, self-aware forms of lying. The first is "the occasional will of the mind to let itself be deceived"; the basic will of the mind is here portrayed affirmatively in its spirited, culture-creating play within a horizon known to be arbitrary and self-imposed, but achieving the goal of "the commanding something" that is spirited mind, mastery over a world it cannot

28. See the reflection on "simplification and falsification" (24) that opens the chapter on the free mind; see also 34.

otherwise overpower. The second more sophisticated subclass of the mind's deceptive mastery is active deception of others, "the by no means unproblematic readiness of the mind to deceive other minds and misrepresent itself before them." This rich category of deception extends from individual acts of cosmetic beautification to "the problem I have studied longest, the psychology of the 'improvers' of humanity," the pious fraud, "the heirloom of all philosophers and priests who 'improved' humanity" (*TI* Improvers 5). Nietzsche calls this activity of the mind "the continual urge and surge of a creative, form-giving, changeable force." As a student of such artful deception by philosophers and priests, Nietzsche claims that the "mind enjoys . . . the feeling of its security in this — precisely through its Protean-arts is it certainly best defended and hidden!"

Nietzsche's clarification of the basic will of the mind stresses the naturalness of custom, of beliefs and practices that misrepresent the world in order to master it. The antinatural is natural to the mind of humanity; it naturally opposes the palpable but indigestible truths of nature such as humanity's animal nature, the truth Nietzsche is bent on letting slip (229). The basic will of the human mind inclines it powerfully to cosmetics, to lying surfaces, and philosophy till now permitted or encouraged that natural inclination.

The clarification of the basic will of the mind comes to an end with an exclamation point and a dash as Nietzsche turns to the reason for the clarification, his explanation of the contrary inclination of the mind of the knower. "The sublime inclination of the knower works against the basic will to appearance, to simplification, to mask, to cloak, to the surface." This opposed inclination "*wants* to take things and does take things deeply, multiply, fundamentally." "Every brave thinker," given to self-examination while examining the whole, will recognize the cruelty of his intellectual conscience and say to himself, "There's something cruel in the inclination of my mind," while adhering defiantly to that cruel inclination regardless of what the virtuous say to him. The gathering argument of the whole chapter — opposition to modern virtue, which aims to abolish suffering and therefore regards cruelty as the ultimate vice — now reaches its sharpest point, the cruelty of the knower, the seeming misanthropy of the will to truth.

Nietzsche's defense of the cruelty of "the intellectual conscience and taste" of the knower unfolds in three stages: Should the knower mask his own inclination to get behind all masks? No, the present task of philosophy forbids it. But then the philosopher must stand trial and defend himself against a charge put by "everyone."

Nietzsche imagines a softer way for "us free, *very* free minds" (preface, 44) to speak: "It would sound nicer if, instead of cruelty, one accused us [*nach-*

sagte] . . . of something like '*ausschweifende Redlichkeit*' — honesty run riot, honesty out of control." It would sound nicer if we were accused of our virtue. The sentence adds two verbs suggested by nachsagte: *nachraunte, nachrühmte* — whispered about, praised about — and nachrühmte leads naturally to *Nachruhm* — fame: "will it perhaps be our eventual fame" to be described in terms of an honesty out of control rather than cruelty? Will Nietzsche's reputation for cruelty eventually be replaced by a reputation for excessive virtue? "Meanwhile — for there's plenty of time till then," Nietzsche returns to the present, where he's bound to be accused of cruelty. "Our whole work till now makes us sick of this moral taste"; the investigator of the natural history of morality finds himself unable to endure the lying labels that deny our animal nature. Nietzsche repudiates the virtuous terms used to describe what moves the philosopher, beginning with Redlichkeit, the very word he had used to name our virtue, and passing to parallel terms used earlier in the book, "love of truth, love of wisdom, sacrifice for knowledge, heroism of the truthful." His repudiation of Redlichkeit certainly looks like Redlichkeit out of control. Virtuous in his loyalty to his inclination but unable to endure moral words to name it, Nietzsche chooses *cruelty* as the designating term, mindful that the future may choose to apply milder terms to him. This is a published report on Nietzsche's private inclination of mind: Isn't it too a kind of moral posturing, bravery turned to bravado? No student of posturing with Nietzsche's subtlety could declare himself an enemy of posturing without posturing.

Nietzsche calls himself names — "we hermits and marmots" — that tie philosophy to human solitaries and shy mammals of burrows and underground passageways — the hermit of Sils Maria finding kinship with the marmots that abound in the hills around Sils Maria and whose shrill cries echo *unheimlich* through the valleys. The names signal the task assigned to the mind opposed to the basic will of the mind after the latter has dominated for millennia: solitary underground discoveries are to be hauled into the open, challenging philosophy's history of moral lying that allowed us to think we're not the animals we are. Secrets kept covered by the agreement of centuries are now let slip; private honesty breaks into the open as cruelty. The hermit's conscience refuses cosmetics, placing cosmetic terms "among the old lying makeup, rubbish, and golddust of unconscious human vanity." The old philologist employs the language of philology for his crucial point: "The terrifying basic text of *homo natura* must once again be brought out and recognized." There *is* a basic text of human nature. It is terrifying. It has been recognized before. It can be made visible by erasing the painted surface of flattering lies. These claims are expanded in the ten-line sentence that brings this section and the whole chapter to its memorable climax.

The cruelty of the philosopher is inseparable from his task. Three verbs set out that cruel task: *zurückübersetzen, Herr werden,* and *machen.*

zurückübersetzen: the philologist-philosopher faces a translation task, translating humanity back into nature; as the next two verbs indicate, the translation task is twofold, interpreting a palimpsest and enforcing the primacy of the basic text.

Herr werden: Nietzsche varies his phrase *basic text of homo natura* by a single adjective in order to indicate what the translation task entails: the terrifying basic text is also *eternal.* Nietzsche, fountainhead of deconstructive efforts to deny the fundamentality of any text, speaks of human nature as an eternal text. Human nature, product of an evolutionary history, is ineradicable by cosmetics, remaining present as the deep-down regardless of what is "scribbled and painted" over it by humanity's writers and artists serving the basic will of the mind. The contrary will opposes that basic will by becoming master over those interpretations, tracing moral misinterpretation back to its premoral text.

machen: the philosopher's task in the present carries forward the task already well begun by great philosophers like Bacon and Descartes: "grown hard in the discipline of science," humanity must now be forced to stand before itself in the very way modern science has already forced it to stand before the rest of nature. Science serves the opposing will of the mind, disciplining humanity through its de-moralizing interpretation of nature. Nietzsche assumes the gains of modern science and defines philosophy's present task as an application of the discipline of science to our species.[29] The task is to make humanity *for* itself what it is *in* itself; it is the task of a knower who surpasses even the heroic knowers of the Greeks, a super-Oedipus, a super-Odysseus who refuses to do what they did. The task is to gaze on the truth about humanity "with unshocked Oedipus-eyes," eyes that are not plucked out even though they see the horrifying truth. And the task is to turn away from tempting tales about humanity "with sealed Odysseus ears," no longer even wanting to hear the Siren song of "old metaphysical bird catchers who have piped at humanity all too long, 'You are more! You are greater! You are of a different origin!' " With eyes open to the truth of human origins and ears closed to interpretations that belie what the eye sees, the hermit and marmot has the task of educating humanity to the truth of human nature. *Retranslat-*

29. See *GS* 109: "When will we complete our de-deification of nature? When will we begin to *naturalize* us humans in terms of a pure, newly discovered, newly redeemed nature?" The whole of section 109 outlines the task of the philosopher in the de-deification of nature.

ing, becoming master, and *making* "may be a strange and insane task, but it is a *task* — who would want to deny that?"

Like so many of the high points in this dramatic theater of a book, this one too draws a response, a question Nietzsche asks on behalf of everyone: "Why we would choose it, this insane task? Or differently asked: 'Why knowledge at all?' " This is *the* question of the book, the question put by the Sphinx or by Oedipus in its very first section: What is the value of the will to truth? Why not rather comforting fictions? "Our Virtues" puts philosophy on trial again, accused by everyone, by the basic will of the mind in profound fear and bolstered by the assurance of secure morality: Why not quiet sanity? Why this insane devilishness?[30]

"And we, pressed this way, the we who've already asked this of ourselves a hundred times, we found and find no better answer. . . ." Than what? The accused has no better answer than the answer just given that there are two natural inclinations of mind. Or the answer given in the following section that philosophy is an inescapable gift of nature. Or the answer given in the whole book that philosophy accords with what it discovers, the way of all beings, and glimpses a new ideal of affirmation of all beings and sets in motion the ultimate politics on behalf of the natural order of the beings. The accusation of cruelty is the accusation already made a hundred times: "Why philosophy at all?"

Section 231   Learning transforms us, section 231 begins, but then argues that at the bottom of us lies something untransformable by learning, "something unteachable, a granite of spiritual *Fatum,* of predetermined decision and answer to predetermined selected questions." The whole of *Beyond Good and Evil* plus autobiographical records such as the preface to *On the Genealogy of Morality* make it clear that *the* predetermined question for Nietzsche was, "Why knowledge at all?" Why commit the crime against the basic will of the mind? Why philosophy, cruel recovery of our animal nature in a silent, surging universe? Because, section 231 answers, such spiritedness is given in us as our

---

30. It was a great event of the twentieth century when the greatest Platonist of recent centuries, perhaps since Alfarabi, Leo Strauss, seemed to deny that this was a worthy task. Strauss publicly sided with Plato and against Nietzsche on the task of opposing the basic will of the mind with a true public teaching about us humans. Strauss's decision found many seconders, as could be expected; the wider rediscovery of the true Platonic tradition that Strauss made possible has consequently been accompanied by a hatred for Nietzsche that Strauss himself did not share. Straussianisms for the people continue to perpetuate "the Platonic notion of the noble delusion" (Strauss, *Natural Right and History* 26), acting as if it were still noble to delude the populace that a moral God rules and that the human tie to nationalist politics is salutary, while acting as if the wholly natural nobility and ignobility of our species dare have no public face.

spiritual fate. In claiming that a predetermined spiritual fate predetermines the answer to fundamental questions, section 231 answers the question of section 230 in a way that befits the transmoral period (32), locating the value of an action or thought in what is unintentional in it. Section 231 thus provides the ultimate, predetermined answer to the chief question of chapter 7 — why cruelty? why philosophy?

"Our Virtues" peaks with an argument on behalf of cruelty that is an argument on behalf of truth or the value of truth. *Beyond Good and Evil*'s sustained opposition to Platonism arrives at one of its key points on this issue of truth and cruelty. Plato and Nietzsche both acknowledge that truth is deadly, deadly to the basic will of the mind. Platonism simply is Plato's response to that cruel fact, Plato's public denial that philosophy is inimical to the fundamental requirements of the city or civil society, Plato's public demonstration that philosophy respects and complies with those requirements. Platonism, that is, holds untruth to be more valuable than truth as a politics for philosophy. Nietzsche denies that the requirements of the basic will of the mind must determine the requirements of society; he denies that the value of truth must remain a private value for the truth seeker, hidden from and irreconcilable with the higher value of untruth for the public.

Nietzsche responds to the cruel fact that truth is deadly to the basic will of the mind with Nietzscheanism, one of whose historical tenets is made prominent here: the recovery of the terrible basic text of homo natura is an irreversible gain of a virtuous, intellectually honest science, a public gain that cannot and need not be reassigned to its private corner. But the chief tenet of Nietzscheanism must be supplied by the reader at this point for Nietzsche does not do it himself; he does not explicitly tie his argument about two kinds of minds, one of which is cruel and driven to an insane task, to the overall argument of *Beyond Good and Evil* that the truth can be made livable, linked to the fundamental requirements of society by a fitting poetry, the celebratory poetry of eternal return. One indication of Leo Strauss's profound understanding of the plan of *Beyond Good and Evil* is his departure from that plan at just this point in order to ask why it is necessary to affirm eternal return.[31] The teaching of eternal return — the ecstatic yet reasonable affirmation of all beings following the discovery of the way of all beings — is also the crucial element of Nietzschean *politics,* a politics of values that enact a new good and bad.

Instead of invoking the basic argument it presupposes, "Our Virtues" turns suddenly to a different topic, "woman as such."[32] Does chapter 7 end on an

31. See *Studies in Platonic Political Philosophy* 189–90.
32. Nietzsche had planned a whole chapter of *BGE* entitled "Das Weib an sich" (*KSA*

issue that is irrelevant to the political character of its whole argument so far? The issue of man and woman gradually comes to light as an indispensable element of Nietzsche's philosophical politics in the service of the value of truth and the enhancement of humanity. Nietzsche's antimodern philosophical politics includes sexual politics.

Spiritualized Justice: Maintaining Womanliness and Manliness
SECTIONS 232–39

As an introduction to Nietzsche's thoughts on woman as such, section 231 wants it "known from the outset how very much these are only — *my* truths." Does this imply that these thoughts can be dismissed as idiosyncrasies of an unteachable male? On the contrary, *my* truths are the thoughts of a thinker whose cruel task it is to recover the basic text of homo natura and use that recovered text in a war against modern ideas. Contrary to modern ideas, maleness and femaleness are differences given deep down, part of the unteachable, untransformable inheritance of our animal and human past. Set at the end of "Our Virtues," these sections argue that the modern virtue of equality as it applies to male and female paints over the basic text of species inheritance. Set in a chapter that emphasizes the criminality of our probity, these sections are part of the crime, "your devilishness and nothing else."

To what degree do the sections on man and woman continue the chief issue of section 230, the two opposing wills of the mind? Does the basic will of the mind belong more to femaleness whereas the opposing will belongs more to maleness? The basic will of the mind seems to transcend gender. But could the opposing will belong to some few males whose task is the pursuit of the woman truth? If so, then the final theme of this chapter, the warfare between the sexes, expresses in the natural divisions of gender the two inclinations of mind, the basic will of the mind to create and sustain artful surfaces and the renegade will to penetrate to true depths. Nietzsche's position with respect to the sexes would then be ontological and epistemological in its roots; the cosmetic or female arts contrast with and are inevitably at war with the willful penetration of surfaces by manly intellect. And yet, as Nietzsche's reflections on this issue constantly imply, the disharmony of the sexes does not exclude a kind of harmony, for it can culminate in productive union as told in poetic tales of the manly and womanly, of Zarathustra and Life, of Dionysos and Ariadne.

Many have thought that Nietzsche's reflections on man and woman do

---

12. 2[50, see also 41, 43, 44]). The corresponding chapter 7 in *HH* is entitled "Woman and Child."

what he says no philosopher has a right to do: perform an isolated act, draw a conclusion that does not derive from the fundamental grounds of his philosophy. But Nietzsche takes pains to argue that his conclusions on man and woman are part of his basic perspective; he calls the problem of man and woman one of "the fundamental problems" which to get wrong proves a thinker altogether inadequate (238). Still, even if his thoughts on man and woman do in fact belong to the natural fruit of his thought, does the rhetoric he often chose for them—pokes to the ribs by a swaggering male—really suit them? Perhaps both content and rhetoric can be better appreciated if the sections are read in their context as the conclusion of "Our Virtues."[33]

The task of a high spirituality (the ultimate product of morality) is to maintain the order of rank of the beings in the face of the modern onslaught to homogenize or submerge significant difference in equality and sameness. Only an immoralist could take up this task, knowing that honesty must draw the charge of devilry. Defiantly pushing on into that cruel task, an immoralist may recover insight into the basic text of homo natura, including the textual difference between man and woman. To see that difference is to be moved to preserve it, to teach that living its tensions enhances the species, driving it forward in a fruitful contest that can reach from the most intimate shared experiences to the broadest forms of public festival. In order to live that basic text it seems impossible to avoid altogether a relapse into Platonism, for one must act as if there were something like "woman an sich," treating the natural history of our evolutionary species as if it had generated something immalleable. Furthermore, to live the preservation of this difference is to tie it to virtue, to principled action in the service of the good where the good is the enhancement of the species. Finally, the preservation of this difference generates a theologizing poetry, mythifying poetry of Ariadne and Dionysos, the basic will of the mind divinized into the most artful of beings, divine womanliness, and the contrary will of the mind divinized into a philosopher god, divine manliness, their marriage the marriage of the two true minds, the radiant and productive harmony of the disharmonious in our species.

Section 232   The opening section, 232, is important as an opening, an introduction to themes elaborated in the following sections and completed in the final section, 239, which shares with the opening the topics of self-reliance, enlightening, shame, fear, uglification, and progress. Also important for understanding all the sections from 231 to 239 is what Nietzsche does not say: he

---

33. Many brief sections on woman and man are scattered throughout chapter 4: 84, 85, 86, 114, 115, 127, 131, 137, 144, 145, 147, 148. I will deal only with what strike me as the main theoretical sections from 232 to 239.

never mentions some of the key elements of his understanding of female and male as elaborated in the works that surround *Beyond Good and Evil*, *Zarathustra* and the fifth book of *The Gay Science*. The partial character of this account is true to the purpose of *Beyond Good and Evil* as a polemic against modern times. The chief issue running through these sections is *Aufklärung*: the democratic Enlightenment inspires women to want to enlighten men about woman as such. Any such enlightenment simplifies and falsifies, reducing a mysterious and nuanced *an sich* to something explicit and unnuanced, the modern ideal of the human. Such supposed enlightenment masks the most basic truths of sexual difference and destroys the useful beliefs the sexes once held about one another, to some degree fictional but edifying idealizations of dangerous difference.

Why engage in such enlightening? For the modern reason of gaining self-reliance. But modern self-reliance or autonomy is, in Nietzsche's language, the autonomy of herd animals, one of the dominant illusions of modern times: "the autonomous herd" is not only the herd without a shepherd but the herd of the supposedly self-reliant who rely on others for self-definition and self-regard. The self-reliance sought by modern woman is the illusory self-reliance of dependent modern males. Not suggested till the end of the chapter and even there not fully elaborated is Nietzsche's view that the material and legal dependence of women on men in traditional aristocratic and military societies is prelude to actual inner independence through superior artfulness. Basic to that independence is a matter never mentioned in these sections but made primary in *Zarathustra*: man is a mere means to woman's true happiness, the child, that which she produces and molds and on whom she exercises her primary creative love.

Why seek self-reliance? The reason, Nietzsche maintains, is the most basic of modern reasons, to overcome fear with the hope of eventually "having nothing more to fear" (201). But the modern fear of fear eliminates the adventure and sense of danger Nietzsche finds basic to the play and dance of male-female relations. Female abandonment of fear becomes possible as males grow harmless under the modern ideal. As females begin to unlearn the "prudence and art" with which they used to deal with males, the result is an "uglification" and "borification" of Europe. The female arts — "of grace, of play, of chasing away cares, of lightening burdens and taking things lightly . . . her refined aptitude for agreeable desires" — were qualities cultivated primarily with respect to males: cleverly, artfully, she played a role flattering to the one she feared and did so at least partly for her own ends.

What does the modern female effort to enlighten males really mean? Nietzsche suggests "among ourselves," among us males, that perhaps woman remains woman while supposedly enlightening us: her abandonment of prudence and art is unbelievable. Nietzsche responds like a suspicious male—in fear: female enlightening must be a new adornment, a prudent and artful attempt to inspire fear of her, "maybe she wants to be master." The nuances of a master-slave dialectic so prominent in everything Nietzsche says of female-male relations point to inescapable forms of slavery on both sides and achievable forms of mastery on both sides: beyond the primary male-female relationship, in the wider world for males; in the creation and formation of the child for females. If male mastery in the wider world extends to possession of females and a kind of mastery within the male-female relationship, the tension of that possession produces the cleverness and artfulness necessary for females to master the master.[34]

Nietzsche suggests that he is moved to his suspicious fear about female enlightening because woman cannot want truth: "What is truth to woman?" Her interests lie with the lie, with appearance and beauty. This interest is not accidental: "We should admit it, we men, we honor and love precisely *this* art and *this* instinct in woman"—it's in gracious response to us that woman makes herself beautiful and indulgent. For who are we? "—the we who have it hard and who for our relief very much like to associate with beings under whose hands, glances, and tender follies our seriousness, our hardness, and depth almost appear like a folly to us." We self-flattering males with such a hard lot in the world find ourselves indulged by females. Indulging us, they indulge our image of ourselves. How could we not like it? And liking it as we do, how should we respond to the new enlightening, the apparent contempt for our hard lot? — assuming of course that we still have a hard lot, that we are adventuresome and lovers of danger in need of recreation, assuming that we are not all already modern males.

Finally, what have women admitted about women? They know women

---

34. Xenophon expresses a subtle understanding of this mastery of the master in his *Oeconomicus:* Socrates tells the would-be gentleman, young Kritoboulos, what he learned of gentlemanliness from the perfect gentleman Ischomachos; Ischomachos's confident efforts to educate his young wife are subtly shown to be male foolishness manipulated by female prudence, by artful cosmetics just when she accedes to her husband's desire for her to stop using cosmetics. Leo Strauss's commentary enables one to appreciate Xenophon's artfulness partly by calling attention to Socrates' female characteristics. See Strauss, *Xenophon's Socratic Discourse,* especially the chapters "Gynaikologia" and "Andrologia." On cosmetics, see *BGE* 145: "Comparing man and woman on the whole, one may say that woman would not have the genius for cosmetics (*Putz,* adornment, beautification) if she did not have an instinct for the *second* role." Relinquishing the *lead* role to the male makes cosmetics indispensable as a means to rule.

better than men possibly can. If they are prudent and artful, they cannot be as charmed by art as its objects are; they know such prudence and art as its practitioners or its rivals. In not conceding profundity to a woman's head or justice to a woman's heart, have women done women justice or told the truth about themselves? Only a male could believe it. So it's a real friend of women who counsels women today: be silent about woman. Prudently silent. Artfully silent. Silent in a way that flatters and enflames males.

While speaking like a male moved by fear to be suspicious of female enlightening and saying what men love about women, Nietzsche chooses not to enlighten his readers about the secret of male love as he did in *Zarathustra* and will do more directly in *The Gay Science* (363): male love loses its ardor when it comes to possess what it most passionately sought; male love is faithless love, letting fall what it gave everything to win. The talk about females in these sections withholds what it knows about males except for its attack on modern males.

Section 236   The beliefs of the greatest poets about women — "the Eternal Feminine attracts us higher" — are not the beliefs of nobler women, for they believe the same about men. Poetic males and noble females believe ennobling things about the other that are to some degree fictional and are known to be such by each. Still, it would be ugly and boring to tell the truth about oneself in the face of the high ideal of the other. It would be ignoble not to try to be what the other believed one to be and wanted one to be. And yet a possessor who loved the possessed with any degree of spirituality would want to be loved in return (194) and not for some phantom of himself, even some idealized image, but for what he is: possession spiritualized has the resources for elevating play between subtle lover and subtle beloved.[35]

Section 237   Echoing the beliefs of Dante and Goethe, men have, until the modern age, treated women "like birds who'd strayed to them from some height: as something more refined, more vulnerable, wilder, stranger, sweeter, more soulful." Fearing they would lose this treasure that came to them in error, they had to lock it up so it would not fly away. Locking up a superior treasure could also take spiritualized forms binding the beloved to a lover who knows himself to possess a treasure of which he may not be worthy.

Section 238   The thought of locking up a bird strayed from a height leads to further thoughts about possession. Nietzsche, the thinker for whom tension

---

35. Nietzsche makes a fitting little joke about this desire to elevate the beloved: "Discovering that one is loved in return really ought to sober up the lover with the beloved: 'What? this person's modest enough to love even you? or dumb enough? or — or — ?'" (*BGE* 102).

is the prerequisite of human enhancement, finds in the relation of man and woman "the most abysmal antagonism." This "fundamental problem" measures the thinker: to deny the necessity of this "eternally hostile tension" is to be "betrayed, exposed," proven "too 'short' for all fundamental problems of life." With this sexual joke against inadequate males Nietzsche introduces the main thought of the section, how a real man thinks about man and woman. Besides depth of mind and desire, such a man has "depth of benevolence." Such well-wishing, however, may not appear humanitarian or philanthropic, for it can easily be taken for mere "severity and hardness," which it finds necessary where the true interests of humanity are not served by what may seem humanitarian. Nietzsche's description of this hard benevolence ties it to the most important of all historical examples.

A severely benevolent thinker must think "*orientally*" about woman and that means "as securable property, as something predetermined for service and perfecting itself in service." In support of his claim Nietzsche refers to "the tremendous reason of Asia . . . Asia's superiority in instinct" and to an example of European dependence on Asia in this regard: "the Greeks . . . the best heirs and students of Asia," the Greeks "from Homer up to the time of Pericles." The Homeric period of Greece, culminating in what Nietzsche regarded as the greatest achievements of humanity in the tragic age of the Greeks, was accompanied by increasing "*severity* against woman." He ends with an appeal: "Just *how* necessary, *how* logical, *how* humanely desirable even, this was: let each reflect on that in private!"

What is Nietzsche publicly inviting us to privately ponder? The larger context for these sections on man and woman suggests that the basic thought is this: the greatest human achievements, those of the Greek age of tragedy, were won by the resistance of certain minds to the basic will of the mind, the cruel refusal of simplicity and ease by minds that found Oedipus's mind or Odysseus's mind heroic. Greek males, trained in the emulation of the heroic by Homer, made contest and surpassing the meaning of their lives. Driven to squander themselves on what could be defined as great, what was out there in the world to conquer, they turned away from the comfortable and pleasant. Greek male contest, Nietzsche seems to suggest, began at home with the most domestic, began with a man's estimation of woman and the womanly insofar as they represented the basic will of the mind. For a male given to contest, the female was a recreation, an occasion for play, but something both more delicate and more wild, something that had strayed from some height and had to be locked up lest it be lost. Nietzsche's counsel to reflect on man and woman is a lesson taught in his new school for the gentilhomme where the gentleman is thought more spiritually than ever before. What will "possession" mean to the spiritual understanding of such a gentleman? Not the crass locking up characteristic of the least spiritual males. In the eternally hostile tension of man and woman, it must mean a possession granted willingly to a male who wants to be loved for what he is, a more spiritual man than the Homeric heroes, a man who looks up to the female as a bird strayed down to him.

The Greek inheritance from Asia led Nietzsche, author of *Thus Spoke Zarathustra,* to ponder how necessary, logical, and humanely desirable this severe perspective on man and woman was. But the Greek inheritance from Asia most prominent in Nietzsche's writing is what *post*-Periclean Greeks, primarily Plato, made possible, the introduction of the most dangerous of all Asian errors, moral monotheism traceable to the Persian prophet Zarathustra but made most exportable out of Asia by Christianity. In speaking of a *pre*-Platonic Asian inheritance of a very different order this section anticipates the very end of these sections on man and woman, the end of the whole chapter on "Our Virtues," a mythic invocation of an earlier Asian inheritance. Zeus lured Europa herself from Asia, tempting away the Phoenician princess by transfiguring himself into a white bull. When Nietzsche makes his final appeal to Europe on the issue of man and woman he appeals to Asian Europa.

Section 239   The final section, 239, seems to be part of what Nietzsche himself privately pondered about how necessary, logical, and humanely desirable Greek severity with woman was: it begins with a critique of the modern notion of women's emancipation and ends by measuring that notion against the Greeks and their Asian inheritance. The section brings the whole series on man and woman to a fitting close by reassessing many of the themes first raised in section 232. Its first words are "The weaker sex," but Nietzsche recolors this phrase toward the end by saying "as one says, the 'weaker sex'" and speaking of the "power and superiority" women exercised over men through "the force of their will."[36] Similarly, the opening speaks of the unusual attention (*Achtung*) now accorded women, whereas the end speaks of a completely different respect (*Respekt*) accorded women in Greek times, respect based not on the modern ideal of equality but on female nature. The difference between the two attitudes focuses on the passion of fear: women have reasonably lost their fear of modern man; Greek males reasonably feared women.

It is easy to understand, Nietzsche says, why modern women have lost their fear of modern men; harder to understand is why women allowed woman herself to degenerate. What strikes Nietzsche as degeneration is the modern aspiration to self-reliance in industrial society compared to the dependent role

---

36. Nietzsche speaks of women having "by far the first rank" "in the eternal war between the sexes" (*EH* Books 5).

of women in societies in which the "military and aristocratic spirit" ruled. Nietzsche describes the self-reliance modern women seek as "the economic and legal self-reliance of a clerk," self-reliance as illusory as that of males in modern mass society. As women enter the labor force seeking dignity in the modern way of work, as they aspire to become *Herr,* Mister or Master, their influence decreases; modern progress is regress. There is an "almost masculine stupidity" about this regress imagined as progress, and just why women, naturally more prudent, would participate in it is what Nietzsche finds hard to understand. He elaborates the stupidity in six separate items, each of which assumes that women have the advantage in the antagonism between the sexes and that the abolition of antagonism is contrary to women's interests. The basic difference of perspective is made starkest in the final item, the contemporary search "for everything slavelike and serflike" in the premodern and modern condition of women, "as if slavery were a counterargument, and not much more a condition of every higher culture, every enhancement of culture." This view of slavery is the basic premise of "Our Virtues" and will be elaborated in "What is Noble?" It is not an argument for the reestablishment of old slaveries but for the recognition of the basic text of homo natura: even the highest drives of the seeker after knowledge, the drive for a free mind, is a form of enslavement, obedience to the unquestionable deep down.

For modern women to condemn their whole past as slavery enslaves them to the modern ideal of autonomy and blinds them to past nobility. How did that happen? Modern education is part of the cause of the "disintegration of womanly instincts," but it cannot be the whole answer because it does not explain why women acceded to the diminished understanding of the human in modern education. The "cultivation" of women in the perspective of the democratic Enlightenment is an example of what "history teaches as forcibly as possible": cultivation weakens the *force of will.* And it is in force of will that women have been stronger: "The most powerful and influence-rich women in the world (most recently Napoleon's mother) owed their power and superiority over men precisely to their strength of will." This claim about history leads to a claim about nature, or how woman's nature forced males into *Respekt* for women. What inspired respect for women, "and often enough fear, is her *nature,* which is more 'natural' than man's" — males have been subject to greater cultivation or denaturing than females. The recovery of the terrible basic text of homo natura includes an understanding of female nature from a respectful, fearing male perspective: "her genuine, predator-like, cunning suppleness, her tiger's claw under the glove, her naïveté in egoism, her ineducability and inner wildness, the incomprehensibility, scope, swerving of her desires and virtues." Man stands before woman as the civilized or weakened before the mysterious and untamed; in fearing woman he fears what he cannot fathom or subject to his control.

Besides fear, a second profound passion is evoked in males by the nature of females, compassion or pity (*Mitleid*) — fear and pity being the passions basic to the experience of tragedy according to the classical analysis. Pity is evoked by appearance: "She appears more suffering, more vulnerable, more needing of love, and more condemned to disappointment than any other animal." Fear of a genuine and uncontrollable naturalness is joined by pity at the appearance of vulnerability. "Fear and pity: with these feelings man stood before woman till now, always with one foot already in tragedy, which tears apart in that it charms." Here lies the secret of woman's power over man. Aware of the fear and pity she evoked in man, woman mastered her ostensible master with superior strength of will and cleverness. Coupling awareness of man's position with awareness of how he perceived her, she exercised mastery over her own apparently swerving, ineducable nature. More mastering than mastered, turned artist of tragic effects by her superior acuteness in the face of brute stupidity, woman till now has known how to make man feel that he has "one foot always already in tragedy." Feeling himself on the brink, fearful and charmed, man has been vulnerable to the seemingly most vulnerable.

Having one foot in tragedy is no cause for lament because real males love danger and play, and the tension of a dangerous undertaking promising sweet victory challenges what is best in him.[37] Reciprocal complementarity of what is best in females and best in males, the play of the sexes, not only serves the continuity of the species, it is a fitting image for the spiritual endeavors of humanity right up to the highest: Assuming truth is a woman, what then? No wonder when gods return at the end of *Beyond Good and Evil* a god and a goddess return.[38]

"What? And that's all over now? And the *breaking* of woman's magic spell is at work? The borification of woman slowly dawns?" With this lament Nietzsche opens his final appeal to women on behalf of our virtues: "O Europa! Europa!" Europa is the Europe addressed in the next chapter by a "good European" speaking on behalf of the European future by invoking the European

37. At the end of *TI* Nietzsche counters Aristotle's interpretation of the experience of pity and fear in tragedy as cathartic: instead of needing a *purge*, such emotion is a stimulant (*TI* Ancients 5). On tragedy, see also *BGE* 29, 30, 150.

38. Nietzsche placed the theme of man and woman at the very center of his next writing, the fifth book of *GS*. He prepares for the treatment of "How each sex has its prejudice about love" (363) with sections on artistry (361) and on manliness (362). The focus of the central section is two kinds of love in which "love thought whole, great, and full is nature." See Lampert, *Nietzsche and Modern Times* 368–87.

past and its Asian inheritances. But Europa is also the Asian princess, the Phoenician girl, whose seduction by a European god, Greek Zeus, was how it all began. The genuinely European began when a male Greek god transformed himself into a white bull and seduced Europa, carrying her off to Crete, where she became mother to Minos, Rhadamanthos, and Sarpedon, mother to the Greek as represented in Homer and the Homerics.[39]

"We know the horned animal that was always most attractive for you, from whom danger always threatens you again." If in our time the old fable of Europa "could once more become 'history,' " it would not resemble the heroic history of the Greeks from Homer to the time of Pericles. If "once more an immense stupidity could become *Herr* over you and carry you off," fable would become history as the boring human future of the "final humans." No god hides in that horned animal but merely "an idea, a modern idea!" the ideal of the herd animal par excellence, the sheep, seducing woman with the new Achtung of equality. Nietzsche offers Europa a different horned animal, one in whom a god *is* hidden, the goat, symbol of Dionysos, god of tragedy, whose being torn apart is the theme of all tragedy, of that poetic view of existence that celebrates the human as mortal, affirming its greatness and mysteriousness within an indifferent marvel of a cosmos. When Dionysos returns at the end of *Beyond Good and Evil* (as at the end of *Thus Spoke Zarathustra*)[40] Ariadne returns with him. The returning gods divinize manliness and womanliness; their marriage composes the sexual difference into a fecund harmony.

39. See the retelling of the tale by Roberto Calasso, *The Marriage of Cadmus and Harmony*. Asking again and again, "How did it all begin?" Calasso displays the many ramifications of Europe's origins in Zeus's seduction of Europa.

40. At the end of the book as Nietzsche conceived it when writing it: the end of part 3, where the return of Dionysos and Ariadne is made most explicit (though without their names) in "On the Great Longing" and continues with their dance in "The Other Dance Song" and their marriage in "On the Seven Seals." For an interpretation that emphasizes the Dionysian themes, see Lampert, *Nietzsche's Teaching* 223–44.

8

Peoples and Fatherlands

The theme of "Peoples and Fatherlands" is the future intellectual and spiritual unity of Western civilization on grounds true to its past.[1] Its seventeen sections cohere as a unitary argument advocating a pan-Europeanism that consciously carries forward the heritage of Greece and Rome and of Judaism and Christianity, Europe's combined legacy of Europe and Asia. The preceding chapter ended with Nietzsche crying out, "O Europa! Europa!" — addressing Europe as if she were still the Phoenician princess carried off by Zeus transfigured into a white bull. In chapter 8 the Europa Nietzsche addresses is an audience already schooled by the preceding chapters on philosophy and religion and on the morals and politics of the new philosophy. When that politics turns to the local, as it now does, it presupposes the argument

---

1. "A Glance at the State" is the eighth of nine chapters of *HH*. A glance at "A Glance at the State" reveals how decisively Nietzsche's ambitions as a thinker have expanded, for the chapter as a whole lacks what this chapter of *BGE* has, a clear sense of what is to be done based on the newly discovered foundations. The section of greatest interest is 475: it advocates good Europeanism against nationalism and sees the Germans as its fitting agent; it also speaks of the peril of European nationalism to the Jews and the corresponding promise of good Europeanism; it credits Jews with preserving "the enlightenment of Greek and Roman antiquity" in the face of medieval Christian efforts to annihilate its very memory.

already made about philosophical politics. Philosophers of the future, experimenters in the ontological and epistemological investigations that are primary for philosophy, must also aim at spiritual rule in order to direct Europe away from the morality of the autonomous herd, the legacy of a failed Platonic philosophical politics. Science and scholarship are the indispensable instruments by which the new philosophy rules through its creation of new values. The new values carry forward a European tradition of virtue, the virtue of free-minded probity secured and undergirded by philosophy in a transition time when the cruelty of that virtue makes it the immoral enemy of the values that currently rule Europe.

Given the prominence already accorded the political argument for philosophy's leadership of science, Nietzsche can afford to write a whole chapter on European philosophical politics without mentioning that core matter again. But as he said in a letter to his sister explaining why Paraguay was unthinkable for a wanderer like him, "Europe is necessary for me because it is the seat of science on the earth."[2] The advancement of science and of the worldview developed by science lies at the heart of Nietzsche's Eurocentrism, *gay* science grounded in philosophy and celebrated by a poetry of the mortal. "Peoples and Fatherlands" treats some of the more traditional aspects of philosophical politics while saying little about philosophy's leadership of science or about philosophy's primary ontological and epistemological concerns. Nor does it speak of that broadest, trans-European political task that Nietzsche clearly stated as early as 1879 when he spoke of "the still distant state of things in which their great task will fall into the hands of the good Europeans: the direction and supervision of the total culture of the earth" (*WS* 87). *Beyond Good and Evil* draws the still distant state of things nearer by grounding that global cultural task in a new ontology and a new highest value. Following that grounding, Nietzsche's task is to call Europe to its own proper task.

The seventeen sections of chapter 8 fall naturally into groups that advance

2. Letter to Elisabeth, 3 Nov. 1886. In a notebook from 1875 Nietzsche wrote, "What is Europe after all? — Grecian culture grown out of Thracian, Phoenician elements, Hellenism[,] Roman Philhellenism, their Christian world empire, Christendom as bearer of ancient elements, from these elements the scientific seed finally sprouts up, out of Philhellenism grows a *Philosophentum* ("philosopher-dom"): as far as science is believed, so far does Europe stretch today. Romandom was eliminated, Christendom was blown away. We're no further along than Epicurus: but his rule is infinitely spread — Hellenization in multiple coarsening and groundlessness" (*KSA* 8.33[9]). See also *HH* 265. On Nietzsche's good Europeanism, see *The Good European* by Krell and Bates, a visual and aural feast that pictures Nietzsche's "Work Sites" in brilliant photographs and words equal to them.

the argument on a variety of fronts. It begins and ends with sections on the local—Wagner's music and the German fatherland. The local opening leads to the more global, for the first four sections pass from German music to German politics to European politics, ending in a four-line section expressing a hope for the future direction of the whole of humanity (240–43). Four more sections on the German follow (244–47ª), two on music, two on prose, music and prose being taken in their broadest function as formative of the soul. The sections on prose lead to a section on genius and to a three-line section on the limits of the knowable (248–49). The second half of the chapter turns to other peoples, with two sections on the Jews (250–51), three on the English and the French (252–54), all viewed from the perspective of the German. The chapter ends with two more sections on the Germans (255–56), concluding with a few rhymes on the theme "Is that even German?"

From the Local to the Global, from Wagner to Hercules
SECTIONS 240–43

Section 240   Section 240 seems an odd opening for a chapter called "Peoples and Fatherlands," because it is a reflection on the experience of hearing the overture to Wagner's *Meistersinger* "once again for the first time."[3] But it proves fitting after all because it expands into a reflection on what is German in Wagner's music, thus opening the theme of the German in the chapter.[4]

Section 241   The rationale for the opening section is provided by section 241: hearing Wagner occasions even in a German who is a "good European" temporary "heartfelt fatherlandishness," a few "hours of national seething and patriotic palpitation"—the first section showed that, Nietzsche says. The

3. In a letter to Rohde sixteen years earlier (27 Oct. 1868) Nietzsche referred to the overture to the *Meistersinger*: "I cannot calm my heart long enough to remain coolly critical of this music: every fiber, every nerve in me quivers; not for a long time have I experienced the lasting transport that occurs when I hear the *Meistersinger* overture." Did Nietzsche attend the premiere of the *Meistersinger* in Dresden, January 1866? (letter to Schuch, Oct. 1885). Section 240 ends by speaking of "what I hold about the Germans: they're from the day before yesterday and from the day after tomorrow—*they still have no today.*" But this, as Leo Strauss noted, is what Heinrich Heine reported to the Germans from Paris as what *the French* hold about the Germans (*Über die französische Bühne,* end of the third letter), Leo Strauss, *Studies in Platonic Political Philosophy* 190.

4. In addition to the Germans, Jews, English, and French, there are mentions in the chapter of the Russian empire (251), the Italians (247, 251), and the Poles (251). See also *TI* "What the Germans Lack," in which emphasis is placed on education and what the Germans lack is an educator.

opening section was therefore an act of writerly daring as Nietzsche risked putting in the most prominent place, putting first, what he gets over in a few hours, a taste of "the insanity of nationalism" (256). But if Nietzsche got over this fever in a few hours, others may take half a year or half a lifetime, he says, even half a century for particularly slow digestions—a standard way for Nietzsche to make fun of fellow Germans. But the point is sober: German nationalism inflamed by German music will endanger European unity for decades. Eventually, however, Nietzsche dares to expect, insane nationalism will come back to "reason," to "good Europeanism."

Having himself come back to reason in these few hours, Nietzsche finds himself a listener again, now to a dialogue between two old patriots speaking of contemporary German politics. Half-deaf, they shout their fevered opposition to one another's opinions about "great politics" and what constitutes greatness in politics. What they shout offers an initial perspective on one of the decisive themes of chapter 8 and prepares Nietzsche's quieter perspective on the great in politics. The first old patriot refuses to call the great politics of Bismarck great because "only great *thought* gives greatness to a cause or deed." The second old patriot scoffs at such a standard: if Bismarck were not great "he couldn't have done it! Was it mad to want to do it? Maybe everything great was mad in its origins!"[5] "An abuse of words!" shouts the first. "Strong! Strong! Strong and mad! *Not* great!" The two old patriots stand loyal to different orders, the first to the old *patria*, to the German profundity that Nietzsche will trace to Luther's prose; the second to today's victories and their promise of increased German hegemony in Europe. Nietzsche quietly reflects on the shouted dialogue—but only after reporting his own station as auditor: happy and beyond, recovered from the intoxication of Wagner's music, immune to immersion in the shouted debates on Bismarck's politics, Nietzsche measures that debate through two thoughts explaining why the distanced auditor is happy: "Soon a stronger would become master over the strong; also . . . there's a balancing out for the spiritual flattening of one people, namely, the deepening of another."

The dialogue and Nietzsche's comment prepare a major issue of chapter 8, a philosopher's reflections on *strong* and *great* in European politics. Though Nietzsche sides with the first old patriot against the second, he will display the limitations of what even that patriot is loyal to while displaying a philosopher's loyalty to something far broader and more ancient than the German past: the total European past brought to consciousness by a novel interpretation that claims to be correct. For Nietzsche's two consoling thoughts amount

5. Compare 227: "Were not all gods till now such holy-grown, rebaptized devils?"

to this: the stronger is the philosopher whose thought gives greatness to the politics founded on it; and the spiritual flattening of the German people will be balanced out by the deepening of the European people through the thought of a philosopher stronger than Bismarck.

Section 242   Nietzsche initiates this widened perspective by stating the view of human history foundational to it. He sets aside as foreground the self-congratulatory words customarily used to describe European difference — *civilization, humanization, progress* — and he sets aside as well the political designation that names European difference without praise or blame, "the *democratic* movement of Europe." Nietzsche describes the process as physiological, an alteration in the very needs and drives of European humanity. This physiological process is an *Anähnlichung*, a "growing-like." Growing like increasingly liberates from local particularities focused on the unlike. European history homogenizes the European mix, a "supranational" type of human being slowly emerging, a type marked by a maximum of the art and power of adaptation.[6] Nietzsche thus looks past contemporary nationalism to what he sees as a deeper tendency in European history: absorption of the local into larger groupings leading ultimately to a globalization of the most powerful customs — the European trajectory thus implies the eventual growing-like of the whole species.[7]

Nietzsche asks, What are the consequences of this global trajectory of homogenization? He answers, The process will probably play itself out into results that "its promoters, the apostles of 'modern ideas,' would *least* like to reckon with." That is, the conditions producing the uniformity of the modern worker are likely to produce as well rare and exceptional human beings of the most dangerous and most attractive quality. The homogenized mass Nietzsche regards as "a type prepared for *slavery* in the subtlest sense," *subtlest* implying that these slaves take themselves to be free or even the first truly free population at the end of a whole history of slavery, the "final humans" of

---

6. In contemporary terms Nietzsche's history of Europe is sociobiological: *Homo sapiens* is a social animal driven by needs and directed by epigenetic propensities to form societies whose conditions then condition the very needs that first generated them — gene-culture coevolution. One feature of this evolution is the tendency to form ever more comprehensive wholes. In the present age that tendency becomes conscious and perhaps capable of rational direction. See for instance E. O. Wilson, *Consilience* 150–83.

7. Nietzsche does not explicitly tie the eventual achievement of the global village to technologies of communication, perhaps seeing these as derivatives of a more fundamental impetus toward the recognition of the shared. As Nietzsche understood it, universalism began with the philosophy of the Greeks, who understood things in terms of their natures, human nature being shared by all members of the species.

Zarathustra's first speech, wage slaves in part, primarily, however, slaves to modern ideas of progress.[8] And the rare exceptions? — "the democratization of Europe is at the same time an involuntary institution for the breeding of *tyrants,* — understanding that word in every sense, including the most spiritual/intellectual [*geistigste*]."

The old patriot who thought Bismarck great is a slave to modern passions welcoming a modern tyrant happy to flatter those passions. The first old patriot is right: Bismarck is strong but not great: innocent of philosophy, not basing great action on great thought, he is not a tyrant in the "most spiritual/intellectual" sense. *Geistigste* is a word laden with precedent in *Beyond Good and Evil,* a decisive word for a thinker whose task is to elucidate and preserve an order of rank among the things themselves and not only among humans (219). The first use of *geistigste* occurs in the first definition of philosophy as "the tyrannical drive itself, the most spiritual/intellectual will to power" (9). What may seem a criticism of philosophy (appearing as it does in a criticism of the Stoics) is in fact a recognition of the highest human activity: the most spiritual/intellectual will to power is exercised by the genuine philosopher. Great strength, the book has long since made clear, is the most spiritual/intellectual strength, the strength of a Plato, who gave his imprint to millennia and in the ruins of whose strength we now live. Democracy is a breeding ground for tyrants of this sort as well, and Nietzsche gives two reasons for democracy's capacity to breed philosophers: its permissiveness and its tremendous variety in practice, art, and mask. Democracy permits the exception and helps it grow through varying perspectives.

Nietzsche is not the first student of democracy to arrive at these conclusions, for they are Plato's conclusions about democracy in book 8 of the *Republic.* And the quieter implication of Nietzsche's account is quietly present in Plato's: democracy, the permissive place of the free and equal, may be the breeding ground for political tyrants, but as the place in which all regimes are visible and all are permitted, democracy is a breeding ground as well for the philoso-

---

8. An enlightening perspective on Nietzsche's view of slavery is found in a notebook, sections of which were incorporated into *BGE*. Asking "the radical question" "*must* there be slavery?" Nietzsche answers, "In truth, there always *is* slavery" and gives as examples, "the Prussian civil servant, the teacher, the monk" (*KSA* 11.25 [225] Spring 1884). If these are slaves, one must ask what Nietzsche means by free, and the answer would have to be a free mind, that is, a free, *very* free mind. Nietzsche therefore revives the view of the Greek philosophers who "went through life feeling secretly that there were far more slaves than one might think — meaning that everyone who was not a philosopher was a slave" (*GS* 18). The account of nobility in chapter 9 hinges on the distinction between slavery and freedom.

pher, the student of regimes who comes to recognize his own vested interest in regimes of a particular, philosophy friendly sort, regimes that at best are not democratic but ruled by an aristocracy friendly to philosophy.[9] Nietzsche thus dares to use the word *tyrant* positively, in the most spiritual/intellectual sense, a philosopher-ruler or philosopher-tyrant.

Section 243   Tyranny in this sense — a new philosophical politics for post-modern Europe and for the global humanity created by the dynamism of modern ideas — is touched upon lightly in the four-line section 243, which brings these opening reflections to a pleasant close: "I hear with pleasure that our sun is in the process of moving swiftly toward the constellation *Hercules:* and I hope that humanity on this earth is doing the same as the sun in this regard. And we at the forefront, we good Europeans! — " Nietzsche hopes that humanity, led by good Europeans, moves swiftly toward a new spiritual/intellectual tyrant generated by modern democracy, an exception who is Strong! Strong! Strong *and* great! *Not* mad! A new Hercules assigned these labors can hardly avoid appearing mad given what necessarily passes as sane. And he would appear even more mad were he to shout these things as their patriot.

The Music and Prose of the German Soul
SECTIONS 244–47[a]

This series of four sections returns to the theme "What is German?" and examines more quietly the positions shouted by the two old patriots. The series peaks by suggesting a rivalry between the literary power that created the older Germanic and a new literary power creating something new in German (247[a]). Section 244 contrasts the old German reputation for profundity with the new Bismarckianism so embarrassed at the absence of dash in the old that it is anxious to abandon it. But the section ends by suggesting that the old reputation be maintained — and the suggestion is put with unmistakable dash, with a panache and swish that mask its own profundity. The little jest that makes Nietzsche's point,[10] his playfulness about German deception, suggests

9. *Republic* 8.557c-558a.

10. Contemporary German openness and honesty is a *Verkleidung,* Nietzsche suggests, an artful costuming that succeeded: the German dresses up in openness, and foreigners mistake him for his dressing gown. Nietzsche explains his little joke: "I meant to say" that we would do well to keep the old dress of profundity whatever may be hidden by it and not trade it in too cheaply for Prussian dash. It's clever for a people to let itself be taken for profound — it may even be . . . profound. And Nietzsche ends with a little German costuming of his own: one should make one's name an honor, he says, and to honor *deutsch* he invents a false etymology rooting *deutsch* in *Täusche* — deceive. Deutsch —

something new in German that Nietzsche sees as the characteristic tempo of philosophic thought (27–28, 213) and that he spelled out a few months later in the fifth book of *The Gay Science* (382): rapidity and brevity don't mean lack of profundity, levity doesn't mean lack of gravity. After a section tracing the downward trajectory of a century of German music from a pan-European to a merely German phenomenon (245), Nietzsche turns to German prose in two important sections.

Section 246   Beginning with how badly books in German prose are written, Nietzsche turns to the German who reads books or *misreads* them, being unschooled in the art of prose, particularly the tempo in which great prose displays its art and purpose. The theme, arrived at through this chastising of the local, is the power of great prose, how truly good books are written and what they can create.[11] Nietzsche says his thoughts on this issue were occasioned by a coarse and ignorant confounding of two masters of the art of prose. Their mastery is described but their names are withheld. The first was able to make his words "drop hesitant and cold as from the ceiling of a moist cave—he counted on their dull, damp sound and resounding [*Klang und Wiederklang*]." But for what? Having just made the question of intention basic to a proper reading of good writing, Nietzsche leaves that question unasked—the intention of the first master, like his identity, seems to be withheld until the end of the following section. The second prose master, likewise unidentified as to person and intention, "handles his language like a flexible rapier and feels, from his arm down to his toes, the dangerous delight of the quivering, oversharp blade [*Klinge*] which wants to bite, hiss, cut." In the Klang of the first and the Klinge of the second, the characteristic style of each seems to ring out. If the first counts on the effect of his dull Klang, the second counts on the cut and dash, the *schneiden* and *Schneidigkeit,* of his Klinge.

Section 247[a]   One section on German style generates another section on

---

deceptive. To be taken in by Nietzsche's etymology would be to mistake a German for his dressing gown. But this dressing gown *says* it's a deception. So the inventor of this deception is not deceptive after all? That is, his appearing deceptive is deceptive? But he's just invented a deception to prove he's not a deceiver. This is a little joke worthy of a philosopher.

11. On the duty to master style in his own German prose, see the twenty-two-year-old Nietzsche's letter to von Gersdorff (6 April 1867): "What is costing me the greatest concern and labor is my German style. . . . I tried to write well and suddenly the pen fell lame in my hand. . . . Above all, a few cheerful spirits must be unfettered in my style, I have to learn to play, as on a keyboard, not merely pieces I have rehearsed but also improvised fantasies—as free as possible, yet still logical and beautiful."

German style, a reader with a "third ear" now addressing readers who've put their "ears away in a drawer."[12] German style generally, Nietzsche says, now has little to do with "sounds and ears" and contrasts unfavorably with "ancient reading" because it is done "merely with the eye." If we take Nietzsche's recommendation to read aloud quite literally, we hear a little oddity about 247[a]: it differs from every other section of the book by having that little superscript *a* placed after the number, visible to the eye but not at all prominent.[13] Read aloud, however, that visually overlookable nuance becomes: *zweihundertsiebenundvierzig a — a?* Why *a?* The superscript *a* suddenly becomes prominent, announcing its oddness, forcing the question of just what it's doing there. An initial answer would be that it provides a pleasant little example of the difference between reading with the eyes only and reading also for the ears. As an unexplained example, it confirms a trait of the writer we're reading, a lover of nuance, of reasons left unspecified, a writer who sows small pleasures of reticence for the reader willing to slow down, the reader learning to trust that his author is careful in many audible ways.

Is that all this little *a* does, establish trust between writer and reader in an exchange of small pleasures? Might this nuance suggest some other, perhaps more significant matter? The recommendation to read aloud leads Nietzsche to consider what was possible for ancient writers whose audiences had active ears. The "great periods" of the speeches of Demosthenes and Cicero depended on a schooled audience, and great writers knew how to play with the expectancies of such an audience.[14] After reflecting on the possibilities open to ancient speech, Nietzsche returns to Germany, noting that the German ear was, after all, schooled in one species of oratory, the pulpit rhetoric of the preacher. Nietzsche has thus built his way to his final point, a point about writing, about "the masterpiece of German prose," the Bible, which "was, till now, the best German book." Culminating in Luther's Bible, this section allows the reader to name the first master of German prose unnamed in the

12. On German style and tempo, see also section 28.

13. Present in the first edition, the superscript has been dropped from many editions, including Colli-Montinari.

14. Some of *BGE* took form as spoken: Nietzsche dictated parts of it to Frau Röder-Wiederholt in Sils-Maria in the summer of 1885. Among the notebooks that have been preserved, W I 6, (*KSA* 11.37) is in her handwriting with corrections by Nietzsche. This notebook contains forerunners of 241, 244, 256. Nietzsche notes in letters that Frau Röder-Wiederholt was "baptized in the blood of 1848" and took offense at his anti-democratic politics (see letters to his mother, von Schirnhofer, Köselitz, and Overbeck, in June and July 1885).

previous section: *Luther* is the master who "dropped words down hesitant and cold as from the ceiling of a moist cave."¹⁵ Adding Luther's name leads to adding Luther's intention: Luther counted on the dull sound and resounding of his words to "grow into German hearts," to form the German people out of a multifarious mix of peoples through the rhetoric of the pulpit; Luther's prose succeeded in forming the German tradition of profundity to which the first old patriot still stands loyal.

If Luther is the first master of the art of prose unnamed in the previous section, who is the master with the flexible rapier? Even Walter Kaufmann, who is not usually attentive to the more outrageous self-advertisements of the writer he is translating, notes that "the second master is surely Nietzsche." And if the first master is Germany's "greatest preacher" who formed the German soul through the cadence of his speech, what is the second master suggesting? Read with open ears and with the indispensable assistance of the preceding chapters, these sections allow the answer that Nietzsche is the contemporary German philosopher whose artful writing aspires to create in the way the best German book till now created, but to do so on a pan-European scale, to form out of European multiplicity a European people.¹⁶

What are these instructions on reading and writing doing in a chapter on the great in politics? What the rapier cut into these sentences on writing goes to the heart of *great* politics, the politics of great thought, which the first old patriot mistakenly supposed lay only in the past and which the second old patriot mistakenly supposed was a mere rebaptizing of words. These sentences claim that prose artistry created the German soul out of a vast mix of peoples, but they go further: they announce an expanded aim by the second prose artist. With these suggestions about great writing, chapter 8 arrives at the deepest level of the political: peoples are created by masterworks of speech, poetry or prose that give their stamp to whole populations, assigning them their unique character, their tablet of good and evil, in Zarathustra's words

15. A note from 1885 tends to confirm Luther as the unnamed master; it speaks of the origins of German prose with its "solemn, dignified, *slow,* grave" character as traceable to the "sons of German pastors" (*KSA* 11.34 [102]).

16. WS 87: "Everyone who is a good European now has to learn *to write well and ever better.* . . . To write better, however, means at the same time also to think better . . . to make ourselves accessible to the understanding of those foreigners who learn our language; to assist in making all good things common property and freely available to the free-minded; finally, to *prepare the way* for that still distant state of things in which the good Europeans will come into possession of their great task: the direction and supervision of the total culture of the earth."

from "On the Thousand Goals and One," where the one, the thousand and first, is the people-forming goal that Zarathustra himself takes up.[17]

The *a* of *zweihundertsiebenundvierzig a* does not make all these points by itself, but it alerts to them, alluding to the presence of the audible, teaching ears that have been retrieved from their drawers that there's much to be attentive to in all these sections, a music of prose, a *Klang* for the man with the *überscharfen Klinge:* no plop resounding into the depths of the German soul, but a hiss, a slice, a cut to the European ear perhaps, by a good European feeling, from his arm to his toes, the dangerous delight of his cutting blade.

The implications of these two sections on reading and writing play in the reader's ear till they sound out the central matter of great politics — the creation of peoples out of words — and this central matter is arrived at just in time for the central section, the next section. Could the periods of great sentences have corresponding periods of great paragraphs and great assemblages of paragraphs? Could the architecture of these assemblages include, among other things, an artful centering of the central matter? The central section of "Peoples and Fatherlands" seems in fact to deal with the central matter. Its theme, expressed with the curtness and cut befitting a writer who writes with a rapier, is two kinds of genius and how they inform the two kinds of creative peoples, a male genius of fathering and a female genius of mothering, a genius of sowing or implanting and a genius of bearing and raising.

The Centrality of Genius
SECTIONS 248–49

Nietzsche places at the center of "Peoples and Fatherlands" an issue he made central on other occasions[18] and had just dealt with provocatively at the end of the previous chapter, the natural difference of male and female based in differently experienced drives of sexual reproduction. At its center, "Peoples and Fatherlands" applies the sexual difference to peoples, fatherlands and motherlands. Maleness is understood as begetting, but more than that as "the cause of new orders of life." Femaleness is understood as being impregnated and giving birth, but more than that as "the secret task of forming, ripening, perfecting." Nietzsche gives ancient and modern examples of peoples of each

17. *Z* 1. On the role of the philosopher as the founder of culture, see the excellent discussion by Alex McIntyre, *The Sovereignty of Joy: Nietzsche's Vision of Grand Politics* 74–99.

18. See *BGE* 194; *GS* 5.363; see also *Z* 2 "The Dance Song"; *Z* 3 "The Other Dance Song."

type — for the first time in this chapter peoples besides the Germans become a main focus.[19] The ancient example of an impregnated, nurturing, perfecting people is the Greeks; the ancient examples of impregnating peoples are the Jews and the Romans.[20] Greeks and Romans are not further discussed in this chapter, but what the Jews represent to Europe is taken up in two sections just after the center. The modern example of the impregnated, perfecting people is the French; the modern example of the impregnating people is put questioningly, "asking in all modesty, the Germans?"[21] The relation between the French and the Germans will be a chief concern of the second half of this chapter, and the core question of that relationship seems prefigured in the gender metaphors of this section: Will the French, that perfecting people which raises, nurtures, and perfects what it receives from others — as it did with Renaissance European civilization, as it did with what arose among the English in Bacon, Locke, and Hume (253) — will the French nurture and perfect what is now arising among the Germans?

The enigmatic little section (249) that follows the central section seems to contrast the knowable and the unknowable. The ultimate unknowability of the self does not refute the knowability of the aggregates of selves who form into peoples through speech that defines their virtue or collective hypocrisies. Here, at the center of the chapter, in the midst of so much that can be known, Nietzsche seems to reaffirm the ultimate unknowability of what is given in one, that great stupidity deep down, that for which one can ultimately only be grateful (231).[22] The mutual togetherness of the knowable and the unknowable seems to belong at the heart of reflections on peoples and fatherlands, knowable things ultimately grounded in the great givens of human sexual difference. "The extreme of the known in the presence of the extreme / Of the unknown," in the words of the Nietzschean poet Wallace Stevens. Or, altering

19. Italy and Italians had been mentioned in 247.

20. The ancient examples repeat three of the four examples from *Z* 1 "On the Thousand Goals and One," Zarathustra's Persians being omitted.

21. Placing Germany with the Romans and not with the Greeks perhaps helps explain the statement in *TI* that Nietzsche owes more to the Romans than to the Greeks (Ancients 2). Nietzsche's comments on Romans and Greeks in that chapter provide an important commentary on the present section. If Nietzsche gives the Romans priority at the beginning of the chapter, the priority concerns Nietzsche's "feeling for style," a significant matter but less significant than what Nietzsche gained from the Greeks as claimed in the final four sections of the five-section chapter: "the wonderful phenomenon that bears the name Dionysos" — a phenomenon that makes "the *sexual* symbol the revered symbol par excellence" (Ancients 4).

22. The same thought seems to be expressed in two epigrams of chapter 4, 80, 81.

the image but still expressing what seem to be Nietzsche's thought and sentiment in Stevens's impassioned words, "How high that highest candle lights the dark."[23]

The Jews

SECTIONS 250–51

The next two sections, 250 and 251, speak of one of the ancient peoples, the Jews. They begin, "What Europe can thank the Jews for?"—Some reader seems to have posed an incredulous question or objection to Nietzsche's placement of the Jews, a non-European people, among the peoples of genius relevant to modern Europe (248). Nietzsche responds as if he were making a case for the defense in an adversarial setting, crediting the Jews with "a lot, good and bad," and narrowing it to "one thing above all that belongs to the best and worst at the same time" (see also 195). Worst is "the great style in morality, the fearsomeness and majesty of endless demands, endless meanings, the whole romanticism and sublimity of moral questionablenesses."[24] Best is the historic consequence of this worst: "the most enticing, most captivating, most select part of those plays of color and seductions to life in whose afterglow the sky of our European culture, its evening sky, now burns—perhaps burns out." This praise issues from a unique perspective acknowledged in the final sentence: "*Wir Artisten*"—we circus performers, we high-wire artists, we jugglers and clowns—"*Wir Artisten* among the spectators and philosophers are, for that reason, *thankful* to the Jews." Not mere fascination matters most to these special viewers of the great historical spectacle—they want to use the tension of the European present to shoot for great future goals. The evening sky of European culture may burn out, but the possibility of that fate impels the philosopher to work for a new dawn in Europe based partly on gratitude to the peoples of genius in its past, Greeks, Romans, Jews.

Section 251 A German *Artist* here shows his gratitude to the Jews. Before speaking of diseased German opinions about the Jews, Nietzsche asks forgiveness for not having escaped the disease altogether himself during a sojourn in a "highly infected area." This remark presumably refers to the anti-Semitism of Wagner and his circle and represents Nietzsche's public apology for his own

23. *The Collected Poems of Wallace Stevens*, "To an Old Philosopher in Rome" and "Final Soliloquy of the Internal Paramour."

24. The preface used similar language to set out this "worst" as the "eternal demands" inscribed in the hearts of Europeans by Platonism, "the worst, most durable, most dangerous" of all errors, carried forward by a popular Platonism, Christianity.

brief descent into anti-Semitic remarks in the 1860s.[25] Nietzsche's report on Germans and Jews states, "I've never yet met a German who was well disposed toward the Jews." By the time he reaches his final recommendation for an alliance of Germans and Jews for the good of the European future, it dawns on the reader that the objects of his attack include a public rabble-rouser whose whole career hinged on anti-Semitism, Bernhard Förster — Förster, who, to Nietzsche's horror, married Elisabeth Nietzsche and with her help recruited Germans to establish a pure Aryan colony in Paraguay in the very months in which Nietzsche was writing *Beyond Good and Evil*.[26] This section, it seems to me, receives its proper gravity only when Förster's speeches about Germans and Jews are heard as the unspoken background to Nietzsche's speech, for then its gravity can be measured by its levity, comic ridicule of the racial hatred Nietzsche said was the greatest danger Germany posed for Europe. "Listen," Nietzsche says, as his ridicule condemns members of his own family, Bernhard and Elisabeth.[27] "Listen," Nietzsche says as he shows himself to be that one German well disposed toward the Jews.[28]

Nietzsche speaks out as a German not simply against its more dangerous forms, but against the very notion of anti-Semitism. The Germans (a "huge mixture and mingling of races," 244) are pictured as a still weak and indeterminate people, even in comparison to modern Italians, French, and English but especially in comparison to the Jews, "the strongest, toughest, purest race now living in Europe." Nietzsche goes so far as to deny the status of "race" to European "nations" like the Germans, while honoring the Jews with that term.[29] As if to confirm and mock Förster's greatest fear, Nietzsche declares "that the Jews, if they wanted — or if they're forced as the anti-Semites seem to want — *could* already have predominance, or quite literally *mastery* over Europe, that's certain." And he adds as if to counter Förster's greatest suspicion: "that they're *not* working and planning for that, ditto." Nietzsche hears in-

25. See Yirmiyahu Yovel, *Dark Riddle: Hegel, Nietzsche, and the Jews*, esp. 120–24, a section entitled "Nietzsche in the Zone of the Disease."

26. On this episode in Nietzsche's life, see Ben McIntyre, *Forgotten Fatherland: The Search for Elisabeth Nietzsche*.

27. In the fall of 1885 Nietzsche read Förster's book, *German Colonies in the Upper Laplata Region* (Naumburg, 1885) (Letters to Elisabeth, 23 Nov. 1885, his mother, 10 Dec. 1885, Förster 11 April 1886), the two latter references call it simply "the green book."

28. See *GS* 377 for Nietzsche's warning to Europe about Germany's racial hatred.

29. Horace's phrase "aere perennius," more enduring than bronze, refers to his own *Odes* (3.30.1) and celebrates his achievement of immortality as their author. See *TI* (Ancients 1), where the phrase stands for Roman style.

stead a desire on the part of the Jews to be accepted in Europe, even to be absorbed and assimilated; and he recommends that this desire be acknowledged and accommodated, adding that such a policy would be advanced if anti-Semitic screamers were *expelled* from Germany — a fine send-off from a philosopher to his rabid brother-in-law just then setting out for Paraguay with his fourteen peasant families to guarantee the "purity" of the German "race."

Nietzsche has an additional recommendation, this one for the Jews: they should *start* plotting the future mastery of Europe. And they should do so in concert with — Germans. And not by some dainty political alliance but by *intermarriage* with German nobility. In a Germany in which plans to breed pure Aryans were widely preached by anti-Semites, Nietzsche imagines an enhanced European future if Jews would only marry into the nobility of the Prussian officer corps, the source of German royalty itself. With this recommendation, Nietzsche breaks off his speech — and calls it what it is: his "cheery *Deutschtümelei und Festrede*," his Germano-mania and holiday oratory for a German Fourth of July, *his* platform speech in the manner of Förster on Germans and Jews. The European future would be advanced, Nietzsche proclaims, if the pure, strong race of the Jews plotted the takeover of Europe through intermarriage with the best of a mixed, weak people, us Germans.[30] Looking soberly at this oratorical performance, long after its subject has ceased being fit for joking, don't we still have to count it among Nietzsche's best jokes?

But Nietzsche's comic performance against German anti-Semites touches on what is serious for him, the "European problem" as he now states it: "the breeding of a new ruling caste over Europe." If Nietzsche's seriousness about the European future is not exactly to be sought in his matchmaking, his arranging of marriages, how *is* the breeding of a ruling caste to be understood? And how would a Nietzschean ruling caste stand to the powers that already rule Europe? The next section turns abruptly to the English, that powerful, empire-building European people, and identifies it as the ultimate source of modern ideas. The following sections turn to the French and the empire the English established even over them, an empire of ideas. These sections show that the new ruling caste can be formed only through a marriage of minds; antimodern, anti-English ideas of German philosophy are to occasion marriages with the French in particular, a mothering people of genius involuntarily prey to the suitors of a fathering people.

---

30. How little the Prussian nobility itself would welcome such unions was well known to Nietzsche: on 6 October 1885 he wrote to Overbeck, "It seems to me that the whole Prussian nobility is crazy about" anti-Semitism.

The English and the French

SECTIONS 252–54

Prepared by the serious mention of a new ruling caste, sections 252–54 turn to the English and the French, the two dominant European peoples in modern times. They focus on Nietzsche's reading of modern European intellectual and spiritual history, and behind the details, occasionally erupting into overtness, lies the chief theme of the whole book, the future of philosophy, or how good European German philosophy can achieve its ends in the growing homogenization of Europe. As the sections move from the English (252), to the English impact on the French (253), to the French (254), Nietzsche's latent argument becomes accessible: the French, a people with a mothering genius to nurture and perfect, must abandon the English liberalism that colonized even them — the modern ideas that are English ideas — and restore instead its own tradition of noblesse. But noblesse is now pronounced *Vornehmheit* so it's necessary to add not only the two final sections on the Germans but a whole chapter — *Was ist vornehm?* — defining nobility in a new way, a chapter that peaks with the nobility of the philosopher, the solitary German wanderer who aims to give the European people a new direction loyal to what mothered and fathered it, Greeks, Romans, and Jews.

Section 252 Nietzsche's argument is historical. England came to rule Europe through ideas traceable to its philosophers Bacon, Hobbes, Locke, and Hume. German philosophy (Kant, Schelling, Hegel, and Schopenhauer) rose up in opposition to those ideas, but its energy drained away into Romanticism. Meanwhile, the English ideas came to be regarded as the modern ideas or even as the French ideas. In the nineteenth century, the English ideas of Darwin, Mill, and Spencer furthered the English colonization of Europe (253).[31]

Section 253 Why is Nietzsche so vehement about this "damnable Anglomania of 'modern ideas'" and its capture of the French — "the apes and actors" of those ideas, their "best soldiers" but also "their first and most thorough-going victims"? Because of what the French represent in the history of the European mind and spirit: looking back from the present, Nietzsche maintains, one "recalls almost with disbelief" the French soul of the sixteenth and seventeen centuries — the centuries of Montaigne, Descartes, Pascal, and the *moraliste* like La Rochefoucauld. Nietzsche is adamant about correcting

31. Methodism and the Salvation Army (founded in 1867 as an independent movement within Methodism) evidently interested Nietzsche, for after mentioning them in section 47 he returns to them here. Methodism is credited with initiating a religiosity that spiritualizes brutes — "alcoholics and sex-addicts" — perhaps a prescient recognition of the growth out of Christianity of recovery religion.

the misreading of European spiritual and intellectual history that interprets the now-dominant English ideas as progress over that earlier French achievement: "One must hang on to this proposition of historical fairness with one's very teeth and defend it against momentary appearances of the eye." The historical proposition he hangs on to with his teeth is this: "European *noblesse* — of feeling, of taste, of manners, in brief, taking the word in every high sense — is the work and invention of *France*."

The battle against modern ideas is a war against the English. German philosophy's initial opposition to English ideas dissipated in Romanticism, which limited the scope of intellect and assigned the profound to intuitions beyond the reach of intellect. The inadequacy of this German response is now evident, "one grew older, — the dream melted away" (11). German philosophy, grown older and not given to dreaming, rises up again against English ideas in the post-Romantic, post-Platonic, postmoral thought of Nietzsche, a philosopher whose historical sense holds on to the historic truth of France's work and invention, European noblesse.

Section 254   Nietzsche's reflections on the French and English in relation to the Germans end by suggesting that the French must embrace *his* thought to regain their cultural superiority in Europe and sustain their tradition of noblesse. French cultural superiority over Europe is evident, Nietzsche says, in its synthesis of north and south, the "Provençal and Ligurian blood," which protected France from "the gray on gray" that is "the *German* disease in matters of taste." But it's Nietzsche who counts the Provençal culture of the troubadours among Europe's greatest achievements and his own "gay science" as a recovery of its spirit.[32] And it's Nietzsche who pictures himself Ligurian, a Genovese explorer like Columbus, who opens new territory for the European. There exists in Germany at this moment, Nietzsche says, an antidote to the disease of German taste, namely, "blood and iron, which is to say, 'great politics.' " Nietzsche placed no hope in Bismarck's great politics — an abuse of words — but seems to lay claim to that dangerous healing art himself as the philosophical counterpart of Bismarck.

There is an openness among the French, Nietzsche says, "to those rare and rarely satisfied human beings who are too comprehensive to find their satisfaction in any fatherlandishness and who know how to love the south in the north and the north in the south, — the born Midlanders, the 'good Europeans.' " If Nietzsche speaks of Bizet, who "discovered a piece of *the south of music*," his

---

32. See section 260, which ends, "the Provençal knight-poets, those magnificent and inventive human beings of the '*gai saber*' to whom Europe owes so many things and almost owes itself. — "

description best fits himself, a German thinker now to be added to the list of Schopenhauer, Heine, Hegel, and Wagner, whom the French tried but failed to resist.

From the Global to the Local: Festive Hercules
SECTIONS 255–56

The two final sections, 255–56, return to the local, to German music, while implying that the pan-European future is found in German philosophy. Section 255 employs the language of *Zarathustra* to depict a postmoral music of the European south and a supra-European, supra-south of deserts and palm oases,[33] a music of convalescence, health, redemption, transfiguration — Zara-thustrian music that knows nothing of good and evil except a traveler's nostalgia for a world left behind.

Section 256   Section 256 provides the fitting finale to the chapter, gathering and punctuating its chief theme that "Europe wants to become one," suggesting again that the means to European unity is German philosophy mediated through the culture of the French. The insanity of nationalism, which alienates European peoples from one another, obscures an already existing pan-Europeanism visible in the greatest minds and spirits of the century — Napoleon, Goethe, Beethoven, Stendhal, Heinrich Heine, Schopenhauer — "and don't get mad at me when I add Richard Wagner," Nietzsche says. The only ones who'll get mad at him for adding Wagner to the list of good Europeans are nationalistic Germans, and they'll get madder still at his reasons, which suggest that one additional name must be added to the list. Nietzsche doesn't add his own name but he forces the reader to add it by describing Wagner's task as the penultimate pan-European task — the ultimate task falling to the author of *Beyond Good and Evil*.

Nietzsche's argument again depends upon a correct reading of history, but now it is recent European spiritual history and the phenomenon of romanticism that concern him. He is somewhat oblique about the relation between Wagner's romanticism and his own postromantic philosophy, but a few months later, in the fifth book of *The Gay Science* (370), he states matters openly: Schopenhauer's and Wagner's "romantic pessimism [is] the last *great* event in the fate of our culture." What's next? A "pessimism of the future — it's coming! I see it coming! — *Dionysian* pessimism." Instead of any explicit reference to the

---

33. See the song of the wanderer and shadow in *Zarathustra* 4, "Among daughters of the wilderness," a song that counters the seductive Wagnerian song just sung by the old sorcerer, "The song of melancholy," the song already countered in prose and in the name of science by the conscientious scientist.

new Dionysian pessimism, Nietzsche ends chapter 8 by returning to a local theme, the German adherents of Wagner, and closes with a little poem taunting them. The poem allows "less refined ears too" to guess what he has against the "final Wagner," whose *Parsifal* preached *"the way to Rome"*: Wagner is not German enough, not barbarian enough. How can you patriotic Germans embrace something so un-German? Chapter 8 ends as it began, on Wagner and heartfelt fatherlandishness, but by now there's no mistaking how totally Nietzsche has gotten over such localism and entered good Europeanism. His patriotic poem will be forgiven him because of his settled view that patriotism to fatherlands is insanity. But — the final poem implies — as long we're dealing with the insane, here's a little verse that may do some good by loosening attachment to a supposedly Germanic hero whose music creates a frenzied nationalism that, without help, might take half a century to get over. So Nietzsche ends merrily, on a bit of clowning that twists a local prejudice in favor of the fatherland to his own vast barbarian trans-Christian, trans-German, deeply European end.

Ever since chapter 5, with its view backward into the natural history of morality, the overriding theme of *Beyond Good and Evil* has been the necessity for new philosophers to rule the European future. Who is fit for that? Having indicated how the philosophical ruler stands to the peoples and fatherlands of Europe, Nietzsche now turns to the final issue, the philosopher's fitness to rule or his nobility. In its most intellectual/spiritual sense *noble* names an aristocracy that philosophers since Pythagoras and Heraclitus have recognized as the highest human type and whose superiority fits it to rule. Nietzsche stands in a long tradition of political philosophy according to which fitness to rule is conferred by nature, by supremacy of spirit and intellect, and rule is won by words, persuasive words that create whole peoples.

9

What Is Noble?

Chapter 9 brings *Beyond Good and Evil* to an edifying end with a portrait of what edifies: high human achievement by a nobility worthy of the admiration it draws. That nobility aims to accomplish the great deeds in morals and politics set out in chapters 5–8. It is a true aristocracy, the rule of the best, of the philosophers of the future, those rarest of individuals capable of bearing responsibility for the human future. Such an aristocracy of rare individuals is possible, however, only if society as a whole is aristocratic, openly honoring orders of rank or gradations of nobility that include at its peak the achievements of wisdom. "What Is Noble?" therefore consists of two halves: the first considers the characteristics of social aristocracy, the second the characteristics of the aristocratic individual. The book thus ends on a portrait of the philosopher as a wise man, wise too in his relations with the less wise.

This book of anti-Platonism thus ends on a Platonic theme, the best social order and the philosopher who rules it. The whole second division of the book, chapters 5–8, has prepared this culmination. The goal of the democratic Enlightenment, the outcome of our whole history of Platonism, the autonomy of the herd, can be overcome only by new philosophers (chapter 5); those philosophers create values that enlist science and scholarship into the service of their moral and political ends (chapter 6); the virtues forged by these values naturalize humanity or compel it to suffer the cruelty of its true condition (chapter 7); such rule by new philosophers is true to Europe's heritage (chapter 8). But the first division of the book, the three chapters on philosophy and religion, also show why the book must end as it does. They argued that philosophy or insight into the way of all beings naturally generates a religion that accords with insight and that will be an instrument of philosophy's rule. The philosopher knows what religions are good for (58), knows how to make use of religion in his project of cultivation and education (61), and knows that the religions that became sovereign through Platonism must be decisively countered (62). So it's altogether fitting that chapter 9's portrait of the philosopher end with Nietzsche speaking as a theologian. The gods who return at the end are laughing gods (294), they are male and female, Dionysos and Ariadne, and their gendered divinity makes high demands on humanity (295). Nietzschean philosophy thus aspires to rule the future as Platonism ruled the past and present, to rule on behalf of philosophy and to rule through religion. But the religion with which the book ends does not turn truth on her head and is not antilife; true to truth, true to life, it is an earthly religion capable of reflecting the hierarchy of natural human experience from the most shared to the most rare; it divinizes human experience from its origin in sexual generation to its peak in philosophy: Dionysos is a philosophizing god who will not readily concede that Ariadne has nothing more to give him (*GS* 363). The book ends as it began, with truth and truth's suitor, and it ends by elevating both, divinizing them.

"What is noble?" — It seems an impertinence for anyone other than Nietzsche to speak about Nietzsche's thoughts on nobility, for here more than elsewhere his subject was himself and his own experiences, and here more than anywhere else good taste and cleanliness dictated that he write obliquely, trusting to the preceding chapters to certify his right to speak of the ladder of rank from its top rung. Yet Nietzsche apparently judged that such seeming impertinence — talk of philosophers' experience by nonphilosophers — is both necessary and desirable, for he forced his readers to confront experiences that could never be their own. But in the playfully riddling aphorisms that convey something of that experience, Nietzsche appeals for courtesy, the courtesy generated by a reverence that knows there are things that are not to be touched, even if they are to be viewed. The philosopher, the most admirable nobility, aware of both the limits and delicacy of the admirable, submits himself to the indignity of being usefully admired.

Robert Eden called chapter 9 "the most beautiful and subtle exposition of Nietzsche's politics," and he exhibits that beauty and subtlety in a valuable account that sets chapter 9 into the context of its classical rivals, Thucydides,

Plato, and Aristotle.[1] I will follow the divisions of the chapter already discerned by Eden, with some small alterations.[2] The first section stands by itself as an introduction to the chapter; the final section stands by itself as an ending to the whole book.[3] The other sections constitute an argument relentlessly focused on the enhancement of the human species. Beginning with a social aristocracy (258–62), the argument pursues the issues of breeding (263–67) and the superior human beings (268–76) and culminates in a singularity, the highest reach of humanity, the philosopher and his task (277–95).

Enhancing Humanity
SECTION 257

"Truth is hard": the programmatic section 257 standing at the head of chapter 9 announces its chief themes in a particularly blunt way — the first sentence states that aristocracy and slavery are indispensable. The goal of Nietzsche's politics is the enhancement or heightening (*Erhöhung*) of the type human, an enhancement achieved by individual souls. Aristocratic society and the slavery it presupposes are instrumental necessities, preconditions of the true aim, the aristocratic individual. The politics of the philosopher Nietzsche, like the politics of the philosopher Plato, serve the interests of philosophy, but these are the highest interests of humanity.

The pivotal point concerns what Nietzsche calls the *"pathos of distance."*[4] *Pathos* carries the connotation of exalted or elevated passion and for a philologist must also retain its Greek flavor of suffering or misfortune. The whole chapter can be viewed as an explanation and defense of the pathos of distance from the perspective of the most distant. One of the most important sections of chapter 9, number 260, acknowledges that that experience is bound to be interpreted from below, from a perspective skewed by envy and hate, ul-

---

1. *Political Leadership and Nihilism* 99.

2. Eden's arrangement of the sections into blocks of five is less persuasive, ibid. 286, n.173.

3. Section 296 was placed at the end very late in the production process of *BGE*. Nietzsche sent a postcard to the printer, C. G. Naumann, with instructions: "The unnumbered piece with three stars that now stands at the beginning of the fourth part . . . should be taken from that spot and moved to the end of the ninth part, that is, to the end of the book. There it is to receive the final number and lose its little stars" (13 June 1886).

4. Introduced here, the phrase is used later at *GM* 1.2; *TI* Skirmishes 37; *A* 43,57. See also *KSA* 12.1 [7,10]; 2 [13, a draft of *BGE* 257]; 11 [363, 377]. On the pathos of distance, see Conway, *Nietzsche and the Political* 39–42.

timately by revenge and *ressentiment.*[5] As an attempt to rehabilitate nobility as a human actuality, chapter 9 attempts to engender respect, even reverence, for what outstrips or stands above one. Suggested in the phrase *pathos of distance* is another major theme of chapter 9, the vulnerability of the most capacious, the likelihood that it will be unable to bear the pathos of its difference and fail to become what it is. As Nietzsche defines it, the pathos of distance is initially the experience of an aristocratic class looking down on what is subject to it and instrumental to its privileges. Absent that social pathos of distance, "that other, more mysterious pathos could not have grown up at all," the experience of distance and difference in the aristocratic soul with its "demand for ever new widening of distance . . . the building up of ever higher, rarer, remoter, more wide-spanned, more comprehensive states."

The opening section also contains a warning about the origins of aristocratic orders, a fitting topic for the opening of a chapter aiming to originate a new aristocratic order: the origins of aristocratic societies are bound to seem criminal, a breakup of settled orders by seemingly heedless barbarians. The singular barbarian of chapter 8, the good European German philosopher with a cultural project for the whole of Western civilization, hurls himself on the established order of the democratic Enlightenment, aiming to replace it with a social order ruled by barbarians of his sort.

First Half: Aristocratic Society

The first half of chapter 9 provides a genealogy of historic aristocracies, setting out their defining qualities. It looks back to societies whose nature it is to look back, honoring themselves in their ancestry. Nietzsche's look back is in part an effort to understand why aristocratic society decayed and was replaced by democratic ideals. A cause that remains in the background is the revaluation of values that occurred as spiritual warfare within the Roman empire, "Rome against Judea, Judea against Rome," as Nietzsche said in *On the Genealogy of Morality:* "So far there has been no greater event than this battle" (1.16). Chapter 9 rekindles that battle with no desire to move backward though consciously honoring both contestants in that war as part of our blood. The new nobility, as *Zarathustra* emphasized (3 "On Old and New Law Tablets" §11–12), looks forward while honoring its ancestors.

---

5. On this point in particular *GM* expands and supplements *BGE,* tracing the genealogy of the condemnation of aristocracy and its pathos of distance.

Aristocracy and Slavery
SECTIONS 258–62

Nietzsche is an advocate of slavery. Nothing discredits him more obviously than this open advocacy, for it unavoidably sounds like a criminal desire to return to conditions that modern ideals worked hardest to eliminate. But just as Nietzsche's advocacy of cruelty must be understood in the most spiritual sense, so must his advocacy of slavery. It belongs to our species to live enslaved — to "truths" or opinions that define the horizon within which life is experienced. Such slavery is natural and insurmountable and was understood clearly by the Greek philosophers: they "went through life feeling secretly that there were far more slaves than one might think — meaning that everybody who was not a philosopher was a slave. Their pride overflowed at the thought that even the most powerful men on earth belonged among their slaves" (*GS* 18). But they kept their thoughts about slavery relatively secret, as Aristotle did in the way he wrote the opening book of his *Politics*. Why did Nietzsche choose to speak openly about slavery? In part, the reason seems to be that the modern understanding of freedom hides the fact of its own spiritual slavery, bondage to ideas that preclude the possibility of truer, more ennobling perspectives.[6] But more than that, the reason seems to pertain to philosophy itself; as the passionate will to true freedom of the mind, philosophy's attained freedom recognizes its own inescapable bondage and ultimately wills that bondage in *amor fati,* the submission of a lover of wisdom to its ultimate beloved. In this respect, Nietzsche could have said with Lessing, There is only one philosophy and it is Spinoza's.[7]

Section 258   To understand the corruption or decay of European nobility one must understand what is basic to a healthy aristocracy: the faith that society exists for *its* sake. Healthy aristocracy "accepts with good conscience the sacrifice of untold human beings who, *for its sake,* must be reduced and lowered to incomplete human beings, to slaves, to instruments." Corruption of aristocracy occurs when it surrenders this sense of its "prerogatives of rule" and becomes a function of another ruling power, such as the monarchy or the

6. Section 260 includes an important reflection of the slavish origins of the modern ideology of freedom.

7. Spinoza is not Nietzsche's only precursor here. When Descartes is read with attention to his artful esotericism it becomes clear that his famous judgment that animals are mere machines, stimulus-response mechanisms, is in fact the still less acceptable judgment that all humans except the very few rational ones, the philosophers, are machines. See Descartes' carefully worded statement in the *Discourse on the Method* at the end of Discourse 5, the end of his account of the mechanical universe. See also Lampert, *Nietzsche and Modern Times* 254–59.

commonwealth. France is Nietzsche's fitting example, given the status accorded France in chapter 8 as the source of European nobility (253). Nietzsche's metaphor of the sun-seeking vines of Java confirms that the highest acts of independence are achievements of the actually dependent; in the philosopher, as that dependence grows self-conscious, it grows graceful and grateful.

Section 259 Section 259 extends and grounds section 258 by stating the ontological grounds of Nietzsche's advocacy of aristocracy: it is the social system akin to life and nature.[8] Once and once only, the chapter on nobility displays its grounds. It does so with a blend of substance and rhetoric that makes it a model of Nietzschean prose. What is the *"grounding principle of society"*? Is it "mutually refraining from injury, violence, exploitation," as modern ideals maintain? To think *gründlich* about *Grund* is to recognize that "life itself is *essentially* appropriation, injury, overpowering of what is alien and weaker; suppression, hardness, imposition of one's own forms, incorporation, and at least, at its mildest, exploitation." As a body within the body politic, healthy aristocracy will act the way any healthy organism acts: it "will have to be the incarnate will to power, it will want to grow, spread, seize, win the upper hand — not out of any morality or immorality but because it *lives*, and because living simply *is* will to power." It will exploit because exploitation "belongs to the *essence* of the living as the grounding function of the organic; [exploitation] is a consequence of the will to power that simply is the will of life." The book's final statement of will to power provides a definitive perspective on its first statement of will to power (9): Who could live in accord with *that*, Nietzsche had asked, when describing nature's indifferent abundance to Stoics, who wanted to interpret nature as benevolent to the best human impulses. The implication seemed to be that no one could live in accord with nature and that philosophy therefore exercised the most spiritual will to power to read nature differently from what it is, as our dogmatic Platonism did. But *Beyond Good and Evil* has argued that humanity matures by learning to live in accord with nature. Politically that means aristocratic rule over slaves — the rule of the philosophers of the future over a human population ordered hierarchically by nature and custom.

Nietzsche is aware of the repugnance evoked by the implications of the will to power teaching for politics. The section opens by highlighting its opposition to the ideal of democratic Enlightenment by using the modern catchword of revolutionary politics since Rousseau: "exploitation." It prepares its first statement of the contrary view with an instruction: "One must ward off all sentimental weakness." After repeating the word *exploitation* it asks, "But why

8. See also *GM* 2.11.

always use just those words in which a slanderous intent has been imprinted for ages?" After twice stating that life is will to power, it adds, "In no point is the common consciousness of the European more averse to instruction than here." After claiming for a third time that life is will to power, the section ends on a final, comprehensive appeal: "Granting that this is an innovation as a theory, — as a reality it is the *primordial fact* of all history: let one be honest with oneself at least this far!" Unsentimental honesty is needed to assess not only claims about the ontological foundation of aristocracy but also the historical claims of the next sections, for if antiaristocratic politics are antilife and antinature, how did they win?

Section 260   Immediately after his call to honesty about will to power Nietzsche offers a defining account of the origins of good and evil, his famous distinction between master morality and slave morality, expanded a few months later into the first essay of *On the Genealogy of Morality*. Nietzsche emphasizes at the opening of *Genealogy* that these "ideas on the *origin* of our moral prejudices" belong among the constant themes of his lifework, receiving their first published form in *Human, All Too Human*[9] but reaching further back as an object of study (*GM* Preface 2). But more than that, his thoughts on good and evil are part of the fruit of his tree of knowledge — forbidden fruit, then, whose taste corrupts. Nietzsche is defiant about publishing them anyway: "Whether they're tasty to *you*, these fruits of ours? What's that to the trees! What's that to *us*, to us philosophers!" *Beyond Good and Evil* too acknowledges the difficulty presented by these thoughts: the pervasiveness of modern ideas makes the truth about master morality "hard to empathize with today," and Nietzsche adds a different difficulty that pertains to his own task: they're "also hard to dig up and uncover."

Will to power, the "*Ur-fact* of all history" (259), shows itself in human history during the moral period as a struggle for power between two moralities. Nietzsche attempts to make clear the spiritual differences separating these two moralities by focusing on their social and psychological origins. Master moralities are marked by honor and reverence.[10] The "noble type of human being experiences *itself* as value-determining . . . it knows itself to be that which confers honor on things; it is *value-creating*.[11] Everything it knows of itself it honors; such a morality is self-glorification." Foremost in noble value

---

9. HH 45 is entitled "*Twofold prehistory of good and evil.*"

10. German links these two words verbally: *Ehre*, honor, is a root of reverence, *Ehrfurcht*, literally, honor-fear.

11. This value creating differs from the value creating of the genuine philosophers (211) in being spontaneous, unreflective, innocent of study, at the origin of a tradition instead of deep into its history.

creation or conferring of honor is "a feeling of fullness, of power that wants to overflow" — words that align this source of value creation with the affirmative aspect of life as will to power; also, "the consciousness of a wealth that wants to give and bestow" — words Zarathustra used for his defining virtue (Z 1 "On the bestowing virtue"). What chiefly divides master morality from modern ideas is the issue Nietzsche made basic in the previous three sections on aristocracy: "the fundamental principle that one has duties only to one's like," that the rest of society exists only for its sake. Among the particular virtues embraced by master morality is the virtue of honesty: the nobility of ancient Greece referred to itself as "We truthful ones," a judgment that makes the Platonic virtue of noble lying especially hard to endure, as indicated by Socrates' admonition on the philosopher's test of endurance (*Republic* 7.537e–539e).

Slave moralities are "probably" marked by a pessimistic suspicion of the whole human condition and "perhaps" by a condemnation of humanity along with its condition. They are suspicious particularly of what is called good by the self-affirming and elevate instead qualities that ease existence for the suffering. Referring to "the famous opposition" stated in his own title, Nietzsche traces the origin of *good and evil* to the identification of evil. The very "power and dangerousness" found by noble morality to be good, to be like itself, is judged by slave morality to be evil or fear inducing. The contemptible that noble morality judges bad, slave morality judges good; ultimately, however, it views its own good with a touch of disdain. Viewed from this moral perspective, the human condition evokes pessimism or condemnation because the range of the human descends to evil while ascending only to a good worthy of disdain.

Nietzsche adds another "fundamental difference":[12] "the longing for '*freedom.*'" Slave morality's "instinct for the happiness and subtleties of feeling free" differs from master morality's "art and enthusiasm in reverence, in devotion" — Nietzsche contrasts freedom with bondage to the advantage of bondage, noble bondage to the higher. The morality of those already free in a social and political sense willfully binds them in reverence and devotion; noble morality freely surrenders to a desired subjection. Nietzsche's example is telling: "love as *passion*." Such love must have noble origins because of the lover's willingness to enslave himself to the beloved, to hold the beloved higher than himself while holding himself high. Noble bondage is given broad historic scope: love as passion is "the European specialty"; "its invention must be credited to the Provençal knight-poets, those magnificent inventive human beings of 'the gay science.'" Chapter 8 claimed that European nobility is

12. The section began by classifying morality into "two fundamental types . . . and one fundamental difference."

the work and invention of France (253); in chapter 9 Nietzsche has already claimed that French nobility squandered itself in the service of the French monarchy, eventually throwing away its privileges on the French Revolution (258). Part of what it squandered was its inheritance of noble poetry that arose in the twelfth century in the south of France, a poetry of lovers pursuing a high beloved, a poetry to which Europe "almost owes its very self." A European thinker who honors his ancestors and diagnoses Europe's betrayal of its best ancestors thus claims noble descent for himself: poets of the gay science who arose in France and gave their imprint to the whole of Europe. Their words and music defined Europe as a civilization of lovers willing to devote the honorable to the still more honorable beloved. Such poetry, the book shows, reaches its peak in philosophy, in which the beloved is truth herself and ultimately the whole that the love of truth uncovers, that from which one does not long to be free, that to which one longs to be bound in the devotion of amor fati.

This defining section thus ends by contrasting slavish freedom and noble bondage. In a setting that argues for the natural unavoidability of slavery it prepares the rehabilitation of reverence from the perspective of nobility, especially in sections 263 and 265 but throughout the second half of the chapter.[13] The rehabilitation of reverence is part of Nietzsche's general task of overcoming slavish suspicion of the possibility of genuine mastery and slavish longing for an unattainable freedom. In his campaign against antinatural fictions Nietzsche aims to replace the modern fiction of human freedom with a true understanding of the human place in nature, an understanding that can accord dignity and even nobility to humans within nature seen as will to power and nothing besides. Nietzsche gave precise definition to his view on human freedom in *Twilight of the Idols* after again refuting "the error of free will" ("the teaching of the will was essentially invented for purposes of *wanting to find people guilty*" [*TI* Errors 7]). "What alone can *our* teaching be?" Nietzsche asks (*TI* Errors 8), and answers by describing the basic implications of his view: "Nobody *gives* human beings their qualities. . . . *Nobody* is responsible for being here in the first place. . . . The fatality of our essence cannot be separated from the fatality of all that was and will be. . . . One is necessary, one is a piece of destiny, one belongs to the whole, one *is* in the whole. . . . *only this is the great liberation*—in this way only the *innocence* of becoming is restored." The new view of what is noble arises naturally out of the new view of nature.[14]

Section 261   What does Nietzsche mean by slavery? Section 261 helps

13. Reverence is mentioned in sections 263, 265, 270, 287, 295.
14. See also "My concept of freedom," *TI* Skirmishes 38.

answer this question by applying the distinction between noble morality and slave morality to the phenomenon of vanity. Nietzsche claims that vanity is difficult for the noble human being to imagine while being almost impossible for the nonnoble person to avoid. If vanity is the attempt to create a good opinion of oneself that one does not have and to believe that opinion when it is reflected back by the other, then vanity is a slavish condition, subjection to the opinion of the other. The noble man, by contrast, confers his own worth on himself, demanding that others share it. The value he confers may in fact outstrip his worth, as in conceit; or it may fall short of his worth, as in "what is called 'humility' or 'modesty' " — "still, all that is not vanity." To understand the foreign experience of vanity the noble man must look to history: in the dependent classes one was what one was considered; even now the common man waits for an opinion about himself and then submits to it. Nietzsche then utters a prophecy: the rising democratic order will encourage ascribing value to oneself, but that ascription will be opposed by a more deeply engrained propensity to vanity, subjection to the value ascribed by others; in this master-slave dialectic within the slavish, the old propensity "becomes Master over the newer one." "Vanity is an atavism," Nietzsche says twice, a return of slavish ancestors.

Why focus on vanity in a chapter on nobility? Perhaps the answer lies in the historic contest over vanity that Nietzsche evokes in every example: the Christian attack on classical virtue claimed that noble pride was vanity or vain posturing. In reviving the argument over noble pride with Christianity's heirs, Nietzsche denies that nobility is vanity and digs up and uncovers post-Christian vanity as an atavistic outbreak of slave morality.

Section 262 Nietzsche sketches the life history of aristocracies on an evolutionary model, a kind of punctuated equilibrium in three phases. First, a fixed kind or type hardens during long periods of constant unfavorable conditions. Second, the type decays when conditions ease and individual variations are permitted to grow; these are "the turning points of history" as new possibilities flourish and compete with one another for supremacy. Third, the newly generated individual variations face extinction from a nonnatural force, moral preachers who strive to preserve the old type morally by preaching it into preservation. What is morally preserved, however, can be only a mediocre reflection of what the actual hard conditions first generated.[15]

Nietzsche's examples are the ancient Greek polis and Venice, but his analysis applies to the whole of human history: we now find ourselves in the unprecedented danger of a comprehensive third phase. The "tensed bow" at

---

15. See *GS* 354 for a later reflection on "the genius of the species" as the species' generation of variety and its generation of the philosopher.

the end of the moral period generates new individual variants whose flourishing is felt by most as a danger. Danger is "the mother of morality" — it mothers moral preachers whose mission it is to stamp out novelty by preaching the perpetuation of the old, inevitably a preaching of mediocrity employing the old noble language of "measure and dignity and duty and love of neighbor." But danger is the mother of immorality as well. Nietzsche, the opposite of a moral preacher, preaches danger calculatedly, with a view to enhancing the species through a culture that encourages a jungle growth of competing variations. But encouraging the dangerous suggests only the destructive half of Nietzsche's task, the half with which his name has been almost exclusively associated. The other, more difficult half employs the dangerous to establish an aristocratic society, and to that task Nietzsche now gradually turns. In the midst of the moral preaching of mediocrity, itself an understandable response to the fearsome decay of a whole civilization, Nietzsche moves in a different direction employing different means. Aiming to forge a new nobility, he employs the charm of the dangerous and different, writing like a pied piper for souls naturally predisposed to the noble. Chapter 9 thus gradually shifts its focus from the social to the individual, from aristocratic classes that once ruled society and looked back upon distinguished forbears to aristocratic individuals separated from the common by experiences based in suffering and looking toward a future for themselves and their like.

Reverence

SECTIONS 263–67

Old words must acquire new meanings if the preconditions of aristocracy are to be met once again. But these are the very words most ruined by the modern attacks on aristocracy and religion, words like *reverence* and *veneration*.

Section 263   Section 263 on the "instinct of reverence" argues that both aristocracy and slavery rightly bind themselves in reverence to what they hold to be higher than themselves. With respect to aristocracy, Nietzsche pictures a "dangerous test" for nobility of soul: cause something of the first rank that is not yet "protected by the shudders of authority against obtrusive grasping" to pass by—those who discern its rank betray an instinct for reverence that belongs to nobility of soul. With respect to slavery, the test is changed: what passes by must bear external markings of authority for its rank to be noticed at all. The authoritatively venerable draws two opposite reactions: hate betrays baseness of soul, reverence betrays what Nietzsche calls "almost the greatest advance toward humanity" that is possible for "the great multitude." This point about slavery is crucial to aristocracy: "much is gained" when the feeling has been successfully cultivated in the multitude that "they are not to touch everything," that there are things worthy of awe and wonder. So great is this gain that the author of the *Antichrist* can praise Christianity for breeding into the European "reverence for the Bible," a book for which he himself feels little reverence in its Christian portion. The section ends on the same thought as the previous one: the preaching of mediocrity by the moral philosophers. Because of what they preach, the post-Christian educated of Europe possess an "impertinence of eyes and hands that go touching, licking, groping everything." Popular piety is preferable to educated cynicism.

Beyond Good and Evil opened with an attack on the revered in philosophy and continued with an attack on the revered in religion and morality. As it prepares to close, *Beyond Good and Evil* emphasizes what was less audible in those attacks: reverence for the truly worthy. This fishhook of a book, itself "unmarked, undiscovered, tempting, perhaps capriciously concealed and disguised," is in part an exercise in the art of "searching out souls" by testing for an "instinct for reverence" for something truly worthy yet identified so easily as demonic.

Section 264   Modern educators are victims of the modern deception that nothing essential is inherited, that everything that matters can be altered by education.[16] Modern education is thus an "art of deceiving — deceiving away the origins, the inherited rabble in body and soul." But even a modern ass who preached, "Be true! Be natural! Give yourselves as you are!" would eventually learn that he has to reach for that pitchfork Horace spoke about and attempt to drive out nature. An educator like Nietzsche, knowing Horace's lesson that nature always returns, does not aim to alter what nature bred in the bone. Consequently, he does not preach truthfulness, a virtue of the noble (260), but honors it through his own arts of deception, as a dangerous test to appeal to the naturally noble who have been educated to believe that natural nobility is vanity.

Sections 265–67   Too concerned about truthfulness to preach it, Nietzsche wants the truth about nobility to be known even if it is offensive: "Egoism belongs to the essence of the noble soul."[17] How does that natural egoism view society — what is its view downward, outward, and upward? Its view down-

16. *GS* 348, 349 develop this theme of the origins of scholars and the influence of those origins on their work.

17. *Zarathustra* also recognizes the resistance such claims about the noble soul will generate; selfishness is the third "evil" that Zarathustra reweighs as a virtue (*Z* 3 "On the Three Evils").

ward is a matter Nietzsche has emphasized since the opening of chapter 9, and he repeats it: "the immovable faith that to a being such as 'we are' other beings must be subordinate by nature and have to sacrifice themselves to it." The noble soul even attributes this necessity to "the primordial law of things,"[18] the same foundation to which Nietzsche himself traced the order of rank that preserved the highest problems for the highest (213).[19] The natural egoism of the noble soul secures itself with a view of natural right, calling it, in the language of virtue, "justice itself." Its view outward is a hesitant recognition that it has peers worthy of the esteem it accords itself. Its view upward betrays that it has no aptitude for "grace," gifts from above not based on merit;[20] it is disinclined to look up. Nietzsche had ended his chapter on the philosopher on just this disinclination (213), and as the book closes he will expand its implications.

By describing the noble view down, out, and up as grounded in an interpretation of nature, and introducing grace at the end, Nietzsche may be invoking once again the historic clash that determined the fate of the ancient view of natural nobility: the clash between Rome and Judea and their competing interpretations of nature and grace. The two brief sections that follow seem to offer meditations on this thought, the first (266) appealing to the authority of the greatest post-Christian pagan, Goethe, the second (267) invoking the perspective of ancient Greece itself.

The Survival of the Commonest
SECTIONS 268–76

Behind Nietzsche's politics of nobility stands an interpretation of human natural history: natural selection favors the common. A politics of aristocracy has the natural trajectory of the species against it.

Section 268   "What is commonness after all?" Commonness is what evolution favors. Commonness is adaptive in the natural history of our species because humans, the most endangered species, survive through communication, and communication depends on the shared or the common. Although

18. This is said by one who, when speaking to physicists, insists on not viewing nature as law-governed (22).

19. There is a close kinship between 213 and 265 as key words attest: primordial law of things, cultivation and birth, origins, ancestors, blood, looking down, justice, rarely looking up.

20. On grace, see also 261 and the foreignness of vanity to the noble soul. On the necessity of grace as fundamental to the Christianity of "Paul, Augustine, Luther," see *KSA* 12.1 [5].

they are the most able to fend for themselves, the highest and strongest individual specimens of our species are also the most vulnerable and the least likely to succeed in enhancing the singular traits that make them noble. The fact of vulnerability does not refute their actual superiority; it merely confirms that superior strength may be inferior to the problem set for it.[21]

The final word of the section, the verb *kreuzen,* is rich in nuance for it engages three senses of *cross:* its general sense of countering or thwarting the powerful forces of natural selection; its botanical sense of cross-breeding to produce new strains; and an echo of the Christian overtones of cross introducing the next section, whose final example concerns Jesus and crucifixion.[22] What Nietzsche crosses includes what became historically victorious over the rule of nobility through the sign of the cross.

Section 269   How can the rare survive? More exactly, how can that one among the rare survive who is a "born psychologist and soul-unriddler" fated to study the fate of the rare? The gravity and indispensability of this theme is indicated by the fact that it is the primary theme of the part Nietzsche added to *Zarathustra* after thinking he was finished when he completed part 3. Now, one year after completing *Zarathustra* 4, Nietzsche again addresses the fate of "the higher humans"; the style and tempo are different but the perspective is the same: that of an investigator tormented by the fate of the higher human beings, almost all of whom surrender to the common, to what is popularly venerated and divinized.[23] Not Zarathustra but Nietzsche himself is now the one who must endure what comes to light as a result of his "incisions" into the souls of the venerated or "noble." "Success has always been the greatest liar," and the student of the human soul must see through the success of the venerated without being corrupted into mere compassion, without losing faith in the possibility of genuine nobility.

21. Nietzsche restates this directly in section 276, bringing the first half of chapter 9 to a close on a chief point of its argument. He returned to this theme in the fifth book of *The Gay Science* (354) "On the 'genius of the species'," in which genius is not primarily the individual specimen but the tendency of evolution to advantage and preserve the common through the inevitable translation of the individuality of experience into the commonality of concepts and words. On the vulnerability of the rare, see *KSA* 13.14[133] = *WP* 684. Entitled "Anti-Darwin," this note is in fact wholly in keeping with Darwinism; see Cox, *Nietzsche* 223–29: "Nietzsche intervenes to complete Darwin's revolution," ibid. 236.

22. "Crucify" in German is *kreuzigen.*

23. The section serves as additional evidence that Z 4 is not what it is often interpreted as being: Nietzsche's deconstruction of Zarathustra's (or his own) difference or superiority, his admission that Z 1–3 had all been a big mistake on his part.

How can the psychologist of the rare endure this sight of the baseness of "noble" souls without succumbing to pity? Publicly, by strategies of masking—an "unmoved face" or silence covered by words of agreement. Privately, by "hardness and cheerfulness." Prepared in these ways, the psychologist turns to "one of the most painful cases" of the ruin of a "great artist" and "higher human being," the "holy fable and disguise of Jesus' life." Nietzsche's psychology of Jesus is introduced by three considerations. First, a statement of woman's faith that "love can achieve *anything*,"[24] a faith that acts to "help and redeem" on the basis of a "boundless and devoted *compassion*" that "the venerating multitude" is bound to misinterpret. Second, a warning from the soul-unriddler: "Alas, the knower of the heart unriddles how poor, dumb, helpless, presumptuous, misguided, more easily destroying than redeeming even the best, the deepest love is!" Third, a caution: "It is possible"—Nietzsche's customary acknowledgment of the experimental quality of soul interpretation—that Jesus was a martyr to his *"knowledge about love,"* a "covert suicide" (*HH* II *AOM* 94). But before dying, Jesus as a great artist created two inventions of love, a Hell for those who did not love him enough and a God who is all love and who takes pity on human love because it is so paltry.[25]

Why present the psychology of Jesus here? It is an appropriate ending for the section as an example of the ruin of the exceptional studied by the psychologist of the rare. But more than that, by providing a genealogy of what was honored and divinized by the venerating multitude of Europe, it carries forward the historic theme of overriding importance to a chapter on nobility by a good European, Rome versus Judea. It indicates the extreme price the species can pay for the ruin of the rare. Moreover, as a theological reflection on Christian love of humanity it prepares a contrast with the theological reflection on love that appears as the penultimate section (295). There too the theme is a god's love, Dionysos's love for humanity. Dionysos alludes to Ariadne when he makes his avowal of love, but he also refers to humanity as a whole. Dionysos so loves humanity that he wants to make it better, still more lovable.

24. A similar reference to Luke 1:37 is an important part of the account of woman's love in Z 1 "On Little Old and Young Women."

25. The importance of this theme is indicated by Nietzsche's treatment of the Voluntary Beggar in Z 4 and especially by the deepened reflections on it in *GM* 1.14ff., and *A* 24–47; Jesus is there absolved of the creative theology attributed to him here and the Apostle Paul made the culprit. A sign of this change of view is evident in Nietzsche's editing of this section for *NCW* in 1888: he omitted the example of Jesus, moving directly from the statement about woman's love to section 270 of *BGE* (*NCW* "The Psychologist Speaks Up").

His artistry does not invent a Hell or a God who is all love, but his manly expression of love is so unpitying that his last disciple must feign to soften it.

The psychologist of the rare must pursue painful matters like the grounds of Jesus' artistic creations. Must he pursue all painful matters? The next sections say No and provide criteria for restraint and respect in the investigation of the noble, relevant cautions as the chapter prepares to address its final theme, the most noble creator.

Sections 270–71 The painful case of Jesus moves the psychologist to ask what it is that singles out the higher humans, that makes noble or separates. His answer is great suffering. Great suffering can be creative in ways very different from Jesus' suffering: it may mask itself by cheerful disguises. The lesson Nietzsche draws from the four cases he cites seems to be a psychologist's guideline for pursuing painful matters: "It belongs to a more refined humanity to have reverence 'before the mask' and not pursue psychology and curiosity in the wrong place." The most painful cases of the ruin of the rare must be pursued; less painful cases, in which separation or nobility is masked by cheerfulness, must not. "Profound suffering makes noble, it separates" (270); "what separates . . . most profoundly is a different sense and degree of cleanliness" (271).[26] Saintliness is not purity (*Reinheit*) but the "highest spiritualization" of "the instinct of cleanliness" (*Reinlichkeit*). Evidence of cleanliness in the sufferer restrains the cleanly investigator, causing him to respect the cleanly mask; what the instinct of cleanliness cleansed from need not be pursued. Great suffering creates, and what it creates guides the psychologist in distinguishing the painful cases he must pursue from the cases that permit him to exercise "reverence before the mask," noble respect for the noble.

Sections 272–76 Other "signs of nobility" prepare for the investigation of the nobility of philosophy in the final half of the chapter. They seem to be concerned particularly with nobility in its rising and in its timeliness, and they end (276) by repeating the chief theme, that the common has a better chance of survival than the rare because of the multiplicity of conditions that must be met for the rare to prosper.

Second Half: The Most Spiritual/Intellectual Nobility

The ending of *Beyond Good and Evil* includes many enigmatic little sections with no directions for interpreting the little dramas of their thoughts and events. Only the setting suggested by the plan of "What Is Noble?" and by

26. On cleanliness, see 58, 74, 210, 284.

the plan of the book as a whole assists in their interpretation. Is philosophy possible? All the basic claims about the philosopher or the complementary human being have already been elaborated in the first eight chapters, and "What Is Noble?" has already indicated the social structure of aristocracy in which the most aristocratic could flourish. What remains as an ending is to describe how the noble peak of human achievement deals with its own ascendancy in such a way as to shelter itself while kindling emulation. The book ends on the edification implied in the thought of the peak of human achievement. When this last assemblage of sections is interpreted in this broad context, the marvelous variety of the individual sections can be appreciated as a series of probes or flares of thought illuminating perspectives on the final theme, the last duty of the noble soul, to share what cannot be shared, the duty of the most admirable to allow itself to be usefully admired. In this beautiful fashion the highest ruler rules.

The general difficulty Nietzsche faced is easy enough to appreciate: as the teacher of a new understanding of nobility he had to find a way to point to himself while respecting the stringent canons of a hermit's taste. It is the problem he solved in *Ecce Homo* in a less guarded manner, obedient to "a duty against which my habits, even more the pride of my instincts, revolt at bottom" (*EH* Preface 1). He who has not made himself a model for himself (281) had to make himself a model for others, though not a model that can be duplicated. He did not strive for nobility, it fell to him unawares and pointing to it himself is tasteless and ignoble. But making it visible remains the last of his tasks. Taste dictates that he mask himself in misunderstanding, duty dictates that he not allow himself to be wholly misunderstood. Here, where it is hardest, his touch must be lightest. Nowhere more than here is paraphrase unjust. It flattens the peaks, turning prosaic what exists as itself only in the acmes of its poetic density. Without paraphrase, however, these thoughts are in danger of being lost as too courteous and too demanding, too deferential to taste to allow us access to their extravagant content.

A Singular Solitude
SECTIONS 277–84

Where does the final theme of the noble as the philosopher begin? Is it section 278 with its direct question, "Wanderer, who are you?" Or is it the preceding section, the halfway point in the chapter: "Bad enough! Again the same old story! . . . The melancholy of everything *finished!*. . . ."? In fact, Nietzsche's not finished; the genuine melancholy of finishing comes only at the end, section 296, and it comes not from having learned something too late;

instead, it comes from the incommunicability of what is best. Even then, however, Nietzsche's not finished because the final poem points to a beginning, the arrival of Zarathustra. And in some basic way a philosopher is never finished but always under way to new depths that become new foregrounds (289). In turning to the final theme of the philosopher, Nietzsche has not arrived at something that only the construction of his book allowed him to learn. *Beyond Good and Evil* follows *Zarathustra* where the essential things Nietzsche learned were already conveyed; it is a book constructed with forethought; what comes last belongs to the theme the book advanced from its beginning, the actuality of philosophy. Because it's not the same old story, the question has to be asked, "Wanderer, who are you?" and it has to be asked by someone who is very inquisitive about the Wanderer.

Dialogues with the Wanderer appear frequently in Nietzsche's books.[27] Here, the one who questions the Wanderer sees him returned transformed from some depth but cannot discern where he's been or what he's become. But he demands an answer, asking a second time, "Who are you?" and adding, "What have you done?" These are the fitting questions to put to the author at the end of a book like this. The inquirer is sympathetic, offering recreation to a wanderer he thinks must need it. Rather than accept the offer, the Wanderer remarks on the questioner's inquisitiveness, forcing him to ask again what he can give the Wanderer. At last he gets his answer: "One mask more! A second mask!. . . . ." Already masked as a mere Wanderer who surely wants to be asked who he is and what he's done, why does the Wanderer need a second mask? And why must it be given to him by the well-disposed inquirer, who wants to help but mistakenly imagines that recreation is the only way to help? Could the only one who can help the Wanderer be the insistent inquirer who forces himself to understand what the mask of the Wanderer masked? And can he help only by a kind of complicity in supplying a second mask, a mask only now to be donned?

What would the second mask be? Judging by the drift of chapter 9 and of the whole book, perhaps the answer is to be sought in the collective of the remaining sections, in the suggestions they make about the philosopher's nobility and its relation to a society that defines itself by what it honors as noble. And perhaps the answer is to be found especially in the actual culmination of

27. The first appearance of the Wanderer is the last section of *HH* (638; see *AOM* 237). Dialogues between the Wanderer and his Shadow begin and end *WS*. The two reappear in *GS* 287 (see 309, 380). Zarathustra himself is "the Wanderer" in the opening chapter of *Z* 3; see also *Z* 4 "The Shadow," "Among Daughters of the Wilderness," and *Z* 2 "On Great Events."

the remaining sections. For a second mask seems to be supplied to the Wanderer at the end of his wanderings by the master of masks, the mask of the last initiate and disciple of Dionysos, theatrical god, god of masks. The wanderer completes his wandering speaking theologically in celebration of Dionysos and Ariadne; the philosopher ends his speaking with religion though without coming to rest, theatrically presenting himself as a devotee of the philosophizing or wandering god. "One mask more! A second mask!. . . . ." Knowing that around every profound mind a mask inevitably grows (40), the new philosopher masks himself in the religion that befits the gay science, suspecting that that science can become a world only around Dionysos and Ariadne.

Section 279   The new philosopher does not belong among the people of profound sadness, unlike the traditional wise who judged of life, "It's no good" (*TI* Socrates 1). The book will almost close on a new criterion for measuring philosophers: their *laughter* all the way up to golden laughter (294). "The Olympian vice" *is* the vice of laughter: the gods are not humane enough to indulge in profound sadness.

Section 280   "Bad! Bad! Can it be? Isn't he going — back?" Has the author of *Zarathustra* regressed in going back to his pre-*Zarathustra* style? He's going back like anyone who wants to leap forward. *Beyond Good and Evil* belongs among the preparatory works for *The Will to Power: An Experiment in a Transvaluation of All Values;* it goes back to the themes and manner of the books addressed to the free minds in order to prepare for the great leap of the magnum opus announced on its back cover.

Section 281   Enclosed in quotation marks, section 281 seems to be a report on Nietzsche's own inner dialogue about Apollo's or Socrates' injunction, "Know thyself" (80–81). He demands that we believe that he has not been preoccupied with the study of himself. Skeptical about "Know thyself," sensing in "immediate knowledge" a *contradictio in adjecto* (16), he is a philosopher who directed himself to look outward in order to understand himself. The riddle that remains may betray his own species to the rest of us: a philosopher seems to be a knower who seeks self-knowledge not simply by introspection but by looking away to the whole to which he belongs. If this betrays the philosopher to others, it seems not to unriddle the philosopher to himself: he seems to want to remain a riddle or a problem to himself, wanderer that he is, finding it good that it be so.

Section 282   If modern times offer particularly unattractive nourishment for the "most spiritual" and help explain why they are so susceptible to ruin, *The Gay Science* (364) will suggest some rules of cuisine to help overcome the problem.

Section 283   Closed to Nietzsche, it seems, is a noble old way of preserving the philosopher's essential solitude by actively provoking misunderstanding through praise of what he disagrees with. Inclined to praise but disinclined to self-praise, he's not permitted the luxury of praising when he disagrees because he doesn't live among the subtle. Lacking subtlety, the praised would ruin his solitude if he lyingly implied he agreed with them.

This section in this setting of sections makes its small contribution to what is surely one of the greatest gains of Nietzsche's disclosure of what a philosopher is: recovery of the history of philosophy as a noble history of human wisdom attempting both to understand the world and to give direction to the human world. The old esotericism of philosophy — its actively provoking misunderstanding through praise of what it disagreed with — is no longer possible or desirable; all that has really changed, Nietzsche implied in one of his most vivid descriptions of old and new esotericisms (*GM* 3.10). The new history of philosophy made possible by Friedrich Nietzsche permits a deeper understanding of philosophers whose esotericism actively provoked misunderstanding. Plato's ideas, Aristotle's teleology of fixed kinds, the apparently Christian stances of Bacon and Descartes, the apparently Jewish stance of Maimonides and the apparently Islamic stance of Alfarabi: all lies open to appreciative reinterpretation as exoteric strategies for the preservation or advancement of human wisdom in a naturally hostile world, as the light and frothy that carries forward what is heavy or profound in the ever-flowing river of time, to use Bacon's image. Armed with a knowledge of esotericism and its necessity rooted in the philosopher's difference — in "the inequality that is between us,"[28] the Nietzschean student of the history of philosophy can read the philosophers of the moral period who had to compromise with the ascetic ideal and be grateful for their nobility: they were the great *Versucher* of their times, philosophers of the future who wrote with a view to the enhancement of the species.

Section 284 If not through misleading praise, how *can* the philosopher Nietzsche live beyond, in *Gelassenheit*, separated from what would ruin his necessary solitude? To preserve the three hundred foregrounds masking his grounds, the master of "his emotions, his for and against," chooses for company only the impish and cheerful vice, courtesy. Mastering his vice, he masters too his four virtues, courage, insight, sympathy, and solitude. If Nietzsche's four virtues invoke the four Platonic virtues, wisdom, courage, justice, and moderation, it is important that courage now comes first and that insight replaces wisdom. Justice, giving what is owed, is replaced by sympathy, which

---

28. Montaigne, "Of the Inequality That Is Between Us," *Essays* 1.42: there is a greater distance between human and human than between human and beast.

is ready to give more than is owed. All these sections concern solitude, and it is the only one of the virtues that receives an explanation. Solitude replaces moderation, the virtue that guided the philosopher's speech and put a misleading public face on the essential immoderation of what he is as inquirer. The virtue of solitude with its silent immoderation is sustained through the vice of courtesy: courteously present, he is inwardly absent; alone when together, he secrets the immoderation of his solitude behind the schooled pleasantness of his company.[29] This would not in the first instance refer to Nietzsche's lauded manners with the English ladies at table in the Hotel Alpenrose but to his primary public presence, his books: he goes public in a courteous way that preserves his solitude.

Society
SECTIONS 285–90

Section 285   The unshareable solitude of the philosopher is a fact of nature: he no more exists for contemporaries than do stars whose light has not yet reached the earth. Yet the thoughts of such solitaries are the greatest events of human history, and the solitaries who think them can be ranked by the length of time it takes to comprehend them.

Section 286   Faust ends with Doctor Marianus looking up; *Zarathustra* ends with Zarathustra looking down and preparing to go down.[30] The opposite type of man to the upward-looking worshipper is the philosopher with the highest view. According to "Before Sunrise" (Z 3), perhaps Zarathustra's most important self-defining speech, viewing the open sky above him gives him his commission of responsibility and frees his hands to act. By ending on the philosopher's descent, *Beyond Good and Evil* ends by reflecting on what it is: a going down following the look up, a speech in the marketplace; though better schooled on its audience than Zarathustra's speech in the marketplace, it is still fully aware that its main public audience does not yet exist and that its fittest audience exists most rarely.

---

29. The rules of a philosopher's companionable solitude are again playfully elaborated in *GS* 365.

30. *TI* Skirmishes 46 begins with the same words from *Faust,* and the reflections that follow again concern the philosopher and his inner duty to go down. The "Skirmishes" end on the elevation of Goethe, but the book adds one more chapter, "What I Owe to the Ancients," in which Nietzsche emphasizes what he owes to Roman decisiveness on behalf of Greekness which is ultimately the Dionysian. "The Songs of Prinz Vogelfrei" in *GS* open with "To Goethe," a reflection on the final choral ode of *Faust* and a challenge to what it looks up to.

Section 287 "What is noble?" Enough seems to have been said to ask the question of the chapter title again and give a precise answer. The view is not free in the overcast skies of our age, but signs can still be read, not signs of actions or "works" but of faith. A kind of post-Christian Lutheran, Nietzsche uses this "old religious formula in a new and deeper sense," offering as the sign of nobility, *"The noble soul has reverence for itself."* Reverence had been a chief theme of the first half of chapter 9 as a mark of nobility in social aristocracies; sections 260 and 263 defined that reverence; section 265, tying it to faith and to reverence for self, ended by looking out from a height preceding a section quoting Goethe (266). Traditions of nobility help prepare a perspective on nobility that outstrips even the nobility of Goethe.

Section 288 High intellectuality/spirituality shelters itself in the courtesy of "successfully appearing more stupid than one is." Such noble courtesy is irony as defined by Leo Strauss in reference to Socrates: "Irony is . . . the noble dissimulation of one's worth, of one's superiority. . . . The highest form of superiority is wisdom. Irony in the highest sense will then be the dissimulation of one's wisdom, i.e. the dissimulation of one's wise thoughts."[31] The one means of dissimulation Nietzsche names is enthusiasm, a category large enough to include virtue.

Section 289 Nietzsche seems to offer a privileged perspective: a hermit betrays the character of hermits' writings, philosophers' writings, given that a philosopher was first of all a hermit.[32] What this hermit writes must itself be treated with caution, for a hermit does not believe that a hermit would "express his genuine and ultimate opinions in books: does one not write books precisely in order to hide what one harbors?"[33] Hiding by speaking is obviously calculated, for he could completely hide what he harbors just by keeping quiet. Instead, he writes books that make what he harbors the object of search for those with a hermit's suspicions. That search is aided by the suspicion that "genuine and ultimate opinions" are not something a philosopher can have: behind every one of his caves lies another deeper cave, "an abysmally deep ground behind every ground, under every 'grounding.'"[34] This is Plato's invitation to philosophy inverted: it does not invite an ascent to the sunlight of permanence but a further descent into the darkness grounding all grounds. But neither is this a deconstruction of the philosopher's opinions for

31. *The City and Man* 51. Strauss too thus seems to replace wisdom with insight.
32. On the philosopher and the hermit, see Strauss, *Persecution and the Art of Writing* 135–41.
33. "*. . . um zu verbergen, was man bei sich birgt?*"
34. "*. . . ein Abgrund hinter jedem Grunde, unter jeder 'Begründung'.*"

it acknowledges their profound groundedness while exercising the suspicion that their truly grounding ground may lie—not elsewhere, not in some altogether different cave, but still deeper, still further along the deepening descent already indicated.

Nietzsche quotes the hermit's suspicion that every philosophy is a foreground philosophy: "There's something arbitrary in the fact that *he* stopped here, looked back, looked around, that he *here* did not dig deeper but lay his spade aside—there's also something suspicious in that fact." Nietzsche's comment on his hermit's speech raises the suspicion that the philosopher did *not* in fact lay his spade aside but only seemed to: "Every philosophy also *conceals* a philosophy; every opinion is also a hideout, every word also a mask." A philosopher's speech is a consciously chosen place to hide himself; what looks like a stopping place conceals from all but fellow hermits that here he dug deeper.[35]

Why conceal? Section 290 supplements the hermit's help by giving a philanthropic reason why "every profound thinker" constructs a hideout of misunderstanding. Misunderstanding merely fails to give a thinker his due; understanding condemns one to share his hard experiences. Sympathy, the virtue replacing justice (284), wants to spare the sufferer. The new and inevitable esotericism shares a basic motive with the old esotericism of the philosophers, the desire not to harm. What follows indicates that limits must be placed on that desire.

Mortals
SECTIONS 291–93

Sections 291–93 are tied together by their openings: *Der Mensch, Ein Philosoph, Ein Mann.* Together, as befits the book's ending, they form a comprehensive and summary reflection on humanity and philosophy. Beginning with what belongs to the species, they move to what belongs to its highest exemplar and end on what that exemplar must do because of his difference: exercise compassion by opposing the religion of compassion. More precisely, as the two subsequent sections (294–95) indicate, he must inculcate a new view of the gods that enhances the type humanity (257).

The human animal (291), lover of simplification and falsification (24), invented the good conscience in order to enjoy his soul as simple. Ten thousand years of morality (32) served that good conscience, sustaining it by audacious

35. Nietzsche expanded this point in *GS* 359, making wisdom itself a hideout in which different forms of spirit could shelter themselves, some to hide base motives, some to invite investigation into themselves.

forgery, by art in a comprehensive sense. Recognizing this truth about humanity, a philosopher will respect the indispensability of art.

"A philosopher" — both sentences of section 292 begin with these words. The first distinguishes the philosopher from human animals generally on the basis of his love of complexity and truth and his constant experience of extraordinary things; perhaps he is himself a thunderstorm and lightning, images Zarathustra applied to the superman and to himself.[36] The second sentence acknowledges that the philosopher as a human being often runs away from himself out of fear, but as a being driven fundamentally by curiosity and not fear he "always again 'comes to himself' " — he comes to *"ein Mann,"* a real man.

A real man (293), standing loyal to what he loves, protects and defends it against everyone. The guiding issue of *Beyond Good and Evil* thus receives another, penultimate formulation: Granted that truth is a woman, what will a real man do? He will take her as his own and act on her behalf. The real man, "a *master* by nature," protects and defends truth out of compassion, compassion for humanity, the species with the ambiguous stance toward truth. By emphasizing compassion, the book ends on the primary theme of its final five chapters, the morals and politics of the new philosophy, or the war of competing compassions (225). That war requires a real man to act against the unmanly religion of compassion, and that means acting to establish a new religion or a new view of the gods — laughing gods hard on humanity.

As a charm against the unmanliness he finds in "the cult of suffering" that captured modern Europe, Nietzsche recommends that "one place around one's heart and neck the good amulet, *'gai saber.'* " This section is thus linked with the defining section on master and slave (260); the natural master's charm is linked to the noble art that captured European poetry and almost created Europe itself. The greatest wars are fought over art, beliefs that charm the heart, and the new lover's art kindles spiritual warfare that serves the gay science.

By ending on the difference of the philosopher's soul and his consequent need to act, Nietzsche indicates that he acts on the scale of a Plato. Like Plato, he teaches a new nobility. Unlike Plato, who pointed away from the truth of the philosopher's soul to fictions of pure mind and a good in itself, Nietzsche

---

36. Z Prologue, 3, 4, 7; Z 1 "On the Tree on the Mountainside"; Z 2 "The Child with the Mirror"; Z 3 "The Seven Seals," 1, 3; Z 3 "On the Old and New Law Tablets" 30 speaks of clouds pregnant with lightning. See *GS* 351: the philosopher dwells in a "thundercloud of the highest problems and the heaviest responsibilities" — Pythagoras and Plato are Nietzsche's examples.

points to the philosopher as the highest nobility. Such a teaching may do harm (290), but it measures that harm against the harm done by Platonic conformity to stupidity, which allowed the human animal simplifying, falsifying toys of an especially dangerous sort. While the philosophical task of schooling gentlemen is Platonic, the new school for the gentleman trains to a non-Platonic ideal in keeping with nature. The ultimate aim, however, is the same: loyal advancement of the love of truth through art.

Gods
SECTIONS 294–95

Gods lie beyond mortals as beings of laughter and cruelty, but they share the highest quality with mortals, philosophizing.

Section 294   Nietzsche's alleged quotation from Hobbes does not seem to be genuine.[37] Did the philosopher of the gay science doctor Hobbes in order to cast an English philosopher in the earnest role of teaching all thinking minds to regard laughter as a vice? If so, it's a comic way of putting English philosophy at the bottom of the new rank order among philosophers while staking a claim for a spot at the top. Nietzsche redeems laughter by recognizing that while it can be the vice of *Schadenfreude,* it can be the virtue accompanying the view from the height where not even tragedy has a tragic effect (30). It's no innovation that gods laugh; the innovation lies in their reason for laughing: they too philosophize, and because they do they laugh in a supermanly and new way.

Philosophizing gods are the ultimate anti-Platonic innovation. Socrates invented wise Diotima to teach that gods do not philosophize because they already possess what wandering philosophers seek. By flattering the gods with omniscience Plato set all philosophers and theologians on the same obsequious track. Nietzsche ends his anti-Platonic book by invoking gods more closely allied to what philosophy actually is. The opposite of earnest, they "like to jeer: it seems they can't keep from laughing even at holy rites." Laughing itself seems to become a kind of holy rite, part of a celebration. In the first section of *The Gay Science* Nietzsche claimed that teachers of tragedy, of a meaning to existence, are eventually driven off the stage by "waves of uncountable laughter" (citing a great tragedian), vanquished by "laughter, reason, and nature." Ten thousand years of moral simplification in the service of a good conscience now become part of a vast comedy whose spectators poten-

37. Leo Strauss, a careful reader of Hobbes, said, "I have never found this passage in Hobbes" (Transcript of University of Chicago Seminar on Nietzsche, Winter 1967, p. 12/6).

tially include a whole species schooled in the good amulet of a gay science. They can laugh at Nietzsche's best joke: "One of the gods announced one day, 'There is only one God. Thou shalt have no other gods before me.' And all the other gods—died laughing. Then there was only one God" (*Z* 3 "On the Apostates"). Laughing gods killed off by the predatory tyranny of the one God prepare their return in Nietzsche's writings.[38]

Section 295 Nietzsche exaggerated when he said he rarely spoke as a theologian, but what *is* rare in his writings are words actually spoken by gods, by Dionysos and Ariadne. This is the first such occasion if their appearance under different names in *Zarathustra* is not counted.[39] Before Dionysos speaks Nietzsche voices many cautions. But hasn't the chief caution already been offered by the book's argument regarding philosophy and its relation to religion? The book as a whole is a necessary preparation for the epiphany in its penultimate section.

38. See Lampert, "Nietzsche's Best Jokes," in Lippitt, ed., *Nietzsche's Futures* 65–81.

39. See *Z* 3 "On the Great Longing," for the arrival of Dionysos from across the sea in the manner celebrated by the Athenians in the festival of the Dionysia; see *Z* 3 "The Other Dance Song" and "The Seven Seals" for the dance and marriage of Dionysos and Ariadne. For the links between these three songs and the traditional tales of Dionysos and Ariadne, see Lampert, *Nietzsche's Teaching* 227–44. The only other appearances of Dionysos and Ariadne together in the published works are *TI* Skirmishes 19; *EH* Books *Z* 8; *Dionysos Dithyrambs,* "Ariadne's Lament." There are only five such appearances in the surviving notes: *KSA* 10.13 [1, p. 433]; 11.41 [9] (a draft for *BGE* entitled "Prologue"); 12.9 [115] (entitled "Satyr play"); 12.10 [95]; 13.16 [40 §2]. On Ariadne, see also *KSA* 11.37 [4]. On the marriage of Dionysos and Ariadne in Nietzsche's writings, see Deleuze, *Nietzsche and Philosophy* 188–89. Marred as I believe it is by its main thesis—that Nietzsche *feigned* his madness as a gift to potential followers—and by the many forced exegeses that strain to support it, Claudia Crawford's *To Nietzsche: Dionysus, I love you! Ariadne* nevertheless strikes me as a remarkable expression of ecstatic empathy with the core of Nietzsche's Dionysian/Ariadnian thought; it is an act of love, passionate, excessive, exuberant, female love for a male. Crawford or Ariadne engages the central passion of Nietzsche's thought—*eros*—while chiding Nietzsche's halfhearted lovers for merely appreciating this or that idea in Nietzsche—and failing to appreciate them. Marred in a different way—by contempt for Nietzsche and by tiresome ridicule of any aspiration he might have had beyond the norm—Anacleto Verrecchia's *Zarathustras Ende* nevertheless provides fascinating glimpses into the weeks surrounding Nietzsche's breakdown in Turin, glimpses that add to the improbability of Crawford's view of feigned madness. See also David Farrell Krell, *Nietzsche: A Novel,* an arresting Dionysian representation of Nietzsche's madness that looks backward from the events of the mad years to recover Nietzsche's life through his letters—beautifully translated by Krell in a way that preserves their vivid immediacy, their quality of having just been written.

What does the return of Dionysos mean? Within the economy of Nietzsche's writings it means the return of the god whose banishment Nietzsche judged, in his first book, the most significant event of Western history (*BT* 12–17). There, Dionysos as the god of tragedy was seen driven out under the lash of syllogisms and taking refuge beneath the sea "in the mystical waters of a secret cult" (12) where he underwent "the strangest metamorphoses and debasements" but "never ceased to draw more serious natures to himself" (17). As depicted in *The Birth of Tragedy*, the cause of that great event was Socrates, "the most questionable phenomenon of antiquity" because he "negate[d] the nature of the Hellenic" as expressed in tragedy (13). *Beyond Good and Evil* shows that Nietzsche remained true to his early judgment about this event while expanding and deepening his conception of just what happened there.[40] The cause of the great event is now assigned more to the strength of the greatest Socratic, Plato, while the event itself is located in the broader sweep of the genealogy of morality and viewed more comprehensively: what Socratism/Platonism cost the West is the whole phenomenon of the Hellenic whose expressions stretch back to Homer and include Sophism and Thucydides, Aristophanes, pre-Socratic Greek philosophy, and Greek science.[41] Plato is now the pivotal player; the culprit is moralism; the victim is the Greek enlightenment. The death of Platonism can mean the rebirth of Dionysos.

Nietzsche's attempts to present the meaning of the return of Dionysos include the brief essay written a few weeks after the completion of *Beyond Good and Evil* as the preface for the second edition of *The Birth of Tragedy*, "Experiment with a Self-Criticism."[42] This essay on what "lies at the ground" (1) of his

40. Nietzsche brings *TI* to an end with a reflection on "What I Owe to the Ancients," and what he finally owes them is "the fundamental fact of the Hellenic instinct," the Dionysian condition. There too Nietzsche ends by noting the trajectory of his career, beginning with the *Birth of Tragedy* and culminating in the deeper understanding and greater explicitness of the later books: "I, the last disciple of the philosopher Dionysos,—I, the teacher of the eternal return . . ."

41. *BT* (13) speaks of Socrates as the individual who dared to negate the nature of the Greek as exemplified in Homer, Pindar, Aeschylus, Phidias, Pericles, the Pythia, and Dionysos.

42. Nietzsche opens his "Experiment" or "Essay" by recalling a decisive moment in his life: the weeks after the battle of Wörth in the "German-French War" (8 Aug. 1870), when the author of *BT* was in "some corner of the Alps"—he was at the Hotel Alpenklub high in the Maderanertal in August 1870, writing an essay entitled "The Dionysian World View" after learning that he would soon be leaving for duty as a medical orderly on the battlefields of the war. "The Dionysian World View" contains many remarkable formulations of the power and loveliness of the Dionysian—a "coexistence of clearmindedness

first book gathers in force till it culminates in its penultimate section (6), where Nietzsche states the two basic matters he now "regrets" about his first book and just how they "ruined" it. The first is that he "obscured and ruined" Dionysian intimations with Schopenhauerian formulations" — "How differently Dionysos spoke to me!" he says after quoting Schopenhauer (6). But "far worse" than this, something he "regrets still more," is the fact that he "*ruined the stupendous Greek problem*" that had opened before his eyes by introducing contemporary issues into it.[43] The stupendous Greek problem is the problem of the value of truth, and there can be no doubt that Nietzsche now thinks that he has grasped that problem properly and pointed the way to its solution. *Zarathustra* and *Beyond Good and Evil* are Nietzsche's proper responses to the stupendous problem faced by the Greeks.

The return of Dionysos in Nietzsche's writings means the return of possibilities for human culture that are not wholly new, for they are the possibilities for art and science already begun on a heroic scale by the Greeks but destroyed by Socratism/Platonism and its ultimate consequences.[44] The return of Dionysos is what Nietzsche sees coming (*GS* 370) as the next great event after the greatest recent event, the death of the god whose ascendancy in European civilization was made possible by the Socratic/Platonic response to the stupendous Greek problem of the value of truth. For Dionysos and Ariadne are, in their way, the true gods. In what does their godness consist? What is truest or most subterranean — the surging will to power that articulates itself into all that is, most spiritually/intellectually into the experiences of the human thinker — comes, in them, to radiant picturing, to poetic formulation in the divination of manliness and womanliness. The appalling fecundity of nature, the eros at its core that has most suffered human denunciation as the cosmically unacceptable, is, in them, gathered into godliness. Around them a mere "everything" of will to power may, perhaps, turn into world, a unitary world that genders itself into disharmonies that may nevertheless marry and be fruitful, a comedy of redemption following the tragedies and the satyr plays.

---

and intoxication" that marks "the high point of Hellenic culture" (§1). It describes how the primitive and chaotic Dionysian energies were tamed and transfigured into collective, communal expressions of beauty and of the human unity with nature in which " 'excess' unveiled itself as truth" (§2). This early essay too, however, needs to be read with the specific cautions Nietzsche raised about *BT* in his new preface.

43. The same two failures are singled out in Nietzsche's review of *BT* in *EH,* in which special emphasis is placed on the phenomenon of the Dionysian.

44. The return of Dionysos himself is now part of what *BT* had pictured as the decisive future event, the rising of some "music-making Socrates" (15, 17).

Section 295, perhaps the most beautiful of all sections in the book, begins with a sentence that never ends. It describes "the genius of the heart," "the tempter god" whose mastery of knowing how to seem gives him access to every soul. Nietzsche reproduced this sentence in a significant place: as his last word before the reviews of his books in *Ecce Homo*, it prepares accounts of his own acts of temptation while prohibiting "any surmise about whom I am describing" (*EH* Books 6).

To certify his right to introduce Dionysos, Nietzsche presents himself as a wanderer from childhood onward, one whose path was often crossed by the god Dionysos. How to present that long-present god to others? Nietzsche had, "as you know," offered his "first born in all secrecy and reverence" to Dionysos, but since writing *The Birth of Tragedy* he has learned much more "about the philosophy of this god" and now, as "the last disciple and initiate of the god Dionysos," he may be permitted "at long last to begin to give you, my friends, a little taste, as far as it is allowed me, of this philosophy." The taste offered must be given in "a half voice," an undertone, partly because of what is said but mainly because of those he must say it to, "my friends."[45] While addressed to his friends the free minds, what Nietzsche says about Dionysos will strike a different audience differently — the philosophers, Nietzsche says, will find it more suspicious and still more offensive. Much in the philosophy of Dionysos is "secret, new, strange, odd, uncanny," but Nietzsche focuses on a single thing, his claim that Dionysos is a philosopher: "Even that Dionysos is a philosopher and that therefore gods too philosophize seems to me a novelty that is not harmless and that perhaps precisely among philosophers might arouse mistrust." Philosophers have all been on the same track since Plato (191), according to whose edict — allegedly taught to Socrates by Diotima — the gods do not philosophize because they are already wise. This is the essential, the indispensable tenet of Platonism: the highest beings must possess pure minds that contemplate the unchanging reality of the good in itself. No wonder a philosophizing Dionysos arouses mistrust among philosophers: if the gods too philosophize, Platonism must be false, the pure mind and the good in itself must be fictions. Leo Strauss helpfully extends the suggestion into a more radical possibility:[46] Nietzsche may be suggesting that it has always been suspected among philosophers, including especially Plato himself, that gods philosophize. Strauss's two references cite occasions on which Plato refers to

---

45. Nietzsche had addressed "my friends" directly only infrequently in the book: 37, 151, 205, and here. See also the references to friends in 25, 27, 40, 43, 44, 209, 212, 217.
46. *Studies in Platonic Political Philosophy* 175.

philosophers as gods;[47] the possibly harmful novelty would then consist in making it accessible to nonphilosophers that philosophy itself is the divine activity.

But if voicing the novelty of philosophizing gods is especially suspect among philosophers, "among you, my friends, there's less against it." Or so it could seem, for Nietzsche recognizes that his free-minded friends would have less against this novelty than do philosophers except for one thing: "*unless* it comes too late and not at the right hour." Nietzsche's talk of gods may be his most untimely meditation for it has been "betrayed" to him that "today you don't like to believe in God and gods." Nietzsche's friends, unbelievers today, seem to have been believers yesterday; they are skeptics turned against all religion by their deliverance from their own. Post-Christian atheism, a welcome emancipation from a most dangerous monotheism, comes at an extremely high cost: renunciation of one of the most ancient and venerable hypotheses, the notion of divinity. Is the way open to new versions and refinements of the divinity hypothesis? Nietzsche is mindful of the "strict habits" of the ears of his friends, the repugnance with which they hear any talk of gods, but he cannot wait the necessary centuries for the aftereffects of our dead God to clear. He has to speak the most untimely word in unreceptive ears, prejudiced against all gods by the character of one. In the frankness (*Freimütigkeit,* literally, free courageousness) of his theologizing tale, Nietzsche may have to go further than his audience would like, but he warns that in unreported conversations Dionysos went very much further than he himself was ready to go — and therefore immeasurably further than he is ready to say.

Nietzsche prepares this first appearance of Dionysos on his own stage with one more qualification: he reports that he has not been permitted to follow human custom and introduce Dionysos by attesting to his virtues. Yet he mentions them anyway, and they're the very virtues most praised in the book, the philosophic virtues: courage of an explorer and discoverer, daring honesty, truthfulness, love of wisdom. The first words we ever hear from Nietzsche's Dionysos are his contribution to a debate about the virtuous words for philosophy that could have been used to introduce him, a philosophizing god: " 'Keep it,' he'd say, 'for yourself and your like and whoever else may need it! I — have no reason to cover my nakedness!' " Reacting to Dionysos's words, the words of a naked philosopher, his disciple adopts the role of virtuous, shocked commentator that he sustains to the end: "One guesses: this kind of deity and philosopher may perhaps be lacking in shame?" Philosophers from Plato to Epicurus were not lacking shame; they chose to clothe their divinities

47. *Theaetetus* 151d, *Sophist* 216b.

in their virtue. The last disciple of Dionysos seems to want to do the same but Dionysos, seemingly shameless, refuses to cooperate. To lack shame is to lack the sense that something needs to be hidden, perhaps because it could cause embarrassment or humiliation if it were seen as what it is. But judging from what Nietzsche's book has said about the philosopher's masks, the shame Dionysos lacks may be shame at being caught red-handed in crime, the highest crime, advocacy of what the reigning gods deem demonic. Dionysos seems shameless; knowing that he always comes to a settled world full of gods, he's always willing to appear demonic and not clothe himself in virtuous words.

Nietzsche's god nakedly embodies the *Versucher* virtues of Nietzsche's philosophy; philosophy is the nakedness of which Dionysos is not ashamed. Still, it's a god who says he has no need to cover his nakedness, and doesn't the nakedness of a god unavoidably mask something — his last disciple and initiate? The penultimate section of "What Is Noble?" masks the nobility of the disciple by hiding him in front of his shameless god. The masking is a showing; while the disciple expresses shocked reservations at the extremes of his god, discipleship gives him away: philosophy, the truly divine activity, is almost shameless, it does us the courtesy of assigning its shameless qualities to a god.

Introduced by this debate about how he's to be introduced, Dionysos converses with his disciple in a way that displays the god's nakedness and the disciple's clothing. Their theme is *der Mensch*, humanity as such, and their dialogue exhibits a god's way of looking down. Dionysos is not a Platonic god, but he's not an Epicurean god either (62), for in looking down he looks for ways to intervene in human history. Echoing Zarathustra's first words, "I love humanity," Dionysos says, "Under certain circumstances I love humanity." He will give other reasons for his love but before he does, it is said that "with this he alluded to Ariadne who was present." When Dionysos returns in Nietzsche's writings he is always accompanied by the mortal Ariadne. Raised to divinity by Dionysos's love, Ariadne, with Dionysos, make up the essential divine pair, womanliness and manliness raised to the highest power. The penultimate section thus returns to the very opening of the preface, but now truth who is a woman appears with a suitor worthy of her, a suitor whom she has allowed to win her though not a suitor to whom she has surrendered — remaining what she is, Ariadne weds the lover who loves her as she is.

"To me, humanity is a pleasant, brave, inventive animal that has no like on earth; it finds its way in any labyrinth." By alluding to the famous story of the labyrinth in Ariadne's presence, Dionysos indicates that it is humanity's heroic quality that draws his approval too, the quality of a Theseus, who, after killing the Minotaur at the heart of the labyrinth with the aid of the sword given to him by Ariadne, got out of the labyrinth with the aid of Ariadne's thread (29).[48] Dionysos is so well disposed toward humanity that he often reflects on "how I might yet enhance it." The god whose epiphany opens with a refusal of virtuous clothing again shows his virtuous nakedness: he acts to enhance the humanity he loves by making "it stronger, more evil, and more profound." The god again seems to have outstripped his last disciple: " 'Stronger, more evil, more profound,' I asked, shocked.[49] 'Yes,' he said yet once more, 'stronger, more evil, more profound; also more beautiful.' " It is when he adds, "more beautiful," that "the tempter god smiled his halcyon smile as though he'd just paid an enchanting compliment." And surely he has, for with this speech too, the tempter must be alluding to Ariadne, who possesses all those qualities herself; to enhance humanity, Dionysos leads it into possession of the qualities of his beloved — he makes humanity truer to what *it* is and to *what is* is.

In his love for truth who is a woman the philosophizing god has come to possess her as no dogmatic philosopher was able to. But more than that, in loving truth he learns to love the true, to love what is, to love nature in all its appalling fecundity and cruelty. Dionysos's pursuit of Ariadne follows the course mapped out in *Zarathustra:* the poetry of that book shows Zarathustra's love of Wild Wisdom transfigure naturally and with the greatest effort into love of Life. Dionysos's enhancement of humanity, making it stronger, more evil, more profound, more beautiful aims to make it more natural, its love of truth transfiguring with great effort into love of the true. The theological tale told at the book's end repeats religiously the very core of the philosophic teaching of the book. At the same time, in being a conversation related by a disciple between himself and his god, it enacts as well the political teaching of the book that philosophy must become political philosophy and set out to change the general taste: Like Plato's Socrates, Nietzsche permits himself to end by telling tales, to end mythologizing;[50] he ends by painting artful pictures of what his book stated in argument.[51]

---

48. In conversations recorded in Nietzsche's notebooks, Ariadne herself is the labyrinth, and the mere hero Theseus loses his way while Dionysos does not. *KSA* 12.9 [115], 10 [95].

49. See *KSA* 11.34 [176], an important programmatic note in which Nietzsche's "philosophy of Dionysos" is linked with reflections on how to succeed in the monumental task of establishing a new moral teaching in the unpropitious context of modern ideas. Also important as a forerunner of section 295 and the philosophy of Dionysos is 34 [181].

50. Plato, *Apology* 39e; *Phaedo* 70b; *Laws* 1.632e.

51. *KSA* 11.34 [232] relates that Nietzsche's youthful experiences with a dangerous

The shocked disciple, far behind his tempter god, has the final word: "One sees here also: this divinity lacks not only shame —;" what *else* does he lack? His words seem to show that he lacks as well what made gods godly, he seems the very devil, tempting us into evil. The disciple continues: "There are anyway good reasons to conjecture that in several matters the gods generally could be schooled by us humans. We humans are — more humane. —" In the theater of this final speech the disciple of Dionysos masks himself in humaneness; feigning the shudder his friends can be expected to experience at his shameless, devilish god, he acts as if it would be an advance to teach his god shame, to teach him a morality that would cover his nakedness and temper his deviltry. But the disciple's feigned humaneness succeeds in acknowledging how an initiate of Dionysos must speak to friends who still have a long way to go to gain a love of humanity like that of Dionysos and his last disciple.

Philosophy
SECTION 296

As beautiful as this final section is and as fitting a leave-taking, it can still seem regrettable that Nietzsche placed it here at the last minute, not allowing his book to end on the appearance of Dionysos and Ariadne and his disciple's effort to mediate between god and man. Yet Nietzsche cannot be wrong about how to end his book. Leo Strauss's words are apt: the penultimate aphorism is followed by the "ultimate aphorism of *Beyond Good and Evil*,"[52] perhaps the ultimate aphorism of philosophy as such, its ultimate speech, acknowledgment of the fate that awaits philosophy's speech, its communication of the feast and frenzy of philosophy's insight. With this reflection on the fate of his "*wicked* thoughts" — the last prose words of his book — Nietzsche returns to the first words of his book, "the will to truth." That his wicked thoughts are in the process of becoming "truths" does not refute the now-vindicated value of the will to truth, however much it means that truth remains a problem for Nietzsche and his friends, a lover's problem, a problem they cannot do without.

---

divinity taught him to be silent and that "one must learn to speak in order to be correctly silent."

52. *Studies in Platonic Political Philosophy* 175.

Out of High Mountains: Aftersong

Nietzsche thought enough of his three-page closing poem to treat it as another chapter, providing it with its own title page. He called it a *Nachgesang*, an aftersong or epode, the third part of the triadically constructed odes of Greek dramatists and lyric poets sung by the chorus.[1] The book that opened with a *Vorrede* ends with a *Nachgesang*, speech turns to song, the speaker having been transformed into a singer by the events of the book. In this respect too *Beyond Good and Evil* parallels *Thus Spoke Zarathustra*, a book of speeches that began with a prologue and ended (in the version Nietzsche published) with the three songs that end part 3. The final song of *Zarathustra*, "The Seven Seals. (Or: the Yes and Amen Song)," anticipates the arrival of "children" (as do the final lines of *Zarathustra* part 4)[2], just as the final song of *Beyond Good and Evil* anticipates the arrival of "friends."

Just what will be required of those friends has been shown throughout

---

1. The epode follows the strophe and the antistrophe, the strophe being sung as the chorus moves in one direction across the stage, the antistrophe as it moves in the opposite direction, and the epode after it has come to a stand. The rhyme structure maintained throughout the fifteen stanzas is ABBAA.

2. The last phrases of part 4 of *Zarathustra* speak of Zarathustra, "glowing and strong, like the morning sun coming out of dark mountains."

Beyond Good and Evil, but it is suggested as well by private events that occasioned the poem in November 1884, almost two years before it appeared at the end of *Beyond Good and Evil.* Nietzsche composed the poem for Heinrich von Stein, and although the private conditions of the poem's origins remained private and could therefore be of no interpretive help to readers of *Beyond Good and Evil,* understanding the poem's origins makes immediately visible a crucial part of its purpose as the final communication of *Beyond Good and Evil.*[3] Stein, thirteen years younger than Nietzsche, was a promising young thinker, a student of philosophy who entered the Wagner circle as tutor to Wagner's son Siegfried; he became a close associate of Lou Salomé and Paul Rée and was the author of many books.[4] A chair in philosophy was established for him in 1887 at the University of Berlin through the efforts of Wilhelm Dilthey, but the apparently robust Stein died of a heart attack at age thirty the day after the chair was established.[5] His close association with the Wagner circle and especially with Salomé and Rée made Stein familiar with Nietzsche long before they met; and Nietzsche knew of Stein, even sending him copies of the parts of *Zarathustra* as they appeared.[6] But their first meeting did not take place until August 1884, when Stein traveled from central Germany to Sils Maria expressly to talk with Nietzsche. Three days of long walks and intense discussion left a powerful impression on Nietzsche, for here was a person of the sort he had long imagined: someone fit to become his follower.

Nietzsche expressed the nature of his hope in a letter to Stein three weeks

3. The original title was "Hermit's Longing"; the published version added two final stanzas to the original thirteen and, among other smaller changes, reversed the order of stanzas two and three, seven and eight, and ten and eleven. The original version can be found in Nietzsche's letter to Stein, end of November 1884.

4. See Janz, *Nietzsche* 2:325–36; on Stein's visit, see Nietzsche's letters to Overbeck (14 Sept. 1884) and Köselitz (20 Sept. 1884). See also *EH* Books 1. In a letter to Overbeck (4 Dec. 1884) Nietzsche said, "Have you read Stein's 'Heroes and World?' Please, do it." Stein's *Heroes of the World* deals with Solon, Alexander, Saint Katharina, Luther, Bruno, Shakespeare, and Cromwell.

5. Nietzsche was greatly affected by Stein's death: "The news of Stein's death . . . has moved me in the most painful way possible, or much more, I'm still completely beside myself about it. He was so dear to me, he belonged to the few human beings whose very *existence* gave me joy. And I never doubted that he was *saved up* for me for later: for such human beings—who, rich and deep, necessarily have a slow development—one must allow a *long* time. And it was not granted to him! Why wasn't I called in place of him? It would have made more sense. But it's all so senseless: and this noble creature, the most beautiful human specimen I ever set eyes on as a result of my Wagnerian relationships—is no more!" (letter to Overbeck, 30 June 1887).

6. Janz, *Nietzsche* 2:287–88.

after his visit (18 Sept. 1884). Counting that visit "among the three good things for which I'm deeply grateful to this *Zarathustra* year," Nietzsche wondered if "perhaps *you* came off worse? Who knows — you may have come far too close to finding Philoctetes on his island. And even something of Philoctetes' belief: 'Without my arrows no Ilium will be taken!' "[7] Nietzsche himself is the Greek hero Philoctetes, who had been banished to the island of Lemnos by the Greeks besieging Troy because of an unbearable condition. But Philoctetes had been given the arrows of Herakles with which alone Troy (Ilium) could be taken — Philoctetes is the necessary man, indispensable to the achievement of Greek goals yet unrecognized by them and hateful to them for what they think are good reasons.[8] Stein is young Neoptolemos, son of Achilles, sent to Lemnos with Odysseus to win Philoctetes' assistance and his arrows for the decisive final battle that would win the war. And Ilium? What is Nietzsche's Ilium but the cultural world to be overthrown by his great task of the transvaluation of all values? Nietzsche's books were written to attract allies and workers, an eventual army to carry out the overthrow with "Philoctetes' " arrows.[9] Two months later, at the end of November, Nietzsche sent Stein the poem "Hermit's Longing" with its distinction between two types of friends, old friends who prove not to be the kind of associates the hermit required and new friends who perhaps are: Lou and Rée would count among the old friends — and Stein? Stein's response (7 December 1884) — declared "dark" by Nietzsche in a letter to his mother and sister — dashed Nietzsche-Philoctetes' hopes for this possible Neoptolemos, at least temporarily as Stein indirectly declared himself un-transformably Wagnerian.[10]

7. See also the letters to Overbeck, 14 Sept. 1884, and Köselitz, 20 Sept. 1884. On the story of Philoctetes, see Sophocles' tragedy *Philoctetes*. Aeschylus and Euripides each wrote a *Philoctetes,* but they have not survived.

8. In a notebook with entries from the fall of 1885 to the fall of 1886, the time of the composition of *BGE,* Nietzsche says, "Every Philoctetes knows that without his bow and his arrows Troy will never be overthrown" (*KSA* 12.2 [64]).

9. See Nietzsche's letter to Overbeck during these weeks: "For I need, briefly put, disciples *while I'm still alive*: and if my books till now have no effect as fishhooks they will have 'missed their calling.' The best and essential allows itself to be shared only person to person, it can and should not be 'public' " (6 Nov. 1884). Much earlier, Nietzsche confessed to another prospective disciple, Reinhart von Seydlitz, that he had, like a pirate, long been *auf Menschenraub* (24 Sept. 1876). Nietzsche imagined a school of philosophy like the ancient Greek schools in which he would teach his philosophy privately to a few select students; see, e.g., the letter to Köselitz, 2 Sept. 1884, shortly after the meeting with Stein.

10. See Janz, *Nietzsche* 2:367–69, 381–82, and Binion, *Frau Lou* 126–27 (who seems

By expressing the hope for new friends, fit friends, the poem placed at the end of *Beyond Good and Evil* expresses Nietzsche's mood of anticipation for those who will be won to his task by the book he had written to entice them. *Beyond Good and Evil* is a "fishhook," *Ecce Homo* maintains, and its final poem depicts the fisherman who cast it, a Philoctetes on his island awaiting the new sons of Achilles for a task of overthrow that they can accomplish only together. *Beyond Good and Evil*'s aftersong depicts the singer in the "midday" of his life and in a summer garden, resting in a "restless joy," "standing and peering and waiting," all expectation for friends who are now to come. The work of the afternoon awaits him upon their arrival, just as Zarathustra's work in part 4 of *Zarathustra* awaited him after the chapter entitled "Midday": perhaps that work could be carried forward by the superior men who had arrived at his cave that morning, but they prove not to be the ears for his teaching.[11] The final poem of *Beyond Good and Evil* repeats in much shorter compass the chief event of *Zarathustra* 4: overcoming the pity and disappointment of realizing that the friends first drawn by his teaching are not those his task really needs — an overcoming that permits hope to survive, hope for new friends.

Although he is not a teacher from the ground up (*BGE* 63) — being a truth seeker before being a truth teller — he has nevertheless "set my table for you" in order to attract friends to his "realm." The ones who arrive discover that he is not the one they expected — just as he discovers that they are not the ones he expected. Drawn to one another through mutual hopes, the two sides draw apart through mutual recognition of one another. Adopting first their perspective on him, Nietzsche repeats three variations of the phrase *ich bin's nicht* — I'm not the one — the second time saying "I'm — no longer the one?" With that variation, the two differing movements of the parties begin to be described: he is no longer what he was, having grown younger; they are no longer what they were, having more naturally aged. He youthens; they age — and their respective movements render them strangers.[12] They suspect that he has been ruined by becoming someone else, that he has unlearned all decency, "unlearned human and god, curse and prayer."

Their perspective on him gives way to his perspective on them in the seventh stanza (as the dash suggests); he beholds them and bids them go, in peace and

---

to have understood the events more clearly than Janz). See Nietzsche's letter to his mother and sister, beginning Jan. 1885.

11. *Z* 4 was composed in 1884–85, after Stein's visit to Sils Maria and before *BGE*.

12. Becoming younger may suggest Zarathustra's experience of recovering the "visions and apparitions" of his youth (*Z* 2 "The Song at Graveside").

not in anger, for they cannot be housed where he's at home. For he, "the *wicked* hunter," is now Philoctetes with his bow and arrows; like the archer of the preface he has drawn his bow completely taut and savors its dangerous tension. Does he know the target, his Ilium? Before turning to that, he warns away those who have arrived: "dangerous is *that* arrow, like *no other* arrow." What happened at the end of the first chapter (23) happens again at the end of the book as each reader is invited to turn away from what is most dangerous. If the author is hurt by turning away those in whom he had hoped but who proved not fit, he nevertheless remains open to new friends. Now grown pale and ghostlike in their withdrawal, his old friends haunt him still with the words, "*Weren't* we the ones?" an echo of his own earlier lament, "Wasn't *I* the one?" *Beyond Good and Evil* ends on its winnowing, selecting function.

In the fourth stanza from the end, he recognizes that his "youthful longing" misunderstood itself, imagining wrongly that a transformation in them had made them akin to him. In the luminous line that summarizes the movement of the whole poem, he claims that "only he who transforms himself remains akin to me" (Nur wer sich wandelt, bleibt mit mir verwandt). Having grown younger and now enjoying a "second time of youth," he awaits new friends, his true allies.

"*This* song is over" — the two final stanzas sing a new song: lament is over, dying on his lips because a friend came at the hour of midday transforming lament to festival. "A wizard did it" but don't ask who; his coming transformed one to two. It's not necessary to ask because the friend who arrives at the right time, the midday friend, is identified: "Friend *Zarathustra* came, the guest of guests!" Together they celebrate the feast of feasts, certain of a united victory. The world laughs rather than weeps as the terrifying curtain is torn — an alteration of the event said to occur at the death of Jesus, the tearing of the Temple veil that separated the Holy Place from the Holy of Holies, where only the high priest was permitted and only on the day of atonement.[13] Like *Zarathustra*, *Beyond Good and Evil* ends by altering a cataclysmic image drawn from the Bible.[14] No death causes the tearing of the veil at the end of *Beyond Good and Evil* but a laugh, a laugh of the world itself as it celebrates its liberation, for the laugh of the world not only tears the veil, it prepares a very special celebration, the marriage of light and darkness. That marriage signals the end of the most catastrophic of human errors, the old Zarathustra's moral

---

13. See Matthew 27:51, Luke 23:45: as the veil of the temple tears in two at the death of Jesus, darkness settles over the whole land (Mt 27:45).

14. Z 3 ends on "The Seven Seals," an apocalyptic image drawn from the book of Revelation.

separation of light and darkness, a separation that made "the fight between good and evil the very wheel in the machinery of things: the transposition of morality into the metaphysical realm . . . is *his* work" (*EH* Destiny 3). With the arrival of "Friend *Zarathustra*" at the end of *Beyond Good and Evil,* the Yes-saying part of Nietzsche's task prepares to succeed its No-saying part. Beyond good and evil, beyond the old Zarathustrianism that is the fountainhead of the Western moral tradition in both Platonism and the Bible, lies a marriage of light and darkness that heals the ancient rift. Like *Zarathustra, Beyond Good and Evil* ends by preparing a marriage, *the* marriage of *the* supposed opposites.

What does the arrival of Zarathustra at the end of *Beyond Good and Evil* mean for Nietzsche's task? Nietzsche's task of finding friends or winning allies for his war is not suspended or rendered irrelevant by the arrival of Zarathustra: Zarathustra too needs companions — not the disciples made in part 1, not the "superior human beings" who come to his cave in part 4, but the children of the marriage celebrated at the end of part 3, the children referred to again at the end of part 4 as Zarathustra prepares his descent to them. *Beyond Good and Evil* and *Thus Spoke Zarathustra* end by pointing back to the books themselves as having solved the same problem: how the wise man plants the seeds of his wisdom, how the genuine philosopher, having awakened to the need to fight, recruits warriors for the great war he alone knows must be fought.

Nietzsche's task at the end of *Zarathustra* and at the end of *Beyond Good and Evil* is the same: he is a wise solitary awaiting the arrival of allies won to his task by his books. The task of waiting is a midday task, a pause in the more active daytime tasks, the morning task that lies behind — the composition of the books that will attract his allies — and the afternoon task that lies ahead. His waiting is shared by Zarathustra; together they are certain of a shared victory; together they possess the arrows with which alone Ilium can be taken: that is the afternoon task, the "great war" whose preparations now include waiting "for those related to me, those who, prompted by strength, would offer me their hands for *destroying*" (*EH* Books *BGE* 1). Only then can the new temple be built; only then can a new day dawn.

Nietzsche's Future

When he sent a copy of *Beyond Good and Evil* to his high-minded and earnest old friend Malwida von Meysenbug, Nietzsche asked her not to read it and even less to express to him her feelings about it: "Let's assume that people *may* be able to read it around the year 2000." Only the turn of a new millennium would make Nietzsche's book approachable, for "the greatest events and thoughts . . . are comprehended last . . . . 'How many centuries does a mind require to be comprehended?' — that too is a measuring rod, with that too we can create the required order of rank and etiquette" (285). *Beyond Good and Evil, A Prelude to a Philosophy of the Future* is timely, written for the near future, the twentieth and twenty-first centuries, a time of nihilism consequent on the death of God. It points its reader to *Thus Spoke Zarathustra*, a book that is untimely, written to help create the far future beyond that nihilism, a human future of experiment and celebration that it is necessary to prepare with the greatest care because the future of humanity is a game in which "no hand, not even a finger of God" plays a part (203).

It belongs to the nature of philosophy itself that the philosopher Nietzsche came into the world unapproachably masked: "Around every profound mind a mask is continually growing, thanks to the constantly false, that is, *shallow* interpretation of every word, every step, every sign of life he gives" (40). Knowing the inevitability of masks, Nietzsche chose to weave his own, the mask of a rash truth teller whose unguarded speech would make him seem an immoralist, a devil, the mask of a super-Machiavelli. That mask, and the vehemence with which its terrible contours would be traced by those who took it to be more than a mask, inevitably assigned a task to his friends, advocates bound by the beauty and rigor of his writings to see eventually that the mask masked its opposite, a new teaching on good and bad by something approaching a god.

Nietzsche's future still lies in our future, I believe, the possible future of a global species hardened in the truth by science and more fundamentally by the philosophy that grounds science, spurring it to the adventure of experiment, steadying it by a rational measure in accord with the way of all beings, housing it within a spirit of gratitude and celebration.

For Nietzsche's philosophy is a love story. He hid that fact because "there are acts of love of such a delicacy that nothing is more advisable than to take a stick to any eyewitness—that'll muddle his memory" (40). While it wants no eyewitness, such love still wants to be known, to be guessed at, to be felt, ultimately to be duplicated by lovers with a similar temper. So it tells the tale of its love in a masking way befitting the nobility of both lover and beloved. For in loving its beloved it loves as well those with whom it may share the lover's tale, those in whom it can kindle love. Nietzsche's philosophy is a love story for lovers.

Other philosophers chose other masks for philosophy's tale of love. Plato's Socrates argued that philosophy is Eros while constrained to mask Eros to conform to the moral faith in opposite values. Spinoza argued that philosophy is the intellectual love of god while describing both love and god without the surge and throb of the blood in them (*GS* 372). Leo Strauss expressed the matter in a way that includes all genuine philosophers: philosophy "is necessarily accompanied, sustained and elevated by *eros*. It is graced by nature's grace."[1]

Nietzsche's tale of the lover is told most fully in *Thus Spoke Zarathustra*, the tale of a lover so ardent, so vehement that he's blind at first to the true identity of his beloved. Thinking she must be wisdom, he learns the truth with difficulty that his true beloved is life herself. Their love story leads to embrace, for the lover wins his beloved by saying to life: You, you are what I want, exactly as you are, an infinite number of times. Their love story ends in marriage and in children, offspring of a teacher who wants life itself to be eternity.

Nietzsche's tale of the lover is told more indirectly in *Beyond Good and Evil,* tempered for minds of an objective, skeptical, critical bent, minds that

1. *Natural Right and History* 40.

can nevertheless be drawn to love's excess not despite the qualities of their minds but because of them. Nietzsche's task in *Beyond Good and Evil* is philosophy's essential political task: in the midst of the most profound natural tendency to hate the natural world morally and live a moral fiction of it, Nietzsche's task is to train in philosophy's most profound passion, love of truth that matures into love of the world.

Works Cited

Ahrensdorf, Peter. *The Death of Socrates and the Life of Philosophy*. Albany: SUNY Press, 1995.

Ansell-Pearson, Keith. *Viroid Life: Perspectives on Nietzsche and the Transhuman Condition*. London: Routledge, 1997.

Augustine. *The City of God*. Translated by Marcus Dods. New York: Modern Library, 1950.

Bacon, Francis. *An Advertisement Touching a Holy War*. Introduction, Notes, and Interpretive Essay by Laurence Lampert. Prospect Heights: Waveland Press, 2000.

———. *Works*. Edited by J. Spedding, R. L. Ellis, and D. D. Heath. 14 vols. New York: Garrett Press, 1968 (1857–74).

Bataille, Georges. *The Accursed Share*. Translated by Robert Hurley. New York: Zone Books, 1991.

———. *On Nietzsche*. Translated by Bruce Boone. New York: Paragon House, 1992.

Beiner, Ronald. "George Grant, Nietzsche, and the Problem of a Post-Christian Theism." In *George Grant and the Subversion of Modernity*, edited by Arthur Davis, 109–38. Toronto: University of Toronto Press, 1996.

Binyon, Rudoph. *Frau Lou Nietzsche's Wayward Disciple*. Princeton: Princeton University Press, 1968.

Bolotin, David. *An Approach to Aristotle's* Physics: *With Particular Attention to the Role of His Manner of Writing*. Albany: SUNY Press, 1999.

———. "The Life of Philosophy and the Immortality of the Soul: An Introduction to Plato's *Phaedo*." *Ancient Philosophy* 7:39–56.

Boscovich, Roger Joseph. *A Theory of Natural Philosophy*. Translated by J. M. Child. Cambridge: MIT Press, 1966.

Calasso, Roberto. *The Marriage of Cadmus and Harmony*. Translated by Tim Parks. New York: Alfred A. Knopf, 1993.

Conway, Daniel W. *Nietzsche and the Political*. London: Routledge, 1997.

Cox, Cristoph. *Nietzsche: Naturalism and Interpretation*. Berkeley: University of California Press, 1999.

Crawford, Claudia. *To Nietzsche: Dionysus, I Love You! Ariadne*. Albany: SUNY Press, 1995.

Crescenzi, Luca. "Verzeichnis der von Nietzsche aus der Universitätsbibliothek in Basel entliehenen Bücher (1869–1879)." *Nietzsche Studien* 23 (1994): 388–422.

Deleuze, Gilles. *Nietzsche and Philosophy*. Translated by Hugh Tomlinson. New York: Columbia University Press, 1983.

Dennett, Daniel C. *Darwin's Dangerous Idea: Evolution and the Meanings of Life*. New York: Simon and Schuster, 1995.

Donnellan, Brendan. *Nietzsche and the French Moralists*. Bonn: Bouvier Verlag, 1982.

Eden, Robert. *Political Leadership and Nihilism: A Study of Weber and Nietzsche*. Gainesville: University of Florida Presses, 1983.

Hegel, G. W. F. *Phänomenologie des Geistes*. Hamburg: Felix Meiner Verlag, 1948 (1807).

Heidegger, Martin. *Was heisst Denken?* Tübingen: Max Niemeyer Verlag, 1962.

Janz, Curt Paul. *Friedrich Nietzsche: Biographie*. Munich: Hanser, 1978.

Kant, Immanuel. *Critique of Pure Reason*. Translated by Norman Kemp Smith. New York: St. Martin's Press, 1965.

Kolakowski, Leszek. *God Owes Us Nothing*. Chicago: University of Chicago Press, 1995.

Krell, David Farrell. *Postponements: Woman, Sensuality, and Death in Nietzsche*. Bloomington: Indiana University Press, 1986.

———. *Infectious Nietzsche*. Bloomington: Indiana University Press, 1996.

———. *Nietzsche: A Novel*. Albany: SUNY Press, 1996.

Krell, David Farrell, and Donald L. Bates. *The Good European: Nietzsche's Work Sites in Word and Image*. Chicago: University of Chicago Press, 1997.

Lampert, Laurence. *Nietzsche's Teaching: An Interpretation of* Thus Spoke Zarathustra. New Haven: Yale University Press, 1986.

———. *Nietzsche and Modern Times*. New Haven: Yale University Press, 1993.

———. *Leo Strauss and Nietzsche*. Chicago: University of Chicago Press, 1996.

———. "Nietzsche and Bacon." *International Journal of Philosophy* 33/3 (2001): 117–25.

Lippitt, John, ed. *Nietzsche's Futures*. London: Macmillan, 1999.

Lyotard, Jean-François. *The Postmodern Condition*. Translated by Geoff Bennington and Brian Massumi. Minneapolis: University of Minnesota Press, 1984.

Machiavelli, Niccolò. *The Prince*. Translated by Harvey C. Mansfield, Jr. Chicago: University of Chicago Press, 1985.

MacIntyre, Alisdair. *After Virtue: A Study of Moral Theory*. Notre Dame: Notre Dame University Press, 1981.

McIntyre, Alex. *The Sovereignty of Joy: Nietzsche's Vision of Grand Politics*. Toronto: University of Toronto Press, 1997.

McIntyre, Ben. *Forgotten Fatherland: The Search for Elisabeth Nietzsche.* New York: Farrar, Straus, Giroux, 1992.

Montaigne, Michel de. *Essays.* Translated by Donald Frame. Stanford: Stanford University Press, 1965.

Parkes, Graham. *Composing the Soul: Reaches of Nietzsche's Psychology.* Chicago: University of Chicago Press, 1994.

Picht, Georg. *Nietzsche.* Stuttgart: Klett-Cotta, 1988.

Pippin, Robert B. *Idealism as Modernism: Hegelian Variations.* Cambridge: Cambridge University Press, 1997.

———. "Nietzsche and the Melancholy of Modernity." *Social Research* 66/2 (Summer 1999): 495–520.

Plutarch. "Life of Nicias." In *Plutarch's Lives,* vol. 3. Loeb Classical Library, 1916.

Rahe, Paul. *Republics Ancient and Modern: New Modes and Orders in Early Modern Political Thought.* Chapel Hill: University of North Carolina Press, 1994

Richardson, John. *Nietzsche's System.* New York: Oxford University Press, 1996.

Ridley, Aaron. *Nietzsche's Conscience: Six Character Studies from the "Genealogy."* Ithaca: Cornell University Press, 1998.

Roberts, Tyler. *Contesting Spirit: Nietzsche, Affirmation, Religion.* Princeton: Princeton University Press, 1998.

Schopenhauer, Arthur. *The World as Will and Representation.* Translated by E. F. J Payne. New York: Dover Publications, 1969.

Strauss, Leo. *Natural Right and History.* Chicago: University of Chicago Press, 1953.

———. *The City and Man.* Chicago: Rand, McNally, 1964.

———. *Xenophon's Socratic Discourse: An Interpretation of the* Oeconomicus. Ithaca: Cornell University Press, 1970.

———. *Persecution and the Art of Writing.* Westport: Greenwood Press, 1973 (1952).

———. *Thoughts on Machiavelli.* Chicago: University of Chicago Press, 1978 (1958).

———. *Studies in Platonic Political Philosophy.* Chicago: University of Chicago Press, 1983.

———. *The Rebirth of Classical Political Rationalism: An Introduction to the Thought of Leo Strauss.* Selected and Introduced by Thomas L. Pangle. Chicago: University of Chicago Press, 1989.

———. *On Tyranny.* Revised and expanded edition. Edited by Victor Gourevitch and Michael S. Roth. New York: Free Press, 1991 (1963).

Stevens, Wallace. *The Collected Poems.* New York: Alfred A. Knopf, 1993 (1954).

———. *The Necessary Angel.* New York: Vintage. n.d.

Verrecchio, Anacleto. *Zarathustras Ende: Die Katastrophe Nietzsches in Turin.* Vienna: Bölhaus, 1986.

Waite, Geoff. *Nietzsche's Corps/e: Aesthetics, Politics, Prophecy, or, the Spectacular Technoculture of Everyday Life.* Durham: Duke University Press, 1996.

Whitlock, Greg. "Roger Boscovich, Benedict de Spinoza and Friedrich Nietzsche: The Untold Story." *Nietzsche Studien* 25 (1996): 200–20.

Wilson, Edward O. *Consilience: The Unity of Knowledge.* New York: Alfred A. Knopf, 1998.

Yovel, Yirmiyahu. *Dark Riddle: Hegel, Nietzsche, and the Jews.* University Park: Pennsylvania State University Press, 1998.

Index